A
Law Unto
Myself

Published by
Mountnessing Publishing

Copyright © 2019 Brian R J O Hughes

All rights reserved

Brian R J O Hughes has asserted his right
under the Copyright, Designs and Patents Act 1988
to be identified as the author of this work

ISBN 978-1-84396-546-6

Also available in paperback
ISBN 978-1-84396-545-9

A CIP catalogue record for this
book is available from the British Library
and American Library of Congress

This book is sold subject to the condition that it
shall not, by way of trade or otherwise, be lent, resold, hired
out, or otherwise circulated without the author's prior
consent in any form of binding or cover other than that in
which it is published and without a similar condition being
imposed on the subsequent purchaser.

Typesetting and pre-press production
eBook Versions
127 Old Gloucester Street
London WC1N 3AX
www.ebookversions.com

Dedicated to my Muse, Ella Watson, without whose prompting this book would never have been written.

A
Law Unto
Myself

Brian R J O Hughes

Mountnessing Publishing

Contents

Preface

1
Chapter One
"Iole"

9
Chapter Two
Greece as a Boy Scout

16
Chapter Three
National Service Edinburgh

25
Chapter Four
National Service Cyprus

37
Chapter Five
Kyrenia

42
Chapter Six
Cambridge in the 1950s

57
Chapter 7
Student Travel to Greece

68
Chapter 8
Surviving as a Student in Greece

73
Chapter 9
Mr & Mrs Robinson

75
Chapter 10
Working in the City

85
Chapter 11
To Israel in 1962

94
Chapter 12
Fifty Years as a Solicitor: Phases 1 and 2

104
Chapter 13
Billericay to Kathmandu by Hughes Overland

112
Chapter 14
Ticket Theft at Shenfield Travel

121
Chapter 15
The Haunted Bed

127
Chapter 16
The Haunted House

133
Chapter 17
Virginia 1980

138
Chapter 18
Billericay, Essex

149
Chapter 19
Billerica, Massachusetts

174
Chapter Twenty
Being a General Commissioner of Income Tax

180
Chapter Twenty-One
The Consequences of Cheek

185
Chapter Twenty-Two
Lifeline: Essex Radio

188
Chapter Twenty-Three
Life with Annette.

197
Chapter Twenty-Four
The Disaster Phase

202
Chapter Twenty-Five
Our Foray into France

211
Chapter Twenty-Six
Resolve Mediation and Counselling

215
Chapter Twenty-Seven
Political Experiences

225
Chapter Twenty-Eight
Lessons Learned: Marriage

228
Chapter Twenty-Nine
The Legal Career, Phase 3: Sorting out the "Baddies"

239
Chapter Thirty
The Legal Career, Phase 4: On the Council of the Law Society

254
Chapter Thirty-One
A Close Encounter with Death

259
Chapter Thirty-Two
Reflections on Survival

266
Chapter Thirty-Three
The Extraordinary Annette

274
Chapter Thirty-Four
Background and Education

279
Chapter Thirty-Five
My Fall from Grace

300
Chapter Thirty-Six
The Intervening Years

320
Chapter Thirty-Seven
Conclusion

Photographic Sections
i
The author at the age of 12
Iole at Cambridge
ii
The Kool Katz disco at which the author met Iole
National Service: Sergeants sightseeing in Kyrenia
iii
Kyrenia Castle: Sergeants together
Cambridge: Poppy Day 1958 – gone fishing!
iv
Members of a BH party en route to Athens
BH party members: suffering 68 hours in railway carriages
v
BH party sleeping out on a mountainside at Delphi
The only vehicle for hire in Athens!
vi
Student protest at the tasteless extension
of Emmanuel College, University of Cambridge
vii
Hazel Wilson, Head Student at
Homerton College. "Anyone for squash?"
Valerie Foulkes: the "late arriver" at Victoria Station, Graduation Day 1959

viii
Andrea, with whom the author fell in love in 1960
Hughes Overland Group: ready to depart for Kathmandu
ix
Hughes Overland "Asiaman" Land Rovers and Transits en route to Kathmandu
The author's Greek friend, Babis, at his holiday home in Kokkino Limenaki
x
The author at 40 years of age
Shenfield Travel: the scene of the theft
xi
Hughes & Co staff photograph
Annette as Manager of the Property Department
xii
Annette at home
Hautefort: view of the Pavillon du Bonheur
xiii
The Pavillon as "Hautefort College"
Annette and the author as family mediators
xiv
The author "on the stump" as the Loyal Conservative Party parliamentary candidate in the 1997 General Election
xv
Viven at the time of our marriage
xvi
Vivien the actress, as "Anastasia"
The author as Cedric, Little Lord Fauntleroy, in "Angels in Love"
xvii
Grandfather Somers: Royal Artillery, 1917
xviii
Robin Tilbrook, Chairman of the English Democrats and a fellow solicitor, with the author
Annette at the Doctorate ceremony

Preface

I have often been told by my friends that I should write a book about my various life experiences and for no other reason than that I have set out a few of them in the following Chapters. All of them are true, however improbable some appear to be.

The book is not intended to be any more than a response to their request that I do so and by the end of it, if you reach that far, you may think that I should perhaps have kept these parts of my life story to myself!

But being over eighty years of age and not much caring what people think any more I offer some possible nuggets of wisdom and details of the lessons I have learned in the hope that you may be able to apply them to your own life and benefit from them.

Brian Hughes
July 2019

1

"Iole"

I first met Iole Syrengela in the Union Cellars at Cambridge.

With my College friends Malcolm Walker, Bobby Morris and Graham Crane I had organised a Jazz Night and Disco for "Kool Katz" in the Lent (January to March) term of 1958: between us we had invited about fifty people – fellow students and their girlfriends: in Cambridge at the time there were seven male undergraduates to every female undergraduate and it was not unusual for the male undergraduates to invite female students from the Language Schools that proliferated in the City to parties they were arranging.

The cellars were dark and noisy with sound reverberating off the walls: everybody was having a great time, courtesy of the Merrydown cider punch we had concocted – which we took it in turns to serve.

After doing a stint at serving I retreated to a quieter corner of the cellars and found myself standing next to an attractive dark-haired girl who appeared somewhat bemused by the whole proceedings.

I asked her name and she said it was "Iole": she was Greek and had been attending the Bell School of Languages: one of my friends had invited her along: in fact I think he had put a poster up in the Bell School inviting any young lady who wished to attend!! Her English was so good that I commented on it and questioned her need to attend a Language School: she said she wanted to perfect her "English English" because she had been taught English by an American!

Since I had visited Greece in 1954 and 1957 we talked about Athens and Greece generally, which I was to visit on many future occasions. She told me her parents lived in Athens and that she had a sister who lived in Persia (as

Iran was then known): she was going to fly to New York after her brief stay in Cambridge to meet her sister and continue her education.

I got the strong impression that her parents were well-off.

I asked what her future intentions were – she was clearly very clever and very modest: when she said she did not know I told her that, being so attractive, she would doubtless find a nice husband and have children: her reply really surprised me: "I will never have children." "Why not?" I asked. "I just know it," she said.

That struck me as a very mysterious reply: it was almost as if she could foresee the fate that would befall her: I could tell that she made the comment not in the sense that she did not want to marry and have children but that, somehow, she would be prevented from having them – as so it proved: it was her fate or destiny that she did not.

Graham Crane had just bought an old London taxi cab for £70 and intended to drive it to Newmarket on the following Saturday to watch the Races: being on a Royal Navy Officer's pay while studying for an Engineering Degree at Cambridge he could afford that sort of extravagance: £70 was the food and accommodation cost for one complete term at my College and the purchase of anything but a bicycle was well beyond the means of most of us.

I asked Iole if she would like to join Graham, Malcolm and me on our trip to Newmarket. "What time are you leaving Cambridge?" she asked. When I said, "8.30 a.m." she looked dismayed. "I never get up before 8.30 a.m," she replied.

"OK, we will drive past your digs at 8.30 am and if you are standing outside them we will take you. If you are not, we will go without you!"

This proved to be one of my earlier lessons in female psychology!! However distasteful getting up before 8.30 a.m. might have been the lure of a trip to Newmarket was too great: she was standing in the road outside her digs when we drove up to them. She jumped aboard and we all had a happy and carefree day, squashed in the back of the taxi for the journey to and from Newmarket.

We drove back as it was getting dark and Graham put the taxi headlamps on: we had only gone about five miles when the headlamps began to fade and we quickly found ourselves driving in the pitch dark: the generator had failed and the battery had gone flat. So much for Graham's engineering studies and abilities!

We could, at one point in what proved to be a perilous return to Cambridge, see a lamp waving in front of us – we must have been going at least five miles an hour!! It was a policeman on a bike. We explained the problem and he told us that, in the circumstances, we could continue our journey but that we would have to take extreme care – which, of course, we did. Iole thought our day out was a great adventure!!

I saw Iole two or three times after that before she flew to New York: I showed her round the Colleges and took her out a couple of times– on my limited student resources. She was very grateful and asked me to look her up when I next visited Athens: her home address was 5 Canaris Street and she said I would have no difficulty finding it.

That proved correct: I asked my friend, Aristides Karamouzis, the Clerk at Thomas Cook who looked after all the group tickets while the group leaders were on holiday in Greece where Canaris Street was: he rolled his eyes and told me to step outside Cooks which was then in Syntagma Square, the main square in Athens, walk towards the Royal Palace and Canaris Street was immediately to the left of it.

So I did and came to a rather expensive looking block of flats: below Number 5 Canaris Street was a huge garage: it was full of "prestige" motors – Mercedes, Cadillacs and a Rolls-Royce. Her Dad must sell expensive cars, I thought!!

There was a man in the garage in a chauffeur's uniform polishing one of these gleaming monsters and I asked him in faltering Greek where I might find Iole. "Press the buzzer," he said "and someone will come". So I pressed the buzzer by what was clearly an entrance door to the flat above and a maid appeared who led me upstairs.

There in a spacious and beautifully furnished lounge stood Iole and her mother. Somewhat overawed and standing there in my khaki shorts and crumpled shirt I wondered what sort of impression I must be making and whether my Greek was up to a conversation with Iole's mother.

I need not have worried: her mother, a tall elegant woman, dressed in the height of fashion, also spoke flawless English: it was then, of course, that the penny dropped: her father was not a car salesman – he owned all the cars in the garage!

Iole explained to her mother in English that we had met in Cambridge, that I had been very kind to her and that she had invited me to call on her when I was in Athens: she then asked her mother if she could take me to an open-air cinema for the evening: "Yes, provided you have a chaperone", she replied!

So Iole and I went to the cinema on a beautiful starlit evening with a rather fat lady who worked for the Syrengelas sitting between us. At least she did not understand English so we were able to converse freely. It was, notwithstanding the chaperone, a happy evening: Iole was clearly pleased to see me and to be able to step outside, even if only partially, what appeared to be a very controlled environment for her – as, indeed, she had been able to step outside it in Cambridge. We said our goodbyes and she asked me to look her up again when I next visited Greece: I promised to do so.

I did not visit Greece in 1959 and she had written to me early the next year to say that she had been married off, at her father's insistence, to the son of a textile manufacturer. I would nevertheless be welcome to call on her.

So in the summer of 1960 I went to see her shortly after my arrival, looking a bit neater and tidier than on my previous visit: she now lived in another elegant apartment in a prestigious part of Athens: she talked nostalgically about Cambridge which she had loved and about her husband whom she did not love.

"Why did you marry him then?" I asked her. "It was the 'dowry system,'" she explained: her father was very rich and she could only marry the son of someone who was equally rich. "Did you not have any say in who you married?" I asked her. "Not really," she replied. "My father is very traditional. You will meet my husband: he is due home about now."

The front door of the apartment opened a few minutes later and in came her husband: she introduced us and we shook hands: it was like shaking hands with a "limp haddock" – cold, with no firmness, nothing. He appeared weak and characterless and not a match for the warm, intelligent and genuine Iole.

As I left, she said, "Better if you do not come again." I wished her all the very best in her future life and left.

I did not hear about Iole for about three years after that but when during a conversation with my Greek "brother", Babis I mentioned her name he looked seriously at me and said, "Have you not heard about her?"

Babis (Charalambos Hesiodos Dendias) and I had become firm friends during my many visits to Athens: on behalf of his father he ran the Hotel Marion in Plateia Vathis – where I sent all my male students. He had a degree in Law from Athens University and a Diploma in Hotel Management from Munich and two sisters, Maria and Heleni both of whom were married to sea captains: Heleni was married to Byron and they had a charming and precocious daughter, Victoria; I never met Maria's husband who seemed to spend his life at sea until, that is, he died.

I understand that he was not popular with his crew and was killed when a container accidentally fell and crushed him to death while his ship was unloading cargo in Vladivostok. One can only speculate on whether the two apparent facts are interrelated.

Babis lived with his mother and father in a flat in Stournara Street, close to the Hotel. "No, I haven't heard about her," I told him. "Well, she is dead," he replied. "She was murdered by her Persian lover. The papers were full of it".

He went on to explain. "Iole had to marry the son of the textile manufacturer because of the dowry system. It is still very strong in Greece and explains why I have not married".

"How so, Babis?"

"When I was on the Hotel Management Course in Munich I met a beautiful Greek girl and fell in love with her," he said. "We wanted to get married and I asked my father if I could marry her." "What is her father?" he asked. "He is a sheep farmer in Thessalonika." "You cannot," my father replied and, when he saw I was clearly devastated by his answer, he said "At least not until Maria and Heleni are married."

In Greece, at that time, daughters had to be married off before a son could marry. Dowries had to be provided for the daughter commensurate with the standing of the person they married and in the eyes of his father a sheep farmer would not be able to provide a dowry commensurate with Babis's status – whether Babis was concerned about the dowry or not!!

I am aware that Babis's father had provided a flat in Athens for each of his daughters as dowries when they married their respective sea captains, one happily and one unhappily. However, by the time that they married, the love of Babis's life had given up hope of marrying him and married someone else. Echoes of this sad outcome are to be found in my own life, save that he never saw his one true love again, whereas I have been fortunate enough to do so, albeit late in life.

Iole had been in the same position as Babis: she would have to marry someone whose parents were equally rich – whether she really liked her potential husband or not. This outdated attitude has led to a lot of intelligent young Greek men and women emigrating to other countries and marrying foreigners for love rather than for appearances. I can think of many of them in the United Kingdom. They did so at the risk of being censured and sometimes being alienated from or disclaimed by their families. This attitude is, of course, still prevalent in many communities, as "Honour Killings" bear witness.

Trapped in a marriage she could not bear she filed for divorce – much to the disappointment of her father: she was "the apple of his eye", the daughter in whom he had invested so much of his own happiness, though not, it would appear, of hers. Her parents concluded, after the divorce, that in order to lessen the adverse social impact of the divorce she should go abroad and live with her sister in Teheran.

Babis explained that Mr. Syrengela owned the oil refinery in Piraeus and that he had married off his elder daughter to a wealthy Persian who would ensure that his oil refinery was supplied with oil: the sister moved in "High Society" in Teheran and I suspect her parents felt Iole might meet someone suitable in Persia and remarry.

Iole's sister introduced her to a number of wealthy Persian families and it just so happened that she was introduced to a handsome, and, it turned out, influential young Air Force officer who was smitten by her. Iole did not welcome his advances, however, and decided that it would be prudent to move back to Athens and leave him behind in his own country.

Being determined to woo Iole, however, the officer persuaded the Persian Government to appoint him "Air Attaché" to the Persian Ambassador in Athens where he continued to pursue her.

And so it came about that he begged Iole to go out to dinner with him one evening at a very fashionable restaurant in Athens and, once in the restaurant, declared his love for her and asked her to marry him, or at least consider marrying him. Iole was very polite and said that she would think about his proposal but that, having been through an unhappy marriage she had not been thinking in terms of remarriage at that moment in time.

She was kind but firm about it and asked him to take her home: she did not invite him in and as she stepped out of the taxi to go into her flat, he also got out of the taxi and shouted, "If I cannot have you, nobody will." With that he drew a revolver from his pocket and shot her three times in the back, killing her instantly.

"Well," said Babis, "that really "set the cat among the pigeons." The attaché was arrested and thrown into jail but within hours he had claimed diplomatic immunity and had been released: he was allowed to return to the Persian Embassy.

Mr and Mrs. Syrengela were appalled at this turn of events and influenced the Greek Government into protesting at the highest level at what they considered a flagrant abuse of diplomatic immunity.

Pressure was brought to bear on the Air Force officer and he decided (or perhaps was ordered) to waive his immunity and allow himself to stand trial for murder.

Now it is an interesting feature of the Greek "psyche" that nothing gives a Greek greater satisfaction than a good argument with a bit of litigation thrown in: Babis indicated that he had decided, after obtaining his Law degree, not to practise as a lawyer because there were 19,000 of them in Athens already and most of them just scratched a living!

What did the Persian officer decide to do? He made an impassioned plea to the court to take him to a place of execution and put an end to his wretched life: "I have lost the only woman I ever loved. Take me, kill me," he cried. "I do not want to live any more."

Now if he had pleaded not guilty or pleaded mitigating circumstances why he should not die this would have given every Greek in the land great satisfaction in pronouncing him worthy of nothing less than a death sentence. But like Welshmen they love a bit of litigation, a bit of cut and thrust – I confess to having Welsh origins myself. We populate the barristers' chambers across the country and many of us become solicitors – so I know how the Greeks think about this aspect of the law.

Putting it simply, the Greeks were embarrassed by this approach and decided to restore his diplomatic immunity and kick him out of the country as a "persona non grata." He therefore left Greece and was never heard of again, his career at an end.

But that was not the end of this story. A year or so after Babis told me about the trial and what had occurred I met a charming and highly intelligent Greek by the name of Costas Vournas. He was what I would call a "smooth man" – cultured and urbane. He had married an American lady and was trying to promote his business, the ACE Bureau. ACE stood for Athens Cultural Exchanges: he knew I was sending hundreds of students from all over the UK to Greece every year and wanted me to join him in setting up cultural exchanges for British students as he had for Americans.

He took me out to dinner one evening and I asked him what he had done before he became involved in cultural exchanges. "I worked as PA for the owner of an oil refinery in the Piraeus," he said. "Who was that?" "I doubt whether you would know him: his name was Mr. Syrengela."

"Oh my God, was that Iole's father?" "Yes, you know about her, you must have read about her murder in the papers". "I knew her", I replied: "I took her out when she was in Cambridge: I met her in Athens before and after she married."

What an incredible coincidence that I should meet her father's personal assistant. "You must tell me what happened after the trial," I said.

"Well," said Costas," "the old man went to pieces. He felt responsible for her death. It literally broke him and he could no longer concentrate on his work. I left him at that point: he was inconsolable, especially at the fact that his daughter could be murdered and that the person who robbed him of her got away scot free." I told Babis about my meeting with Costas and we both put her fate down to the will of the Gods, a real twentieth Century Greek tragedy in which I am now the belated Chorus.

That concluded the tragic story of Iole for me but, as the reader will have gathered, I have never forgotten her and would want her fate to have lessons for us in the present time.

Wealth does not bring happiness: forcing young people into relationships that are more for the social standing and "mores" of the parents is essentially counter-productive. Women are not chattels to be traded (or "had" as the Persian Officer said): life has to be lived with kindness and compassion, not selfishness and self-absorption. Too much to expect, perhaps, in this far from perfect world but I hope her story will give pause for thought and reflection as it has for me throughout my life.

2

To Greece as a Boy Scout

When I told Iole, in the Union Cellars in Cambridge, that I had been to Greece in 1954 I probably mentioned that I went there as a Boy Scout (a "proskopos") at the advanced age, in Scouting terms, of eighteen.

The path that led me to that particular visit, the consequences of which affected me for the whole of my life, was a strange one: it commenced when I was thirteen.

Having passed the 11-plus and having secured my pre-existing place at a grant-maintained school (my father could not afford more than two terms' fees) I gravitated from lower one in which I performed well to upper two in which I performed badly.

I performed badly because my mind was on other things. I had become the "Dinky Toy" dealer of my year. Model cars and planes passed through my hands (including, I recall, the Imperial Airways, "Mayo" – a flying boat with a smaller plane on top – probably worth quite a lot now!) Had any schoolmaster cared to lift the lid of my desk he would have found neat rows of Dinky Toys where exercise books should normally be. But how else was a twelve year old to make an honest living?

The headmaster wrote to my parents at the end of my last term in upper two and told them that if I did not buck up my ideas I would have to leave the school. I got the message, gave up "second hand car dealing" and leapt from 29 out of 32 to 5th in my first term in classical three.

On entering classical three the form master, Mr. Martin, an authoritative figure with aquiline features ("Polecat" to the boys for obvious reasons!) stated that sixteen boys would have to learn German and sixteen Greek. "Who wishes to learn German?" Thirty one of us put up our hands. One boy, John Rist, who subsequently became Professor of Classics at Toronto University, wanted, not surprisingly in retrospect, to learn Greek.

"Well, in that case, every alternate boy in the class register will learn Greek and if any of your parents object tell them to write me a letter and I will see what can be done. Hughes, you will learn Greek."

I have to admit that I was disappointed at the time: my father spoke good German. At family Christmas celebrations and, after a few drinks, he would stand on the dining room table and sing "Die Lorelei" or give recitations in German – much to my mother's acute embarrassment. "Get down, Rob, immediately," she would hiss at him. But he was irrepressible, and when the Muse was in him and he had an appreciative audience it took more than a hiss to get him down! His consumption of alcohol, apart from Christmas, was monitored and strictly limited by my watchful mother!

Fate often takes a hand in life and it is strange how the decision of Mr. Martin affected my future. This book would not have been written, I would doubtless have gone to another university and would never have had so many remarkable experiences. There was to be no going back on his decision. Greek it had to be whether I liked the subject or not!

To me the torture of having to assimilate Latin and Greek from the ages of thirteen to sixteen was pretty intense. On the other hand, Latin teaches one to be logical and think straight and Greek helps one to explore human frailty.

It was not until I reached the sixth form, lower six Classics, that we were introduced to ancient history. That subject switched on an intense light in my brain and illuminated and justified all those arduous years of study.

Ancient history was amazing: when studying the histories of Greece and Rome one could see how the mistakes of past civilisations are replicated throughout history: one could also absorb the thoughts and study the ambitions of men who over two thousand years ago were as clever and gifted as we are today.

Through a combination of Latin, Greek and ancient history one enters a world of Gods and Heroes, of fate and "hubris", of great art and architecture, of power and the corroding influence of it. Just as importantly it generates a huge desire to visit Italy and Greece and see at first hand what remains of Greek and Roman civilisations. The opportunity to do so occurred, thanks to the School Scout troop, earlier than I expected.

My only previous connection with Scouting had been as a twelve year old Billericay Sea Scout. Billericay was a strange location for a troop of Sea Scouts, being so far from the sea. Moreover, although we at one stage had a dinghy on the boating lake known as Lake Meadows, it had sunk shortly before I joined at the age of twelve.

The Scoutmaster ("Skip") was, frankly, a rather suspect character. He had been a Petty Officer in the Royal Navy: he seemed to enjoy taking young Sea Scouts to his flat in Southend and "entertaining" them. I received such an invitation myself and was taken by "Skip" to see Bert Ossirati – Southend's champion wrestler, fight at the Kursaal.

Bert Ossirati was like a rubber ball – bouncing off the canvas as he was hurled onto it by his Irish opponent who clearly won the bout. When Bert Ossirati was given the decision a riot broke out, with chairs being thrown into the ring and the Irishman giving an impassioned harangue to the furious crowd. "This fight has been fixed," he shouted, and it was clear that most people agreed.

I was led outside as bare knuckle fights broke out and spread from the ring towards the back of the hall. As a child I thought this was really exciting!

It was when "Skip" offered to dry me after a swim that I felt something was wrong: I politely declined and dried myself. I left the troop shortly afterwards but not before I had achieved my "Second Class". The Scout Troop was disbanded a few months later.

There were no CRB checks in those days: too much trust and perhaps naivety was shown in the appointment of people as Scout leaders. Times have certainly changed and perhaps we have gone too far in the opposite direction in preventing perfectly respectable parents joining the Scout movement.

Mr. Rowswell ("Perk" to the boys), the Scoutmaster at my school, Brentwood School, was completely different. Short and stocky and full of energy, not only was he a teacher but he also controlled the issue of textbooks to every boy in the school. One could often find "Perk" in a largish room next to the cloisters in the "Old School" (and it really was old!) behind huge piles of books that he issued to classes and retrieved at the end of each school year.

He had decided in 1953 that the school Scout troop should be the first in the country to visit Greece immediately at the end of the Greek Civil War, and to travel there via Milan and Brindisi. As soon as I heard that the school Scout troop was going on this ground-breaking adventure I approached him and asked if I could join as an "ex Boy Scout".

"No", he replied, "you have to be a member of the school Scout troop and become a First Class Scout." "OK, how do I become a First Class Scout?" "You have to pass a number of tests and undertake a two-day twenty mile hike and write a log on what you saw and did during those two days." "It is November now and we are going in March: I cannot see you being able to do the hike before then."

"If I do the hike and pass the tests will you take me?" He looked at me quizzically. "If you do, I will let you join the trip."

Fortunately I had three things in my favour – wonderful parents, determination and the fact that another boy at the school who had been in the school Scout troop for two years but had not achieved his First Class, also wanted to go to Greece.

My mother, who controlled the family finances with the precision of an accountant, decided that she would help me raise the necessary fare by going out and doing a post round. Moreover I was used to the cold. When we moved into our new home, Pink Cottage, at the end of 1947 it was still drying out: the walls were damp, the winter of 1947/8 was bitter and all I had was a single-bar electric fire set in a tiled surround on the wall upon which my father had placed a wooden plaque. It read, "One inch of joy surmounts of grief a span, because to laugh is proper to the man." That, and a couple of blankets, were intended to keep me warm and sanguine!

And so it was that in February 1954, with my fourteen-year-old companion, I was driven to Kent and deposited somewhere not too far from Cobham. It was a sunny day but it was intensely cold and I have to admit to being the first Boy Scout in the country to abandon shorts for corduroy trousers.

As it started to become dark we stopped at a farm and asked if we could camp in the farmer's field. He offered to put us up for the night but we bravely declined. What would "Perk" think if we had "cheated" by spending the night in a farmhouse!

We nearly froze to death that night and when we tried to fold the little green bivouac tent in the morning it would not fold – it was like a board, frozen solid! We ultimately packed it and set off again.

During the morning we came to a hamlet – a church and about four or five houses. I have since tried to find it because I hope it was not a figment of our joint imaginations.

In the wall of what appeared to be a Georgian house I noticed some thin red tiles that appeared to be Roman and we decided to knock on the front door and ask if they were. It would be something to add to our log.

The door was opened by a slim blonde young lady in a grey dress with a white collar: she looked about twenty five.

"Sorry to bother you, but do you know if the tiles in the wall of your house are Roman?" Yes they are." "You both look cold. Would you like to come in and have a cup of tea. I can then show you one or two other interesting things about the house."

We gratefully accepted the offer and went inside. She was apparently governess to four young children whom we never saw

After the cup of tea she led us into a room which just had a great hole in the middle with a solid beam in the centre of it: on the beam were what appeared to be iron shackles. "Do you know what this room is? It is a bear pit and on the opposite wall you will see an Anglo Saxon window.

"But that is not all: follow me." She led us into a gallery that was part of a mediaeval hall and pointed to the wall. There, scratched into the wall and behind glass, were pictures of 13th century ships with wording in what was clearly an early form of French. The pictures and the wording had obviously been made by children. We were gobsmacked by what we saw and we thanked the young lady effusively for what she had shown us.

I have since purchased the OS sheets for the Cobham area and have driven all round it but I am blowed if I can find that hamlet and that house! Google indicates that there is only one "open air" bear pit in Kent, not one inside a house! The location of that house is a complete mystery.

Having braved the elements and submitted my log I was allowed to travel to Greece. Once across the Channel we all sat in the train from Calais to Basel and from Basel to Milan. After an eight hour stopover in Milan and an evening meal in an Italian restaurant at the station we set off to Brindisi, at the heel of Italy.

Two days after our departure from Victoria Station we boarded the "MV Miaoulis" – a brand new and very beautiful but small passenger ship operated by Nomikos Lines. It had been presented to Greece as part of the reparations Italy made to Greece for occupying parts of the country during the Second World War. By the time I stopped travelling to Greece via Brindisi some twenty years later it had been replaced by much larger passenger ships and was probably used subsequently for passenger travel between the smaller islands.

Regrettably I left my mark on the ship by lighting my small primus stove upside down on the pristine planking. Hopefully the crew never realised how the marks appeared on the deck!

As a school Scout troop we were taken to the Army camp at Vouliagmeni and accommodated in tents. It is hard now to imagine an Army camp at Vouliagmeni, populated as it is by massive hotels and expensive villas. But in those days one could buy two kilos of fresh oranges for roughly 6d (2 1/2p) – not sure now how many hundred drachmas we paid but at the time there were 80,000 drachmas to the £ sterling. As youngsters we felt quite rich with these high denomination notes even though they were worth next to nothing. The Greek Government subsequently decided to knock off the "thousands" and make it 80 drachmas to the £ sterling.

Because it was such an unusual visit to Greece, the British Ambassador, Charles Peake, attended our camp and the Greek Government arranged for a number of young Greek students to visit us. Among the students was an attractive young lady by the name of Lydia Hadjidakis with whom I was able to converse – she in her faltering English and me in my faltering Greek.

One of the things that interested me in her, apart, admittedly, from her good looks, was her name. "Hadji" is Turkish and her family must have been part of the Turkish population which dominated Greece until 1820. Lord Byron was one of the champions of liberty during the Greeks' struggle for independence, hence the popularity of the name in Greece. Most Turks were driven out of Greece at the time (in the same way as the Greeks were driven out of Turkey a century later when Kemal Atatürk came to power).

Some Turks, including Lydia's family, must have stayed in Greece and become assimilated into the Greek population. I was later to experience the antipathy of the Greeks towards the Turks and vice versa during my military service in Cyprus.

As Scouts we had to entertain the Ambassador and Greek dignitaries with renditions of Scouting songs, and it is probably fair to say that we were at the very forefront of the subsequent popularity of Greece as a tourist destination.

Returning from Greece the same way as we had arrived after visits to Mycenae and Epidaurus and, of course, the Acropolis, I was full of enthusiasm for the country and probably to the surprise of my teachers achieved a state scholarship in Classics and a place at Cambridge.

I do not claim credit for that success, however. The credit goes to our extraordinary teachers. Five out of the eight boys in my upper sixth form, second year, achieved scholarships in Classics. That has to say as much for the quality of the education as for the abilities of the people who were taught.

It is such a pity that teaching Classics has fallen by the wayside because it gives such a remarkable foundation to later studies and the ability to rationalise and put life into perspective. I can only hope that one day this is appreciated and that study of the Classics makes a comeback. I doubt it will but one can always live in hope!

3

National Service: Edinburgh

What I did not mention to Iole in the Union Cellars, or indeed ever, was that during my National Service I had been attached to the Special Branch of the Cyprus Police as part of a Military Intelligence Unit in Kyrenia, a resort on the north coast of the island.

The unit consisted of a Major Peter Purves, Detective Sergeant Jim Herlihy from New Scotland Yard, a retired English Lady of the Realm who acted as our Secretary and myself. Our secretary's husband had been awarded a knighthood, as a senior member of the Civil Service, and they had settled in the island on his retirement.

Our remit was to keep an eye on the known EOKA suspects and sympathisers in the Kyrenia area and to pass back such information as we were able to Military Intelligence Headquarters in Nicosia: we had, for example, paid a "surprise visit" on the Bishop of Kyrenia and had uncovered a great deal of information, literature and posters relating to EOKA in his Palace.

EOKA was the mainland Greek organisation that wanted Cyprus to unite with and become part of Greece, led principally by Colonel Grivas, a famous partisan from the Second World War.

Union (Enosis) with Greece was realistically and practically impossible for two simple reasons: with its large Turkish-Cypriot population Turkey would never have allowed it and Cyprus, as an island, was wealthier and had a much higher standard of living than Greece: there was no real reason why the bulk of the population would wish to tie themselves to a poorer, and, in the case of the Turkish population, an alien country.

In terms of subsequent history the invasion by Turkey of the north of

Cyprus and the division of the island into Greek and Turkish sectors bears witness to the fact that Turkey would never have countenanced Enosis: the fact that the Greek sector has not sought closer ties with the mainland since partition is also evidence of their lack of enthusiasm for "ever closer union".

We knew that, as a unit we were under surveillance by EOKA members and sympathisers, which made the whole situation a bit "cat and mouse". We were aware that Emilios Georghiou, one of our Special Branch policemen was an EOKA sympathiser, and probably an EOKA member, and I am sure that he knew we suspected him by the way we prevented him from entering our offices in the Special Branch Headquarters. But more of my experiences on active service in Cyprus in the next chapter.

When I was called up in September 1954 to do National Service I was posted initially to the Royal Artillery Regiment Training Camp at Park Hall, Oswestry. Among our "intake" it was obvious that some of us were more used to the disciplines of army life than others – to whom they were going to come as a considerable shock!

Between the ages of sixteen and eighteen I had been on a number of signals courses with the Royal Corps of Signals in Colchester, learning about wireless and telephone communication systems and had been a Colour Sergeant in charge of the Signals Platoon of the School's Combined Cadet Force for two years before being promoted in my last term to Company Sergeant Major in charge of Support Company.

To me it was exactly what I had expected: to others it was a traumatic experience: "hard nosed" NCOs made you march backwards and forwards across a vast parade ground seemingly for hours, threw all your kit on the floor of your barrack room if anything laid out on your bed was fractionally out of place made you sweep leaves across the parade ground, only for them to blow back again or else they put you on canteen detail where you had to peel several hundredweights of potatoes: all this constituted "training" and was supposed to instil discipline in those who were unused to it!

Medical checks were carried out on our arrival at Park Hall and when being inoculated we all stood in a long line in nothing more than our pants while a medical orderly walked along the line plunging a hypodermic needle (the same needle) into the arms of the recruits. Every so often one of the recruits would faint and collapse on the ground in anticipation of having the needle thrust into him!

It was at Park Hall camp that we were summoned to a WOSB (War Office Selection Board) if we were considered "Officer material". With a number of others I was sent for assessment and given a "Deferred Watch". In other words the assessors – mostly senior officers – were not sure about my suitability to be commissioned into the Royal Artillery but would assess me again after a further three months.

Having risen to the rank of Company Sergeant Major in the school's CCF I was surprised when I was deferred but I had made it clear that, if commissioned, my choice of regiment was the Royal Artillery. My grandfather had been in the Royal Artillery, laying telephone lines to forward observation posts (FOPs) during the First World War and I wanted to follow in his footsteps and join "the Gunners".

Although I did not appreciate at the time that I was what one might call "psychic" (and I ask the reader to suspend belief on that assertion until you have read the later chapters of this book), I always had a gnawing suspicion that I could not explain, except in terms of a deep revulsion at the loss of so much life in the trenches, that the man whose spirit I may have inherited was killed on the front line during the First World War. Fanciful perhaps but there was no getting away from a strong sense that I had lived before and this was one of the reasons why I had myself "regressed" (taken back to what might have been a previous life) when I was in my early forties.

When, therefore, on the Deferred Watch I was offered the chance of officer training and gaining a Commission, not in the Royal Artillery but in an infantry regiment, I turned it down. Turning down the offer of a Commission in an infantry regiment might be seen by many as short-sighted and somewhat arrogant – and perhaps it was: but fate had clearly intervened in my decision and had led me to do so.

In terms of rationalising my decision, hostilities in the Korean War had concluded in 1953 but a peace treaty had not been signed and if I was to see active service in Korea I wanted it to be in a regiment of my choice. I had no wish to go into the PBI ("poor bloody infantry") and be ordered into action by officers for whom I might not have had a great deal of respect: the lives of subalterns were cheap, as I was well aware. I would choose how I died if I was going to – as, indeed, I nearly did!

The upshot of my decision was that I remained at the Royal Artillery Regiment in Edinburgh to which I had previously been posted and was put on a TARA Course. The Regiment, the 51st Heavy "Ack Ack", was being converted into the 38th Medium Regiment equipped with 4.5 inch guns (similar to those on a Royal Navy destroyer) and later with 5.5 inch guns mounted on their own tractors (instead of being towed behind three ton trucks).

TARA's were "Technical Assistants, Royal Artillery" and responsible for aligning guns on targets up to 14,000 yards away by means of logarithmic tables. I had never understood logarithms at school but when lining up these huge guns they made perfect sense: we were the "intelligentsia" of the other ranks and nearly all of us were waiting to take up places at university at the end of our two years' National Service.

During the first few months at Edinburgh I managed to avoid guard duty by becoming "Stick man" six times in a row. The "Stick man", the smartest soldier on parade, was excused guard duty and thereby avoided having to stay all night in the guardhouse. Consequently my best boots had a "glass-like" finish because they were never used except for these parades. I made a point of standing rigidly to attention or "at ease" from the moment we lined up on the parade ground for inspection – because I knew that the parade ground could be seen from the Officers' Mess and the Inspecting Officer would have had a look at us before he appeared on the parade ground.

My best boots gleamed because, being canny, I had brought my CCF boots with me as a third pair. When, therefore, the CO ordered everyone to wear their best boots on manoeuvres – to prevent what he considered an obsession with keeping "best boots" for special occasions – I just wore my "second best" boots which looked as good as everyone else's best (because I did not wear them much either!)

By this means I ingratiated myself with my Battery Sergeant Major, "Danny" Kaye, a former sparring partner of Jack Gardner, a British heavyweight boxing champion. The Sergeants' Mess also overlooked the parade ground and after being "Stick man" on three consecutive occasions the sergeants started betting on me. Danny told me triumphantly that he had won £30 on me on the sixth occasion and offered me a permanent place serving as a waiter in the Sergeants' Mess. I turned down his offer saying that the only way I would come back into the Mess would be as a sergeant! Strangely, I just missed out on this!

Shortly after that offer I was promoted to bombardier (two stripes) having come out at the top of an NCO's "leadership course" where all but three of the participants were promoted to lance bombardier (one stripe) or not promoted at all.

Promotion to bombardier meant that I had to take over the duties of the "regular" sergeants who lived out of barracks with their families: these duties included getting all the other ranks up in the morning, getting them to bed before lights out and acting as Guard Commander at the barracks (Redford Barracks in Colinton) and at Edinburgh Castle.

Redford Barracks in Colinton, a suburb of Edinburgh, were based on a design used for barracks in the Raj during the Victorian era. The design was unfortunately totally inappropriate for a cold and windy city on the east coast of Scotland. The barracks were draughty and poorly heated and, once in a warm bed, few of us relished getting up in the morning.

As a bombardier I had my own room but every morning I had to wake up the sleeping gunners at 6.30 am and rouse them from their beds. I would therefore go through the three barrack rooms on my floor, fully dressed, telling everyone it was time to get up. Those who demurred, after ten minutes' "grace", received short shrift. I would vigorously bang the end of their beds with the pick axe handle I carried: it always had the desired (jarring) effect! Sometimes I had a violent reaction but not often and nothing I was incapable of handling.

Another duty was to ensure that everyone was in bed by 11 pm and, one evening, an inoffensive young Gunner by the name of Humphreys staggered into one of the barrack rooms at about 11.30 pm covered in blood. He had been set upon and beaten up in Leith, the port area of Edinburgh, just outside one of the pubs there. I dressed his cuts and bruises and made sure he had no broken bones, before putting him to bed.

The next day I was approached by Cassidy, one of the Gunners who had opted for three years' military service instead of two years in prison. He was an experienced lock picker – whose skills I once used when I inadvertently closed my locker with the key inside. He asked me if I would turn "a blind eye" to the fact that no one in Humphrey's barrack room would be in bed at 11 pm that night. The entire barrack room proposed to pay a visit to Leith. As long as they could get back into the barracks after 11 pm without being seen I had no problem with his request.

At about midnight twenty or so Gunners reappeared in Humphrey's barrack room, all very pleased with themselves. Humphreys had been avenged! I gained considerable respect for "turning a blind eye" and I also gained respect by never letting the "f" word pass my lips and by going to church every

Sunday. With my friend, Kenneth Gubbins, I attended the "Ice Cream Parlour" in Morningside, the name given to the Church of Scotland, where we both acquired a lot of friends and, in particular Archie and Moira Thomson and their parents who offered us a "home from home". The church was called the "Ice Cream Parlour" because of the pastel shades in which the interior had been painted.

As mentioned previously, acting as Battery Orderly Sergeant included acting as Guard Commander at Redford Barracks and at Edinburgh Castle in the absence of the regular sergeants who lived outside the barracks. Other than having to be aware of an undefined (at the time) threat of IRA terrorism guard duty at the barracks was uneventful. I did, however, have some interesting times as Guard Commander at Edinburgh Castle and I can recall one occasion vividly.

At about midnight one particular night there was a banging on the outer door of the castle and I sent a member of the guard to find out what the noise was all about. He returned saying that an elderly lady wished to commit suicide by throwing herself off the battlements.

"Go back to her and ask if she would like a cup of tea before she commits suicide. If she says 'yes' bring her into the guard room while you" (I pointed to another member of the Guard) "go and find a policeman. Otherwise tell her she cannot come in."

She did want a cup of tea, which we took some time to prepare and it was not long before a policeman arrived to take her away. "Hello, Molly", he said. "Up to your old tricks then. Come on dear, I will take you back to the Home." Problem satisfactorily resolved!

The reader may be wondering what we all did during our days at Redford Barracks and the answer is not a great deal. Making young men, mostly between the ages of eighteen and twenty, undertake National Service was an interesting concept and was intended to supplement the manpower resources of the British Army, Navy and Air Force during the Cold War.

When I was conscripted in 1954, apart from Korea, there had not been a war as such since 1945: National Servicemen had been deployed from the end of World War Two in Malaya, Kenya and Cyprus to fight "terrorist" insurgency but, for a Royal Artillery Regiment with "big guns" there was little it could be called upon to do.

Inactivity saps morale and lowers awareness of danger and what it is like to be in a "battlefront" situation: two years in the Services was a period of "marking time" for most National Servicemen. Nevertheless it did change many of them from boys into men.

As a regiment we did occasionally go on manoeuvres to the Otterburn ranges near Morpeth in Northumberland and three incidents stand out in my mind while we were there.

The first relates to my job as a TARA. Each battery had a "three ton" command post truck which we (the TARAs) had converted to take a large sloping board or table top at the front of the enclosed canvas area behind the driver's cab. On this sloping area the two TARAs for each of the three batteries placed Ordnance Survey maps of the area in which we were located at the time. We marked the position of the guns of our respective batteries on the maps and their alignment – basically pointing forward and not backwards!!

Each regiment had a survey officer, in our case a Lieutenant MacDonald, and I recall he came to our truck on the morning after we had arrived at a particular location and told us that our guns were pointing in the wrong direction!

As "lead TARA" I demurred and Battery Sergeant Major "Danny" Kaye was summoned: he listened to what Lieutenant MacDonald had to say and then turned to me. "Are the guns 180% out, as he says, or not?" To which I replied "No, Sergeant Major, they are not."

"Get out of my battery", Danny shouted at the unfortunate Lieutenant MacDonald. "You cannot speak to an officer like that", said the piqued lieutenant. "I can speak to you any way I like," retorted Danny and, with that, the Lieutenant was unceremoniously shown off the premises!

Danny came back to me immediately afterwards and said, "I hope you were right." "Don't worry, Sergeant Major." I had already checked the alignment of the guns with John Wilson, my "university-bound" counterpart in the adjoining battery. Lt. MacDonald was subsequently made Regimental Catering Officer, a role for which he was doubtless better suited!

The second incident related to an "inept" performance by a Sergeant Jones who was ordered to fire ranging shots into a range between 12,000 and 14,000 yards away. As TARAs we passed him the coordinates, the angle of elevation of the guns and how much explosive charge he needed to hit a target some 13,000 yards away.

Our brigadier had come to see how accurate our shelling of a target would be and sat outside a concrete command post at the 12,000 yard mark. He radioed the battery to say that he was in position and waiting for our battery to fire into the range ahead of him.

Fortunately for him, Nature intervened and he decided to visit the loo in the command post. When he came out of the loo he was concerned to note that his radio had disappeared and that the shell from one of Sergeant Jones's guns had landed where he had been sitting!

He drove back to the battery and demanded an urgent explanation. As TARAs we were able to demonstrate that the correct information had been passed to the guns. He then insisted on an examination of the gun that had fired the "rogue" shell. The shells were not small and, if one stood immediately behind and in line with the barrel of the gun, one could actually see the shell leave the barrel and zoom into the air – an impressive sight.

The barrel of a 4.5 inch gun weighs about two tons and the elevation had to be locked, once set. The unfortunate Sergeant (subsequently Gunner) Jones had failed to ensure that the barrel had been locked and the weight of it had reduced its elevation by one or two degrees. The last we saw of Sergeant Jones was his being led off by two Royal Military Policemen (RMPs). He was very lucky he did not kill the brigadier and that he was merely demoted back to the ranks!

The third incident was a strange one. We had parked our three ton TARA truck in a deserted churchyard way up on the moors near Otterburn. The mist swirled around our truck on a cold early winter's night and I was ordered to do guard duty between midnight and 2 am with just a torch for company.

The thought of wandering round a misty cemetery in the dead of night in pitch black conditions was not an attractive one. I had visions of a ghostly Magwitch suddenly appearing from behind a tombstone but when I started my midnight watch I was really surprised.

The atmosphere was so friendly – there is no other word for it. I could not understand it: it was as if the spirits of all the people whose bodies lay in that cemetery had appeared to welcome me. It was such a contrast to what I had expected that I have never forgotten it. My fellow TARA who did the 2 am to 4 am watch was not so happy about standing guard in what he considered such a "spooky" place.

The boredom, overall, of my duties in Edinburgh and the loss of sleep occasioned by my having to act as Guard Commander at least once a week led me to employ a stratagem I had been taught by one of my schoolmasters. It was to propel me from Edinburgh to Cyprus, to active service and to a much more interesting and exciting time in the Army

4

National Service: Cyprus

"If you want to do anything in the Army tell them you can already do it," said Mr. Riddiford, our Latin master. Mr. Riddiford ("Bubbles") was always giving us sage advice and would quite happily come into the classroom for a Latin lesson and say, for example, "Let's forget about Latin for the moment: I am going to tell you about Italian coffee bars." And off he would go, striding round the classroom pointing out a "Gaggia" coffee machine over here and wines and spirits behind an imaginary bar over there, while we sat entranced by his enthusiastic description of life in Italy, particularly life in coffee bars!

"When you go into the Army if you want to drive a truck," he said, "tell them you can already drive a truck. They will then put you on an M.T. course. It is how the Army operates."

"Take my example. I wanted to go out to Italy during my National Service, so I told my C.O. I could speak fluent Italian. It was an absolute lie but before I knew it I was in Trieste and up before a Major in the Intelligence Corps."

The Major was not impressed and said, "Riddiford, I am going to give you a month to learn Italian. If you do not, I will send you on the first flight back to England."

Bubbles continued: "So I really set myself to the task of learning Italian: I put an ice pack on my head as I sweated over the words and phrases I had to be able to pronounce.

"At the end of the month I went before the Major desperately worried that I would be flown home."

"Not bad Riddiford," said the Major. "You have done well but you need to brush up your colloquial Italian. Get yourself a woman!"

"So I did," said Bubbles," and now have a wife and two bambini: I married the daughter of a engineer in Mestre, near Venice and my life could not have turned out better for me."

We boys were impressed and I made a mental note of his stratagem.

In fact our schoolmasters were all full of advice to us and this perhaps is one of the advantages of a public school education. For example, Gerald Cluer ("Tom"), one of our Greek teachers, came into our classroom one day and said, "Boys, I want to tell you all about matrimony." We wondered what he was going to say.

"When you get married you will look into her eyes and what will you see?" "Don't know, sir," we replied. "You will see marital bliss. And she will look into your eyes and what will she see?" "Don't know sir. "Three square meals a day!" We all came to the conclusion that poor Tom was not happily married.

So when boredom in Edinburgh set in I asked for an interview with the C.O. "Sir, I speak fluent modern Greek and would like to be posted to Cyprus to act as an interpreter." It was an outright lie but I guessed the C.O. would not speak or even understand Greek. "Well done, Hughes," said the C.O. "I will notify the War Office immediately." At this time Enosis and EOKA were beginning to grab the headlines in the national papers and I guessed that the Army would be looking for interpreters.

Within a week I received a travel pass to a Military Intelligence Unit in Chester where I met about thirty other National Servicemen who had Ancient Greek at "A" Level. All except myself and one regular Royal Artillery Sergeant had absolutely no desire to go to Cyprus. I discovered this by asking them all before the interviews began They said, "We are all happy where we are. We don't want to be posted to a dangerous place like Cyprus."

"In that case," said I, "you must all pretend to be as thick as possible while I and the Sergeant here (whose name, strangely, was John Smith) try to impress." They all thought this was a great wheeze and so, shortly thereafter, I was taken in to see a Major Costanza.

Major Costanza, a sallow-faced man in his forties thrust a Greek book in my hand: "Read that," he said. I had been to Greece in 1954 and had purchased a Greek phrase book in Edinburgh before I got on the train to Chester. I also had Ancient Greek at "A" level so I read the book to him in passable modern Greek. During the course of the interview I had twigged that he was Maltese and did not speak or understand Greek at all. It was not difficult, therefore, to impress him.

The other Servicemen, all very bright, came back into the barrack room in which we had been put, falling about with laughter at the deliberate mistakes they had made in reading and translating the book they had been given.

So, not surprisingly, John Smith and I found ourselves on an RAF transport plane, each with a rifle, heading for Nicosia a week or so later.

As our plane taxied down the runway on arrival I noted the burnt-out Hermes transport plane at the side of the runway: it had been blown up by terrorists.

We were collected by an Intelligence Corps sergeant and taken to see the Brigadier to the Chief of Staff. He was a very engaging man indeed – extremely bright with a twinkle in his eye.

"We have been trying to stop you two boys coming out to Cyprus but you have somehow arrived," he said. "It was quite obvious to us that neither of you would be in the Army long enough for us to train you to speak Greek and act as interpreters.

"But you have both shown considerable initiative and I am going to offer you two choices. I can either send you both to a Royal Artillery unit on the island or you can come into Military Intelligence." "Military Intelligence, sir," we said in unison!

"In that case I can post one of you to Nicosia and the other to Kyrenia. Which is it to be? "Kyrenia, Sir," (a seaside town) we replied in unison.

"Well, you will have to toss for it.". With that he took a coin out of his pocket and flicked it into the air. I was lucky on the toss of the coin and won Kyrenia!

"Well that is settled. I will arrange the postings," he said. "Excuse me, sir. Could I ask a question?" "What is it?" the Brigadier replied.

"He is a Sergeant, sir. Is there any reason why I cannot be a Sergeant as well?"

"I suppose not", said the Brigadier. "I will see to that too."

I have always operated on the principle that if you do not ask you do not get and my somewhat "cheeky" question resulted in a very satisfactory outcome: promotion to Sergeant secured several advantages, not only through an increase in pay but in much better living conditions.

And so it was that I was taken by truck to Kyrenia Castle and a billet with the Wiltshire Regiment.

The next day I was collected and taken up to the Special Branch headquarters where I was introduced to the "dramatis personae."

The first person I met was Detective Sergeant Jim Herlihy from New Scotland Yard. He had been seconded to Special Branch in view of his passing knowledge of Greek.

Jim Herlihy was, in fact, a very interesting man: during the war he had been in the SBS (Special Boat Service, the counterpart of the SAS) and he struck me as more of a soldier than anyone in an Army uniform in Cyprus at the time. While we were holed up in the Pentedaktylos range of mountains which separate the north from the centre of the island trying to locate terrorists he told me about his experiences in the SBS. The six (or eight) crew members would bring their MTB (motor torpedo boat) or equivalent at the dead of night into a cove of a small island and make their way towards the German garrison in the town: they would then work out which road the German troops would use to make their way to the harbour in the morning and then lie down on either side of the walls bordering the road in wait. As the German troops marched past they would lob hand grenades over the walls into the road and after they had exploded rake the Germans with Sten gun fire, killing them all. They would then head "hell for leather" towards their MTB. He said they would always leave an SBS beret behind because the remaining Germans would otherwise have massacred the islanders as a reprisal. Hitler had ordered that no SAS or SBS personnel should be taken prisoner: they should be executed on the spot. They knew they had to make a clean getaway before a German spotter plane was sent out and strafed them.

Jim had also acted as a royal protection officer to the Duke of Edinburgh during the Royal visit to Australia in 1954 and since what he did in private on the visit doubtless falls within the compass of the Official Secrets Act, all I can say is that, according to Jim, it was very difficult to protect someone who did not really want to be protected!

The Duke of Edinburgh, being an ex-Naval Lieutenant Commander had a mind of his own where protection was concerned. Jim did teach me some useful things, however: how to kill a guard dog that is attacking you by using its own momentum against it; how to disarm someone with a knife and break their arm at the same time and, perhaps more useful, how to open a letter without anyone knowing it had been opened and read.

I have come across many wives in my time who were intrigued to find out how this was done but my response has been, "If I tell you, I will have to kill you." That has the effect of switching the conversation on to other subjects!

Major Purves was an Intelligence officer serving out his time. He had not been demobilised in 1945 and my guess is that he had joined the Army as a regular before the outbreak of the Second World War. He had been posted to Kyrenia because not a great deal more was expected of him. He had a photograph of himself as a Major, with Field Marshal Montgomery and a group of other officers in 1945 on his desk and it was pretty clear to me that he had not progressed since and he was not going upwards in rank.

One of our most valuable supporters was Brigadier Cummings VC, who was in charge of the Special Constabulary, an auxiliary police service in Kyrenia.

Brigadier Cummings had won his VC in Burma. When giving a briefing to his senior officers at a command post in the jungle a Japanese soldier managed to crawl up to the front of the command post and lob a hand grenade into it. Brigadier Cummings had coolly picked it up and thrown it back out of the opening through which it had arrived, killing the Japanese soldier.

He was an amazingly sprightly man, in his sixties, and came to target practice with us. We took all the Greek-Cypriot Special Branch policemen with us to demonstrate that we could hit targets, of whatever kind.

At one practice, Brigadier Cummings had borrowed a 9mm Schmeiser pistol from the Wiltshire Regiment Major at Kyrenia Castle and fired at his target making the shape of a heart in it with the bullets. Our Cypriot compatriots were very impressed. No one ever bothered him!

Another great character was Sergeant George Wright from the Warwickshire Constabulary. he was your typical Midlands police officer – well-built, friendly-looking and very competent – a "switched on" version of "Dixon of Dock Green". Shortly after I arrived he won enormous respect from the town of Lapithos, a hotbed of EOKA activity in the north- west of the island. It was part of his "patch" and he would drive there in his khaki shorts and jacket (KDs) black police belt and black police hat in his Land Rover on a regular basis.

As he was approaching Lapithos one day he heard an explosion and headed immediately towards it. There in the road he found four seriously injured young children. They had found a cache of hand grenades hidden in a wall by the side of the road and one of the children had pulled out the pin of one of them. George immediately put tourniquets on the injured children and without further ado drove at top speed to the nearest hospital. The children survived and after that he was called Sergeant "Georgios tou Lapithou" (Sergeant George of Lapithos). Nobody went near him subsequently. He became a hero to everyone in the town.

Of the Wiltshire Regiment personnel only two stood out – CSM Peter Martin and Sergeant Douglas Puffett. Peter Martin had eight or nine "O" levels and was determined to make the commissioned rank of Major before he left the army. He was always immaculate (except when I once wrecked his uniform – of which more anon) and extremely capable. He and I got on extremely well and I owe the fact that I was not arrested and thrown into jail to his timely warning (of which more also anon!).

Sergeant Doug Puffett and I became friends in a different way.

After spending a couple of days in a large and somewhat airless stone barrack room on the north side of the castle as a Bombardier my promotion came through and I was taken to the Sergeant's quarters. These consisted of a row of cell-like rooms facing on to the parade ground in the centre of the castle.

The Wiltshire Regiment Sergeants thought they would put a "snotty-nosed public schoolboy" in his place by pouring a couple of buckets of cold water over his bed! When I found my bedding was sodden I said, "Whoever did this did not make a very good job of it. He should have done it like this." With that and with Sergeant Puffett shouting, "If you throw that on my bed, look in" I threw a bucket of water over his bedding. To cut a long story short he then went to find a fire hydrant, I another, and we, Sergeants all, spent a night sleeping on tables outside our cells, having given the other ranks and the officers ringside entertainment at a massive water fight.

Doug Puffett and I and the other Sergeants all "came to an understanding" after that incident – and we all became very friendly. All "japes" were then directed principally by myself toward the three young subalterns.

I was accepted into the club (and I have to say that Sergeants do extremely well for themselves – often better than the Officers). I, for example, being an Acting Sergeant on active service received more pay than a Second Lieutenant, paid no mess fees and, courtesy of the Quartermaster, tended to eat better food than the officers. The officers' and sergeants' shared the same cook, Loucas, and the same kitchen. I can remember one occasion when the Sergeant Major looked at a plateful of anaemic-looking thin pork strips, floating in brown oil-tinted water that purported to be gravy and said, "I am not eating this muck. Q, let us have a Chinese. What have we got in the stores?" With that the Sergeants, having just returned from Hong Kong, prepared an excellent Chinese meal while the Officers ate or threw away Loucas's unappetising offering. I had already gathered from serving for a few days in the Sergeants' mess in Edinburgh that Sergeants looked after themselves and I have no doubt that this still goes for the entire British Army!

The tradition of pointing the tomato ketchup bottle towards visiting Sergeants arose from my not winding down the top of the ketchup bottle before passing it on. One morning at breakfast in the Sergeants' Mess Peter Martin picked up the bottle, shook it, and a plume of ketchup rose into the air and landed on his immaculate uniform.

Considering how inconvenient and embarrassing this was for him he was remarkably good about it but decreed that in future everyone should shake the ketchup bottle with the lid pointing at myself: they all did this until I left them!

As far as avoiding jail is concerned I regret to say that I was a disruptive influence in Kyrenia Castle. When a Daily Mirror correspondent paid an overnight visit to the castle I made an apple pie bed for him and I was nearly caught fixing a "tarantula" that I had made out of pipe cleaners and boot polish on to the light switch on one of the Officer's bedrooms. I had not appreciated that one of the Officers sharing the bedroom had gone to bed early and as I was fixing my "spider" to the light switch he heard me, said, "Who's there?" When I said nothing he reached for his revolver. At that moment I thought it prudent to disappear but not before I had said "Curses".

About half an hour later a deputation of subalterns came down to the Sergeants' Mess and complained about my activities. They said they would be reporting me to the Major.

The next day I went to the Special Branch headquarters and received a phone call from Peter Martin. "Brian, make sure your revolver is unloaded when you come into the castle tonight. It is an offence to bring a loaded weapon on to military premises and two RMPs will be waiting for you." They were indeed waiting in the shadows as I walked into the castle and I was able to show them that my revolver was not loaded. I thanked Peter for his timely warning.

This was shortly followed by a summons to appear before the Major "in residence" with his Sergeants: we all stood to attention in a row in front of him and he shouted, "I know my Sergeants. They would not get up to all the things that have happened here since you arrived. If I had my way I would kick you out of my castle." I looked sideways and they were all nodding their heads vigorously. "I am reporting you to the Colonel. Dismiss."

After that we all had a drink, with the Sergeants apologising to me for not taking any of the blame with me. But they were all regulars and could not afford to blot their military records. I was quite all right about that – all the disruptive ideas had been mine even though they went along with them!

The day of the summons to Harcha, the principal barracks of the Wiltshire Regiment duly arrived and I had to appear before the Colonel who, in fact, was an extremely pleasant man. The RSM who had led me in to see the colonel stood ramrod straight beside me.

After discussing my future place at Cambridge University and regretting the fact that I had clearly annoyed all the Officers at Kyrenia Castle he told the RSM to discipline me.

This was not before I had pointed out to him that there was absolutely nothing for the men to do at the castle, that they were not allowed out into Kyrenia and that, accordingly, morale was low as a result of the boredom they all felt.

The RSM marched me to the vast parade ground and then marched to the other side of it. He was your typical RSM, short, stocky, trim moustache with his baton quivering under his arm. "Party", he screamed across the parade ground, "Quick march." When I reached the middle, he screamed, "Party halt," and marched across the parade ground, halting within inches of my face. He then shouted so that anyone within two hundred yards could hear, "One more squeak out of you Sarn't Hughes, and I'll knock yer dahn." With that he gave me the most enormous wink! "Party, about turn, quick march," and off the parade ground I marched. After that we went for a drink in the Sergeants' Mess and not long after that the privates and NCOs at the castle were informed that, if they had "civvies", a trip to Beirut had been arranged for them. The Colonel obviously got the message.

I only had one more "run in" with the Colonel and that arose from a Sergeants' Mess party at the main barracks. We drove from Kyrenia in a one-ton truck with a turret: we drove through a ravine on the way up to and back from Kyrenia. The Sergeants all drank themselves "under the table" and I had to help them into the back of the truck where they all collapsed – four sleeping beauties! I stood in the turret on the way back and as we were driving down the ravine to Kyrenia the Colonel was driving up it.

I did not salute him: instead I kept my eyes firmly on the sides of the ravine looking for any reflection from metal. The Colonel obviously thought this was insubordination and I was summoned before the Major on arrival in Kyrenia.

"Why did you not salute the Commanding Officer?" he asked. "Because it was a perfect ambush position, sir, and the perfect moment to have opened fire on us was when we were saluting." "Oh," said the Major. "Dismiss."

I had been up in the mountains looking for terrorists: the troops were all cooped up in Barracks and more interested in etiquette than the realities of the situation. In this connection it is worth pointing out that Lance Bombardier Francis, the CO's driver, was killed and the CO of my old Royal Artillery Regiment was seriously wounded by terrorists when the regiment arrived in Cyprus for the Suez operation, just before I left the island. The threat was real.

As for the operations I undertook while attached to Special Branch, two stand out, and in one I nearly died.

The first operation was photographing a riot. We had an old metallic green Vauxhall Velox and we drove up close to a riot in Kyrenia – in woodland just on the outskirts of the town. I was deputed to take photos of the rioters while the police tried to restore order. Most of the rioters were young – about eighteen to twenty years of age – brandishing EOKA slogans saying "Thanatos sto Harding" ("Death to (Sir John) Harding", the Commander in Charge in Cyprus).

One particular young female rioter in the centre of the riot was hurling abuse at us and Sergeant George Wright, a well-built man, strode up to her and pulled her away from the other rioters. She went with head held high, looking every inch a heroine until he spun her round, bent her over and smacked her on the bottom: he did it very neatly and quickly let her go. I have never seen a young woman so embarrassed. From being a heroine she looked like a naughty schoolchild who had been smacked on the bottom for misbehaviour and propelled back to her fellow rioters.

When, however, they spotted that I was taking photographs they all started throwing rocks at me and it was at this point that we considered a strategic withdrawal would be in order. As Jim and I rushed for the Vauxhall, stones whistled past our ears and as we drove off rocks were bouncing off the roof of the car!

The other operation in which I nearly lost my life took place in the Pentedaktylos range of mountains.

One day I was sitting in my room at Special Branch headquarters when the double doors giving access to it opened and there stood Sergeant Christophides. As he moved towards me I said, "Stop right there." "You know you are not allowed in this room." "But you are my friend and I wanted to have a word with you." "In that case," I replied "we will have a word outside" and I ushered him rapidly out of the room.

Sergeant Christophides was a man in his fifties, a regular policeman who had worked in the Cyprus police for over twenty years, long before the days of Enosis. When I asked him what he wanted to have a word with me about he was shaking – he was obviously terrified about something. He gave a few incoherent and inconsequential mumbles and walked away.

There was no doubt that he wanted to gain access to my room and that he had been pressurised into doing so – probably by Emilios Georghiou. I immediately went to see Major Purves and told him that someone was clearly putting pressure on him. Major Purves agreed and told me to ensure that no one gained unauthorised access to any of the Special Branch Offices.

Every morning I had been picked up by our trusty metallic green Velox, driven by Ahmed, our Turkish-Cypriot driver, and when I was not standing in a ditch near the castle with my revolver in my hand I was inside the Cyprus police station just outside the castle.

It was there that I met and became friendly with Stelios Kozanis, a police sergeant from Greece. He had been a policeman in Thessaloniki but because he was well educated and spoke good English he had joined the Cyprus police. "I would not trust any of these Greek-Cypriot policemen further than I could throw them," he said and I knew exactly what he meant. They were not to be trusted and my encounter with Sergeant Christophides reinforced this view.

A few days after this incident Major Purves called Jim and me into his office and said, "I am sending you both off on an operation in the mountains." And to me, he said, "Draw a sterling submachine gun from the Wiltshire Regiment armoury."

As far as I was concerned this was an intelligence-gathering operation but Jim had had a more comprehensive briefing. We therefore headed off to the mountains one hot summer's evening with Ahmed, our Turkish-Cypriot driver. Jim and I were both dressed as terrorists. I had a rucksack with an Enosis flag attached to it and we all wore scarves over our faces.

As we walked through a Turkish-Cypriot village I wondered whether this was a good idea but, apart from a few villagers, saying "poor EOKA" or words to that effect, nothing happened. I half expected someone to lob a hand grenade at us but, in retrospect our Turkish-Cypriot companion had doubtless been recognised! The villagers had joined in the charade.

From the intelligence point of view I did wonder whether Military Intelligence headquarters in Nicosia wanted to find out whether Turkish villagers were likely to report the presence of EOKA terrorists in the area but that was the only sensible conclusion I could draw from doing something quite so provocative.

As it was we carried on up into the mountains and spent the first night in the undergrowth under the stars: after a quick snack in the early morning light we headed towards a quarry and laid in wait overlooking it.

The quarry workers turned up and started talking between their hammering of the rocks. Jim asked Ahmed, "What are they talking about?" "Well," said Ahmed, "One of the wives in their village is having an affair with one of the married men in the village." "That is hardly military intelligence," said Jim and after a couple of hours' listening to tittle-tattle we decided to move on.

We headed towards one of the paths over the Pentedaktylos range and picked out a good ambush positon. As it got dark Jim said, "I want you, Brian, to mount guard over the path between 12 midnight and 2 am. Wake me if you hear anything."

And so, at 12 midnight I began to listen out for footsteps in the pitch black of that summer night.

At about 1 am, I did indeed hear footsteps and as I reached over to wake Jim, one of my CCF boots, which had Blakeys on them, clinked against a rock. Blakeys are metal studs which one can fix on to the sole of a boot to reduce wear. The footsteps stopped immediately.

"Where did the footsteps come from?" asked Jim. "They were coming up from the south – from the bottom of the mountain."

"Right, Ahmed and I will go in that direction while you stand guard over the path."

This left me standing in the pitch dark with my Sterling sub-machine cocked and ready to fire should I encounter whoever was walking along this path at 1 am in the morning: someone who, moreover, appeared to have taken his own boots off because there was not a sound from him!

As I stood there I could just detect after a few minutes a looming figure about three feet away. I had to think quickly: if it was the terrorist and he was armed he would fire as soon as he realised I was in front of him: on the other hand if he fired my finger was on the trigger of the Sterling and my almost automatic reflex, when shot, would be to pull the trigger. I would doubtless hit him.

If it was not the terrorist and I said nothing Ahmed or Jim would probably shoot me!! So – what to be done? I said, taking a chance, "Who is there?"– and it was Ahmed!

"If you had not said, 'Who's there?' " I would have shot you" said Ahmed. It was a fairly hairy moment!

We spent some time looking for the "traveller" after that and concluded that if he had had the savvy to take his boots off and tiptoe away he was probably an experienced terrorist – in fact it could even have been Grivas himself.

That would have explained why Sergeant Christophides was desperate to come into my room to find out if we had any knowledge of terrorist movement in the area that he would have been under pressure to pass on to EOKA. As I have said previously it was "cat and mouse" at the Special Branch headquarters.

We were picked up the next day by a detail from the Wiltshire Regiment. Jim was concerned that we did not disclose our presence until the detail officer called out to us but he need not have been so concerned: he had been in serious combat, the Wiltshire Regiment privates had not. I knew how half asleep and vulnerable they were.

It was one of my regrets that we did not catch the "midnight walker" but it had been an exciting experience and I did fall in love with the mountains and forests of North Cyprus. It was also the closest I came to being killed but not the closest to dying: this came later.

5

Kyrenia

Between the First and Second World Wars Kyrenia had been a pleasant place for the British administrators of the island to spend the weekend or even to go on holiday. On the north side of the island, facing Turkey, it boasted a pretty harbour and a splendid (at the time) hotel, the Catsellis Dome hotel.

By the time I arrived there it had also become a popular "home from home" area for British expatriates: our secretary at Special Branch headquarters and Brigadier Cummings were typical examples.

From the time we first administered the island the balance between the Turkish and Greek populations had altered significantly: whereas in 1850 the majority of the population were Turkish, by 1950 the majority were Greek: but they were not Greeks from Greece. Most of them had come from Egypt when that country was part of the British Empire.

They were traders and entrepreneurs and over the one hundred years they had acquired much of the 85% of land that had previously been owned by Turkish-Cypriots: there was a simmering resentment on the part of the Turkish- Cypriots in that they were gradually being marginalised by their Greek-Cypriot counterparts.

The position was exacerbated by the fact that, as in the case of Protestants and Catholics in Northern Ireland, the Christian and Muslim populations were educated in different schools. There was no effort to make education non- sectarian or society cohesive – or, if there had been any effort, it had clearly been abandoned by 1956. The two communities were steadily growing apart and it was only in certain areas of administration where "colonial" rules applied, for example, the Cyprus police, that this was not quite so evident.

From being the virtual owners of nearly all the land and resources in the Island the Turkish-Cypriots were becoming the "poor relations." A number of Greek-Cypriots felt that in order to cement their position they should seek union with Greece, a country with which they had a historic connection and a common language but nothing more.

To me the tension between Turk and Greek was quite obvious: the risks to the expatriate community and to British Servicemen were equally clear. While I was in Kyrenia two British RAF sergeants were gunned down in Ledra Street in Nicosia and there were terrorist incidents across the island. Shortly after I left, a Lieutenant Gray was murdered on a beach a few miles to the east of Kyrenia and, as I have already mentioned, the C.O. of my former Royal Artillery Regiment was severely injured and his driver killed on their arrival in Cyprus to take part in the Suez operation.

Behind the apparent serenity of Kyrenia therefore there was an undercurrent of fear and tension between the Turkish and Greek-Cypriot, and the Cypriot and British populations. I felt sorry for the British expatriates who thought that they had found the ideal place to retire – away from inclement weather in England in a pleasant English-speaking island. Kyrenia was particularly popular with the yachting fraternity who frequented "Lottie's Bar" on the harbour front and who lived "out of town."

The EOKA terrorists were not really interested in the civilian British population, only the British authorities and the armed forces, but it must have been nerve-racking for most elderly expatriates to know that violent change could be on the way, given the antipathy of many members of the Greek-Cypriot population towards the United Kingdom.

Being on the north side of the Pentedaktylos range of mountains and being much more wooded than the south of Cyprus, Kyrenia enjoyed a better climate than Nicosia which, in the summer, was parched and baking hot. It also boasted the impressive Venetian castle in which a detachment of the Wiltshire Regiment was housed and to which I was taken.

There were two police stations in Kyrenia, one near the castle in which the regular police had their headquarters, and one about a mile out of the town from which the Special Branch operated. The latter had clearly been a family home of generous proportions at some stage. Now the British operatives were on the first floor and the Cypriot members of staff on the ground floor.

On arrival in Kyrenia I was issued with a .38 Webley revolver and a shoulder holster that was intended to be worn under a jacket. While, in the winter this was practical, it became extremely impractical when the weather improved and all one could comfortably wear was a short-sleeved shirt.

After wearing it under my shirt for a few days I discussed the problem of access to my revolver with Jim Herlihy. One could hardly wait for a terrorist to hold fire while you undid the buttons on your shirt and reached inside for it!

He told me what to do: keep the revolver in your right hand trouser pocket attached to your belt by a lanyard no longer than eight inches in length – long enough for you to whip it out of your pocket and fire from the hip but short enough to prevent a terrorist from creeping up behind you, taking it out of your pocket and shooting you in the back.

When walking round the streets of Kyrenia in my "civvies" you will appreciate that I kept my right hand in my trouser pocket all the time and stood in the ditch next to the headquarter's police station, waiting to be picked up by the Special Branch car, with the revolver in my hand, every weekday morning.

Jim Herlihy was billeted in the Hotel Bristol at the end of the main street and I did not envy him the insecurity he must have felt at night, with the Cypriot population knowing he was attached to Special Branch. The bar there was another popular watering hole for British expatriates.

He and I wore civvies whereas all the troops in the castle wore uniform. The only personnel allowed to wear uniform outside the castle were the senior NCOs billeted with their families outside the castle and the major in charge of the Wiltshire Regiment detachment in the castle.

In fact the other troops were not allowed out of the castle at all and although a sergeant from the Education Corps turned up at regular intervals ("Scholar" to the troops) to give English lessons – basically reading and writing – there was little for the privates and junior NCOs to do, apart from play football and basketball.

By 1956 the fear of terrorism had pervaded the island, particularly Kyrenia, where the Bishop of Kyrenia was a strong advocate of Enosis and the overthrow of the British occupation of the island. In fact it was from his palace that I acquired the "Death to Harding" flag that I wore on the back of my rucksack when Jim, Ahmed and I went off to the mountains on our "operation."

One sergeant – and I can only recall one, who lived outside the castle – invited the other sergeants to his rented home and we spent a very pleasant day at Bellapais, a mediaeval monastery in ruins, some six or seven miles from

Kyrenia but that was our only outing. The town itself was "off limits" to all but Jim and myself and the senior NCOs.

One of the first things I did on arrival at Special Branch headquarters was suggest that I purchase a camera and after a couple of weeks Jim and Major Purves thought this a good idea and gave permission to drive to a camera shop in Ledra Street in Nicosia. We drove down a crowded Ledra Street until we came to the camera shop. Ahmed stopped outside with engine running while Jim stood at the door with his revolver in his hand and I stood at the counter with my revolver in my belt. The terrified shop keeper was much relieved when I quickly purchased a Zeiss Ikon Contina camera, paid him the exact money and left, all within the space of a couple of minutes!

The camera was subsequently used to photograph rioters and scenes of army life at Kyrenia castle: it was a prized possession which I kept for many years. Being honest, I declared it when entering the United Kingdom from Cyprus. The import duty was more than I had on me at the time but the Customs officer took pity on me and let me pay £9.10.0, leaving me with a few pence and a travel warrant to Woolwich Barracks, the headquarters of the Royal Artillery in London.

Boredom was one of the principal challenges of life in the Army. National Servicemen had very little to do and most of us kept a chart ticking off the days we had left to serve. I had one on the wall of my office in the Special Branch offices and the end of my Army career could not come quickly enough.

The main problem in Cyprus was the heat of the summer sun: walking through woodland in the elevated areas of the Pentedaktylos range of mountain was very pleasant – cool and shaded – but the sun blazed down every day on the open area within the castle and one really had two choices: stay in a room at the castle and read whatever was available (I once snapped the quartermaster reading Beano!) or go for a swim. Prickly heat was very common – a reaction of the body to intense heat.

The rooms in the Special Branch headquarters, were tolerable, with fans to blow fresher and cooler air towards us. The cell-like rooms at Kyrenia castle were embedded into massive stone walls and also protected us from the heat.

There was a small sandy beach between the castle walls and the sea and CSM Peter Martin, his wife and children and the other sergeants were able to take advantage of this. I swam whenever I could and it is one of my regrets that I did not report to the authorities the amphorae I saw on the sea bed some hundred yards or so from the beach to the east and about thirty feet below me.

The amphorae turned out to have come from a very ancient Greek cargo ship that foundered off the coast. It was remiss of me not to have said anything at the time but, fortunately, the shipwreck was subsequently located.

The only other incident I recall while swimming was to be told in no uncertain terms to "clear off" (or words to that effect) by an armed naval rating when I swam out to a Royal Navy cruiser anchored offshore! With my flippers and goggles I may well have looked like a terrorist planning to attach a limpet mine to one of Her Majesty's warships! I was, however, able to assure him that I was a Brit and would leave his cruiser (which I think was "HMS Kenya") alone!

Until the age of 71 swimming was one of my ways of de-stressing. Thereafter, following my "near death" experience, it became problematic, as you will discover in a later chapter.

6

Cambridge in the 1950s

The student mix at Cambridge during the 1950s was an unusual one. Whereas the colleges were all single-sex establishments this has changed and most colleges now accept male and female undergraduates. Consequently there is a much greater parity in numbers between men and women within the university.

The male undergraduates were, in 1956, a mixture of worldly young men, like myself, who had been in the Army or the Royal Air Force for two years, doing their National Service and "wet behind the ears" eighteen-year-olds who were fresh from their grammar or public schools and from living either with their parents during their school days or between school and university in the case of former boarders from public schools.

In this respect some of the colleges had a greater intake from "top echelon" boarding schools than others, notably Trinity and Kings Colleges, whereas my own college, Downing, had a preponderance of young men from grammar schools. My school, Brentwood School, being independent but essentially grant maintained fell half-way between the extremes of fully fee paying and totally grant maintained or county funded grammar schools. It had "fee payers" and boarders, but not many of either.

Most colleges had particular traditions, for example, in oarsmanship or sport of some kind. In 1956/57 Jesus College attracted oarsmen, Christ's College, footballers and Downing, tennis players. Downing was not then the "rowing" college it has since become.

The reputations of colleges in the academic sphere usually rested on the fact that among their past and present professors and fellows could be counted eminent writers, researchers and lecturers in particular fields, for example in science, literature, languages, engineering or law. Downing, like Trinity Hall, was known as a college for aspiring lawyers, boasting numerous famous authorities on the subject, notably, in the case of Downing, Professor F.W Maitland (an authority on the English legal system) and Professor Kenny (an authority on criminal law) whose works were standard textbooks for law students at the university.

In my time Downing also had Professor Clive Parry, not only a brilliant and highly entertaining lecturer but a world-leading authority on international law, and Dr. F.R. Leavis, a famous and controversial fellow who lectured and pronounced on figures in English literature. The latter's combative style was exemplified, to me, by the way in which he rode his bike round the gravelled paths of the college, head down with the single-minded determination of a Kamikaze pilot! He was not disposed to steer round students who had to jump out of the way as he approached them.

The fresh "out of school" undergraduates mixed slightly uneasily with their more worldly "ex-National Service" counterparts but all bore with fortitude the rigours of a spartan existence within the college. The late Georgian rooms were poorly heated and you had to share the arctic (in winter) washing and toilet facilities with everyone else on your floor. There were few well heated rooms and none with "en suite" facilities and TVs, as there are now.

Apart from the two year difference in age the basic distinction at Cambridge was between the "Arties" and the "Hearties". The Arties were the intellectuals who did not involve themselves too much in sport whereas the Hearties were dedicated sportsmen who for the most part played rugby or cricket or rowed for their colleges, some of them also for the university.

The two types were lampooned by an exceptionally bright cartoonist, Timothy, in the university newspaper, Varsity. In his cartoons about "Rick Runcorn, Twenty Third Citizen of the Space Age", they were called the "Hahtis" and the "Ahtis" and both lived on another planet! Sadly, Timothy died just after he left Cambridge. He would doubtless otherwise have become quite famous if one is to judge from his perceptive series of cartoons on a number of aspects of university life.

In between the Arties and the Hearties were what I suppose one would call the "half Arties" and the "half Hearties," like myself, who enjoyed both aspects of university life – engaging in sport to a reasonable extent while not overlooking the wonderful opportunities that existed for broadening the mind.

In terms of broadening the mind and, apart from studying one's own chosen subject, there were free lectures on a range of subjects at the Senate House on Saturday mornings. Any undergraduate could attend provided he or she was wearing a gown. One of the first books I purchased at university was "Art and Reality" after hearing the author, Joyce Cary, speak at one of these lectures.

Another way of broadening the mind was to attend the Sunday evening services at Great St. Mary's Church where Reverend (later Bishop) Mervyn Stockwood offered the religious equivalent of "bread and circuses". He invited all sorts of controversial figures to give sermons, for example Joe Gormley from the National Union of Mineworkers, the sceptic (at the time) Malcolm Muggeridge, Billy Graham, the famous American evangelist, and so on.

I can vividly remember him addressing the congregation after one particularly fiery sermon and putting what he considered a simple question to it. "How many of you will be voting for the Labour Party at the next General Election? Please put up your hands." He pronounced the word "hands" as if it had an "ey" in it (heyands") and party as if it had two" "e's" at the end of it: he was always very theatrical. About 15% of the undergraduates put up their hands. "And how many of you will be voting for the Liberal Party? Please put up your hands." About 20% put up their hands. "And how many of you will be voting for the Conservative Party? Please put up your hands." About 65% of the congregation put up their hands.

"To those of you who intend to vote Conservative," he boomed, "all I can say is: God help you when you are sixty."

There were, of course, many other ways of broadening the mind, the Arts Theatre, the Arts Cinema, the University Dramatic Society, among them. I became a habitué of all three. There were also musical performances and concerts and one of my big regrets in this respect is walking past the Corn Exchange in 1958 and seeing a poster for the first ever performance in England of "Carmina Burana" by Karl Orff and not buying a ticket. Maybe I could not afford one but anyone who has ever heard this particular work cannot fail to be stirred by the music and I had to catch up with a live performance of it, extraordinarily, in a church in Rome many, many years later.

The Cambridge Footlights were generating the comedians and satirists of the future, such as Jonathan Miller, David Frost and Peter Cook, while the University Dramatic Society was honing the skills of people like Margaret Drabble whom I saw perform with great intensity in the Tennessee Williams play, "Camino Real". There was plenty in Cambridge to challenge and activate the mind if you were prepared to go out and look for it.

On the sporting front I rowed for a year or so at "2" in the Downing second boat which, at the time, was well down in one of the lower divisions but gave that up in favour of cycling down to the college boathouse at about 7.15 am and taking out a single scull – a one seater – for a quick row down the river before breakfast. It was always a wonderful experience to be skimming over the Cam in the silence and beauty of the surroundings with the swirls of water left by the oar blades marking one's progress.

The public perception of Oxford and Cambridge universities over the years has been that they are elitist institutions and that the undergraduates of both are somewhat out of touch with the lives of ordinary people. Nothing, however, could be further from the truth for most of them, and particularly so as far as members of Downing College were concerned.

Cambridge has always been a "power house" of learning and we all knew we were so privileged to be able to go there and benefit from the dynamism of the place. There were undoubtedly among our intake a few undergraduates who regarded themselves as God's gift to civilisation but the vast majority of us felt we were extraordinarily lucky to have secured a place there. There was nothing superior about us: we had just worked harder than everyone else to get in.

The university had, moreover, since the end of the Second World War, done its best to ensure that its students kept their feet on the ground and did not lose touch with the realities of life. In this respect I would refer the reader to a later chapter on Mr and Mrs Robinson. When, also, I arrived at Downing in 1956, admittedly feeling rather pleased with myself that I had been offered a place there, I attended, within the first day or so, a Freshers' meeting at which we were addressed by Professor Clive Parry. "Do not think," he said, "that you are superior to anyone else in achieving a place at Cambridge university. You may think that you are brighter than most of your contemporaries but imagine what the university would be like if it were stuffed full of eggheads. It would be quite awful. We have to leaven every intake in order to give the university balance. And you may be part of the leaven!" That comment should have brought down to earth any undergraduates who had illusions about their own superiority.

Downing, in any event, comprised about 70% undergraduates from grammar schools, mostly in the north of England with a large contingent from Manchester Grammar School. The rest came mainly from independent grant maintained public schools, such as Brentwood, where not many were fee-paying boarders. Very few indeed came from the expensive public schools where all the pupils were boarders and had their fees paid by their parents. There was, therefore, no noticeable sense of elitism among us: we were lucky young men from modest backgrounds who had worked extremely hard to achieve the "A" or "S" grades one needed to get into Cambridge. The only thing we had in common was the quality of the education we had received at our respective schools, a quality which in later decades most comprehensive schools have been unable to replicate.

Having spent two years at Kettering Grammar School and eight years at Brentwood School, having turned down the chance of a commission in the Army after being promoted company sergeant major at my last CCF camp at the end of my school career, and then coming up through the ranks in the Army after that, I had no real problem in getting on with anyone and treating people as equals whether they were college Porters, members of the kitchen staff who helped me organise the catering for the Downing May Ball or the "Bedders", the ladies who cleaned and tidied our rooms when we were out at lectures.

Lest the reader conclude that everything was sweetness and light in Cambridge I have to point out that relationships between Town and Gown could be difficult at times. The university owned, or had owned, pretty well every building in the centre of Cambridge at one time or another and its influence was immense. It even had its own MP until 1950. Many residents of the town were employed in subservient and not very well-paid roles by the colleges that were the town's biggest landlords. The Lodging House Syndicate, a body administered by the university, controlled the rents paid by undergraduates to private landlords.

The university was a community within a community but its tentacles spread through and affected most aspects of life in Cambridge. This "Ivory Tower" and dominating presence gave rise to resentment on occasion and an inevitable coolness between the university and the general population of the town. One bone of contention, for example, was that although the colleges and the university (including the members of the university) enjoyed all the facilities available to the residents of Cambridge neither was liable to pay domestic rates on their buildings to the local authority.

Moreover, some undergraduates, who were identifiable by the gowns they wore at all times, were not quite as considerate to others (probably including their own parents) as they should have been: their behaviour and appearance sometimes antagonised younger members of the town community. There was, therefore, the occasional fight between the testosterone-fuelled young men of both sides. None of this ever affected me but I was aware that the divide existed.

There is no doubt that the attitudes of the townspeople in the 1950s were based partly on a lack of understanding of the university's charter and the ways in which the colleges and the university functioned. In recent years the university has done its best to present a friendly face to the town and now has an "Open University" weekend early in September when college and university buildings and gardens are thrown open to members of the general public so that they can see what goes on within those previously hallowed precincts and begin to understand the relevance and use of one part of the university to another.

My first step, on arrival at Downing in October in 1956, was to get into my room, unpack my trunk and complete the registration formalities. As soon as I had done this I went to my future Classics tutor and told him that I had forgotten pretty well all the Greek and Latin I had ever learned!

This came as a bit of a shock to him but I was well aware that, if I had told him before I arrived, my place at the college would have been withdrawn and offered to someone else. It is always better to get one's feet "under the table" before making that sort of announcement!

"Well, what do you want to read?", he asked. "Law," I replied. "In that case, you had better go and see the vice-master who is the college law tutor and find out whether you can do so."

Hyde Charnock Whalley Tooker, the vice-master, had fought in the First World War as a young man and suffered throughout his life from "shell shock". He was a decent, kindly man and, after a moderate amount of "huffing and puffing" about my getting into college under false pretences, agreed to accept me as an undergraduate member of the law school.

Although he was not to know it at the time, several of my fellow law students never actually became practising lawyers, like myself, so I do not feel particularly guilty about the way in which I secured my place at Downing.

Having secured my place my next step was to have a chat with the porters and find out, from them, the best area for "digs" in my second and third years. "Freshers", like myself, were in college for the first year but had to live outside college after that. Most of them at this stage were too engrossed in the novelty of their present surroundings to consider where they were going to live in future years and I knew that I would have a head start if I started looking straight away. The porters suggested that I investigate the Orchard Street area on the far side of Parker's Piece, the large park opposite the entrance to the college.

Orchard Street was a pretty street with picturesque cottages down one side of it and one of the houses on the opposite side of the street, Number 24, was on the college accommodation list. I knocked on the door and asked Sidney Cable, the landlord, whether the accommodation was available. "I am afraid you are too late", he said. "What, for next year?" I replied. "Oh, I thought you were asking for this year. Yes, the rooms will be available next year." I put my name down for them immediately. Mr and Mrs. Cable could not have been kinder to me during my subsequent two years there and their home was only two minutes away from the college gates. I will explain the relevance of this later.

People with better literary skills than my own have written a lot about student life in Cambridge in the 1950s. All I can add, apart from a number of personal reminiscences, is that it was a really lively place with future "prospective" (mostly male) politicians dominating the University Union, future academics involving themselves enthusiastically in learned societies and future national sporting figures improving their skills while representing the university.

I fell into none of the above categories but I was worldly and had organising ability and during my first few weeks in college I threw myself into assisting with the construction of the college float for the Poppy Day parade and the planning of other fund-raising activities.

In the 1950s the Poppy Day parade was as much a carnival as a day for collecting funds for the British (now Royal British) Legion and each college built a float for the hour long parade and dreamed up other static fund-raising events. In other words, the day itself was more humorous than serious. As previously stated many of us had been in the Forces, the post-war period had been very drab and Poppy Day was considered a day for letting one's hair down and having some fun. It was, in many respects, similar to the more modern "Rag Days" at other universities.

As a result of my involvement in the 1956 Poppy Appeal in which we came third out of twenty three colleges in terms of monies raised I was voted College Poppy Appeal Organiser for 1957 (and subsequently for 1958) and with my team of helpers had to think up humorous but fund-raising activities for both years.

Although my team helped create two features for the parade and two day-long static events in 1957 the only static event that stands out in my memory was "Buy a Slave in the Slave Market". I seem to recall that it was the brainchild of the college rugby club!

The large flat-bed trailer that we had used for the parade float was parked in front of the Guildhall in the main market square. On it was a large cage and a rugby player dressed as an Arab with a microphone in his hand. A number of burly rugby players dressed as Arabs stood in the crowd watching the young couples who stopped to see what was going on. Two of the Arabs would sidle up, position themselves on either side of a young lady and whisk her on to the trailer and into the cage before either she or her male companion could really object. The young lady would be told that she was helping raise funds for charity and would be described in glowing terms by the Arab "dealer". He would then offer to sell her to the highest bidder. Non-Arab "plants" would bid for her up to 2/3d (roughly 12 1/2p), leaving her companion with little option but to bid 2/6d (half a crown) if he wanted to stay in her good books! Although it was a "crowd puller" I felt it was somewhat insensitive and dropped the event in 1958 in favour of a much more profitable raffle.

In fact it was as a result of the raffle in 1958 that I realised I was psychic. This observation may strike you, the reader, as odd but it is, in fact, true.

I registered the raffle and set about gathering some decent prizes by writing to all the major retailers and food manufacturers I could think of and by approaching hotels, restaurants and off-licences that might be prepared to assist in raising funds for the British Legion. A dinner for two at a leading Cambridge hotel was the first prize (there were few restaurants in the town in those days). I managed to accumulate about fifteen other prizes of various kinds. I sent a couple of our college students to the various pubs in Cambridge to sell the tickets and also went out myself. While in a pub on the outskirts of Cambridge I had got down to my last ticket when the barman rang the bell for closing time. The number of that last ticket was 0320. "I have not bought a ticket in my own Raffle," I thought. "I will buy this one for myself."

And so it came to pass that the raffle took place and the numbers were drawn. I had managed, courtesy of the college porters, to find a big bag full of wooden pellets with numbers on them: quite what their original purpose was I have no idea but they proved very handy for the raffle. Terry Allen, the President of the Junior Common Room (the JCR), the senior undergraduate in the college, sat at the far end of the room with the bag while I sat in a low armchair just inside the door at the opposite end.

The drawing of the numbers proceeded normally until, all of a sudden, I had an overwhelming sense that I would win the next prize: the feeling was so strong that I put my left hand on the arm of the student sitting next to me. He looked at me rather strangely but I indicated "don't move" with my right hand.

Terry drew the first number "zero", the next "three", followed by "two" and "zero". Having collected the prize – a Boots leather stud box – I returned to my chair and said to the student next to me, "I apologise for putting my hand on your arm but I had to prove to myself, if not to anyone else, that I knew one thousand per cent I was going to win that prize." It so surprised me that I should have had this feeling of total certainty that I have never forgotten it.

One other memorable incident occurred during my fund-raising activities for the Poppy Appeal. After returning from one of my "pub tours" selling raffle tickets I went to have a quick cup of coffee with Tony Denton, the student secretary of the JCR. He had rooms in college, and as we sat talking I heard the clock on the Catholic Church in Lensfield Road start to chime twelve. That electrified me because the college gates were locked at midnight and I had to get back to my digs. "Sorry, Tony, I have to dash." I raced to the gates where the head porter was poised, keys in hand, to lock them. "You will have to let me out," I said. "I will have to report you, sir, for leaving the college after midnight," he replied. Without further comment I left him and cycled like a mad thing to my digs. As I burst into the hall of 24 Orchard Street, my landlord appeared. "I have just left the college after midnight, Sidney. I am afraid you will have to report me for arriving back here after midnight." "Oh no, sir," Sidney replied. "I will confirm that you got in at 11.59 pm."

A few days later I received a summons from the dean – would I go to see him in his rooms. "I am going to get a severe ticking off," I thought. When I arrived, the dean was sitting behind his desk, looking very serious.

"Hughes, you appear to have broken all the laws of physics. Can you please explain how you left the college at one minute past twelve and arrived at your digs two minutes earlier at 11.59 pm?"

I realised that this little conundrum appealed to him as an academic and that the summons was not as serious as I had first thought. We had a chat about what the college was doing to raise funds for Poppy Day and there the matter rested.

Although we were one of the smaller colleges we had once again punched well above our weight in 1957: we came sixth in the total amounts raised by each college and sixth in terms of per capita contribution to the appeal.

We raised £488 which would, at the time, have equated to the salary of a secretary for a whole year or one quarter of the cost of a three bedroomed semi-detached house.

Having felt challenged by Mervyn Stockwood's comments about the number of Conservatives in his congregation I decided to give Liberalism a try and find out what the Liberal Party really stood for. I started appearing at the University's Liberal Club meetings and asking leading questions from the floor. This was quite a good technique for getting oneself noticed and it was not long before I was invited to join the committee. It was also a good technique on the part of a political party for silencing someone who is asking difficult questions! I am not sure whether the same applies today!

The committee decided to send a team down to Purley in Surrey to help campaign for a prospective Liberal Party candidate at the next general election and I joined it. The candidate was a very pleasant person and such was the persuasiveness of the team that I could see it was beginning to make substantial inroads into what had been a massive Conservative majority. This caused me slight unease and, of course, not long afterwards Eric Lubbock won Orpington, previously a Tory stronghold, for the Liberal Party.

Not long after this successful foray into electioneering I was promoted librarian – keeper of all the club's literature (books and pamphlets setting out and explaining Liberal Party policies). It was at this point, I am afraid, that the rot set in. Any librarian worth his salt should know what the books in his care are about so I decided to read them. As I read through them all I was forced to conclude that, however well-intentioned many of the policies might be, they did not really make economic sense.

After staying on long enough to meet luminaries from the parliamentary Liberal Party, such as Jo Grimond, the party Leader and well-known personalities like Peter Wildeblood, the author of "Against the Law" and "The

Main Chance", I resigned from the committee. Peter Wildeblood, a well-known journalist, had been dragged through the courts and prisons for his "abominable crime", namely his homosexuality, and it was much to his relief and many others of his kind that Sir John Wolfenden, the former headmaster of Uppingham and Shrewbury schools and Vice-Chancellor of the University of Reading, published his famous report in 1957, advocating a more tolerant attitude towards homosexuality.

My only previous brush with the topic of homosexuality had been as a result of my decision to buy a pair of moss green suede shoes from Joshua Taylors, an "up market" store in the centre of Cambridge, just after I arrived there. They looked great to me and I bought them. The first time, I wore them, however, one of my fellow lawyers came up to me and said, "Brian, don't you realise that only gays wear suede shoes?"

No, I didn't know and I told him that I did not particularly care what other people thought! I liked them and that was that! I think it was that remark that made me aware of the narrowness of people's thinking before the publication of the Wolfenden report.

Once I had gained freedom of choice in what I wore no one was going to put me in a sartorial straitjacket ever again: my mother, who had controlled the purse strings until I went up to university, believed that undergraduates should wear Harris Tweed jackets, grey flannels and brown or black leather shoes! The time had come for her son to choose his own clothes and footwear. I was therefore so relieved by the explosion in choice in the early 1960s when men, gay or straight, could wear whatever they liked.

While on the subject of clothes, one of my great friends at university and still a great friend, had been in the Royal Artillery with me in Edinburgh. His mother was a Scott Moncrieff, one of Scotland's noblest families, and I shall never forget his comment when I bought him a tie for his birthday. "Brian. Why have you bought me a tie? I already have a tie." He was quite serious and, for someone who has made a point throughout his life of buying ties of almost every conceivable colour and design I found his reaction quite extraordinary. I wondered at the time how much more Scottish one could get than that!

A sense of humour is a great asset and when I was walking back from a free Saturday lecture at the Senate House on 1 March 1958 and saw that the Cambridge University tiddlywinks team was playing the Goons in the Guildhall I decided to see whether I could blag my way in. Of course there was no such thing as a Cambridge University tiddlywinks team but I admired the cheek and enterprise of the group of students who had thought up this particular wheeze and had persuaded the Goons to visit Cambridge. I regarded it as an equivalent test of initiative on my part to witness the match if I could.

There were a lot of students besieging the main entrance of the Guildhall but I calculated that there must be another staff entrance somewhere towards the rear of the building. Surprisingly the door to this particular entrance was unguarded and I gained access to the building. I was quickly spotted by a member of staff who told me to leave. I told the gentleman in question that during my active service in Cyprus the Goons had been the only real source of entertainment on the radio for the Armed Forces and that they were comedy heroes to people like myself. I told him that I would be very discreet and well behaved and he somewhat reluctantly let me proceed to the council chamber where Peter Sellers, Spike Milligan, Harry Secombe, Wallace Greenslade, Max Geldray and others were causing great mirth and amusement with their Goon Show impressions. They clearly thought the tiddlywinks match was great fun and the air was constantly punctuated by Harry Secombe's slightly maniacal laughter! I do not know whether the match ever reached a conclusion but it was wonderful to see them performing so close at hand.

Of the fair sex I have said little in this book but I had become a firm friend of Valerie Foulkes who, together with her two travelling companions, I had chaperoned during her four-week trip to Greece in 1958 (see next Chapter). I was constantly being asked by Greek men how I could have three "girlfriends" but little did they know how my three Newnham ladies regarded me. I was a useful guide and protector who spoke a bit of Greek but that was all. I subsequently attended many of the sherry parties thrown by her and her friends at Newnham. In those days it was, of course, "no sex please, we are British". All friendships had to be platonic. Valerie was the daughter of a director of a large department store in Nottingham and ultimately married into the "Fenwicks of Bond Street" dynasty. I guess an attraction towards owners of department stores must have been in her genes!

I also went out for a time with a young lady who was even more energetic than myself and, dare I say it, considerably more mature. Her name was Hazel Wilson and she was the senior student at Homerton teacher training college, chosen by the college to accompany the Queen Mother and to thank her when she visited the college to open its new wing in June 1957. She, again, was an extraordinarily charming young lady but I neither fell in love with them nor they with me.

That awe-inspiring sensation crept up and hit me hard on my return journey from Greece in July 1960, a few weeks after I received news that was to dash my hopes of marrying the young lady in question.

Having gained a reputation as organiser of the college Poppy Appeal and of student travel to Greece I was invited to join the Downing College May Ball committee in 1958 and to make all the travel arrangements for the Downing College cricket tour of UK military bases in Holland and Germany in 1959.

The May Ball committee decided to go "up market" and the ball was advertised as "The Best May Ball in Cambridge". It undoubtedly was. We booked the famous Joe Loss orchestra as our principal dance band and a separate jazz band to play in another part of the college. A large marquee was hired and erected in the college grounds with a sprung floor for ballroom dancing. We offered a champagne reception with the Master, Professor Guthrie, at the start of the evening and a full English breakfast at the end of the night – the only college to offer food at 6 am in the morning. Contrary to their name "May Balls" are held in early June: ours took place on 9 June, at the very end of term.

The price of each ticket was six guineas – a lot of money in those days. Our advertising poster showed an elegant young man in tails stepping out of a Rolls-Royce (belonging to Mr. Ashton, one of our lecturers) with an attractive young lady in a ball gown on his arm. In the background were the impressive Greek columns of the Master's lodge. We knew we had to sell tickets outside Cambridge as well as in college if we were to cover our overheads for this ambitious and expensive event and used recent graduates as contacts in the London Stock Exchange and elsewhere in the City to boost ticket sales.

One of my roles was to liaise with Mr. Robson, the kitchen manager, on the catering aspect of the ball and he really did us proud. He carved a beautiful swan out of a block of ice as the centrepiece of a magnificent array of food. When I asked him where all the amazing meat dishes had come from and how we could have afforded them – duck, pheasant, a stuffed roast pig and more, he gave me a wink and said, "It all fell off a lorry." I did not pursue the subject!

My other main involvement as a committee member was with the floodlighting of the college when it got dark. My friend, Neil Hardman, and I arranged for the college chapel building to be floodlit in magenta and white, magenta being the college colour. We also placed a large number of honey jars which we had acquired and in which we put nightlights round the parapets of the building. We waited for the sun to go down and lit the nightlights: the college looked quite spectacular.

There were, of course, no health and safety regulations in those days and our clambering over the roof of the college placing the honeypots in position and then lighting the nightlights in the dark in evening dress was as nothing when compared with the exploits of other students who regularly put the tops of Belisha beacons and chamber pots on the spires of King's College chapel or those who managed to park an Austin Seven on the roof of the senate house in the centre of Cambridge. The fire brigade had to cut up the vehicle while on the roof in order to get it down!

This latter type of operation required considerable skill and expert timing – between the beats of the police constables who regularly pounded the streets of Cambridge.

In this respect I do recall knocking on the door of the room next to my own in college late one evening in spring 1957 in order to borrow some coffee. Pat McCreight, an officer in the Royal Engineers who was at Cambridge on an engineering scholarship, answered my knock dressed in full battle fatigues with a Commando woollen hat on his head. "What are you doing, Pat?" I asked him. "Better you do not know", he replied. I took his jar of coffee and left wondering what he was about to do and I have never found out since!

We covered our overheads and made a small surplus. The ball had fortunately, been a great success.

Although I was not a cricketer and merely made all the travel arrangements the Downing College cricket tour proved to be, shall I say, very interesting. We arrived for our first match at an RAF base near Nijmegen and when put in to bat declared at about 150 for two wickets which we thought should be enough. The host RAF team were all out for about 85 runs and from that match onward we were referred to on Forces Network Radio as "Cambridge University" and not "Downing College, Cambridge"!

The upshot was that Yorkshire and Lancashire League players doing their National Service were rapidly drafted from all over Europe into the Army and Air Force sides we subsequently played against. The Downing side coped admirably with the stiffer opposition but it was quite amusing to be advertised as the actual Cambridge University cricket team who were infinitely better players.

There are three other memories of that tour which stand out in my mind. The first is the extraordinary generosity of the Dutch who, despite their comparative poverty at the time, laid on a splendid buffet at a reception given by the mayor and citizens of Nijmegen. The second is the fact that whatever shop one visited in Holland the young girl at the till spoke excellent English, and the third is my visit to the open air swimming pool at Nijmegen.

One had to walk through a slipper bath to get to the main pool and there, by the side of the slipper bath, was a little boy, who could not have been more than two years old, assiduously emptying it with a toy plastic bucket into the main pool. "They start them off young here." I thought. It was as if draining land was innate! He probably grew up to be an engineer, creating polders!

As will have been gathered from all my activities at Cambridge including, incidentally, finding 88 students in my last couple of terms for three parties to Greece, after I had left Cambridge in the summer of 1959 I did rather overlook the aspect of study. I was rescued by having a photographic memory and by a number of frantic thirteen-hour revision sessions during the four weeks prior to my final tripus examinations. In fact, I learned so much during those last few weeks (when I ought to have been revising what I should already have known) that I could doubtless have achieved a better degree if I had studied everything earlier.

But you cannot have everything in life and I had fun!

7

Student Travel to Greece

Having been to Greece as a Boy Scout in 1954 and to Cyprus as a National Serviceman in 1956 I really wanted to return to Greece when I was an undergraduate at Cambridge.

During the Lent (pre-Easter) term in 1957 I noticed an advertisement in the personal column of "Varsity" the student newspaper. It read "Athens, £19 return by train. Mon 26th June to Sun 25th July. Apply Rosemary Bishop, Girton".

"That sounds interesting" I thought and without further ado borrowed my best friend's bike (!) and rode out to Girton College on the outskirts of Cambridge. There were, in my day, two misconceptions about the College and the young ladies within it. The first was that it was built there to discourage male visitors and I have to admit that the twin red brick towers at the main gate and guarded entrance hall made it appear somewhat forbidding. The second was that the female undergraduates there were more "jolly hockey sticks" than those at Newnham and New Hall, probably because they had to cycle a couple of miles each day to get to and from the University!! They were alleged to have built up stronger leg muscles as a result!! Stereotypical labelling and very untrue!

Having signed myself in and having been scrutinised by a suspicious female doorkeeper – in those days we had to sign in and sign out – I strode the labyrinthine corridors of Girton like Theseus in search of the Minotaur – except that the Minotaur, in this case, was Rosemary Bishop! She turned out to be a charming young lady, dark haired and bright eyed with strong features and obviously a lot of drive and determination: she was the sort of person cut out to run a Civil Service Department and probably did so. I could not see her settling down to a quiet married life!

She had absolutely no idea what the journey would be like but she was reading Classics and had a great yearning to see Greece: she could get there free of charge if she could make up a group of sixteen students: that was all she needed for a leader's free ticket. All she now needed was a bit of moral support to get her proposed venture off the ground. I offered to become her assistant and to help her in whatever way I could and she willingly accepted my offer. We decided on a series of tea parties and over tea and crumpets, a favourite student dish, we persuaded seventeen other students to take the plunge and join us. No-one else had ever organised a student trip like this before and what an exciting picture a journey across Europe on the Tauern Orient Express must have been conjured up in the minds of our fellow travellers. The journey would take 68 hours in each direction and we would be free to do whatever we wanted in Greece until we caught the train back to London some three weeks later.

My only problem at the time was that I did not have any money but I resolved the matter of the train fare by writing to my old school and applying for a book grant of £20: the school kindly sent me a cheque for this amount.

The question of the cost of accommodation then arose: most of the time I would be able to sleep on the decks of ships travelling between the islands or on the roofs of buildings but there would be occasions when this would not be possible: I therefore joined the Cambridge University Rover Crew, as a "back up" measure, in order to obtain an "International letter" which would enable me to sleep in Scout huts across Greece. I had been in the Scouts, had attained my first class and did not consider this too unethical!

In fact I went to the University Rover Crew meetings for a couple of terms until they decided to build a replica of a "ballista". A "ballista" was a huge wooden catapult used by the ancient Romans to hurl rocks and fireballs over the defensive walls of towns they were besieging: having been a TARA and having been involved in firing shells from 4.5 inch guns up to three miles I could not muster a great deal of enthusiasm for this particular project!

The reader will doubtless be reassured to learn that I have repaid my debt to Scouting for this "low cost" facility by having been President of my local District Scout Association for over thirty five years!

I scraped together another £23 with which I intended to live and travel round Greece for the three weeks: it was also optimistically going to feed me on the return journey!!

The great day arrived, Monday 26 June. The train left Victoria Station at 3 pm and we were all there by 2.30 pm. Nearly everyone, apart from myself, was there in sports jackets or summer dresses, more suitable for an afternoon on the backs at Cambridge than the trek across Europe that was in store.

The utter impracticality of most of the students was obvious: some had brought suitcases and others bags full of sandwiches for a three day journey. Others were bland and remote, thinking that the sixty eight hours would drift away into mere nothingness if one was "enveloped" in Kafka, Dostoievsky or Jean Paul Sartre. The majority of the group was female, as was the case with all my subsequent groups. This is because women are usually more definite and certain than men about what they want to do. Men are often "non committal" until they make up their minds too late!!

The journey down to Dover was comfortable in British Railways best rolling stock, designed to impress the foreign Tourist on arrival: there was a buffet car with cups of tea and sandwiches and a bar service. The first signs of discomfort were evident on the ferry crossing from Dover to Ostend: the sports jackets, shirts and ties were letting in the cold wind and the short sleeved summer dresses were looking and obviously feeling inadequate in the breeze!

On arrival in Ostend we passed through a neat station, walked along the low platform where the trains rear up over one's head and clambered aboard our carriage from ground level through massive swinging doors. The train itself was a bit of a disappointment: the carriages were split into a series of compartments with rexine seats: the plastic numbers above each seat identified our compartment and our reserved seats: we were eight persons per compartment, more than a bit crowded but not too bad. The compartment was at least warm and we settled down for the first part of the journey. The precision of Belgian Railways was impressive, also the speed of the train: the journey will not be too bad if the rest of the journey is like this, I thought. The evening sandwiches were not too bad either, a bit dry but welcome and edible.

But at about 10.30 pm came the crunch: it was time to think how we were all going to sleep and be comfortable. Most people had brought a sleeping bag or a blanket but space was limited and everyone was behaving very formally: there was the sad realisation on the part of those who had brought their pyjamas that they would not be putting them on that night or on any other night of our journey!! Shoes off, belts loosened, skirts discreetly unzipped – that was it!

Any expectation of sleep was, in any event, rudely shattered by ticket inspectors who, every hour or so, demanded to see our tickets and, when we reached the frontier with Germany, our passports and our luggage. As previously mentioned the compartments were well heated and soon became stiflingly hot for the six people lying across the seats with the luggage piled up in the middle: we therefore opened the windows a little, only to freeze the two young ladies we had put in the luggage racks!! After an uncomfortable and sleepless night out came the, by now, cardboard sandwiches – with curled slices of cheese and butter inside them that tasted like yoghurt!

We arrived at 9 am on the second day of our journey at Munich, giving us seven hours to look around the City before boarding the Hellas Orient Express. It was and still is a bustling City full of beer houses but I was on a shoestring budget so had a couple of drinks and a welcome sleep on a park bench before returning to the station. The crowd of people waiting for the train was immense and we were not quite sure where our reserved seats would be: there were Germans, Austrians, Yugoslavs and Greeks all fighting to get on the train and capture any unreserved seats! The crush was intense and once we had found our seats, and ejected the passengers who had tried to claim them, we realised that we were "land locked". Getting down the corridor of the carriage was virtually impossible!!

We spent another uncomfortable evening and night and arrived in Zagreb the next morning after crossing the Alps: the one major compensation was the crisp and brilliant coldness of an Austrian dawn – the freshness of the air being replaced by a sultry heat as we entered the Yugoslav plains. If we had thought the train was full, it became even more so at Zagreb and, worse still, the diesel engine had gone, to be replaced by a steam train. From then on things got tough, with choking fumes and smoke in the tunnels, crowded corridors with gnarled old women hunched on wicker baskets covering fruit, chickens (dead and alive) and bric a brac of all kinds, with young women clutching their babies wrapped in sacking, and cloth capped men, whose dark eyes smouldered through their tanned skins, and who silently stood or sat chewing or smoking tobacco through their yellow, stained teeth.

We arrived in Belgrade. It was as impossible to move down the corridor over the bodies as it was futile. The loos on the train were filthy and stank and there was no water in the taps. Arrival at any station after Belgrade came as a welcome relief where, at the risk of being left on the platform, if one could actually get off the train, one could buy a bottle of beer, a frankfurter or a piece of stale salami and a dusty roll after haggling over the amount one should pay in the local currency.

The journey by this time was taking its toll. The production of tickets and passports at all times of day and night had exhausted our group: the bright and artificial conversation of the first day had dimmed by halfway through the second night. "War and Peace" would get no further than page 66, the card school had folded like a collapsing pack, the pretences and the guards had been dropped! But strangely enough a camaraderie was developing, born of common suffering and a "rubbing off" of the sharp-edges that would continue throughout that month long holiday.

We reflected on the wealth of Western Europe and the contrast between Austria and Yugoslavia, Austria with its neat farms and villages nestling in green valleys being replaced by what seemed the tedium of the Yugoslav plains, the dirt and the dust, the lack of water, the heat causing the chocolate to melt and drip through the handbags and the rucksacks, the ragged villages and the barefoot children straggling along the railway line, the ox carts and the mud brick, faded ochre houses dotted about in a shimmering haze of brown hills and blue sky.

The efforts to be presentable had gone and the stiff British upper lip had sagged as we came close to reality. At the end of the third day we were still in Yugoslavia. Would the journey ever end? And then, late at night, we arrived at the Greek border where we had a nerve racking wait in "no man's land". The war had not long ended between the Greeks and the communists who had been supported by President Tito. The train had seemed to empty just before we arrived there and once we had crossed the border a surprise was in store: the Greeks attached a Restaurant car to the train! It was panelled in rich mahogany, with a large chandelier, tables with table cloths, table lamps and waiters. We could hardly believe it – our image of the Orient Express captured for a few hours in a pre-War dining car where we could sit and luxuriate and drink Turkish coffee. It has long since gone but the memory of it remains.

Our first real contact with Greece came at 3 am in the morning when we arrived in Thessaloniki: from that point there were only a few enjoyable hours to go as we passed Mount Olympus, admiring the majesty of the mountains and meandered down to Athens. The heat, the noise and the smell hit us as we got down from the train exhausted but enlivened by the thought that a bed was not far away! It was a voyage of self discovery for most of our group and one I am glad I did not miss.

As previously stated, I had scraped together another £23 for the holiday and lived and travelled round Greece on this meagre amount for the three weeks I was there. Being literally penniless on the homeward train journey I survived courtesy of the scraps of food given to me by a particularly kind group of young ladies from Newnham College. My parents were shocked by my gaunt appearance when I returned home but I had had a wonderful time.

This trip gave me an idea. Why not organise my own group in 1958 and go back to Greece? I approached Rosemary and she had no objection. She planned to organise a group to go by train to Istanbul.

The group I organised in 1958 turned out to be the launch pad for what became a substantial programme of student travel to what was then an undiscovered paradise. The students I sent to Greece over the next fifteen years were "trailblazers" for the subsequent boom in popularity of Greece as a holiday destination.

In 1958 I obtained the free leader's ticket for having a group in excess of fifteen persons: I charged each student an extra £1 for organising the trip and finished up with a group of over thirty of them: the financial requirements of travelling to and surviving comfortably in Greece were thereby resolved.

One of the interesting things one can do at Cambridge is attend Honorary Degree Ceremonies: Robert Frost, the famous writer and poet was being given an Honorary Doctorate at the Senate House in June 1958 and I decided to go along and watch the Ceremony. Since my undergraduate gown was very old (it had an "e" label on it and had been given to me by a friend of my father) I borrowed a Graduate gown from my friend "Gus" Donnell: he was studying for a Post Graduate Degree at Cambridge, having gained his first Degree at a Northern University. An "e" label, incidentally, was an "economy" label that appeared on clothes manufactured during or shortly after World War II.

Perched on one of the balcony seats I found myself sitting next to a very attractive young female undergraduate who looked at my gown and said, rather puzzled, "that is a Post Graduate gown." What College are you at?" "Downing", I replied. "Oh, do you know an undergraduate by the name of "Brian Hughes? I am going on his group to Greece". "Yes, I know him". "What is he like" she asked. "Oh, he's alright", I said, "quite an interesting chap. I believe he has been to Greece before". "That is good to know", she said. "I hoped he knew what he was doing". "I am fairly confident that you will be alright", I replied, keeping a straight face throughout!

With that we parted until, of course, the day the group assembled at Victoria Station. The name of the young lady was Valerie Foulkes and she was travelling with two friends from Newnham who had made the booking on her behalf. When, twenty minutes after the latest assembly time and ten minutes before the train was due to leave, she had not appeared I took the group to its reserved seats and went back to the ticket barrier.

At 2.55 pm, five minutes before the trains was due to depart, I spotted her and called her over. She was, of course, completely taken aback at finding out who I was but nevertheless said, when I reminded her that she should have been at Victoria by 2.30 pm, "but I am four minutes early"!

"I will have to watch this one" I thought. Which I did!! I reunited her with her two friends from Newnham and accompanied the three of them throughout the bulk of the holiday. I could not escape being "ribbed" for not telling her who I was at the Senate House but I did at least ensure that she and they arrived at the railway station in Athens in good time for the return journey!

At Athens railway station I found that I was one person short: I was missing Jeremy Brisley, a really charming and lively young man from Magdalene College. I remembered him well: he had come round to my digs in Cambridge with three or four other potential travellers during the summer for my "sales pitch", during which I offered toasted crumpets, tea and Battenburg cake. Most potential travellers were persuaded to sign up and join the group after the free tea!

On my return to London I telephoned Jeremy's parents: "I am afraid Jeremy did not turn up at Athens Railway Station for the homeward journey. I have no idea why he did not do so and hope he has managed to get home". I was totally unprepared for Mr. Brisley's reply: "Thank you, Brian, for phoning but I am very sorry to tell you that Jeremy is dead".

That was like a bolt from the blue. "How did he die?" I asked, taken aback by the news. His father replied. "Jeremy met two Greek student friends in Athens and they decided to hire a caique and sail it from Piraeus, the Port of Athens to Poros. They set off in good weather but half way across the bay to Poros they ran into a squall. They must have tried to turn the caique into the wind but the rudder fell off and they were all pitched into the sea. Jeremy's body was washed up three days later on the shore at Poros".

I must have sounded very shaken because he added "Jeremy's death was not your fault so do not feel bad about it". I could not help feeling bad about it, however, and the memory of Jeremy and what happened to him is embedded in my brain, as also in my memory is Stephen Blundell.

Over the years news of my groups spread throughout all the Universities in the United Kingdom and Stephen joined one of my groups when I was sending over two thousand students a year to Italy, Greece and Turkey. He, like nearly every visitor to Greece – whether they be student or adult – wanted to visit Myconos and Delos, two little "pearls" in the middle of the Aegean. .

Stephen and his three companions arrived by "inter island" ferry from Piraeus and once ashore at Myconos they decided to go for a swim. The four swam out a hundred yards or so and then turned back towards the beach. Two young French Tourists who had already been for a swim were watching them and when one of the four started waving frantically they dived into the sea and swam out towards them.

They met three swimmers coming back and said "are you all OK?" "Yes, we are OK" replied the three: it was only when the three reached the shore they said "where is Stephen?" He was missing.

To their great credit the two young French swimmers put their masks and snorkels on and swam out once again to where they had seen Stephen: sadly they located him under a rock about fifteen feet below the surface: they managed to get him ashore but it was too late and he lay lifeless on the beach.

His three companions went immediately to the Police Station on the Island to report his death and to ask for assistance. Much to their consternation the Police said they could do nothing unless the expense of putting him in the morgue was covered by payment or guarantee of payment: the students had insufficient money to cover the expense and there appeared to be no way the body could be moved from the beach until the British Consulate in Athens gave the necessary guarantee.

However, news of Stephen's death spread like wildfire and came to the attention of Yehudi Menuhin, the famous violinist who had a villa on the Island. He immediately went down to the Police Station, berated them for their insensitivity and guaranteed payment of the morgue expenses himself. Stephen's body was then collected from the beach and taken to the morgue.

I have the greatest of admiration and respect for Yehudi Menuhin as a result of that incident and would like everyone to be aware of his humanity and generosity of spirit. I happened to be in Athens at the time and received a telephone call from the British Consulate asking for the address and telephone number, if possible, of Stephen's parents and telling me what had occurred. A brief call from myself to Billericay elicited the required information from his booking form which I passed on to the Consulate.

Of the 15000 odd students I sent abroad mercifully only two died. Others caused problems and I can recount two incidents which may be of interest.

At the end of September in about 1964 I was bringing a group of just over eighty students back from Greece via Brindisi: it was the last of the season on that particular route: there were about 55 female students and about 25 male students in the group.

As we approached Brindisi I got all the young ladies together and said "When we arrive in Brindisi we will be met by a number of American Servicemen who will be waiting to take the "Brian Hughes gals" for a drink at one of the local Bars: they know my groups arrive every Friday afternoon and they will be on the quayside waiting for you. My advice to you is not to go to Bars with them, but, if you do, you must ensure that you are at the Railway Station in Brindisi which is at the far end of the town by 20.30 hrs latest. The "Expresso del Levante" comes from Lecce and departs Brindisi at 21.03 hrs. It does not stop for more than a few minutes and we have to find our reserved seats very quickly. Do not, repeat not be late".

When 2030 hrs arrived I was about eleven young females short. I entrusted my ruck sack to a member of the group, stepped outside the Station and grabbed a taxi. "take me to every Bar in Brindisi", I said. With the help of the obliging taxi driver I tracked down the eleven missing young women. "Do you want me to tell your parents that I left you drinking in a bar in Brindisi? Get up to the Station at once". One or two of them had had so much to drink that they were quite reluctant to leave their amorous USAF hosts. I had to put the more inebriated ones in the taxi!! With about five hair raising minutes to spare they were all at the Station and I breathed a sigh of relief.

On another occasion I received a telephone call from the leader of one of my Istanbul groups: "one of our group was refused access to Bulgaria unless he had a haircut: he refused and was thrown off the train". I have to admit that I was worried about ringing up his father and having to tell him that his son was somewhere in Turkey: the father was a Lieutenant Colonel in the British Army and I thought he would be extremely perturbed: his reaction, however, was totally unexpected. "Bloody good job", he exclaimed "I have been telling him to get his hair cut for ages"!!

There were of course many other incidents, during my fifteen years of organising student travel, like, for example, the earthquake in Skopje when we had a group of well over fifty students heading towards the epicentre of the earthquake and no certainty that the railway lines had not been damaged by it. We spent the night before the group left manufacturing armbands for each of the three parties that made up the combined group.

Overall, however, rail and rail/boat facilities to Greece via Idomeni and Brindisi worked well and I often bump into former "Brian Hughes" travellers – now in their sixties and seventies – who have fond memories of their holidays in Greece and Turkey despite the rigours of travel there in their youth!

With so many parties travelling out to Greece, Italy and Turkey I had to select someone within each group capable enough and responsible enough to hold the group ticket during the outward and homeward journeys: Thomas Cook offices held them during the students' holidays in the respective countries.

I chose the leaders on the basis of their handwriting: the person with the clearest, boldest and most well formed handwriting, whether male or female, was asked to lead the group and hold the party ticket: he or she invariably agreed and I never lost a party ticket. Judging people by their handwriting clearly works!!

On one or two occasions the students whose handwriting appeared to mark them out as potential leaders were reluctant to take on the responsibility until I pointed out that, in the hands of someone less capable, the group ticket might be lost!

I did not have to use this stratagem very often but I do remember one tall elegant young man from one of the Cambridge Colleges on a train journey to Istanbul who reluctantly agreed to hold the ticket on one condition, namely that he could address the group of thirty odd students before they left Victoria Station.

That was unusual but I had no objection and he said as follows: "Brian Hughes has asked me to hold the group ticket. I am prepared to do so but if you have any queries or any worries or concerns throughout the three day journey I shall be much obliged if you will kindly keep them to yourselves". I knew, at this point, that I had chosen correctly!! He turned out to be an excellent leader!

8

Surviving as a Student in Greece

On my first trip to Greece as an undergraduate in 1957 I had taken £23 for my holiday there: this had to include boat travel to and from the islands and sustenance on my homeward journey. Survival during my 24 days there was therefore predicated on my eating very low-cost food and sleeping outside – on roofs or the decks of ships – as much as possible.

Living was, of course, incredibly cheap at the time.

In 1973, sixteen years later, sleeping on the roof of a hotel cost 20 drachmas (25p): one could have the luxury of a bed in a "four bed" room in student accommodation for 40 drachmas (50p)!

Low-cost food consisted of bread or yoghurt with honey, fruit (mostly melons) and the occasional moussaka, which I discovered on this particular holiday. Omelettes were also cheap and were usually served with cheese, potatoes (sometimes called "smashed potatoes") and "muala". While visiting an inexpensive restaurant, the Ideal in Venizelos Street, I confidently ordered omelette with "muala". I did not know what "muala" were but thought that since they were on the menu they must be all right. When I returned to the hotel and looked up "muala" in my Greek dictionary I discovered they were sheep's brains! But, apart from feeling vaguely ill at the thought of eating them there was no adverse reaction. Milk shops (galaktopoleia) were also cheap and the water in Athens was drinkable.

One rapidly learnt where and where not to buy red melons and not to eat overripe fruit. Red melons have a poor filtration system and if there are any impurities in the soil, eg. sewage, where they are growing the red melon sucks them up in its race to ripen!! Eating a suspect red melon would result in a severe reaction after you had eaten it!

I subsequently advised all my students to take a bottle of Dr. John Collis Browne's Chlorodyne (or equivalent) or a liquid preparation by Allen and Hanburys that was very soothing for minor upsets. The Chlorodyne would normally "bung them up" sufficiently until their stomachs had recovered from the reaction!

The other most common cause of severe stomach upsets was, strangely, self-inflicted. Many members of my student groups, on arrival in Athens, would gulp down far too much iced water from the dispenser in the entrance hall of the X.E.N (the Greek equivalent of Y.W.C.A.). Young male students feeling parched on their long walk from their hotel to meet their female companions at the X.E.N would help themselves liberally to the iced water, giving their stomachs a chill.

I also had a number of students collapse on me through eating too little and trying to do too much. Being on their own in a hot and foreign country they had embarked on a "learning experience" in more ways than one!

It was as a result of joining Rosemary Bishop's group in 1957 and organising my own in 1958 that I decided students needed advice and guidance on many aspects of their holidays before they even left the United Kingdom and this is how the "Brian Hughes Handbooks" on Greece, Italy and Turkey came into being.

In addition to telling students what they had to do before they set foot on Victoria station the handbooks also advised on aspects of travel such as what to take with them and what not to take with them. Before I advised against it many a student found his/her clothes in their rucksack covered by a sticky brown mess as the chocolate they had packed away for the journey melted in the heat of travel through Yugoslavia.

After the trip in 1958 I wrote to all my student travellers asking them for good tips on cheap hotels and restaurants wherever they happened to have travelled. Their replies were extremely illuminating and informative and after three or four years I had a remarkably comprehensive handbook for each country full of useful advice and information for students, including details of restaurants and hotels, and train, bus and boat fares in most areas of Greece and the islands. For example the outward boat fare from Piraeus to Herakleion in Crete in 1973 was 110 drachmas and 123 drachmas back (£1.35p out and £1.50 back for a twelve to eighteen hour trip). Students were, however, advised to purchase their return tickets in Athens to avoid paying the extra 13 drachmas – 15p(!) – and to avoid Saturdays and religious festivals when the boats were more crowded than usual.

One aspect of the holidays that caused most students to remember them were the train and boat journeys. Apart from the extraordinary sensation one experienced when sleeping on the deck of an inter-island ferry as it slid into harbour, with engines hardly audible, and seeing the stars or the breaking dawn above, often the most memorable memories were the 68 hours they spent on trains between Victoria and Athens via Yugoslavia on the Tauern Orient Express (not to be confused with the Orient Express). The handbook notes on how to survive are to the point: "You may possibly be six but probably eight per compartment on the journey Ostend to Munich and Salzburg to Ostend, definitely eight per compartment Munich to Athens and Athens to Salzburg. Provided you can hang luggage on the hooks by the door and window and there are only six of you, two people can sleep in the luggage racks, two on the floor and one, or in the case of eight people, two on each seat", provided they do not have smelly feet. "Alternatively, all the luggage can be put in the middle (between the seats) to sleep four to six across, two aloft. Banishing people, if necessary, to the corridor will always alleviate the sleeping problem for those left in the compartment. However thefts from luggage left in the corridor overnight are not infrequent, especially in Yugoslavia, between Ljubljana and Zagreb." Women were usually banished to the luggage racks because their hips fitted between the struts that held them up!

The same general rules applied on the Brindisi route except that trains were not quite so crowded and sleeping places easier to find.

These journeys engendered a camaraderie that seems to have lasted over many years for a number of my former student travellers.

The handbooks grew in popularity every year as the comments flowed in. By the time they had reached twenty-four pages (in the case of Greece) packed full of useful information they accounted for most students opting to travel "Brian Hughes" rather than by the National Union of Students service that could only offer more expensive air travel to these countries. Many N.U.S travellers telephoned to ask if they could purchase one of the handbooks but were told they were only available free of charge to "Brian Hughes" travellers, and were politely refused.

I was not the only student to run short of money while on holiday in Greece and one of the tips in the handbook on Greece was about selling blood for cash: "If running short of money, sell some blood – 237 drachmas for 300 cc." (Roughly £4 a pint and enough to keep an impecunious student in food for two days). Students were advised to take a "blood donor" card if they possessed one to the blood bank, close to the "men's hotel".

One other piece of advice which is as relevant today as it was then was as follows: "Beware jellyfish and sea urchins: the spines of the latter burrow well under the skin's surface if you tread on one without plimsolls on and may take several days to come out. I am told that hot candle wax dropped on the spot helps to draw the spines out or make them more easily extractable (and if this does not work consult a doctor immediately. Olive oil rubbed well into the stricken area will soothe inflammation from a jellyfish bite. Although neither snakes nor scorpions will go out of their way to attack you, you might easily be bitten if you accidentally tread on one in long grass."

With their advice on sunburn, calamine lotion and on taking a couple of plasters my students should have been prepared for most eventualities (albeit with heavier rucksacks than most intended to take with them)!

Because of the contribution the British, in particular, had made to the liberation of Greece after the Second World War members of "Brian Hughes" parties invariably encountered friendship and hospitality from the people of Greece.

In 1958 memories of German atrocities during the war were still fresh, however, and, on my way home with my group in that year, two adventurous students told me of a worrying incident when they tried to climb the principal mountain in Crete – Mount Ida. They had nearly reached the top when a bullet ricocheted from a rock above them and assuming they might be in trouble if they continued upwards they decided that discretion was the better part of valour and started to descend.

A few hundred feet below them they found a Cretan dressed in traditional garb holding a rifle which he pointed at them. When they told him in the best Greek they could muster that they were British, he could not have been friendlier and made it clear that he only shot at them because he thought the blonder student of the two was German!

Fortunately attitudes have changed perceptibly since the 1950s but modern readers will doubtless have noted that Greeks are not particularly enamoured of EU interference (mainly attributable to German influence) in the economy of their country.

Ladies were advised to be "cautious of the charmingly hospitable unmarried Greek males" who seemed to make a point of attaching themselves to the female members of my groups and entertaining them. I pointed out that, as with Iole, it was customary for the lady to have a female chaperone whenever she was taken out by a "casual male" acquaintance."

Fortunately I never lost one of my young ladies as a result!

The author at the age of 12
The end of banana rationing!

Iole at Cambridge

The Kool Katz disco at which I met Iole

National Service: Sergeants sightseeing in Kyrenia

Kyrenia Castle: Sergeants together – self-attached to Special Branch

Cambridge: Poppy Day 1958 – gone fishing!

Members of the BH group en route to Athens

BH party members: suffering 68 hours in railway carriages

9

Mr & Mrs Robinson

It is strange how minor incidents in life can alter one's perceptions quite profoundly.

When I was at university I volunteered to visit elderly couples in the Cambridge area and talk to them in an attempt to ease their isolation. I had previously volunteered at school to join the school's Docklands Settlement project and felt rather guilty that, within my hectic schedule of activities, I had not found the time to spend on it.

I was allocated a Mr and Mrs Robinson and cycled out one afternoon to a rather "down at heel" part of Cambridge – off the Hills Road.

Mr and Mrs. Robinson lived in a very small terraced house and were clearly very old and very poor. When I came into their tiny living room they were both huddled round a coal fire; both wore thick black clothes and it was obvious that they had next to nothing in terms of possessions.

"We knew you were coming so we bought a packet of biscuits," said Mrs Robinson. It was a kind and generous gesture that must have cost them a shilling and I was touched by it. But even more touching (and disturbing to me at the time) was their obvious happiness in the midst of poverty. I am afraid to say that, as a callow young man, I could not come to terms with that. I stayed talking to them for an hour or so and they said they looked forward to my next visit.

As I left them, however, I thought to myself, "How can a couple like this be so happy and yet so poor?" My whole life to that point had been predicated on achievement and that achievement bringing with it wealth and happiness: that was why I had worked so hard to get into university and read law. My attitude clearly needed a rethink – wealth does not necessarily bring happiness but love and kindness do.

Although, as a result of my feelings, I was not brave enough at the time to go back to Mr and Mrs Robinson and confront the situation again, they left an indelible impression on me. My reaction had been to reject the concept of being happy, though poor, but after going down the ambition route and finishing up divorced with my two young sons in the mid-1970's the memory of my meeting with Mr and Mrs Robinson kept coming back to me. They had something I did not have and was unlikely ever to have with my mindset at the time.

Over the years, however, that mindset has changed and although I have always been happy – apart from a brief period as a truculent teenager – I have also tried to be kind and not to bother too much about wealth – except insofar as it can do good.

My second wife, Annette, constantly told me that, with my abilities, I could join a legal practice in London and earn a fortune, but to what end or purpose? It was far more rewarding in happiness terms to work in a small town, not charge any more than I needed and spend time on family and community activities.

My two sons came to live with me permanently not long after my first wife and I divorced and I would not have been able to look after them as I did if I had worked in London and been a City lawyer on a much higher salary.

The moral of Mr and Mrs Robinson is that life is what you make of it: you should not think that it is wealth that makes you happy. All one really needs is enough to get by on: wealth should not be an end in itself.

10

Working in the City

Leaving university is a bit like leaving school – a big step into the unknown. Into what sort of future? After school I knew I was destined to go into the Army or the Air Force: for most school leavers in 1954 it was a matter of conscription and obligatory National Service.

After university there was no certainty. The successful or unsuccessful choice of a future life or career could only be predicated on what one felt one was capable of achieving in a particular area of interest or expertise and on fortune. As a classicist steeped in Greek mythology I had already developed a strong sense that fate – what we call chance – plays a big part in our lives and that feeling has never left me.

There is no doubt that in the late 1950s and early 1960s a number of career options existed, but which option should one take and where would it lead? This is what everyone leaving any university at any time has to decide and, given its significance and effect on one's future, it is a question that should really be answered after considerable thought.

A lot of young people, however, trust to luck and I probably fell into that category, although, in my case, I was more of an ancient Greek than most. By this I mean that I felt my life was already mapped out –predetermined, irrespective of the decisions or choices I thought I was making on my own! Whatever, I knew I had to earn a living somehow but how to do so, be happy, useful and fulfilled I really had no idea. "Fate" would doubtless lead to whatever was in store for me.

Most young people look at their parents' careers and try to gauge how happy and fulfilled they have been. It was obvious that my father's options had been restricted by his having to leave school after "matriculation" (the equivalent of "O" levels or GCSEs). His own father had not even been prepared to pay for a school uniform for him and had forced him to give up any idea of staying at school beyond the age of sixteen. In fact my father had to wear his Scout jersey at school because he had no school uniform and was nicknamed "cabbage" as a result.

On the other hand, my father had been very bright: he had a quick brain and was a good organiser. Without further education and a professional qualification, however, he had been passed over for promotion once he had reached a comparatively senior level in local government. Younger, qualified solicitors with far less experience and ability were taking over the roles he would have been perfectly capable of fulfilling. This restriction on his ability to progress undoubtedly affected him deeply and his heartfelt advice to me was always, "Whatever you do in life get a professional qualification behind you. You will not then be overtaken by younger and less competent people with qualifications."

Because he had been involved in the legal and administrative aspects of local government and because he recognised the need for me to have a qualification of some sort he had influenced me into reading law at university and into heading towards a professional qualification in the law. But is that what I wanted? I was very much in two minds. After hearing what my father had to say about "small town" politics and the suppressed frustration of most of his fellow local government officers at the antics of headline-grabbing councillors I decided that local government was not for me!

If I was to try and become a high street solicitor I would have to find a solicitor who would give me articles of clerkship without demanding a premium, as they often did in the late 1950s. My parents could not afford to pay a premium on my behalf and if no premium had to be paid then I would probably have to work for a pittance for three years.

Becoming a barrister had its attractions but, there again, one faced the cost of pupillage. Moreover, if I went down that route – as many of my university colleagues did – I was not at all sure that I possessed the intellect to become a QC or a judge of some kind. It would also doubtless have meant that I would have to live somewhere in London in a shared flat with a number of other impecunious trainee barristers and survive as best I could on whatever I was paid as a trainee. Travel to and from London every day would have been expensive and beyond the resources of my parents and myself.

Obtaining articles of clerkship in the City of London, however, where I might also get paid seemed a distinct possibility and I discussed this option with my father. He suggested that he contact Arnold Willis, my godfather and the best man at my parents' wedding. He was now a partner in a firm of stockbrokers in the City and might know someone who could offer me articles.

Arnold Emery Willis who, to me was "Uncle Arnold," was an extraordinary man and I am not just talking about his looks. He was a stocky, completely bald figure with a long flaming ginger beard and looked like a cross between an Old Testament prophet and a Viking! I suspect he wore this amazing beard in order to divert attention from his baldness! He and my father had been close friends when they were at school in Westcliff and right up to the Second World War. Their paths diverged substantially, however, when my parents moved to Northamptonshire in 1939.

Arnold had obtained employment as a clerk in the administrative offices of the London Stock Exchange on leaving school and, like so many young men in the City, had been conscripted into the HAC – the Honourable Artillery Company – and commissioned at the outbreak of the war. The HAC have always regarded themselves as a cut above the Royal Regiment of Artillery in the same way as the Royal Regiment of Artillery have considered themselves somewhat superior to the infantry, the regiments "of the line". I am well aware of that because I was in the Royal Artillery during my National Service!

It made no difference to any sense of superiority when Arnold was captured with other members of the HAC at Tobruk in North Africa in 1941 and shipped across to Italy with hundreds of other prisoners of war. However, while being marched in a long column of prisoners of war through a town in southern Italy Arnold saw his chance and stepped into an alleyway unnoticed by the guards and "headed for the hills" where he joined up with a group of partisans. He spent the next two years with them blowing up railway lines and sabotaging military installations and having a thoroughly satisfying time!

When the Allies invaded Italy in September 1943 he was determined to slip through the German lines and re-join the British Army as soon as he possibly could. He successfully achieved the first and most dangerous part, and, to his great relief, came across a British night patrol in "no man's land." His relief was short-lived, however, because within minutes of joining the patrol it was ambushed by a German patrol and he was taken prisoner for a second time.

The Germans did not lose prisoners of war in the same way as the Italians and he soon found himself in an offlag, a prisoner of war camp for officers in the middle of Germany.

Among the officers in the camp was David Hellings, a former junior partner in a firm of stockbrokers in the City of London with whom he struck up a friendship. David offered him a partnership in the stockbroking firm he intended to establish after the war was won by the Allies and when they could return home. Arnold therefore joined David Hellings as a partner in Rowe Swann & Co. after they had been repatriated. In addition to offering a normal stockbroking service the partnership set out to bring companies that needed capital to the London Stock Exchange by way of "flotations" and Arnold became the partner in charge of new issues. Most of these companies were successful medium-sized enterprises that would benefit greatly from the exposure a Stock Exchange listing would bring them.

When Arnold joined Rowe Swann & Co. he was not at all well off but fortune was, again, on his side. His big break came in 1954 when the Conservative Government decided to denationalise the steel industry. With the help of David Hellings, Arnold was able to borrow £250,000 from merchant bankers Samuel Montague, who at the time had offices in the same building in Austin Friars as Rowe Swann & Co. He used this money to purchase one million Steel Company of Wales shares at their flotation price of five shillings (25p) per share, selling them not long after flotation for up to forty five shillings (£2.25) per share. This "sure fire" transaction turned him into a millionaire within weeks and with his new-found wealth he created a company, Augustine Investments, and put into it a number of businesses he snapped up at the time, including Dolland and Aitchison, the well-known opticians.

I had never had a great deal to do with him, apart from occasional visits with my parents to see him, his wife and children in the impressive Victorian rectory he had purchased in the north of Essex but he was always well disposed towards me and was happy to arrange for me to meet the solicitor who acted on behalf of Rowe Swann & Co. His name was Hilary Scott (later Sir Hilary Scott) the senior partner of Slaughter & May, an eminent firm of City solicitors.

I was taken by my godfather to meet this austere man in his splendid wood panelled offices, not a stone's throw from the offices of Rowe Swann & Co. and, in a private interview without Arnold being present, we discussed my achievements and interests at Cambridge and the possibility of being articled to him or one of the other partners. After a fairly cerebral exchange of views with Hilary Scott who was subsequently awarded his knighthood upon being elected President of the Law Society (an honour conferred automatically on all presidents until Margaret Thatcher put her foot down and ended this archaic practice) he undoubtedly concluded that I was not of the requisite intellectual calibre for his firm and politely turned me down. It was clear that he was looking for graduates with first class degrees and I did not have one!

He was pleasant and had clearly interviewed me as a favour to my godfather. As a member of the Council of the Law Society for ten years, representing all the solicitors in my Essex constituency I regularly walked past the painting of him in the Law Society's impressive headquarters in Chancery Lane and wondered what would have happened if he had decided to accept me as an articled clerk. This book would certainly not have been written and I would not have had so many stories to tell!

Somewhat crestfallen I walked back to my godfather's offices with him. He had kindly waited for me while I had the interview. He could see that I was disappointed and said, "How much do you think Hilary Scott earns?" "It must be somewhere between £5000 and £6000 a year." I replied. That would have been about five times more than an assistant solicitor and about twice as much as partners in most medium-sized legal practices in the City would earn, as far as I could gather. "Chickenfeed," he said. "Why don't you come and work for me? You could earn far more than that in stockbroking".

This was an offer I could not refuse so, ignoring my father's sound advice I accepted it! It was not long after the offer had been made that I was inducted into the statistical analysis department of Rowe Swann & Co. where I remained for nearly two years. The purpose of the "stats" department was to assess the future profitability of Stock Exchange listed companies and advise clients on "best buys". Many of the clients were very wealthy and relied on the dividends from their investments to keep them in the style to which they had become accustomed.

The department was populated by a mixed bunch, all male, headed by Eric Lyons who invariably wore smart and undoubtedly very expensive, medium blue suits which stood out from the more sombre dark grey attire of the rest of us. In this respect the first thing my godfather did when I turned up wearing a new Burton's grey suit was to pack me off to a tailor in Savile Row where I was measured up for what I thought was an incredibly expensive "City gentleman's suit", complete with waistcoat, at forty five guineas (£47.25) and then to Locks, the hatters in St. James Street, Mayfair for an equally expensive bowler hat made of genuine rabbit fur! Only "staff" wore Burton's suits and Austin Reed bowler hats apparently: "gentlemen" wore Savile Row suits and bowlers made by Locks! Never were boundaries so clearly defined as in the City of London in those days, as I was to find out.

Locks still had the last admiral's hat made for Sir Horatio Nelson in a glass cabinet on the ground floor. I believe he was killed at the Battle of Trafalgar before he could collect it. Locks, would put an extraordinary wooden contraption on a client's head that measured the contours of his or her skull: in this way they were able to produce a hat of whatever type that fitted perfectly. Before Annette, my late wife, died we met the director of Locks on holiday in Italy who, as a young man, had sold me my bowler. It was a remarkable coincidence and he invited us both back to his premises in St. James's where I once again encountered this unique head measuring device!

The stats department staff consisted of Eric Lyons, the manager, who I felt always looked more appropriately dressed for selling expensive motor cars in a West End showroom, Henry Jackson, Eric Kohn and Alastair Hitchens. Henry's real name was Heinrich Jacobsen and his parents had owned a major tyre factory in Germany before Hitler launched his assault on everyone and everything Jewish. His parents had had the good sense to send their son abroad before they lost everything including their own lives. Henry had qualified as a chartered accountant in England and was quiet, thoughtful and methodical. Eric Kohn, on the other hand, was a very exuberant individual, intellectual, aware of business trends and opportunities and very tuned into the political scene: he could always spot which way any particular market was going. He was a great talker and would have made an excellent university lecturer in economics or business studies. He was passionate about Mahler, his favourite composer.

Alastair Hitchens, another young graduate like myself, garnered information from company reports and Extel (Exchange Telegraph) cards that contained factual summaries of the past performance of stocks and shares of companies quoted on the London Stock Exchange. I was given the same job as Alastair: we, in effect, did the spadework for the other three and it was Alastair who facetiously called me an "Encyclopaedia of Useless Information"!

Although my salary was only £12 a week the firm paid regular bonuses and during the time I was there I was earning the equivalent of £900 a year, not much less than a newly qualified assistant solicitor in the City of London.

Working in the stats department moreover gave me an excellent overview of the stock market and an opportunity to invest in stocks and shares that I thought might appreciate in value. My only problem, during my first few months in the Department, was that I had no money! It took me three months to pay off the cost of the Savile Row suit and the bowler hat! So how was I to raise some money with which to buy some stocks and shares? The answer seemed obvious: organise some more student parties to Greece!!

Bernard Baruch, the famous American financier, a precursor of Warren Buffett, said that he made his fortune by buying shares "too late" and selling them "too early". He would invest in shares which had started on an upward trajectory, wait for them to rise another ten per cent and then sell them, however much further they looked likely to appreciate. In other words "never be greedy". If the shares went down he applied the same rule. His remarkable ability was to spot the shares that were likely to go up rather than down!

One of my earliest purchases, and the reader will be able to gauge from it the modesty of my finances, was 100 Tecalemit shares at about 14 /- (70p) a share: they looked a good bet but, to my surprise, they started going down, rather than up! I asked my godfather what I should do – hang on or sell? "Brian, you have to learn to accept a loss in stockbroking and move on," he said. Since this advice was pretty much in line with Bernard Baruch's approach to selling and buying I reluctantly sold and lost a minute £8.19.10d (just under £9.00), but that was quite a lot to me at the time! Within a couple of weeks, however, they had appreciated to well above my original purchase price. From that moment on I decided never to ask anyone for advice on the stock market but trust my own judgement. As a result that was my only loss in thirty two transactions!

There is a Greek saying "the bag fills bean by bean" and by adopting a cautious approach and not gambling too much on any particular transaction I had soon accumulated enough to pay my father £60 for his car, an aged 1936 Austin Ascot de luxe: it was twenty four years old, the same age as myself, and was, in essence, a "dressed up" box on wheels with a twelve horsepower engine which one could only start by cranking the engine with a starting handle. My father was happy to sell it because he had a bad chest and had found starting it on cold mornings very difficult. He upgraded to a 1939 Wolseley Sixteen, identical to the Wolseley's in "Foyles War", which had a starter motor.

Once I had the car which was, in fact, very reliable, I devoted one day nearly every weekend to driving to Cambridge, Oxford and London University colleges and pinning posters, advertising my Greek parties, on every student notice board I could find or to answering letters from students who enquired about travel to Greece.

The steady process of accumulation went on and I was able in 1961 to sell my father's antique Austin and purchase a second-hand Wolseley 1500, with same engine in it as an MG sports car. This enabled me to travel further and faster to universities I had not previously been able to reach in one day. The money I had saved also gave me the ability to rent a bedroom in a modern four bedroom flat belonging to Isaac Ascher in New Cross Gate, which I used as a "pied a terre" during the week when I left Rowe Swann & Co. and commenced articles of clerkship in September 1961. The flat that I believe Eric Kohn had told me about was at the top of a hill in a predominantly West Indian area on the borders of Lewisham: that did not bother me in the slightest but the location of it would doubtless have caused a few raised eyebrows had I stayed with Rowe Swann & Co!

Isaac (Ike) Ascher, to whom I will refer again in my chapters on Israel and my political experiences, was a very pleasant single man in his mid-thirties who let out bedrooms in his well-appointed flat to graduates as a supplement to his income as a lecturer in politics at Goldsmith's College: he was a good and fair-minded host and I met some very interesting people as a result of renting a room there.

But again, I digress!

As previously mentioned my godfather became the partner whose principal role was to bring medium- sized businesses to the stock market: in the early 1960s there was a great desire for capital in order to fund further development of successful businesses and the way in which this was achieved was very similar to the way in which the Government subsequently sold shares in British Gas to the general public. You will doubtless remember "Sid".

A prospectus would be issued by a firm of stockbrokers. Rowe Swann & Co. were not the only ones bringing these companies to the market. The stockbrokers would underwrite the issue of shares and invite members of the public to apply for them. By this underwriting of the issue of the shares the company coming to the market would know that the money it expected from the sale of its shares would be guaranteed because if not enough people subscribed for the shares the stockbrokers would have to take up the unissued shares themselves.

The invitations to apply for shares would normally state that, if the number of shares applied for was more than the number available, subscribers would receive shares pro rata. Since the shares in nearly all the companies coming to the market in this way were likely to appreciate there was usually a stampede for the shares: the people who wanted to make a quick return on their money were called "stags" and like the other members of the stats department and all the other brokers and dealers in the Stock Exchange I often became a "stag", applying for shares, and, if lucky in the allocation of shares, selling them shortly after they were traded.

One of my great "misses" in this respect was my godfather's suggestion that everyone in the firm should apply for shares in a company that he was responsible for bringing to the market. The name of the company was Racal Electronics and Rowe, Swann & Co were underwriting the issue of their shares. I did not have £100 to spare but the shares, when floated on the Stock Exchange, appreciated very quickly and not long afterwards the company was able to make a "scrip issue" to shareholders of shares in a subsidiary it had formed. The subsidiary was a telecommunications firm by the name of Vodafone! The original shares in Racal Electronics and the shares it issued in respect of its subsidiary grew enormously in value as Vodafone expanded and must now be worth a fortune!

I have to contrast this, of course, with the many share flotations that have flopped over the years where the stockbrokers who underwrote companies coming to the market finished up with egg on their faces and most of the shares!

To purchase shares by filling in an application form and selling whatever number one received after they had floated and appreciated in value struck me as perfectly acceptable. We in the stats department were doubtless in a better position than most to be able to assess whether or not the companies coming to the market were likely to be successful but, in essence, everyone took the same risk.

What I took a very dim view of was using the clients of the firm to make a profit. Eric Lyons was constantly asking Alastair and me to prepare reports on companies for circulation to clients. He once asked me in particular to prepare a report on Edgar Allen and Company, specialist steel manufacturers in Sheffield, which was sent out in the usual way. I recall that the shares were priced at just over 30/- (£1.50) a share and I was gratified to see the price of the shares move up almost immediately to about 37/- 6d (£1.87). I was not at all happy to discover subsequently, through the share dealing department, that Lyons had purchased a tranche of the shares before asking me to prepare the report and had then sold them when the price had moved upwards. The fact that they subsequently peaked at over £2 per share was neither here nor there as far as I was concerned. I did not want to be part of that particular money-making scheme.

Placing what was, in effect a bet, using one's own judgement was one thing but creating or assisting in the creation of an uplift in the price of a share in what was a restricted market and then profiting from it was not for me. I doubt whether the partners who were all pretty strait-laced were aware of this particular practice and I only found out by accident. Nor do I know how often Eric Lyons did this but I was disappointed with what he had done. This practice and any other form of insider trading has since been banned by law but at the time I have no doubt that some people in other stockbroking firms were doing very much the same.

I went to see my godfather shortly after this discovery and asked him whether I could become a "blue button", a trader on the floor of the Stock Exchange, but there were no vacancies: alternatively could I join his new issues team, but there again, the recently graduated son of a partner had stepped into that role. It made me realise that being a godson was not likely to help me become a partner in the firm: one had to be the son of a partner to progress! Nepotism was the order of the day.

When it became obvious that I was never likely to break through the glass ceiling and progress to becoming a partner and that I would probably have to carry on writing reports until retirement I decided belatedly to take my father's advice and qualify as a solicitor. The next phase of my life was about to begin!

11

To Israel in 1962

When Ike Ascher knew that I intended to visit Israel during my stay in Greece he gave me the name of a colonel in Israeli military intelligence with whom I might be able to stay for a short time.

Little did I realise how extraordinary my eight days in Israel would be.

Ike had relatives in Israel and the colonel was one of them: not only was he a senior officer in the Israeli Army but he was also a principal lecturer at Kfar Galim just outside Haifa.

Kfar Galim had been established in 1953, as part of the settling enterprise for young immigrants during the establishment of the state of Israel: it was set up as an educational centre in order to educate and train these young people, "in the spirit of the values of labour and agriculture, democracy (which many of them had never experienced), tolerance (also) personal fulfilment and settlement."

Kfars are, in essence, training camps where young people learn the agricultural skills that they will need when they go to kibbutzim – community farms which produce much of the nation's foodstuffs – for internal consumption or export.

I wrote to the colonel and asked him if I could possibly stay for a day or two at Kfar Galim: he willingly agreed and told me how to get to it.

My reason for going to Israel was twofold: my student travel business was growing fast and I wanted to be able to offer advice and information on the facilities that existed on the ground for students. I was also curious about this extraordinary country whose future appeared to be very much in the balance. ISSTA, the Israeli Student Travel Association, had already approached me with a view to offering my students cheap student flights to Israel from Athens and it was clearly sensible to see what Israel had to offer them.

It is difficult to imagine nowadays but in 1962 only fourteen years after it had come into being, Israel was a pariah state. Arab nations throughout the Middle East had been intent on stifling it at birth and during its infancy refused access to anyone who had an Israeli customs stamp in his or her passport.

This meant that any UK citizen determined enough to visit the country had to obtain a second British passport that was valid for Israel only. We were not, of course, alone in having to deal with this attempted boycott: the same barrier was placed in the path of the nationals of other countries whose governments had to devise similar ways round it.

I therefore applied to the Passport Office in Petty France, explained the purpose of my visit and was issued with a second "slimmed down" version of the standard British passport for presentation to and stamping by Israeli customs. Armed with two passports I could now safely fly from Athens to Tel Aviv without having to forego any future visits to the Middle East.

The ISSTA charter flight from Athens was not quite what I expected. It was in an antiquated Douglas DC3 (a Dakota): these planes had been used extensively by the US Air Force during the Second World War and this particular plane had probably been sold off at the end of its military career!

It seated about twenty four people in an unpressurised cabin that was very basic: the toilet at the back of the plane was over a hole in the fuselage through which one could see the sea glistening a few thousand feet below as one relieved oneself!

The plane flew into Tel Aviv (Lod) Airport on a Thursday afternoon and from Tel Aviv I caught the bus to Haifa. On the plane I had sat next to an enthusiastic young Socialist from Jerusalem who had been to Yugoslavia to study how the Communist system worked under President Tito. We had had an animated conversation on the plane about the respective merits of capitalism and Communism which we obviously approached from different ends of the spectrum! But we had got on very well and he invited me to visit him and stay the night with himself and his wife at his flat if I was able to do so. I thanked him for his kind offer and said I would visit them if I could.

The first things I noticed when the bus arrived in Haifa were the parking meters along the sides of the main streets – which I had never seen before, also the supermarkets which, again, seemed so American: this was before

Mr. Cohen opened his first Tesco supermarket. In England, at the time, one queued at the counters of the International stores or the Home and Colonial stores, bought the unwrapped cheese, butter and ham or whatever dairy or meat produce one wanted straight from the display counter and either paid over the counter or at the till at the exit.

These were the days before Sainsburys and Mr. Cohen (the "Co" in Tesco stands for "Cohen") revolutionised British shopping habits and introduced the American style supermarket. Given the strong American influence in Israel it is perhaps not surprising that supermarkets opened in Israel before they opened in the UK.

Another bus ride brought me to Kfar Galim where I was greeted in a most friendly way by the colonel who put me up in his bungalow. That evening we discussed the threats facing Israel and the attitudes of the great powers towards the country. The attitude of Israel towards Great Britain was ambivalent – the Balfour Declaration in 1917 had been welcomed but not the British resistance to the inflow of migrants from Europe into the country following the Second World War, as exemplified by the fate of the SS Exodus in 1947.

I woke next morning after a good night's sleep at about 7.30 am: the sun was pouring in through the windows and it was clearly going to be another hot day. I heard the sound of marching feet and looked outside. About twenty young people were marching past the bungalow. "Are they going to work?" I enquired. "No," said the colonel, "they are coming back from the fields: they have already been to work." It made sense in that heat to start to work early but that must have been really early!

The obvious thing to do that day, Friday, was to go to Caesarea, a little way up the coast and look at the Roman remains there. On the bus from Haifa I bumped into two other British students and we decided to spend the day together and return later in the day to Haifa on the bus. It was after about an hour of standing at the bus stop that we discovered there were no buses after 4 pm to Haifa on Friday afternoons: the Jewish Sabbath starts on Friday afternoon in Israel, not on Saturday morning!

I suggested that we head for the Caesarea golf club and try to hitch a lift back to Haifa: once arrived we positioned ourselves on the long drive leading from the club house and thumbed a number of large cars: they all drove straight past us.

"OK," I said. "The only way of getting a car to stop is for one of us to lie down on the drive. A car will then have to stop." "Not us" said the other two, so I lay down on the road as a large American car came round the bend from the club house. The car came to a halt, as I hoped it would, and I asked the driver if he would be so kind as to take us to Haifa if he was going in that direction.

"Of course, I will," came the response. We all piled into his vast American car. "My name is Shubinsky," said the driver. "I own the Sussita car factory of Israel." My response was immediate: "I saw one of your cars on display at the Earls Court Motor Show last year. It had a fibreglass body on a Ford chassis and had a Ford engine. I was quite impressed by it."

"Good boy. You must try one." "Come to my factory on Sunday and I will let you have one for your holiday in Israel." That was a really amazing offer which I readily accepted!

I went to his factory on the Sunday and waited there until the two Americans to whom he had previously loaned the car returned it. It was a sort of fibreglass Land Rover –cheap and cheerful with a white body: but it turned out to be very practical and reliable. I suspect that it was the under-powered pick-up truck he had launched at the New York Autoshow in 1960 (and which he did not go on to produce in any number). But it was fine for me!

Once he had completed the paperwork I drove off in it towards Tel Aviv, the principal city of Israel. Apart from the limited number of highways and the streets within the cities the roads were of poor quality but there was little traffic on them and I was able to travel from place to place quickly and without difficulty.

Once arrived in Tel Aviv which, at the time, had a population of about 400,000, I located the offices of ISSTA at 7 Petah Tikva Road, met Zvi Ravon, the manager and secured an agency for student flights from Athens to Tel Aviv. After this a visit to the Israel Government Tourist Corporation offices in Mendele Street where I met and spoke to one of the staff. The staff had great plans for the expansion of tourism to Israel but were very much aware that if these plans were ever to come to fruition they would have to overcome, in some way, the natural reluctance of anyone to visit a country which faced a constant threat of invasion by its adjoining Arab neighbours.

The Israelis were clearly hoping that tourism would in due course boost their economy which, although expanding rapidly had, to that point, been dependent on restitution and reparation payments from West Germany, the sale of Government development bonds, loans from wealthy Zionists and private investment. Much of the money received by the state of Israel was going into the purchase of military hardware, including Dassault Mirage jet fighters from France and tanks from the United States.

The need to build up its defences to protect itself from invasion must have accounted for the somewhat neglected state of many of the roads and the generally run-down appearance of the villages through which I passed. Ensuring survival as a nation had to be the first priority: tourism and the development of hotels and tourist sites had to take a back seat. Nevertheless, I collected as much information as I could on the country and on all its potential tourist attractions. After a busy morning in Tel Aviv I set off for Jerusalem via Ramlah, arriving in Jerusalem late in the afternoon.

Before the Six Day War in 1967 Jerusalem with a population of about 160,000 and quite a lot smaller than Tel Aviv and Haifa was at the end of a hilly promontory jutting out into Palestine. Like the "Finger of Galilee" in the north it was very vulnerable to attack on three sides. I found the small apartment of my Socialist friend in a recently built development on the west side of Jerusalem and asked him if his kind offer still stood. Now that I had a car it would be no problem for me to find alternative hostel accommodation if it did not.

He and his wife, however, insisted that I stay the night with them and took me out for an evening meal. The next day my host took me sightseeing in Old Jerusalem. Tourism was virtually non-existent but I did obtain the usual certificate from the curator attesting to the fact that I had ascended Mount Zion, "in keeping with the ancient tradition of pilgrimage to the Holy City"!

As we walked along the terrace behind the defensive ramparts marking the boundary of the Jewish area of the city I peered over them towards East Jerusalem: no sooner had I put my head above the parapet, however, than my host grabbed me and urgently told me keep my head down. "Did you not see the Jordanian soldiers a few yards away on the other side?" he said. "They were likely to shoot at you if you kept looking at them." I had indeed seen and looked at the soldiers with their red and white head-dresses and black headbands with their rifles in their hands but I had not for one moment thought that they would take a "pot shot" at me! This was my first real indication of the sense of ever-present danger and of the siege mentality felt by the Israelis. This experience was to be repeated later when I visited the north of the country.

Having thanked my Socialist friend and his wife for their great kindness and hospitality I set off once again for Ramlah. After a brief stop for a bite to eat in Ramlah I pressed onward towards Hadera. Being constantly on the move and having no time for proper lunches I lived on what I could buy at the roadside or on the streets of the places I visited: that suited me because I did not have much money anyway!

It was in Israel, therefore, that I encountered shashlik (charcoal broiled lamb on skewers), kebabs, falafel (ground chickpeas formed into balls and deep fried), houmous and bourekas (unsweetened paper thin pastry filled with cheese or spinach – which I had already come across in Greece). I have never tasted better houmous than in Israel nor enjoyed food like shashlik or bourekas more!!

My immediate objective was to visit Nazareth and view the Church of the Annunciation. The road between Ramlah and Hadera lay in the narrow coastal strip which linked the northern and southern parts of Israel and which was less than ten miles wide at one point. In 1962 the Arab nations could well have cut Israel in two had they possessed the military resources and the resolve to do so. As it turned out the Israeli Army was better trained, equipped and motivated and, when the country was actually invaded five years later in 1967 in a war initiated by President Nasser of Egypt, General Moshe Dayan, the Israeli Commander-in-Chief inflicted a crushing defeat on the Egyptians and the Syrians. He appeared, sporting his black eyepatch, on virtually every newspaper in Europe and America after his extraordinary victory. The Israelis had responded to the invasion by throwing the Egyptians back in disarray across the Suez Canal, annexing the area of Palestine to the west of the River Jordan (the West Bank) and seizing the Golan heights in the north from the Syrians.

I arrived at the Church of the Annunciation in Nazareth as it was closing: the Arab caretaker was just locking up. I asked if I could possibly have a quick look inside and the Arab caretaker said that unfortunately he had to catch a bus home.

"If I drive you home will you unlock the church and let me have a quick look inside?" I asked him and he agreed. As I drove him home I found out that his family owned the Arab Cigarette and Tobacco Company, formerly "of Palestine" and now "of Israel." I believe it was the "Tatli-Sert"cigarette factory in Nazareth.

"How are you Christian Arabs getting on now that Israel is a fully fledged state free from British influence?" "Not too well," he said. "We are gradually being edged out of business opportunities. It was fine under the Mandate but we Christian Arabs are being marginalised in the new state of Israel.

I expressed my regret and when we arrived at his home he invited me in for a cup of tea and the opportunity to meet his family: most of them spoke good English and they were clearly very pro-British and, in particular, pro Winston Churchill. In fact I stayed the entire evening with them discussing the Middle East and going through the caretaker's books on our former Prime Minister!

As I was about to leave the caretaker asked me if I would like a guide to take me round Gallilee – and to show me Capernaum and Lake Tiberias: his nephew was a medical student at the university in Tel Aviv and would be happy to act as a guide. Again, I accepted the kind offer.

The nephew spoke good English and I had another extraordinary day driving from Nazareth where Frank Sinatra seemed to be more prominent than Christ (if one was to judge from the massive billboards on the main roads) to Capernaum. My host was well informed about the history of the area and I also learned a lot about the difficulties encountered by non-Jews in the professional field: he intended to qualify as a doctor and then consider emigration.

The history of Israel since 1962 bears witness to the fact that he would have been well advised to emigrate on qualifying as a doctor since Christian Arabs have subsequently had little or no opportunity to secure a reasonable livelihood there.

Having visited Capernaum, the Mount of the Beatitudes and Lake Galilee and having been very impressed by what I had seen I decided to drive further north the next day and visit Metulla, the small town closest to the Lebanese and Syrian borders on the Armistice Line: this was the Armistice Line agreed by the United Nations in 1948 when the foundling state of Israel was established.

Metulla was built on a ridge of hills with a view of Mount Hermon. It was a quiet and tranquil place, but well within the range of hostile artillery.

Although there was not a great deal to see in Metulla the area around it was very pleasant being some hundreds of feet above sea level and well wooded and consequently cooler than Jerusalem and the cities on the coast. I decided therefore to drive back down this outcrop of Israel (called the "finger of Galilee") along the border with Lebanon via Kiryat Schmona to Qedesh and then swing inland to the mountain town of Safad, in those days an artistic centre noted for its painters and potters.

I had not driven far down the road from Qedesh when I was flagged down by two heavily armed members of the Israeli Army who pointed out that I was within sniper range from hostile Lebanese militants on the other side of the border. No one in their right mind would travel down this particular road if they wanted to stay alive! I heeded their warning and turned inland straightaway. I subsequently found out that Kiryat Schmona was a regular target for rocket fire and cross-border attacks.

I used youth hostels or cheap hotels for my overnight stopovers and, after looking round Safad, a picturesque little town, I booked into a nearby youth hostel. It was unusual for any young person to turn up in a car at a youth hostel and I immediately attracted the attention of a pleasant looking but slightly odd young man in his mid-twenties who, in good English, asked me where I was headed the next day. "To Haifa," I said. "I need to go to Haifa," he replied immediately. "Can I come with you?" "I don't see why not," I said but I got the strong impression that if I had said I was going to Tel Aviv or Jerusalem he would have needed to go to one or the other. But it was when he indicated that he would like to drive the car that the alarm bells started ringing! That comment did not sound too healthy to me and I went to find out at what time the gates of the courtyard of the hostel were opened.

The manager of the hostel confirmed my suspicion that the young man suffered from a personality disorder and indicated that I would be well advised to disappear before he woke up. The gates opened at 5 am and I therefore told the young man that we would be leaving at 7 am. Having lain awake pretty well all night I was out through those gates like a flash a few seconds after they opened at 5 am and headed south west along the winding wooded roads towards Haifa.

In fact I was so half asleep that after a couple of miles I was stopped by an Israeli policeman in an old Land Rover. He wore the Colonial uniform the Israelis had inherited from the British – khaki drill shorts and jacket with the usual police driver's black cap: he was in his fifties and reminded me very much of Sergeant George Wright of the Warwickshire constabulary.

He told me that he had stopped me because I was driving somewhat erratically. I explained why I was on the road so early after hardly any sleep, and why I was in such a hurry to get away from the youth hostel and the very odd young man. I was concerned to return the car to Mr. Shubinski in one piece. My reference to the car belonging to Mr. Shubinski impressed him and he decided to send me on my way. He did make me promise, however, to have a strong cup of coffee at the next coffee shop I could find. That was not difficult because in August, at the hottest time of the year, everything in Israel opens early. I took his sage advice and kept my promise to him.

The fact that Mr. Shubinski had lent me the car for nothing undoubtedly impressed all the people I met during my stay in Israel but I have to say that all the Jews and Christian Arabs I encountered were, without exception, incredibly generous: all in all I received nothing but kindness from everyone I met in Israel.

I spent the rest of the day driving back to Mr. Shubinski's factory where I handed back the car and thanked him immensely for his extraordinary generosity. He wanted to know what I thought of it and I told him that I had been very impressed. He seemed very pleased. I found out later that, although he had some good years producing cars in the 1960s, he ultimately went bankrupt in 1971. But I will never forget that big hearted-man.

One last night at Kfar Galim before I headed for Lod airport and a flight back to Athens in the same antiquated DC3!

Overall I had an amazing time in Israel. There was a constant sense, however, of the country having to be on virtually a war footing – hemmed in, as it was, by a hostile Egypt in the south, a hostile Syria and Lebanon in the north, with Jordan waiting in the wings to join any hostile invasion if it considered it opportune to do so. Like the other Arab countries it was no friend of Israel but it was led by a king who was more astute and more interested in preserving the Hashemite dynasty than destroying Israel. He may well have been aware that if he could not defend himself effectively his neighbouring Arab allies would turn their attention to disposing of him.

It was an extraordinarily educative trip that I will never forget.

12

Fifty Years a Solicitor: Phases 1 & 2

My long legal career spanning well over fifty years breaks down into four distinct phases.

Phase 1 commenced when I became "articled" to Brian Hugh Hobson Cooke, a partner at Bircham & Co in the City of London: he probably agreed to my becoming his articled clerk because of the similarity in our names.

In the early 1960s one was lucky to obtain "articles" without having to pay one's principal a premium for the privilege but Bircham & Co were forward-looking in this respect and actually paid me £6 a week in my first year of articles, £7 a week in my second year and £8 a week in my third year. By comparison, my secretary, who could not have been more than twenty-one years of age, was earning in my third year £10.15.00 (ten pounds fifteen shillings) a week. For an aspiring articled clerk it was very much a case of "jam tomorrow"!

I was put into the department dealing with the Staff House Purchase Scheme of the North British and Mercantile Insurance Company and thoroughly enjoyed the conveyancing work carried out by the department. Apart from a few weeks under the tutelage of Mr Lambert, the wills and probate partner, I spent pretty well my entire time at Bircham & Co buying and selling residential property.

On one occasion, however, Brian Cooke, asked me to transfer a property in Rutland Gate, Kensington from the North British and Mercantile Insurance Company to the Commercial Union Assurance Company for £1m (one million pounds). That was a lot of money in 1963 and I was worried about making a mistake during the transaction: he assured me, however, that there was nothing complicated about it and that I was perfectly capable of dealing with the transfer.

When I received the deeds packet relating to the property I discovered that with the Land Registry certificate there was a large bundle of old deeds. The Land Registry certificate was certificate number three and the property had first been registered in 1863: the bundle of old deeds with it dated back from 1863 to the mid-1750s.

I read them through and discovered that the freehold had been owned by Queen Victoria's uncle: his signature was on one of the beautifully handwritten conveyances. With the deeds was a map or plan which also fascinated me: it was dated 1759 or thereabouts, was hand-drawn and showed two features that I can vividly recall: one was a drawing of a man on a horse below which appeared the words "the Knights Bridge"(Knightsbridge) and the other was "Mr Shakespeare's House" to the north of what is now High Street Kensington. If photocopies had existed in those days I would have copied the map but, being scrupulous, I put the plan back into the deeds packet and sent everything to the Commercial Union Assurance Company.

In later years I have written to the Land Registry asking whether land certificate number three still existed but sadly it does not and the deeds have probably been destroyed. The significance of that land certificate was considerable, however, because I believe it marked the outcome of "behind the scenes" lobbying by Prince Albert before he died in 1861.

Prince Albert had been impressed by the system of land registration in India, then part of the British Empire, and wanted to introduce it into the United Kingdom.

The "Colonial system" was straightforward: the buyer and seller of an area of land would arrange for the district surveyor to visit the land and peg it out: the wooden pegs would have had the "WD" arrows on them, of the same design as those appearing on prisoners uniforms in the 19th century.

The district surveyor would prepare and give to each party to the transaction a plan showing exactly what the dimensions of the land were (which they had agreed with him) and he would keep a copy of the same plan: he would transcribe the copy on to the map of the district, which he kept in his office.

He would advise both parties at the time of the land transfer that if either of them subsequently tried to alter the position of the pegs in their favour one or other would be hanged! Respect for this system and the potential outcome of infringing it was great, although I doubt whether Prince Albert had such a draconian penalty in mind for the clients of English and Scottish conveyancers!

The system of pegging out the dimensions of areas of land in the City of London had been employed after the Great Fire in 1666: it was not exactly a novel concept.

Although the size of each area of land in the City of London had been established after the Great Fire their ownership and the rights and restrictions affecting each area some two hundred years later was another matter.

In the 1850s evidence of ownership of land in London was a complete mess – with various "ownerships", freehold, copyhold, episcopal, etc. having different types of title documentation: rationalisation of them all was desperately needed. Someone with Prince Albert's detachment, political influence and intellect was necessary to give a spur to those who, like him, wanted an orderly system of land ownership. As a nation we had already mastered the art of mapmaking and a Land Registry was the logical next step.

But again I digress! In my last year at Bircham & Co, in addition to my student travel activities I managed to earn over £4000 for the practice, of which I received £400 and my secretary approximately £550.

When to the surprise of my principal I passed all seven heads of the Law Society's finals and handed in my notice I do not think that either I or the practice felt "short changed" in any way. The practice had helped me to qualify and I had earned my keep while working for it.

As previously indicated I left the City practice because I concluded that no solicitor in his right mind would employ someone who had a very substantial interest in organising student travel: that meant setting up on my own in Billericay with effect from January 1965.

As a sole practitioner I would have to tackle every type of legal problem thrown at me, unless I decided to refer prospective clients elsewhere: I would have no experienced partners or legal executives to assist me and I faced the considerable risk of making mistakes unless I was extremely careful.

With that in mind I concentrated, at first, on simple residential conveyancing and wills and probate but as the years went by I gradually expanded the range of my work and my knowledge. I started to take on criminal work in the Billericay Magistrates' Court where personal clients were involved and one particular case stands out in my memory.

I was instructed by Twolyn Hire Ltd for whom I had dealt on a commercial lease to appear on behalf of one of their drivers who had been charged with driving the wrong way down a "one way" street. The "one way" signs had apparently been obscured when he did so.

"I noted the accused on his motorbike," said the police constable, "travelling the wrong way down a one way street. I stopped him and cautioned him," he intoned, and then proceeded to read the rest of his evidence from his notebook. When he had finished giving his evidence I asked him whether it was correct in every detail. He gave me a somewhat disdainful look and replied "Yes, sir."

"Then would it interest you to know, constable, that my client was driving a one and a half ton truck at the time you have stated he was on a motorbike? At this, the constable looked distinctly uncomfortable and referred once again to his black notebook. "Oh, I have referred to the wrong set of notes. I should have referred to the earlier set which I can now read to the court." My response was immediate: "You have given your evidence on oath and have previously confirmed to the court that it was correct in every detail. I accordingly ask for this case to be dismissed."

The magistrates who, by this stage, could hardly conceal their mirth, responded, "Case dismissed." It was an important lesson in not necessarily believing what a policeman asserts to be the truth, whether under oath or not, and it stood me in good stead, particularly in relation to divorce litigation thereafter where divorcing policemen were concerned! I subsequently enjoyed excellent relationships with the police when working with them on fraud cases but when dealing with cases involving their personal lives I had to treat their evidence of matrimonial disharmony with many pinches of salt!

The end of the first phase was marked by my move from my first floor offices at 106a High Street Billericay to Foxcroft. The second phase of my legal career was one of consolidation and expansion of my burgeoning practice and lasted from my purchase of Foxcroft, the former children's home, until the sale of the practice in 1989, principally at the suggestion of my late wife.

During this period I tackled most aspects of high street practice and learned what could and could not easily be done within a traditional legal framework.

In terms of what could not be done within a traditional legal framework but could be done effectively and successfully outside it I will never forget the case of a client whose son had, let us say, "fallen into the clutches" of a taxi driver's daughter. This was a matter of putting into my client's head a course which I could not advise him to take, as a solicitor, but one which might give him pause for thought! I had known the father at school: he was a very nice person but a trifle unworldly, like his son.

My client was divorced and had been divorced for some years: his young son had chosen, at the time of the divorce, to live with his father but as he grew into a teenager and beyond he had found his father's attitude towards staying out late and partying somewhat restrictive. I am sure that his father had his best interests at heart but my client tended to wear coloured bow ties and cravats and was very old-fashioned.

The young man had become besotted with the young lady in question whom he had met at a disco: being of a romantic disposition and after meeting her a couple more times at discos and parties he had proposed that they become engaged. Her physical charms had been all too apparent throughout. She, being flattered by the advances of this good-looking but inexperienced ex-public schoolboy whose father she clearly thought was rich, had accepted his proposal of marriage: his father, however, was very worried indeed about what his son had done and tried to dissuade him from marrying the girl. In order to counter the father's opposition the young lady had invited the son to come and live with her mum and dad and share her bedroom and her bed at her parents' council house. The taxi driver and his wife thought their daughter was "on to a good thing" and allowed him to move in with them: he needed no second invitation!

The son accordingly moved all his belongings, including his clothes, his record player, his CDs and other personal items, much to his father's concern, into the council house. It soon became apparent, however, to the taxi driver and his wife that he was, in fact, completely unsuitable for their daughter: rich his father might or might not be but a good marriage prospect he was not. He was, in their view, a bit of a waste of space. They therefore threw him out with his clothes but held on to the rest of his possessions.

My client asked me what could be done to recover them: would I be prepared to take the taxi driver to court and force him to hand over his son's possessions? I explained to him that I could, of course, issue proceedings but by the time we reached court and obtained the necessary order he would probably have spent more than his son's possessions were worth and his son would probably have purchased replacement items in any event.

The taxi driver, if not dishonest and intending to keep the son's possessions and sell them off, appeared to be holding them as some sort of lien, rather like a hotel owner who can hang on to your luggage until you have paid your bill.

Was this to compensate his daughter for her "hurt feelings" or did he assume that the boy would not have the resources to pursue him legally?

Why not, I suggested, do the same – hold something of his as a "lien" until he handed over your son's possessions? I told him that the taxi driver would probably not take much notice of a court summons and that my client would undoubtedly waste a lot of money getting nowhere.

So why did he not consider the "sixteen brick solution"? At this point my client looked perplexed. "What exactly is the sixteen brick solution"? He asked. As a solicitor I could not really give him "non-legal" advice but he had to consider the psychology of the taxi driver and a potentially quick, easy, but slightly hazardous, way of recovering his son's possessions.

"I have already given you your legal option but have you thought about going round to his house at 3am, when it is nice and quiet, with sixteen standard size bricks?

"You will carefully and quietly take the wheels of his taxi and put four bricks under each axle, ensuring that you do not damage the vehicle in any way." This was in the days when most vehicles did not have wheel locking nuts.

"You will telephone him at 7 am the same morning and ask him if he is going to work that day. He will probably say 'yes' and you will then suggest that he goes outside and has a look at his taxi. Which he will undoubtedly do. When he comes back, furious and threatening to put "the law" on to you, you will tell him that there is no need for that. If he puts all your son's possessions carefully and neatly on the lawn outside his council house and keeps an eye on them until you arrive at 8.30 am his wheels will be returned. But he must put everything outside and nothing must be damaged. You will take with you a schedule of your son's possessions and you will check them off. When you have retrieved all your son's possessions you will tell him to go inside his house and await the return of his wheels: you will telephone him when they are on his lawn."

I assured him that, if the police turned up in the middle of the night, which was most unlikely, he would have to assure them that he had no intention permanently to deprive the taxi driver of his wheels and was merely exercising a lien, against the value of items the taxi driver had failed to relinquish. But the involvement of the police was remote if he telephoned the taxi driver early enough.

With that, my client left my office but he telephoned a day or so later!

"That idea, which I accept I have to claim as my own, worked like a charm. My son got all his possessions back this morning undamaged. We collected them at 8.30 am. Thank you for helping put that idea into my head after explaining the costly legal option and the risk involved."

Of course, I could not claim any credit or make a charge for, let us say, encouraging my client to think "outside the box" but I did ask him to consider some basic points in devising a strategy to deal with this type of problem: weigh up the psychology of your opponent, assess his weak points and work out whether litigation is going to be too expensive or counter-productive in terms of time and money costs. Is it going to be worth your while to spend your precious time to recover something that you can probably afford to replace? Is there some other way of achieving a satisfactory result?

My client and his son were lucky and were able to exploit the taxi driver's weak point in the same way as he had hoped to exploit the son's weakness. I cannot recommend or advise anyone to do the same but it turned out to be a useful, cheap and cost-effective outcome to what could have bogged my client down in litigation, probably to no good purpose for a long time.

On the other hand, doing things outside a legal framework when they should have been done within it can prove very costly and I have frequently told my clients that doing things "as a matter of principle" without checking the law can be extremely expensive. In this respect I can recall one case in particular, where a client had acted "as a matter of principle", rather than following the letter of the law.

My client, a company director, had fitted tracker devices to his fleet of vehicles: in this way he could tell exactly where any of his vehicles was at any particular time, so that he could direct the nearest vehicle to a job that needed carrying out. When one of his employees appeared to be spending a lot of his time "on the road" between jobs, far more than any of his other employees, he decided to check where that employee's vehicle was on a number of occasions. When he did so and compared the driver's time sheets with those of the other employees it quickly became apparent that the employee had parked his vehicle outside his own home for many of the hours he claimed to be on the road and for which he had claimed payment.

Incensed, my client had called the employee into his office, told him what he had discovered, accused him of theft and fired him on the spot – for fraud. When my client subsequently received a caim from an employment tribunal for "unfair dismissal" my reply to his telephone call to me was: "You should not have done that. Your employee had employment rights and you should have given him oral and written warnings and the opportunity to explain himself." "But it was a matter of principle," he said. "I cannot have fraudulent employees ripping off the company like that." My response was brief: "principles can be very expensive" and so it proved.

I obtained the services of a barrister who was very experienced in employment law for my client: he spoke eloquently before the tribunal of gross misconduct but you will not be surprised that the aggrieved, idle and dishonest employee won his claim for unfair dismissal. As my client left the tribunal he muttered, "Is there no justice in this bloody country?" (He was apt to speak his mind!) "I catch this bloke at home, probably watching TV, on more than one occasion, submitting bogus time sheets and I have to pay him over a thousand quid – that is not fair."

"That is the way the cookie crumbles," I replied. "You have to abide by the complexities of employment law even though he may well have been the most dishonest person you have ever employed. He clearly knew employment law better than you did and may well have been sacked by other employers for the same reason."

This same client came to me on more than one occasion suggesting tax savings schemes, which, without putting too fine a point on it, were not schemes of which HMRC and H M Treasury would have approved! When I rejected them and told him why, and asked him why he came to me with these dubious schemes he said, "Because you are the most honest solicitor I know!" I suppose he thought other solicitors, of whom there are a number, would take his money and let him face the consequences later. Also that I would tell him to his face and not send him a bill! Fortunately this particular loophole has been closed by the government by making financial advisers and lawyers in general responsible for the "duff advice" they give to their clients, like advising them to participate in "shell" film-making companies and to claim big tax allowances or refunds of tax. These advisers usually take substantial fees and have, in the past, left their clients as the "responsible taxpayers" to face the consequences in terms of massive penalties for tax evasion. My client knew, in any event, that, as a General Commissioner of Income Tax, I would give a "straight" response to his dubious proposals!

Dishonest solicitors usually end up before a solicitors' disciplinary tribunal where they are "struck off". This means that they cannot practise as solicitors any more. The proportion of dishonest to honest solicitors is about the same as with other professionals. Sometimes they start off by drawing monies from their client account that they are not entitled to: sometimes they send clients exaggerated bills for work they have done, knowing full well that, if challenged, they will be found to have, in effect, helped themselves to client monies by doing so.

More importantly "legally dishonest" solicitors usually face a criminal investigation. In some cases the Law Society cooperates with the police in uncovering the extent of the theft of client monies and this is where the third phase of my legal career started, when I was appointed a Law Society Intervening Agent. I cover this aspect of my career in the next chapter.

Before I move on to the third phase I should perhaps mention another amusing case. I had been instructed to represent a leading and highly reputable employment agency in the centre of London that advertised for and carried out the screening of potential job applicants for posts in a number of government departments.

The role of the agency was to whittle down the very large number of applicants for any advertised role to four persons who would then be interviewed by the government department concerned.

There could often be over fifty applications for any advertised appointment and it made sense for the outside agency, which had already agreed the appropriate employment criteria with the department , to select those most likely to be able to perform the required role and then leave it to the department to decide which of the four applicants it might wish to employ.

A Nigerian lady, having failed to reach the final four applicants for a particular post brought a claim against the agency for "racial discrimination." She presumably felt she should have been included in the final four.

We appeared before the employment tribunal in Woburn Place, just off Tottenham Court Road. The tribunal chairman, a female QC, asked the Nigerian lady, who was representing herself, to outline her claim. What evidence did she have of racial discrimination? What were her reasons for making the claim? It was up to her, as claimant, to explain the reasons.

At this, the lady pulled a plastic bag out of the large shopping bag by her side. "This is the evidence," she cried, and spilled the contents of the plastic bag on to the table in front of her. We all looked at the contents – the bag had been full of corks from wine bottles. "You can see with your own eyes that this agency has driven me to drink."

We all looked at each other disbelievingly, scarcely able to restrain ourselves from a mixture of mirth and annoyance: this lady had cost my clients a lot in legal fees and wasted the tribunal chairman's time.

Nevertheless the tribunal chairman was extremely polite and explained that her "evidence" did not constitute a valid basis for her claim. She thereupon dismissed the claim without further ado!

Given the ease with which claimants could take employers, potential employers and even agents of potential employers to an employment tribunal, at no cost to themselves, it was not surprising that the Ministry of Justice introduced a fee structure for bringing employment claims. Any claimant who wished to pursue a claim after discussing the merits of it with ACAS had to pay a fee to bring his or her claim to an employment tribunal.

The introduction of a fee dramatically reduced the number of claims, many of which were speculative in the sense of the claimants hoping that their employers would settle a claim rather than spend a fortune on legal fees.

The introduction of a fee structure also resulted, however, in a number of applicants not being able to pursue perfectly valid claims through inability to pay the appropriate fee.

In view of the manifest injustice of not being able to pursue a perfectly valid claim it was subsequently determined by the Courts that the Ministry of Justice had acted "ultra vires" (beyond their lawful powers) in imposing fees on claimants. The interests of Justice were not being served by making a claim unaffordable for genuine claimants. As a result employees have, once again, been enabled to bring claims as before. There is, however a worrying trend on the part of Government to make claimants pay the cost of maintaining the judicial system and it is one of which every citizen should be aware.

13

Billericay to Kathmandu by Hughes Overland

Although Hughes Overland became one of the largest and most reputable trek operators in the United Kingdom with overland tours and expeditions to Greece, Turkey, Morocco, Russia and Eastern Europe it is probably best remembered for running a "bus service" between Billericay and Kathmandu!

It is doubtless the juxtaposition of the names "Billericay" and "Kathmandu" that generates laughter and a sense of disbelief. Who, one might, ask would want to travel between these two places? The answer was "quite a few!"

When acting as a sidesman in the college chapel I was once asked by the chaplain to look after the Bishop of Ely, an elderly and clearly nervous old gentleman, who had been invited to give the sermon at one of our Sunday evening services. "And where do you come from, my boy?" he enquired. "From Billericay, sir," I replied. "Oh, I haven't been to Northern Ireland for years." It would have been impolite of me and embarrassing for him to point out that Billericay is in Essex, some twenty five miles from the centre of London. Quite how Billericay got its strange name no one is sure although I do have my own theory as to its origin.

By 1966, some eight years after my first student train group to Greece, I was sending about three thousand students and recent graduates abroad each year to Greece, Italy and Turkey during the Easter and summer vacations: I had also set up a student travel office in Athens offering coach tours in Greece and student flights to Israel and other destinations.

Having noticed some "ads" in the Observer and the Sunday Times for treks to Morocco and North Africa and being interested in exploring innovative ways of travelling across Europe it occurred to me that I should organise a "pilot" trip to Greece by minibus.

On a purely experimental basis I therefore purchased a twelve-seat Commer minibus and employed a very capable young driver by the name of Paul Renouf to take the first tour. He was, in effect, charged with assessing the viability of the route out to Greece and back in the middle of the summer. On his return he gave me an excellent assessment of what had turned out to be a very successful tour and I decided to organise some more in 1967. Paul did point out, however, that the Commer minibus lacked stability when heavily loaded – with a large roof rack holding all the luggage and the tents. As a result Ford Transits and long wheelbase Land Rovers were purchased for all subsequent tours.

The Ford Transits were fitted with heavy duty suspension and the radiator systems were adapted for hot climates: they proved to be reliable in all but the most extreme conditions and were ideal for tours within Europe. Long wheelbase Land Rovers were subsequently acquired for the more rugged expeditions to Morocco and the Far East.

After three years the trek programme had expanded substantially and the long drive at our first marital home could no longer accommodate the number of vehicles we had to put on it! If the programme were to expand further we would need substantially more parking space and a manager to oversee what was becoming a large and quite complex operation.

Vehicles had to be purchased, signs written with our "Hughes Overland" logo, serviced and insured, drivers with good mechanical skills and the right personalities had to be found, tents and other equipment needed "en route" had to be purchased and checked, and advertisements and brochures had to be produced and distributed, etc. By this time I was offering our student travellers thirty-five day coach tours to Greece and Turkey for £48 in conjunction with BATO of Belgium, a subsidiary of FIAT, and no other ABTA member was offering three-week tours by minibus to Greece. It was at this point that I employed David Smith as Operations Manager and as a director of Hughes Overland Limited, the company formed to run the entire operation.

David proved to be an excellent organiser but some of his ideas were very ambitious – over-ambitious in terms of our loss-making expedition from London to Cape Town. We nevertheless got on well together and he expanded Hughes Overland Limited into a substantial business, taking on sub-contract work for another large trek company and buying additional Transits for their North African and Greek tours, in addition to buying the fleet of vehicles required for our own tours.

At the end of each summer holiday season we had, unsurprisingly, a large number of vehicles to find parking space for or dispose of.: David came to me with a novel and partial solution. Why not send some of them to Kathmandu and back? It would use the vehicles and keep them out of Billericay for several months. It would also enable us to hold on to some of our more experienced drivers. I did a costing exercise and the idea seemed feasible, particularly for our fifteen-seat Transits and long wheelbase Land Rovers – provided we had no major breakdowns or accidents. Moreoever, advertising the trips in the national press when no one else was offering trek holidays would be good PR, if nothing else.

And that is how our "Asiaman" series of Billericay to Kathmandu treks came into being. Because Kathmandu had links with Bangkok by air and because Bangkok was a hub airport for flights to Australia, New Zealand and the Far East we were reasonably confident of attracting hardy Australians and New Zealanders who wanted to see a bit of the world on their way to or back from the United Kingdom. And so it proved.

Our first Asiaman service left Billericay on 6 March 1971 and the second on 18 September 1971. The trips were planned in four stages. Stage one was from London to Istanbul, taking in Cologne, Salzburg, and Belgrade – 2100 miles in nine days. Stage two was from Istanbul to Teheran via Ankara, Samsun, Trabzon, Erzerum and Tabriz – 1650 miles in nine days. Stage three was from Teheran to Kabul via Isfahan, Persepolis, Kerman, Zahedan, Quetta and Kandahar- 2000 miles in thirteen days while stage four was from Kabul to Kathmandu via Lahore, Delhi, Agra and Benares – 1700 miles in twelve days. The total journey time for what we called the "direct route" was 43 days and the one-way fare was £85.

In terms of the journey itself Stage one was on reasonably good roads and enabled passengers on the "outward" route to get used gradually to the degree of comfort on offer! But our "cross continental" service was never intended to be a luxury tour and the terrain we covered could not, by its nature, ever be considered an easy ride! The whole trip could, however, be enormously rewarding and exciting provided it was entered into with a spirit of adventure and a realisation that discomfort would be involved at times.

The route for Stage two took our Ford Transit minibuses and long wheel base landrovers over several high mountain ranges and along the southern shores of the Black Sea. Trabzon had a good beach but was often cut off by snow in winter, forcing our vehicles to take an interesting diversion along the banks of a river for several miles. Mount Ararat, upon which, according to the Bible, Noah's Ark came to rest on its 16,000 foot peak, came into sight as they approached the border with Iran. Over the border into Tabriz and then a fine highway into Teheran, the last point of real civilisation for Eastbound travellers.

Stage three found our vehicles heading southwards to Isfaham, a beautiful city, and then onto Persepolis, the ruins of which are one of the greatest wonders of the Ancient World, being the former capital of the ancient empire of Darius and Xerxes. After Shiraz, across the desert, the mountains and the salt flats to Kerman and Zahedan. From Zahedan into Pakistan and through the desert of Baluchistan before reaching Quetta and a well deserved rest. From Quetta north into Afghanistan and along the fine new (at the time) highway to Kabul.

Stage four marked the final leg to Kathmandu. The road from Kabul wound through the Kabul Gorges, eventually arriving back in Pakistan. Passengers were forbidden by the Afghan authorities to take any photos of the Khyber Pass: the penalty for doing so was the confiscation of one's camera!! From Lahore our vehicles entered India and joined the Grand Trunk Road arriving in Delhi a day later. From Delhi to Agra where our passengers visited the Taj Mahal and onward to Benares, the holy city of the Hindus on the banks of the Ganges.

From Benares our vehicles headed north into Nepal where a really mountainous road took them up several times to over 8000 feet before they finally descended into the Valley of Kathmandu and our destination.

We later ran treks that spent twenty one days on stage one – visiting Paris, Zurich, Milan, Rome and Athens and spending two days sunbathing on the Greek island of Thassos – 2600 miles for £100 single.

Air travel from Kathmandu to Bangkok and onwards from Bangkok to the Far East was arranged through Thai International Airways, BOAC (as it then was) and Quantas. Even at this distance of time the trips can clearly be seen as offering incredibly good value for what was included in them.

Each expedition carried tents and cooking equipment and a range of spare parts and on each expedition one driver was a fully trained mechanic. A locker in the back of each vehicle carried tea, coffee, sugar, rice and powdered milk towards the cost of which each passenger contributed four pounds (£4): the individual baggage limit was 35lbs and passengers were advised what best to wear. It was so cold camping out in the Turkish mountains, for example, that the primus stoves used for cooking had to be placed under the engines of the vehicles to stop them from freezing at night. Vaccinations were obviously necessary and we insisted on medical insurance cover.

Passengers included Lord and Lady Hunt and a number of Sherpas (Lord Hunt had masterminded the Mount Everest Expedition in 1953 when Sir Edmund Hillary had climbed it). Most of our passengers, however, were young British, Australian and New Zealand travellers. We did, nevertheless, have one passenger, an elderly farmer from Billericay, Eric Rolfe, who not only endured the arduous 43 day outward journey but decided to come back the same way. He must have been very tough!

Lord Hunt was kind enough to write to me on arrival in Nepal and I quote from his letter:

"Our journey to India in a Hughes Overland minibus was an unforgettable experience from my wife and myself. Going by road, with an itinerary and timetable which are flexible, has the great advantage of making it possible for the traveller who is not in a hurry to see and learn a great deal along the route, in a relaxed way. But quite apart from the interest of new places and meeting people who live there, we enjoyed the special kind of companionship with our fellow travellers which a journey like this creates; it is an opportunity to step aside from the 'rat race' and share the simple life with good companions, which many people seek today".

One cannot run a tour operation like this without having a few "hiccups" and we had a number of unusual experiences, the most notable of which was an incident in Persia (Iran). Our driver on one of the Asiaman trips telephoned the office to say that the engine of his Ford Transit had blown up. I asked him where he was. "Some miles out of Zahedan in the middle of the Persian desert," he replied.

"In that case you will need a new engine. Will you be able to fit it?" He said he would so David and I immediately contacted Fords to check whether they had any crated engines. Fords confirmed that they had crated Transit engines in store at Slough. We therefore stripped the seats out of one of the Transits, drove to Slough, purchased the engine and drove it to Heathrow. It was put on a commercial BOAC flight to Teheran for onward transmission on an internal flight to Zahedan.

The driver had been told to strip out the blown-up engine, buy some oil for the new engine and hire a flat bed truck to transport it into the desert. He would have to clear customs, which, in the event he did in the usual way, by greasing the palms of the officials at Zahedan airport. The engine arrived on the second day and was fitted and working within forty eight hours of the driver's initial phone call. The tour caught up on its schedule within the following few days and arrived in Kathmandu on time.

On another occasion one of our fifteen-seat Transits had diverted to Karachi. The first set of kingpins had broken in Afghanistan and the reserve set also appeared to be on their last legs. We immediately boxed up another set in a wooden box which we painted white with the red cross of St. George emblazoned on it. It was sent to our driver in Karachi labelled "British Everest Expedition: most urgent." It arrived quickly and the tour once again arrived in Kathmandu on schedule.

The only disaster we had was a crash not far from Benares in India. The lead driver of our convoy of three vehicles on their way back from Kathmandu saw what he thought was a slow-moving lorry ahead. At that moment he had to move off the single metalled carriageway to make room for a bus coming towards him. Both vehicles were half on the metalled road and half on the verge and the oncoming bus sent up a great cloud of dust which obscured the road ahead.

What our driver did not appreciate was that the lorry ahead was stationary, had no rear wheels and carried a large load of coal. He drove smack into the lorry, knocking out the jacks that supported the rear of the lorry, causing several tons of coal to smash through the windscreen and completely disable our vehicle. The coal took off the top of the driver's thumb, which had been on the steering wheel, and the impact threw all the passengers violently forward: most of them sustained hip injuries. They were all insured and were taken to a hospital in Benares where they were well treated. Their insurance upon which we had insisted paid for their flights to the United Kingdom.

As a result of this incident we were left with one "written off" and two serviceable fifteen-seat vehicles on to which we had to load all the equipment and luggage that could not be taken with them by the injured passengers. We immediately asked our most capable spare driver, Tony Eady, who had already acquired the nickname "Speedy Eady" to drive as fast as he could to Teheran in a twelve-seat minibus and meet the other two vehicles there. Tony, then a law graduate, drove the 3750 miles to Teheran in record time, loaded all the excess luggage and equipment from the disabled minibus into it and returned to England with the other two vehicles.

The Indian Customs authorities demanded substantial import duties on the Transit we had had to leave behind in Benares, despite the fact that it was completely unroadworthy and I concluded that the Asiaman service was too high risk and too low return to be viable.

Strangely our vehicles were very popular in India and Nepal because they had saffron coloured bonnets and rear doors and white bodies (or vice versa) because we swapped the bonnets and the rear doors of the vehicles. Saffron is the Buddhist colour and white the Hindu.

Our twin-colour vehicles were seen around Billericay quite a lot between 1967 and 1973 and it is interesting to note that Basildon Council and taxi services in the Billericay/Basildon area have adopted the saffron and white colouring for their vehicles, a constant reminder to me of Hughes Overland and my decision to switch the bonnets and rear doors of our Transits.

Although the dispute with Indian Customs did not, in itself, lead to the end of the Asiaman service it brought home the difficulties of dealing with foreign officialdom and the expense and loss incurred as a result. At this point in 1973, after two years of comparatively successful tours with Ford Transits and long wheelbase Land Rovers it had become apparent, moreover, that we would have to change our entire fleet of vehicles and invest in Mercedes eighteen-seat coaches in order to comply with new Common Market regulations: all our drivers would also need PSV licences.

The cost of a Ford Transit was not much more than £2000 but the cost of a Mercedes coach was over £8000. Given that such a substantial investment would be required to maintain Hughes Overland as a large trek and tour operator I decided to sell the company and sought a buyer. By great good fortune I was approached by Sir William Bolton, a very wealthy man, who wanted to buy it for his nephew.

The nephew took over the company, moved its offices to the Earls Court area and renamed it "Jet Trek". David Smith stayed on as Operations Manager under its new ownership. The service to Kathmandu continued for a short time but, unfortunately, on its very first tour with a Mercedes coach, the coach plunged into a river bed in Nepal and had to be written off. I believe the company with its large European operation was sold on to Treasure Tours of Australia.

In retrospect Hughes Overland never let any of its passengers down, not even in the middle of the Belgian Congo when we had to pay the prison governor in a small town to release a Belgian mechanic who had murdered his mistress so that he could carry out a substantial repair on one of our long wheelbase Land Rovers! The story of our London-Cape Town expedition would fill another book in itself!

The company maintained an efficient, roadworthy fleet of vehicles and the quality of service remained high until it was sold. In fact, Intourist, the Russian tourist organisation, chose it for a promotional film on holiday tours by minibus in Russia and one of our Russian tours was followed by a film crew throughout its entire time in the Soviet Union.

Attempts have been made in recent years to replicate our Asiaman service but no one has succeeded in doing so: there was talk of an "Ozbus" taking Australians and New Zealanders from London to Kathmandu but it is doubtful whether the Ozbus quite made it as far as Kathmandu: the owners of it no longer appear to be advertising the route and it must, in any event, be so much more dangerous than it was in the early 1970's.

As originator of the first, and doubtless last, successful regular overland passenger travel service operated by an ABTA member between England and Nepal, I was subsequently elected to Fellowship of the Royal Geographical Society. I had not expected this: it was a most welcome and much appreciated acknowledgement of my efforts in trying to initiate a regular service on a route that had not been attempted before.

14

Ticket Theft at Shenfield Travel

A potentially catastrophic event occurred at Shenfield Travel Bureau in mid-October 1974.

In the 1970's travel agents who were authorised by IATA, the International Air Transport Association, could write out and issue tickets supplied to them by most international airlines. Each airline had its own tickets and ticket covers: the actual tickets which had a number of counterfoils were blank when sent to the travel agents and were validated by the agent's office stamp in the top right hand corner before being handed to the passenger.

One of the counterfoils was for the passenger to hand over at the "check-in" desk on the outward flight, another was for any return flight or onward flight and one was for the travel agent to send with his monthly return and cheque to the airline in question. Because the tickets were blank they had to be kept in something that was reasonably secure. In the case of Shenfield Travel Bureau they were stored in a locked steel cabinet in the manager's office

One particular morning Gordon Forster, my co-director and manager of the bureau, arrived to find that the bureau had been burgled and that most of the blank air tickets and the office's validating stamp had been stolen: a thief or thieves had gained access to his office through a small toilet window high up in the wall at the rear of the building and had broken into the locked cabinet. Nothing else had been stolen and it was clear that the thieves knew exactly what they were looking for: they had taken nearly 1000 blank air tickets with a potential "written up" value of £1.5 million.

The first thing we had to do was report the theft to the police station in Brentwood and request their urgent attendance. A police constable from the CID office duly appeared. To our astonishment, however, his view was that blank air tickets were only pieces of paper and that all we had to do was report the theft to the various airlines. This was despite our pointing out to him that blank air tickets were extremely valuable. He was not particularly interested in the theft and did nothing to investigate it subsequently. He could not be made to understand that a blank airline ticket in the wrong hands could be written out for travel to any destination in the world served by the particular airline: all the ticket required was the validation stamp and this could be forged, if not stolen.

We discovered, for example, during the subsequent investigation of the thefts, of which ours was just one, that one British Airways ticket with a face value in excess of £3000 was written out for first class flights from London to Sydney and back. It was sold to a member of the Scottish aristocracy in a bar in Chelsea for £400. The noble gentleman in question claimed that he did not know the ticket was stolen and because of his status and wealth was able to retain a leading firm of London solicitors to get him off a charge of possession of a stolen ticket.

One might reasonably conclude that his acquittal was a prime example of privilege and money successfully negating the effectiveness of a criminal law system that applies to everyone else. One would have had to be remarkably dim not to have realised that one cannot purchase a ticket worth more than £3000 from someone in a pub, albeit the pub, being in Chelsea, called itself a bar – but perhaps some members of the Scottish aristocracy are a bit dim. I make no further comment since the gentleman in question was found not guilty!

We did, of course, notify the airlines of the theft immediately and ask them to do everything possible to put a stop on the use of the tickets. We also notified the Association of British Travel Agents (ABTA). It soon became apparent that six other travel agencies had recently been broken into within a period of fourteen days and that over 9000 tickets had been stolen in total. The potential "written up" value of these tickets was in excess of £10 m and the theft from Shenfield Travel Bureau was just part of a well-planned criminal operation.

The immediate reaction of the airlines whose tickets had been stolen was to protect their position by notifying all seven travel agents that, according to their IATA agency agreements, they had accepted liability to reimburse the airlines for any loss the airlines might incur as a result of the use of the stolen tickets. This was notwithstanding the fact that within hours of being advised of the thefts the airlines had received full details of the numbers of the stolen tickets and would have been able to prevent their use when presented at the flight check-in desk of the airline in question.

In the 1970s there were no computers, no instant means of checking whether or not a ticket was stolen when presented at an airline check-in desk at an airport: there was, for example no method of scanning tickets on presentation. There need be no pre-booking of seat numbers and a passenger could turn up for a flight at any airport with an "open" ticket written out by a genuine or a bogus travel agent and ask to be put on a flight to the destination shown on the ticket, provided of course there was a spare seat on the plane.

Alternatively the bogus travel agent could telephone the airline reservation desk, quoting the travel agent's identity number on a stolen or forged validation stamp, reserve a seat on the plane and sell the ticket. The airline reservation desk would include the passenger in the number of people on that flight in the same way as anyone booked by a genuine travel agent. Provided the ticket bore an agent's stamp or what looked like an agent's stamp no questions would be asked at check-in. The check-in desk would assume that the ticket had been paid for and that the agent would be sending payment for the ticket, plus a counterfoil of the ticket with his monthly sales return to the airline.

The obvious flaw in this system was that, in the case of a stolen ticket, the travel agent's counterfoil would not be sent to the airline and no payment would have been made. How then would the airline be able to check the amount it had lost if the counterfoil was not sent? The checking system was rudimentary. The tickets presented at the check-in desks were sent to the accounts department of the airline in question and random checks would be made on approximately ten per cent of all the tickets received from the check-in desks.

One could envisage a situation where tickets were stolen from a travel agent at gun point and the agent being held liable by the airline for the consequent loss of revenue to the airline notwithstanding the fact that the airline was informed of the theft and did nothing to prevent the use of them. As a lawyer this struck me as manifestly unfair and I immediately called a meeting of all the travel agents affected by the thefts. All of them had approached their local police stations: none had been particularly interested in what each considered had been a "one off" theft of blank pieces of paper.

I suggested that, in the circumstances, we should make a joint approach to the police, to IATA, to ABTA and to the thirty seven airlines affected. It was obvious that we could not meet the demands made on us by the airlines. Even if only ten per cent of the stolen tickets were traced we would jointly be facing a bill of nearly £1m that we clearly could not afford. The joint approach was agreed and with the wholehearted support of the agents who faced potential ruin I prepared a sixty eight page confidential dossier which I circulated to all the airlines involved as well as to IATA and ABTA.

The dossier listed all the stolen tickets, the details of the thefts, details of the staff and security arrangements adopted by each of the agents and an overview of security generally. The overview dealt with the relationship of IATA to the police, the attitude of the airlines prior and subsequent to the thefts, the attitude of agents prior to the thefts and recommendations to airlines for the improvement of security. The dossier also contained a request for clarification of IATA attitudes towards the relationship between airlines and their agents.

As a result of the dossier and a meeting between myself and Eric Engledew, the Chief Executive of British Airways, a moratorium was agreed on the enforcement of the IATA agency agreements while the full extent of the loss to all the airlines was established. There were a number of reasons for the moratorium. The first was that enforcement was likely to put the travel agents out of business on the basis that the potential loss could be £10m, a figure that was not disputed by the airlines at the time. The second reason was that agents could not justifiably "prefer" the claim of one airline over that of another airline when the agents were well aware that they did not have sufficient assets to cover all potential claims.

There were also questions about the tenuous contractual relationship between the travel agent who had entered into an agency agreement with IATA and the airlines with whom he had not. Could the airlines pursue the agent directly or would they have to do so through IATA of which they were members?

I also raised the matter of division of the travel industry into two camps, namely agents and principals. The problem of theft was one that should be met by agents and principals jointly and I pointed out that it would be a retrogressive step if the airlines attempted to enforce the passenger sales agency agreements in order to protect themselves while affording no protection to the agents: the considerations of natural justice would also have to apply.

In this respect I was supported by ABTA, the Association of British Travel Agents who made it clear that if any airline ignored the moratorium it would put all such resources as were necessary at the disposal of any agent who was sued by an airline for recovery of the loss arising out of the theft of a stolen ticket and would also give maximum adverse publicity to that particular airline.

But what could be done about the theft of over 9000 tickets in a well-planned criminal operation when seven "local" police constables in seven different locations appeared completely unconcerned about it? The police had to be galvanised into doing something and it was here that my acquaintance with Eric Moonman, the Labour Party MP for Billericay, proved incredibly helpful.

Eric Moonman had previously approached me, as an organiser of student travel to Greece, and asked for advice on arranging classical tours to Greece for adults. This was something he was contemplating should he lose his seat in Parliament. As a result of his approach I introduced him to Babis, my Greek "brother" with whom, surprisingly, he appeared to develop an instant and, I feel, genuine friendship.

Having explained our problem to Eric I asked whether he would be prepared to table a question in the House of Commons, namely: "What are the police doing about a robbery which is greater than the Great Train Robbery?" We both felt this would generate a positive reaction and it certainly did!

Within two hours of tabling the question I had an irate response from Lord Harris at the Home Office. "What the hell is this all about?" he growled at me. So I explained the significance of the loss and the total inactivity of the local police and he calmed down. "I will have a word with Sir Robert Mark", (the Metropolitan Police Commissioner) he said, and, true to his word, he did. Within six days a specialist ticket fraud squad, comprising ten members headed by Detective Chief Inspector Cressy, had been set up by the Metropolitan Police and I had received a request to attend a preliminary meeting with the squad in a disused school building close to Victoria coach station.

I had to enter the school playground through a gate in a twelve foot high metal mesh fence which surrounded the apparently unoccupied building and was taken to a room in the centre of it to meet D.C.I. Cressy and the members of his newly formed squad.

His squad were all male but one would never had guessed that they were policeman: from the perspective of their ages and their casual clothes one would have passed them in the street without even glancing at them. The building itself was also totally anonymous, looking as though it was about to be demolished which it probably was, and had been fenced in securely to prevent vandalism. It was, however, undoubtedly an ideal place from which to conduct a discreet investigation into a large-scale theft of airline tickets or from which anti-terrorist activities might be conducted. No one would associate it with New Scotland Yard or any other police establishment.

Having explained the content of the dossier, the potential value of the tickets and the financial risks faced by the seven travel agents (we had, collectively, already received notification of the use of many of the stolen tickets) I left DCI Cressy to get on with the task of apprehending the criminals and finding the tickets.

He did, however, keep me closely in touch with progress and asked me to continue as liaison with the other six travel agents while he communicated with the airlines themselves and with the agency investigation panel of IATA in the United Kingdom.

Although the local criminals had, on occasion, used unsophisticated methods to effect "break ins" (the thieves at Leyton Travel had knocked a hole through the wall when they could not get in through the doors or windows!) they were sufficiently knowledgeable to leave behind "out of date" airline tickets and travellers cheques.

For example BOAC and BEA had only recently merged in March 1974 and their tickets had been replaced by "British Airways" tickets. British Airways had not, however, requested the return of the BOAC and BEA tickets. Since members of the general public were aware of the merger and British Airways would not have accepted BEA or BOAC tickets in any event there would have been no point in taking them. Travellers cheques were also more easily identifiable as stolen than airlines tickets and, when encashing them, the holder could well be required to produce evidence of identity. That would be an unnecessary risk as far as the criminals were concerned.

It was obvious that the police were up against a sophisticated criminal organisation and it soon became apparent that the originators of the scheme to steal so many tickets were based in the United States and that they intended to use the tickets for flights from airports all over the world. They appeared to have "sales outlets" across Europe, Africa, North and South America.

I am aware, for example, that stolen SAS, KLM, Lufthansa and Iberia tickets were used liberally in Europe; PanAm and TWA tickets in America and Air France tickets in South and East Africa: upon them appeared the forged or stolen validation stamps of travel agencies within the country of that particular airline. A stolen Air France ticket would be used for a flight from Johannesburg to Rio de Janeiro using the validation stamp of a travel agency in France. A stolen PanAm ticket for flights from London back to London via Boston, Los Angeles and Miami would, for example, bear a forged Thomas Cook, London validation stamp, a stamp that would give a "check in" desk confidence that the ticket was genuine. I have seen copies of the above.

How were the criminals going to profit from the theft of so many tickets? As indicated, they sold a lot through their distribution networks to other criminals in other countries. Others were written out for long and costly flights from England or America, for example, London to somewhere in Australia. The ticket would then be presented to an office of the particular airline with a request that the ticket be amended for a flight to a closer destination and that the difference between the cost of travelling to the two destinations be refunded.

Some airlines refunded the difference in cash but most gave credit vouchers that could then be used to buy a bona fide ticket to another destination at a later date. In this way, for example, a number of unsuspecting American students purchased "discounted" credit vouchers in New York, advertised for sale on college notice boards, for travel to Europe.

What made the use of stolen tickets so easy? It was basically down to the fact that, during the 1970s, load factors on most airlines worldwide were comparatively low. Flights were rarely full to capacity and the chance of getting a seat on a flight, even with a forged "open" ticket were high. In those days many airlines, being national flag carriers were subsidised by their governments and could therefore afford to operate with lower numbers of passengers per flight than nowadays. As the reader will be aware many national airlines have either been privatised or gone out of business since 1974 and those that remain have had to achieve much higher ratios of passengers to seats on their flights in order to survive in a very competitive market.

Of the thirty seven airlines whose tickets were stolen in 1974 well over half have, in fact, disappeared. At the time however, there was no great problem in turning up at an airport with an "open ticket" and no prior reservation: "standby" passengers invariably got on to the flight of their choice and no questions were asked at "check in" if the validation stamp appeared to be genuine.

Not only did I act as liaison between the police and the other travel agents, DCI Cressy also asked me to assist him in dealing with the Press by feeding "non-attributable" information to newspapers, which they would doubtless print! After about three months into the investigation, for example, he asked me to telephone the Crime Correspondent of the Daily Mirror and tell him on a "non-attributable" basis, that the police were very close to making a number of arrests in connection with the theft of the nine thousand air tickets. "And are you close to making these arrests?" I asked him. "Not exactly, but we are keeping close tabs on a couple of our suspects and we want to see what they do when the article appears in the paper." I duly made the phone call and a couple of weeks later DCI Cressy reported to me that nearly 8000 tickets had been recovered from a lock-up garage in Romford Road, Bow. Simultaneous raids had been carried out by the police in several parts of the country, as well as in New York and Los Angeles. Printing equipment that produced forged validation stamps was also seized and a number of arrests were made. DCI Cressy told the newspapers that his investigations had led to a "ticket trail" across Europe and East Africa and that his squad had unearthed sufficient evidence of other travel frauds to keep it going for a year!

The rest of the 1000 tickets that the police had been unable to recover kept trickling in and by mid-1976 the notional loss to all the airlines amounted to just over £100,000. In view of the fact, however, that the dossier had been instrumental in prompting the police to take such effective action against the thefts referred to in this and other types of airline fraud, the airlines decided to write off their notional losses, to the relief of myself and the other travel agents. The actual loss to the airlines had been minimal, in any event, because the scheduled flights would have departed from airports whether or not one of the passengers had a forged ticket. It was only where they had made a cash refund that they were actually out of pocket.

IATA subsequently reviewed the agency agreement and made it less onerous on travel agents when thefts that they could not prevent took place. Computerisation of ticketing procedures has effectively done away with printed tickets and the problems encountered in 1974 no longer exist.

It had been a worrying incident at the time and I was pleased and relieved that we had all emerged from it unscathed.

As a footnote to the ticket theft I was subsequently asked by Eric Moonman's wife whether I would be prepared to join the Management Committee of the Women's Refuge in Basildon as a legal adviser on a pro bono basis. The Refuge had been set up to provide a "safe house" for the wives and female partners who had been traumatised by the men with whom they cohabited: most of them had suffered continual violence and abuse and I was only too happy to go down to "The Triangle" in Basildon, a Community Centre and attend the Committee meetings.

After attending for about a year, however, I concluded that the Refuge was well managed and that there was not a great deal I could contribute to the management of it. It was, moreover, an all female Committee who, not surprisingly, appeared not to have a very high opinion of men in general! My own practice was expanding rapidly, my personal time was limited and I therefore tendered my resignation from it: being on the Committee nevertheless gave me a sobering insight into the lives of "battered" women and the effect of violence and abuse on them and on their children.

BH party sleeping out on a mountainside at Delphi

The only vehicle for hire in Athens!

Student protest at the tasteless extension of Emmanuel College, University of Cambridge

Hazel Wilson, Head Student at Homerton College. "Anyone for squash?"

Valerie Foulkes: the "late arriver" at Victoria Station, Graduation Day 1959

Andrea, with whom I fell in love in 1960

Hughes Overland Group: ready to depart for Kathmandu

Hughes Overland "Asiaman" Land Rovers and Transits en route to Kathmandu

My Greek friend, Babis, at his holiday home in Kokkino Limenaki

15

The Haunted Bed

Every November Babis used to fly over to England with the accounts he had prepared. We were partners in the British Travel and Student Service, a travel agency we maintained in Stadiou Street in Athens.

Babis booked the coaches we used for student our trips to Delphi, sold student air and boat tickets and operated as an advice centre for members of Brian Hughes parties.

At first he stayed with an elderly widow, a Mrs. Reading, who "mothered" him and looked after him extremely well. Mrs. Reading also acted as an unofficial "Nanny" to my two sons, and my first wife, Vivien, and I took her on holiday with us to France: she was a very kind-hearted person and the nearest my sons had to a grandmother.

After Vivien and I separated and divorced by mutual consent I bought a maisonette in Chapel Court, Billericay. Chapel Court was known jokingly as "Divorce Court" because nearly every person in it had been divorced!

It was a large maisonette with three bedrooms and I decided to ask Babis to stay with me rather than place him with Mrs. Reading after I had purchased it.

The reader has to be aware that Babis did not really like coming to England in November: it was much colder than Athens and nowhere near as pleasant. He therefore insisted on my giving him a bottle of whisky every year that he could take to his bedroom to fortify himself against the low temperatures he felt he would experience during the night.

He arrived on a Wednesday in mid-November 1974 and all went well for the first couple of nights. Babis and I went through the two sets of accounts he had prepared and agreed them: one described very accurately the trading records of the travel agency, the other showed exactly half the turnover and half the income.

"Why have we got two sets of accounts, Babis?" "Well, Bri-yann," (his way of saying "Brian") "one is for us and the other is for the tax inspector in Athens". I asked: "Why are they not the same?"

"The answer is very simple" said Babis. "When I show the inspector the accounts, he will not believe me and will increase everything, including the tax, by 100%."

"So what you are saying is that we will finish up paying the right amount of tax." "Exactly," replied Babis!

In the light of this revelation one can hardly be surprised at the economic muddle in which Greece finds itself most of the time! But I digress.

The maisonette had three bedrooms and before Babis arrived I needed a bed for the guest bedroom. I had a Victorian pine military chest in the guest bedroom and decided to look for a Victorian bed.

The best place to look was at an auction sale of antique and Victorian furniture and one Tuesday evening after work I drove up to Clare in Suffolk to view the items in a "Boardmans" sale. As soon as I walked into the sale room I saw exactly what I was looking for – a beautiful Victorian brass bed.

"How much is this bed likely to go for?" I asked the auctioneer. "About £100," he replied. "Can I leave you with a bid for this amount?" "Yes, that would be no problem – just give us your details and we will let you know if your bid is successful."

I drove home with the sale catalogue and thought about my bid: perhaps I had been wrong to leave such a low bid: it was item number 4 in the catalogue. Could I afford to drive to the auction next day and bid for it myself? To hell with it, I will do that and miss a couple of hours' work!

So next morning I was sitting in the auction room at 10 am and by 10.15 am the bed was mine! I had paid £105 for it. The euphoria was quickly tempered by the realisation that I had no way of getting the bed back to Billericay and I had to collect it the next day, Thursday!

They say that "necessity is the mother of invention" and I went across the High Street in Billericay to John Mahoney of MacHart Furnishers, clients of mine and asked him if I could borrow one of his furniture vans. Thursday was, in those days, "early closing day" and he had no objection at all.

So, on Wednesday night, I drove the furniture van via Kelvedon to Clare in

Suffolk. I had booked accommodation at a guest house in Clare and called in on Bill Rough, a retired director of Plessey turned antique dealer, in Kelvedon en route. We talked a lot about antiques and antique dealers and he assured me I had made a good purchase. I only mention the visit because when I arrived in Clare the guest house was closed! After banging on the door, the proprietress, an elderly and rather annoyed lady, appeared at the front door in her nightdress and let me in. I had visions of sleeping in the van!

The next morning I drove to the auction rooms. "You do realise, don't you, that this bed comes with a virtually brand new mattress." "No, I did not realise that."

"It belonged to an elderly lady, a Miss Clements, who died in the bed: the bed was part of her Estate."

"I will take the mattress," I said "It looks fine to me." And so this beautiful gleaming Victorian bed plus mattress was installed in the guest bedroom at Chapel Court.

I showed the bed to Babis and said "This is your bed, Babis. I hope you enjoy sleeping in it." And, indeed for the first couple of nights he did.

On Saturday morning there was a knock on the front door at 8.00 am. I guessed it was the milkman, picked up a £1 note and went down the two flights of stairs to the front door. There were two flights because the maisonette was on the first and second floors of the building: there was a single bedroom flat beneath it.

"It is more than £1," said the milkman. "It is £1.20." This meant having to go up two flights of stairs again and when, by this time thoroughly awake, I got to the first floor I noticed that all Babis's sheets and blankets were in the "downstairs" first floor hall.

That was strange. I picked them up, carried them up to the guest bedroom and opened the door. Babis was fast asleep, in his vest and pants, uncovered, on the bed. Rather than wake him I threw the sheets and blankets on the floor and shut the door.

I went to the office for a couple of hours and on my return spoke to Babis about the sheets and blankets.

"I can only suppose, Babis, that you decided to go to the loo during the night, that you forgot there was a bathroom upstairs, that you wrapped the sheets and blankets about yourself and went to the loo on the first floor. You must have done this in your sleep."

"Bri-yann that cannot be true. If I walked in my sleep my parents would have told me. I have lived with them all my life."

"Well that is a mystery Babis. I have no explanation for it."

The following Tuesday I had gone to my office, which was only a couple of hundred yards away, when at about 10 am I received a telephone call from Babis.

"Bri-yann, you must come back to the flat immediately." He sounded panic-stricken. What was it this time?

"Bri-yann, come to my bedroom. I must show you something." We went up the staircase to his room. Babis dramatically threw the door open and pointed at the military chest upon which he had placed his suitcase. "Feel my clothes," he said.

So I did. They were sodden – completely soaked. I picked up the top item and smelt it – it was definitely water, not what I thought it might be, given the fact that he had probably drunk quite a lot of whisky before he went to sleep!

"Explain that," Babis said. "Well, Babis, when you arrived you put your open suitcase under the window (which was of the "swivel" variety). It rained the other night. You left the window open, the rain bounced off the window and on to your clothes before you moved your suitcase."

"In that case," said Babis" "the floor on each side of where I put the suitcase will be wet." We felt the floor: it was bone dry.

"Well, Babis, there is a radiator under the window and it must have dried the carpet."

That reply did not satisfy him at all. Babis had previously talked about spirits and ghosts: he had a particular fascination for the story about Anne Boleyn's ghost walking the Tower of London with her head under her arm. The story had been in an English Tourist Board brochure in Athens, advertising the sights of London.

"Bri-yann, spirits have done this. They have come in through the window and have done this. From now on I am going to sleep with the window shut."
"As you wish, Babis." The pine military chest still bears the water stains from this incident and that is mildly annoying, but more of that anon.

The following Saturday marked the climax of these strange "goings on." I left for the office as usual for a couple of hours when the phone rang again.

"Bri-yann, you must come home at once." This time Babis, who had been a lieutenant in the Greek Army during his National Service, sounded really worried. I raced home to find Babis standing in the kitchen, fully dressed and in a state of great anxiety.

"Something very serious has happened," said Babis. "What is that, Babis?"

"When I went to bed last night I put my cigarettes and lighter on the chair by my bed and ash tray under the chair." When I woke up this morning the cigarettes and lighter were not on the chair."

Babis was a chain smoker and I had, on occasion, stayed with him and his parents in their flat in Stournara Street. In the bed next to mine a body would be completely covered by a sheet. It would stir and a great hairy arm would slide out from under the sheet: a great hairy hand would describe a delicate circular movement until it alighted on the packet of cigarettes and the lighter on a small table next to the bed. The arm, cigarettes and lighter would disappear under the sheet. There would be a "click, click" sound and a puff of smoke would come out of the hole through which the arm and hand had previously appeared. That was Babis waking up!

"So where were they, Babis?"

"I rolled over on the bed and looked under the chair and I saw my lighter and cigarettes under it. But there was no sign of the ashtray. So I got out of bed and looked around for it. I found it empty under the centre of the bed. Not only that, there was something on my back and when I felt my back I found three cigarette stubs were sticking to it."

Babis paused. "But that is not all. Look!" With that he lifted the sheet and there, down the centre of the bed, was all the ash from the ashtray. He had been lying in it.

"This bed is haunted," declared Babis. "We must examine it."

So we took the mattress off and there, on the frame, was a small brown label attached by a piece of string, with the words "Miss A E Clements, Deceased."

"Take that label off," said Babis (which we did). "We must now get the priest."

So we went downstairs and I rang David Greaves, the vicar. "David, we have a problem. I have a haunted bed and the lady who died in it is terrifying my guest. Can you come and exorcise it?"

David, who had come into the priesthood as a result of acting as a padre to prisoners of war who were forced to work in one of Hitler's slave factories, was sympathetic but said, "Brian, there are a lot of psychic phenomena in Billericay at the moment. I cannot come round immediately but if you have any more problems let me know and I will do my best to help you."

I said to Babis, "The priest says there is a lot of it about at the moment: he is very busy but he will come round, if necessary."

I could see that Babis was not happy with this so I walked to the foot of the staircase and shouted up it. "Look here, Miss Clements, I am not prepared to let you haunt my guests like this and if I have any more trouble from you I will have to have you exorcised."

Babis stood open-mouthed. He could not believe what he was hearing! In fact, he was so disturbed by the three incidents that he left Billericay shortly thereafter, never to return. Henceforth I had to visit him in Greece.

After he left I went upstairs and sat on the brass bed and said, "Miss Clements, I do understand how you felt. As a spinster who loved your bed, you did not like a short, fat, hairy Greek who went to sleep in it in his vest and pants and who chain smoked and drank whisky. But you must bear in mind that although you are very attached to this bed it is no longer **your** bed. If I have any more problems with you damaging the furniture or haunting the guests I really will have to have you exorcised."

The only way of finding out whether Miss Clements "got the message" was to put someone else in the bed: the opportunity arose shortly afterwards.

As a member of the local Rotary Club I entertained a student from the Commonwealth Institute. He was a polite, well-mannered, well-spoken Indian student studying English literature at London University. In the evening we sat, discussing English literature, particularly poetry in which we shared a common interest.

"I have a lovely bed for you to sleep in," I said and showed him into the guest bedroom. "This is it," I thought to myself!

The next morning he appeared, unfazed, and I asked casually: "Did you sleep all right last night?"

"Oh, I had a wonderful night's sleep," he said. "Thank you so much for your hospitality." Miss Clements clearly approved!

Subsequent to the visit of the young Indian student I have to say that Miss Clements behaved impeccably and many a guest has "unwittingly" spent a comfortable and incident-free night in her bed.

Although I am now satisfied that Miss Clements has given up her proprietorial attitude towards it I do still treat the bed with great respect and make sure that it is neat and tidy at all times!

16

The Haunted House

At the age of forty, with two young sons to look after every weekend, a busy practice and a strong desire to move from a maisonette into a house I started to look round for somewhere to purchase – somewhere I could take on as a project.

As I walked past the offices of Thain and Richardson, estate agents, in Billericay high street I saw a black and white photo of a house that appeared to have been "in the wars". Its white plastered exterior had grey patches in it where the plaster had fallen off the walls. The house had an incredibly gaunt and run-down appearance. I went inside and asked where it was and the asking price.

The house was in Stock Road and belonged to the Baptist ministry (the Retired Baptist Minister's Housing Association). The asking price was £25,000. The Association could no longer afford to maintain it and was moving the three retired ministers out of it.

I went to see it and concluded that the association had never spent any money on it in the first place. It was divided into three primitive flats and on the first floor there were buckets to catch the rainwater that came through the ceiling. The house had a second floor with twin eaves and the lead guttering between the eaves had not been replaced since 1957, some nineteen years previously.

On the second floor was a 79-year-old minister who was not at all friendly. His name was the Reverend Moule. "I have been living on this floor since my retirement fourteen years ago and I do not want to move," he said. "Your ministry has decided to sell the house and is apparently going to move you to better accommodation." "Well, that is as maybe, but there is something about this floor." "What is that?" I asked. "You'll find out," he replied.

The house appeared to be a brick-built Victorian or Edwardian structure and was clearly an extension of the Tudor house attached to it. I could only assume that at some point in the past the farmer who owned the Tudor house and Hill House Farm had a family he could not accommodate in it and had decided to build the "additional wing".

The rooms on the ground and first floors of the extension were large. The rooms in the eaves were not small but only had four inch by two inch floor joists – presumably designed for servants who would only have had a tin box for their clothes and an iron bed to sleep on: no other furniture would have been allowed.

The land around Hill House Farm had been substantial and in 1931 part of the back land was sold to the local council for recreational purposes. The land in question is now called Lake Meadows, the local park.

A Major Spitty owned Hill House Farm until he died in 1898. The farm was subsequently acquired in 1917 by Robert Spurling, who sold off all the farmland as building land in the 1920s and 1930s. In the 1940s the house, by then called Hill House, was acquired by Mr William and Mrs Alice Cater: he was apparently a wealthy stockbroker.

When he died in 1956 his widow, who had purchased on behalf of the town a small house in the High Street as a museum (the Cater Museum) decided that the house was too large and wished to give away the non-Tudor wing. She approached the Congregational Church, which declined the offer on the grounds that the cost of conversion would be too great. She then approached the Baptist ministry, which said the same – but that it would take the house if she converted it.

Mrs. Cater did reluctantly convert it – in a most primitive fashion and the three retired ministers moved into the non-Tudor wing, by now named "Green Pastures". The Baptist ministry then promptly sold off half the garden as prime building land for £12000!

How the Reverend Moule managed to survive on the top floor, reached as it was by the steepest staircase I had ever encountered, I shall never know – but he did and he was clearly happy in his rooftop eyrie.

Not put off by his mysterious remark I asked my architect, Ron Ketley, to look at the house and tell me whether he thought I could do things with it. He came back full of enthusiasm. "We can do so much with it: it is an ideal project. You must buy it."

And so I purchased and moved into Green Pastures. The first task was to make it weatherproof: this entailed renewing the lead guttering between the eaves, removing all the external plaster to expose the cream coloured bricks and then re-rendering it completely. It was cold in the house during the winter but we all got by with coal fires and electric heating until 1983 when the conversion of the house took place.

But that is to jump ahead and I must first tell you of the reason why the conversion took place as it did.

When I first moved into the house (with my sons joining me every weekend) we used the top floor as a storage area – old carpets, suitcases, anything for which we had no immediate need.

One October evening in 1977 I returned from work and stepped into the hall. The house had a strange atmosphere: I was convinced someone was in the house: I shut the front door and went to the next house in the road. "Would you mind standing in the hall of my house for a few minutes? I am sure there is someone upstairs." My neighbours looked puzzled but obligingly did so. I went through the upper two floors: no one was there!

Strangely, exactly the same "atmosphere" occurred in the house every year thereafter (and I managed to pin the date down to 16th October) until, one day, I had been up to the second floor for something and, as I was walking down the steep stairs, I realised what was causing the atmosphere.

Whenever, over the previous five years, I had walked down those stairs I had felt "eyes in my back." I was being watched. I said aloud, "I've got it. You are afraid of me falling down the stairs." At that moment the atmosphere lifted and I promised to do something about them.

Not long after this light-bulb moment I asked Ron Ketley to return and discuss the conversion of the house: I had saved up enough to do it. "Ron, I have come to the conclusion that the top floor is haunted and that whoever haunts the house died on those steep steps leading to the second floor."

"I knew it was haunted because the old priest on the top floor told me," he replied. "Then why did you not tell me?" "I did not want to put you off the purchase," was his response. "Thank you, Ron. What else did the priest tell you?"

"He told me that she, definitely a 'she', appears as a white wraith crossing two of the bedrooms on the top floor."

I told Ron about my experiences and said, "I want a staircase no one can fall down, with bannisters on both sides, with a maximum angle of descent of 40 degrees."

"In that case we will have to chop away part of the top floor to fit it in." "No problem, do that."

And so a staircase was fitted with a reinforced metal frame that was not only easy to ascend and descend but sufficiently fire resistant to enable safe passage to the lower floor.

At the same time central heating was installed. My two sons, who had by this time been living with me full time for nearly three years, wanted me to install a small billiard table on the top floor. I consulted Ron Ketley. "The top floor with only two inch by four inch floor joists will not take a billiard table but if you double up the strength of the joists this would be possible".

"In that case, Ron, we will double up the joists."

"You do realise don't you that this will mean that the floor will rise by two inches,, he replied.

And so, the one inch thick oak flooring was stripped out, the additional joists were inserted and a new pine floor was laid.

Central heating was going to pose a problem and I consulted the painter and decorator, James Mackenzie, whose father had carried out some building work for me previously.

"You have lath and plaster walls and the central heating will dry out the walls and make them unstable. You will need two coats of strong anaglypta paper to hold the plaster in place".

"In that case two coats of Anaglypta it will be."

Imagine now a bare room with a new pine floor with the walls newly wallpapered and painted – everything pristine, no cracks, no crevices – all surfaces new.

Imagine, therefore, my surprise when, the day after James Mackenzie had left the house, I walked into the room only to be stopped short by a small, gleaming, silver object on the floor: it was a mint-fresh Victorian threepenny piece, dated 1897.

It was not tarnished: it looked brand new. It could not have fallen out of any crack in the wall or hole in the floor– there were none. I decided to try and find out more.

I took the coin to a friend, Robert Easton, for an explanation. Robert, who investigated psychic phenomena, explained: "Four things travel through time and space: books, keys, money and bread, and don't ask me why bread," he said. "This was clearly a 'thank you' from whoever died on the staircase."

I had no reason to disbelieve him and I can confirm that within three weeks the coin had tarnished and lost its mint condition.

Determined to find out more I wrote to the Registrar of Births, Deaths and Marriages and asked him whether anyone had died in Hill House on 16 October 1897. His reply was interesting. "On that day a maidservant by the name of Ada Rolfe had died in Stock Road but no address had been given."

Rolfe is a Billericay farming name. I once had a retired Billericay farmer by the name of Eric Rolfe who went to Kathmandu on my Billericay to Kathmandu bus service; he must have been tough because he went out and came back by minibus – 43 days out and 42 days back!

So I now had a name, a date, a young woman whose spirit had spent over seventy or eighty years anxiously watching people go up and down the staircase and a "thank you."

The next thing was to get someone who could determine whether or not my theory of the death of Ada Rolfe was true. My conjecture was that she had been called downstairs one October evening, as it was getting dark: she had inadvertently caught the hem of her long skirt in her shoe and had pitched forward down the steep and narrow staircase and had broken her neck at the bottom of it. The only problem with my theory was that the non-Tudor extension was apparently built after 1897!

Nevertheless, I obtained the services of a Medium who came to the house. "Can you please go round the house and tell me if anyone died traumatically in it.? Let me know where."

She went methodically around the house and then led me to the top floor. Looking over the newly installed banisters she pointed downwards. "Somebody died there." It was exactly at the bottom of the staircase which had been removed.

That might have been the end of it but one evening my son, Alex, who by this time was sixteen, was sitting in his bedroom on the first floor when he heard a crashing sound outside his bedroom door. He ran to the bedroom door and opened it. At that point somebody screamed right in front of him but there was nobody there. He confirms that he was so terrified by a scream coming out of thin air that he slammed the bedroom door shut, took out his air pistol and sat with his back to the radiator in his bedroom facing the door until I returned home from the office a few minutes later.

It was an October evening and I guessed immediately what it was. Nevertheless we checked whether our immediate neighbours were in – there was no reply from them and it transpired subsequently that they were out. I decided to tell Alex the entire story and all I can surmise is that it was some kind of replay of what occurred.

The words "followed by a scream" haunted me for some time until I realised that people who break their necks do not scream but the person who found the dead young women would have done so.

This took me back to the time Annette moved into our home. We had been on honeymoon in Portugal with our five children – as you do, apparently – and had bought a large white china vase with flowers painted on it. The vase had pride of place in the hall.

Annette was in the front bedroom sorting out her possessions while I was in the main bedroom clearing one of the large cupboards for her clothes.

She came into the room and asked why the Portuguese pot was in front of the bedroom door. I had no idea nor had any of the children who were scattered about the house. We thought it might be a prank but they were all quite serious – no one had transported it upstairs.

What is more Annette said she had just had a strange experience: a musical box which her father had given her on a holiday in Switzerland when she was nine and which had not worked for years suddenly started playing when she took it out of the box in which she had packed it.

I may well be wrong but I cannot help feeling that there was the spirit of a little girl in the house who was delighted when Lucy, probably about her age, moved in and it was the little girl who had screamed.

There has been no sign of her for thirty years and I assume she has "moved on."

The house is friendly and kind – the atmosphere is welcoming despite the fact that things can appear and (disappear) within it. I would not be anywhere else.

17

Virginia 1980

Strange and seemingly inexplicable things seem to happen when I am least expecting them: what occurred during a holiday in Virginia in 1980 was no exception.

I have always been very close to my sons, Chris born in 1967 and Alex, born in 1969 and when my first wife, Vivien, and I separated and divorced in 1974 I took them on a series of holidays, initially close to home and gradually moving further afield as they grew older and I built up confidence in taking them abroad.

We started with the Isle of Man and by the time Chris was twelve and Alex was ten we had reached the West Coast of America via Jersey, Limerick, Malta, Majorca, Tenerife and Rhodes. America proved to be a very popular holiday destination for them and from 1979 to 1981 we spent three weeks every summer on the East and West Coasts of the United States.

During our holiday to the East Coast in 1980 we flew into Washington from Boston on 21 July, hired a car and drove straight to the Old Colony Inn in Alexandria, a town close to the capital. Having peered at the White House through the railings, as all tourists do, and having visited the Capitol, the Lincoln Memorial and various exhibitions at the Smithsonian Museum we decided to head off in our hire car in the general direction of the Shenendoah National Park and the Blue Ridge mountains.

Before, however, we left Alexandria we paid a visit to Gunston Hall, a period property near the River Potomac: it had originally been the home of a wealthy plantation owner, George Mason, one of the Founding Fathers of the

United States of America, and the house was built in the Georgian "Colonial" style. Quite why I decided on a visit to Gunston Hall, as well as Mount Vernon, I cannot recall but, as we parked the car I said to Chris and Alex, "I have an odd feeling about this place." Perhaps the feeling was triggered by the sight of what appeared to be a replica of a late 18th century or early 19th century wooden school house in the grounds. I added: "When we go through that side door I am sure we will go into a room with a large fireplace like this," and I described it to them: it had an unusual overmantel. My sons were quite used to my mystic pronouncements and looked at each other with resigned expressions that said, "Here is the old man going off his rocker again!"

But, to their surprise, when we went through that side door and into the room beyond there was the fireplace, exactly as I had described it. To be honest that also surprised me and I thought, "Could I possibly have seen that fireplace in a book somewhere?" But, frankly, I doubt it.

Alternatively, could I have seen it or a design for it in a past life? The thought was not quite as fanciful as one might imagine because it appeared to link in with the regression I had experienced in London only a year or two previously. In that regression I had the sensation that I, or perhaps somebody linked to me in some way, had lived near Alexandria and had been the private tutor to the children of plantation owners. A regression, incidentally, is either the product of a fertile imagination during a period of semi-hypnosis or does actually reveal a past life of the spirit that I suspect takes up residence in us during our lifetimes. I hope to be able to tell the story of that intriguing experience in another book but need to research the story first in order to gauge whether or not it might be true.

Having had that "odd" experience at Gunston Hall we left Alexandria shortly afterwards and drove towards the Appalachians. When we arrived in Luray we stopped at a McDonalds set in a wooded area with benches and tables scattered among the trees: having found a convenient table I asked the boys what they wanted for lunch: they gave the hardly unexpected reply, "Hamburgers, French fries and coke." So off I went into McDonalds and stood in a long queue waiting to be served.

I could not fail to notice that the young lady serving my queue looked just like my cousin, Jacqui. Not only that she seemed to have the same, for want of a better word, "aura". I said nothing at the time but when they got through their cartons of coke rather quickly and both asked for another I told Chris and

Alex I would get some more coke for them on condition that they came into the restaurant with me. I wanted them to come with me and tell me something. "What do you want us to tell you?" "Wait and see," I replied.

I took them to the same line and then said: "Can you see the young lady serving our queue? Who does she remind you of?" "Auntie Jacqui," they both said at once. She was not, strictly speaking, their aunt but they referred to her as such. "OK let us have a word with her."

As I purchased the coke I addressed the young lady behind the counter: "Forgive my saying so but my two sons and I think you are the spitting image of my cousin." She looked intrigued. "What is her name?" she asked. "Her name is Jacqui," I replied. With a look of shock, she said, "But that is the name of my baby daughter." I offered to put her in touch with my cousin and she gave me her name and address: her name was Paula Pates.

Of course, I had to tell my cousin Jacqui when I returned home, and she was not at all fazed. "She was probably my doppelganger." "What," I said, "is a doppelganger?" Well, she was very matter of fact about it and I have to confess that I half believed her because it brought back to my mind an experience I had during my National Service.

After 4.30 pm on Fridays we Gunners were allowed out of Redford Barracks for the weekend: we would put on our "civvies" and catch the tram from outside the barracks and go down to Tollcross, the tram terminus in the centre of Edinburgh. Although I did not make a habit of going there, I had been standing in the bar of the North British Hotel at the far end of Princes Street one evening when a young man of roughly my age had bounded up to me and, in a broad Belfast accent, had said, "Hi, John, what are you doing here?" I looked at the young man whom I had never seen before and said, "I am not John." "Stop kidding me," he replied. "Of course you are John, and where did you get that accent?" "I am not John," I repeated. "Yes, you are. You are John from Belfast." "No, I am Brian from Billericay." He walked away scratching his head in disbelief and I had not the wit to pursue him and ask him who, exactly, John was!

"But," continued Jacqui, "where you saw Paula Pates is most interesting." "Why is that?" "Well, you probably don't know this because they tended to keep it to themselves, but our Uncle Gerald, Uncle John, Auntie Mabel, Uncle Ted and Grandad used to meet at Sheppey Road on Saturday evenings and go on the Ouija board. Gerald told me that one evening they asked whether they had ever lived before. The answer was that they had and that some of them had lived in Virginia."

As a trained lawyer I have to treat what she told me as "hearsay" evidence but the whole subject is intriguing and has prompted me to research it further. Looking at the "doppelganger" experience logically and rationally there can be no doubt that among the many billions of people on the planet there have to be a lot of them who bear a striking resemblance to someone else: there are only so many configurations of the human face, and the same shape of face, hair and eye colourings and complexion must be replicated somewhere within such a large world population.

No human being will, however, share the same genetic structure as another unless he or she is an identical twin and the comment about Virginia has puzzled me ever since. You, the reader, may consider that this is all "stuff and nonsense" but in a later chapter I will refer to cautious belief in what one does not really understand, for example "Virgin birth" and the limitations we place on ourselves by accepting without question beliefs that provide us with a comforting framework for this all too temporary life.

I am reassured by the fact that it is not just myself who has these strange experiences: I am usually with someone when they happen. Moreover, my gardener, Neville, who is about as sane and well balanced as anyone, recently approached me and said, "I did not know whether to mention this to you, but I spoke beforehand to your son Chris who assured me that you are into this sort of thing and would not be disturbed by it."

"What sort of thing?" I asked. "Well, while I was sweeping up the leaves in the garden on 26 October (2016) I happened to look up and there, about twelve feet away, was a lady, not looking at me but in the direction of the drive. She was standing quite still and did not appear to notice me. She was quite stout, about 5 feet three to 5 feet four inches in height, about sixty years old and wearing a black bonnet, black veil and black dress with a small bustle at the back. She was clearly from a wealthy background and appeared to be in mourning."

Neville who noted the time as 11 am referred to her, rather surprisingly as being "in the Old Orchard by the big tree." I do not know whether he is aware of the fact that the area in which he saw her appears as an orchard on the Chapman and Andre map of the Billericay area dated 1776. He went on to say that her image fractured and dissolved in front of his eyes: her dress was late

Victorian or early Edwardian.

Be that as it may, he went home to do some research of his own and concluded that it was a "paranormal residual phenomenon." I accepted his conclusion and also did some research of my own. It would appear to have been the widow of Major Spitty, a previous owner and former Lord Lieutenant of Essex who lived in the house of which my own now forms part: he died in 1898 and his widow would have fitted the description that Neville gave me.

18

Billericay, Essex

The history of Billericay is well documented, not least because of its connection to the "Mayflower".

There are, however, one or two aspects of that history that do not appear in history books because they relate to individuals or to events that can so easily be overlooked.

Take, for example, the death of Basil Brookes, JP who lived at Burghstead Lodge in Billericay High Street: he was a wealthy and influential member of the community, Chairman of the Magistrates and highly respected.

He and his wife decided to go on holiday to the Far East in 1953. On their homeward flight from Singapore their plane touched down at Rome Ciampino Airport early in the morning of 10 January 1954 in order to refuel. The plane was a De Havilland Comet, the third of its type, and the pride of the BOAC fleet. The Comet was the first jet-propelled passenger aircraft in the world, a beautifully designed aeroplane that would have been able to compete strongly with any American and European rival.

It took off for Heathrow at about 10 am and between the Islands of Elba and Montecristo suffered explosive decompression and fell out of the sky. Mr and Mrs. Brookes were killed instantaneously.

In their respective Wills Mr and Mrs Brookes had put the following words: "if my wife/husband does not survive me I leave everything to my children".

The executors of the estate of Basil Brookes took the view that because the deaths of Mr and Mrs Brookes must have been simultaneous Mrs Brookes could not have survived her husband: accordingly estate duty would be payable on his estate alone.

"Not so", said HM Inland Revenue. "Mrs Brookes did survive her husband as far as we are concerned and you will therefore have to pay estate duty on her estate as well."

"That is nonsense," said the executors. "How can Mrs Brookes have lived any longer than her husband when they were in an aircraft that literally exploded thousands of feet in the air?" And so they entered into litigation with HM Inland Revenue and took their argument to the House of Lords. What do you think happened?

"The Inland Revenue are correct," said their Lordships. "We must have a rule in this sort of case: from the legal perspective we have to determine that one of them survived the other. It is impossible for us to say who survived whom: we therefore have to determine that the wife survived her husband because women have greater life expectancies than men."

The costs of fighting the Inland Revenue, after paying the two sets of estate duty, exhausted the monies left in the two estates and the children were obliged to sell Burghstead Lodge and that is why the property is now owned by Essex County Council and houses the offices of the public library.

From that moment on every solicitor in the land who had not already done so made sure that the wording of clients' wills read "if my wife or husband does not survive me **by 28 days** I leave everything, etc" thereby avoiding the fate that befell the estates of Mr and Mrs Basil Brookes.

If married heterosexual couples do not make wills and die simultaneously the wife is deemed to survive the husband: in the case of same sex marriages no one yet knows what the rule will be but it is more than likely that the older will be deemed to have died first. The same rules will apply to civil partnerships, which are recognised by the State.

There are many other interesting stories about Billericay people and one that I thought was apocryphal until recently relates to Fred Eales, the saddler, who lived in the middle of Billericay High Street in the small house on the right hand side of the Cater Museum: it is, at the time of writing this book a jeweller's shop.

In the 1920's Fred delivered post by pony and trap to outlying parts of Billericay but by the late 1940's he had effectively retired and confined himself to "pottering" in his little shop and watching the world go by. When I say "the world" I mean the occasional pedestrian and the even more occasional car that passed his front door! It is difficult to visualise how quiet Billericay was in the

1940's. For example, even in the early 1950's the Eastern National Bus used to park for at least twenty minutes in Chapel Street between St. Mary Magdalen Church and Goodspeeds, the fish shop: no one ever went up Chapel Street! That street is now so busy as a "bypass" for an even busier high street that nothing is allowed to park or stop in most of it.

As a child I remember Fred – a short, tubby little man who sat on a wooden kitchen chair just inside the door of his shop. He wore carpet slippers, a pair of baggy black trousers, a white shirt without a collar and a black waistcoat: he invariably wore a flat cap.

"C'mere, boi," he would say to me as I walked past his shop as a twelve-year-old schoolboy in my short grey trousers, dark blue Brentwood Grammar School blazer and maroon school cap.

"Did yer know there were a "BillyRicky" Grammar School?" he would ask. "No, Sir," I would reply. "C'mere." With that he would reach inside his shop and produce two large books with brown leather covers: inside the cover of each was a frontispiece with the words "Billericay Grammar School" printed on it.

He did this to me three or four times and I only realised some years after I had to sell Foxcroft that my old office had been the Billericay Grammar School in the 1860's.

But that is not the story: it is just an illustration of the fact that when he had nothing to do he would invariably be sitting at the front door of his shop watching what, if anything, was happening in the High Street.

It is not surprising therefore that in 1928 he should have been sitting at the door of his shop and should have been asked by a party of German visitors who had arrived by train from London the whereabouts of Great Burstead parish church and that he should have offered to take them by pony and trap to the cemetery in which the crew of Zeppelin L.32 were interred. Zeppelin L.32 had been shot down by Second Lieutenant Frederick Sowrey over Billericay on 26 September 1916. It was such a notable event that the Great Eastern Railway had laid on special excursion trains from Liverpool Street to view the wreckage. Fred, who doubtless offered the German visitors a cup of tea after he had brought them back from Great Burstead, subsequently received an engraved glass bowl from them with a note expressing their "deepest thanks for the kindness and friendship you rendered to us."

Although the Zeppelin had been on a bombing mission and had been shot down by a very brave Royal Flying Corps Officer great respect was shown to the twenty two Germans who died and full military honours were accorded to them when they were laid to rest in 1916.

From 1928 onwards German ex-Servicemen regularly visited St. Mary's Church, Great Burstead and in 1936, on the twentieth anniversary of the downing of the Zeppelin twenty three of them came over to Billericay to attend a special memorial ceremony as guests of local British Legion branches.

Swastika emblazoned flags were raised alongside British Legion standards and not a few Nazi salutes were given by the visitors. In the aftermath of the Second World War it is, perhaps, difficult to visualise such a ceremony but the Great War (as WW1 was called at the time) was thought by many to be the war to end all wars.

Going back further in time and to something I can vouch for, having seen the actual documentation during my career as a solicitor in Billericay, is the way in which the railways sought to populate the towns and villages through which their recently constructed lines passed.

Billericay in the 1870's was the "back of beyond", a small town with a modest population. The Red Lion and the Crown Inn, a coaching inn, in the centre of the town, had for many years, benefitted from good business from travellers, including visiting attorneys (or solicitors as they were called from 1876); soldiers on their way from Colchester to Tilbury Fort had marched through the town: stabling for officers' horses had been provided in Crown Yard, opposite the Red Lion, also dormitory accommodation for the foot soldiers until they could travel to London and out to Tilbury by train.

The cellars of the Crown Inn – under Crown Yard – stored the beer that was brewed for the inn and its outlying public houses. The Coach and Horses in Chapel Street was the tap room for the inn and doubtless a favourite drinking place for the soldiers who were billeted in the dormitory accommodation. The locals could pop into the tap room and fill the jugs they brought along with beer. There was a separate entrance for such purchases.

The Crown Inn was able to brew its own beer because, on the opposite side of Chapel Street, there were a number of springs that provided the necessary fresh water for brewing. Seven pints of water were required for each pint of beer: the Crown Inn brewed and sold the beer to a number of "tied" public houses in the area.

The developers of Chapel Court encountered these springs when they started to build maisonettes on the site and had to pile extra long foundations into the soil in order to stabilise the development.

But I digress! The late Victorian era was a dynamic period of industrial and commercial expansion when railways were changing the face of the entire country. New homes were being built as far out as the town of Romford and the village of Barking to house the burgeoning population of London who could now get into the City by train. Southend was also rapidly taking the place of Rochford as the most important town in the south-east of Essex.

Southend and all towns and villages in between therefore became the target of the railway companies of the day and 1884 saw the laying of the track between Shenfield and Billericay by the Great Eastern Railway.

Until the first passenger train stopped at Billericay on 1 January 1889 people had travelled to and from the town by stagecoach. At least one stagecoach had visited Billericay three times a week from 1777. Between 1777 and 1779 it had left The Three Nuns in Whitechapel on the edge of London on Tuesday, Thursday and Saturday mornings at 8 am and had stopped at Billericay on its way to Rochford: it returned from Rochford on Wednesday, Friday and Monday mornings. The return fare to Rochford was, I believe, eight shillings at the time.

In 1780 the service switched its departure point to The Bear public house: there must have been improvements in the route because the stagecoach then left Whitechapel at 2 pm in the summer on the same days of the week as before but at 10 am in the winter.

In 1782 Billericay did not have any resident lawyers and John Vanderzee was the first attorney to visit the town from London on a regular basis. He is known to have first visited Billericay in 1782, arriving by stagecoach from London and staying overnight at the Crown Inn. He would have seen clients in their own homes or doubtless in the Magistrates Room (the Assembly Room) in the inn before returning to London.

Attorneys were sworn attorneys or "side clerks" of the barristers who had chambers in the Inns of Court in London: they visited outlying towns and took instructions on behalf of their chambers. As the population of England was dispersed and towns and cities outside London expanded attorneys were gradually differentiated between London attorneys attached to and part of chambers and country attorneys who were independent of chambers and who conducted legal work on their own. The attorneys in London who had become independent of chambers set up the "London Law Institution" in 1823 when many of them sought to raise the reputation of the profession by setting standards and ensuring good practice. "London" was dropped from the title in 1825 when country attorneys joined the institution.

The institution formed a committee of management in 1825 and in 1831 acquired its first royal charter as the "Society of Attorneys, Solicitors, Proctors and others not being Barristers practising in the Courts of Law and Equity of the United Kingdom". As this was a bit of a mouthful the society changed its name to The Law Society in 1903!

By 1821 three attorneys were making a point of visiting Billericay on a much more regular basis – John Delamere who appointed Clare & Dickinson as his agents in London, George Shaw who appointed Milne and Parry, and Henry Stanley who appointed Shepherd & Pacey. The fact that three attorneys thought it worthwhile to visit Billericay is an indication of growth of the town between 1782 and 1821. In 1876 country attorneys and London attorneys who, by this time, were entirely independent of chambers unified under the "brand name" of "Solicitor".

The wealthy had been using coaches to convey themselves around the country for centuries but by 1747 the idea of travel between towns by stagecoach (and the delivery of post by stagecoach) had become popular. The Government, ever ready to tax people, therefore introduced a coach tax on 25 March 1747. Nothing changes!

So how were the railway companies to recoup the massive investment in building railways? It had to be by a direct assault on the stagecoach industry and the system of moving goods by horse and cart and by canal. It had to be on the transportation of goods, principally during the night, and the transportation of passengers during the day. However, in order to generate passenger revenue the Great Eastern Railway had to persuade the population of London to visit and, if possible, set up home in the towns and villages that were becoming accessible by these advancing lines of steel.

At this point some enterprising estate agents and entrepreneurs came up with a clever plan. They would go down to the towns and villages on the two rail routes between London and Southend and buy fields from farmers who, as a result of the arrival of the railways, were finding it hard to make a living. Farmers had previously been able to sell their produce in London without much competition from farmers in other parts of the country but the expanding rail network had changed all that: goods were flowing into London from areas that had previously been unable to send them there.

The fields would cost very little and could be subdivided into plots. The plots would be advertised as a cheap way of acquiring an idyllic retreat at the weekends away from the noise, smell and bustle of London. I will refer to the noise and smell later in this chapter.

The railway company would provide special excursion trains on a Sunday to all the destinations on their new railway lines: the cost of an excursion ticket for a family would be one shilling. Brewers would provide free beer for each excursion – as much as you could drink. In return the breweries would be allocated a free plot or plots for a public house on the proposed "Estate". The Great Eastern Railway, the estate agents and the public houses would all promote the excursions as a wonderful way of having an inexpensive day in the fresh air of the countryside whether or not one bought a plot.

You can imagine what happened! The families, whose parents had undoubtedly drunk too much free beer, were picked up at Billericay and other towns and villages on the routes of the new railways by a horse-drawn charabanc. They were taken to a large field that had been marked out in plots, and offered the opportunity to acquire their own little piece of the countryside. They could (at first) put whatever they wanted on their plot, whether it be a static caravan, a hut or other permanent or semi-permanent structure of some kind. The cost was initially five pounds per plot. What a brilliant idea these happy and inebriated visitors thought – their own plot in the country in somewhere like Queen's Park on the outskirts of Billericay.

The reference to the Queen in Queen's Park may well have been a reference to Queen Victoria and an allusion to her homes in Sandringham and the Isle of Wight: the name of the estate was obviously designed to impress!

The same strategy was being adopted by the rail company on the Fenchurch Street to Southend line. HW Iles, estate agents in Stratford concentrated on buying land in and around Billericay. Entrepreneurs like Richard Ramuz, for example, bought huge areas of land in the Southend area on the Fenchurch Street line. Inevitably a lot of people were tempted to buy plots and subsequently used the railways to get to them. While London prospered the plots continued to be sold.

These holiday plots are to be differentiated from the plots nearer to the centre of towns and villages that were intended to be close to community facilities and have drainage and permanent water supplies.

The rapid advance of the railway lines towards Billericay in the late 1870's and early 1880's not only affected the stagecoach companies and farmers; it also affected the owners of the Crown Inn.

By the 1870's there had been three stagecoaches a day taking passengers to London and to Rochford but as more and more towns were connected to London by rail the need for stagecoaches diminished.

By 1878 the railway lines had been laid all the way out of London to Shenfield and all the residents of Billericay needed in order to travel to London was a stagecoach from Billericay to Shenfield: 1884 saw the laying of the track between Shenfield and Billericay and the writing was on the wall for the Crown Inn.

One can also appreciate the consternation of the residents of Billericay when an army of workmen turned up to dig the huge culvert to enable the rail tracks to be extended to Wickford. The culvert cut off all road traffic – horse, cart and stagecoach – that normally travelled between Billericay and Chelmsford, the county town and principal corn and cattle market. It was only when the bridges over the culvert were built that normal travel to the north of Billericay via the High Street could be resumed.

It is sobering to reflect on the fact that the last stagecoach left Billericay for Shenfield in 1888 less than fifty years before I was born. The first goods train arrived in Billericay on 19 November 1888 and the first passenger train stopped at Billericay six weeks later on 1 January 1889.

Once the railway line had reached Billericay and had accepted passenger traffic few people would want to stay overnight as they had in the past: travelling to and from London no longer took two days. Visitors would simply travel to and from London, returning the same day. Troops no longer had to march through Billericay to Tilbury when they could be transported by train from Colchester via London.

The decision had already been taken to close the inn and the brewery and relocate the inn as a hotel to the bottom of the High Street in Stock Road close to the railway station where it would have to compete with The Railway public house to be built in 1885 on the opposite side of the road.

The arrival of the railway had also spelled the end of another lucrative source of income for the Crown Inn from the farmers in the area. Early most mornings – until the arrival of the goods train service – horses and carts would line Billericay's long High Street before setting off for London with hay. The horse population of London was vast and horses needed hay. The drivers of these horses and carts would have a beer (or two) at one of the many pubs in the High Street and the Crown would get a share of the takings.

Having had a drink and it being very early some of the drivers of the carts would climb up on to the hay and catch up on their sleep. They relied on their horse following the cart in front of it – as it would have done had the driver been sitting on the board that passed for a seat. Sometimes, however, one of the horses in the long column of carts would stray "off course": chaos ensued if the driver was asleep on the hay and there are records of magistrates in the Billericay court fining these irresponsible characters a shilling for being drunk in charge of a horse and cart!

The long line of hay wagons that regularly left Billericay for London was just one of the many that wended their way to the City. The horse population of London was huge and grew as quickly as the human population. Between 1861 and 1911 the human population of London rose from over three million to over seven million: the horse population also more than doubled.

The arrival of the railway in Billericay meant that, in future, any hay required would be transported to London by rail, thereby relieving congestion on the poorly maintained roads. Farmers in the Billericay area then had to compete on the price of hay and other produce with farmers from other parts of the country. The Crown Inn consequently lost beer sales from yet another source.

It should be borne in mind that the massive horse population in London caused immense problems. When we watch Victorian dramas on television we are looking at a sanitised fantasy world in which cobbled streets are relatively clean and we gain no impression of the smells and noise that assailed the noses and ears of our forebears.

By the early 1890's, for example, when hay started being taken up to London by goods train, London had 11,000 cabs and several thousand tramcars: the tramcars used twelve horses per day: more than 50,000 horses were needed for public transportation alone. Add all the horses required for the carriage of the food (and beer) and the personal, domestic and business commodities (including coal) that were demanded by a rapidly expanding population and you reach a figure in excess of 100,000 horses on the streets of London on a daily basis.

Each horse produced between fifteen and thirty-five pounds of manure per day and at least two pints of urine, both scattered liberally over the streets of London. Urban streets became minefields and had to be navigated with great care.

Crossing sweepers stood on street corners and for a fee they would clear a path through the manure and urine for pedestrians in dry weather. Wet weather, however, turned the streets into swamps and rivers of filth. The bottoms of women's skirts would be impregnated with manure and urine if the street was not cleared in front of them as they crossed it. Iron horseshoes on cobbles made conversation impossible on busy streets and the inescapable stench of over 200,000 pints of horse urine per day, plus the other smells of London made life there very unpleasant. The manure was, moreover, an ideal breeding ground for flies.

I will end this distasteful view of life in the City by observing that in 1894 there was the "Great Horse Manure Crisis". Writing in The Times one writer estimated that in fifty years (1944) every street in London would be buried under nine feet of horse manure! How fortunate, therefore, that the petrol combustion engine was invented at the end of the nineteenth century!

The unpleasantness and congested nature of London was a great driver behind the desire of many to enjoy fresh air and, if only for a short time, a healthier lifestyle in the countryside. When the railway companies offered these Sunday excursions there was no shortage of customers for them. Towns like Billericay had greater attractions than we can appreciate in our "smell-free" and "noise-free" society.

Unfortunately the events of the Great War and its aftermath conspired to turn these "holiday plots" in the countryside into something very different. Many plot owners had lost their lives fighting in the Great War, the influenza epidemic in 1920 had killed off many more and a large number of soldiers returned from the front to find that there were no jobs for them.

Welfare benefits were minimal and for many of the unemployed, including the widows of dead servicemen their only real asset was their modest home in London or outer London – which they were obliged to sell or vacate in order to survive. These unfortunate people often retreated, with their families to the holiday plots they had purchased in happier times and set up home in old caravans, railway carriages or whatever small and usually basic properties they could afford to put on their plots.

Where their owners had been killed in the Great War or died subsequently the abandoned plots became overgrown: the estate roads were not made up and, in the winter, turned to mud. There was no mains drainage and, in most cases (in the 1920's) no water supply. Slatted wooden boards along the sides of the unmade roads, called "duckboards," were the only means of access by foot to the dwellings on these estates. My father, who worked for the Council, took me to some of these estates, in Laindon and Pitsea in the late 1940's and, as a student, I delivered mail during the Christmas holidays to the single storey and mostly wooden dwellings on the old Queen's Park estate in Billericay between 1956 and 1958. There were no streets as such and one had to remember each property by its name and roughly where it was located in order to deliver the post to it!

In fact, between 1946 and the mid-1950's most of the roads – even on the more permanent estate developments – between the main roads in Billericay were unmade. Hillside Road, off Chapel Street, behind Waitrose and the High Street was, in 1948 a muddy track that led down to a farm at the bottom of the hill. In that year the farmer who lived there was prevailed upon to tow my father's car back up to Chapel Street with his tractor when my father let his 1936 Austin roll down the track in third gear in order to start the engine, rather than use the starting handle! The engine had started but it proved impossible to reverse up to Chapel Street because of the mud!

The street scene in Billericay has changed so materially since 1948 that it is difficult for residents in the twenty-first century to visualise how quiet and how undeveloped the town was until the electrification of the railway line in 1953 led to a massive growth surge in the population of the area and the adoption by the local authority of all the side roads.

As for the "holiday plots" these have all disappeared from Billericay and from the Basildon District: the steadily rising value of land and the construction of the new town of Basildon from 1951 onwards has seen to that.

Echoes of these plots remain, however, in the restrictions and stipulations that appear on the registered titles of many properties but, those apart, there is little to remind us of the development of the town in the late nineteenth and twentieth centuries.

19

Billerica, Massachusetts

In the autumn of 1973 Albert ("Bertie") Quirk of "Abbotswood", Norsey Road, Billericay, was leaning on the handrail of a Nile cruise ship, looking out over the river, when he started to chat to a friendly American tourist in his fifties who happened to be standing next to him.

"What part of America do you come from?" asked Bertie. "I come from Massachusetts," the American replied. "I can tell you are British. What part of England do you come from?" "I come from Essex," said Bertie. "A place called Billericay, some twenty five miles from London. "Good God," said the American. "I come from Billerica." And so, from that coincidental meeting arose my connection with Billerica!

Bertie was my sister Angela's father-in-law and he passed on to me the name and address of the friendly American: his name was Gordon Brainerd and he was a selectman, the equivalent of a town councillor in Billericay, and a leading citizen in the town. He lived in a period property in Concord Road, Billerica.

I had not previously heard of Billerica and my curiosity was aroused. How could it be that there was a town in America with an almost identical name? What was the connection? I would have to find out and the easiest way of doing so would be to fly to Massachusetts and visit Billerica. In view of the fact that I was a director of a travel agency at the time there would be no problem in organising the flights, the car hire and the hotel accommodation. But, apart from finding out how Billerica got its name and how it compared with Billericay, there would, I felt, have to be some additional point to any visit. Not only would I, hopefully, be able to convey greetings from Bertie and his wife to Gordon Brainerd I would also be able to research the historic links between the two towns and, as a member of Rotary International, visit the Rotary club of Billerica for lunch!

Because of my work commitments any such trip would have to be brief, but I would just be able to fit it in between the Monday luncheon meetings of my own Rotary club. The plan I formulated would be to fly to Boston on Tuesday, hire a car and drive the twenty or so miles to Billerica, stay at a hotel in the town or nearby, visit the council offices, library and local museum on Wednesday or Thursday, meet Gordon Brainerd, attend the Rotary lunch on Friday and fly back on Saturday.

I was motivated by my sense of humour to fit the visit between the Monday luncheon meetings of my own club. The established custom in Rotary is that if one visits a club in another country as a guest one should present one's own club banner to the host club. In turn the host club presents one of its own banners to the visiting Rotarian who passes it on to his own club. Billericay club and many other clubs attach these overseas banners to large display boards or tableaux and put them on display during meetings to emphasise the international nature of Rotary. I could visualise the surprise and possible confusion of members of my own club if I were to present it with a banner from Billerica, Massachusetts when only a week previously I had been lunching with my fellow Rotarians. But when could I do this?

1974 had been a turbulent year for me as a result of the disruption caused by our divorce and the need to find new homes but the opportunity to put my plan into action arose in 1975. I wrote to the Secretary of the Billerica Rotary club early that year, telling him about Bertie's chance meeting with Gordon Brainerd and asking when would be the best date for a visit. He replied that the club luncheon on Friday, 2nd May would be an ideal date because the club was presenting a new flag to the town and that many selectmen, including Gordon Brainerd, would be in attendance. The presentation would take place, moreover, at the Manning Manse Tavern, a timbered building erected in 1696 and used for special occasions: it was a very well-known historic eating house in North Billerica.

I therefore wrote to Gordon Brainerd introducing myself and telling him of my interest in Billerica and how delighted I would be to meet him at the Rotary lunch and pass on greetings from Bertie and his wife. Very much to my surprise he had, on receipt of my letter, taken it upon himself to persuade the Board of Selectmen to make an official presentation to me at the luncheon. So, from being an inquisitive casual visitor from England I would become representative of Billericay, a guest of the town and part of the presentation ceremony! He also contacted the local historical society on my behalf telling them of the reason for my visit!

But I was not to know this when I checked into the Burlington Holiday Inn on Route 3, at the Massachusetts turnpike, just outside Billerica on Tuesday 29th April. The lunch was three days hence and my task in the intervening two days would be to compare the two towns, investigate the historic link between them and look around the area. You can imagine my surprise early the next morning when the first road sign I saw in the centre of Billerica read "Chelmsford – 9 miles" – exactly the same as in Billericay!

I quickly discovered that Billerica, which covers an area of 26.4 square miles, is divided, like Gaul, into three parts! These are the south of Billerica, known as Pinehurst, "central" Billerica, known as Billerica Center, and North Billerica. Within the boundaries of the town there are also a number of defined residential and commercial areas.

The drive into central Billerica from the Burlington Holiday Inn took me through Pinehurst and, although I did not visit it at the time, I subsequently became aware of the claim to fame of this part of the town. It boasts what was, in the seventeenth century, called "Nutten's or Nutting's pond" but what is now known as Nutting Lake. It is not an ordinary lake and it is certainly not a "pond" in the accepted sense of the word. It covers seventy-eight acres and put Billerica on the map as a tourist and holiday destination for decades.

The average depth of the lake is five feet with a maximum depth of twelve feet. Until the 1970's the water in it was so clear that one could see the bottom. It is bisected by the Middlesex turnpike and has a larger west basin and a smaller east basin. It currently has and always has had a beach now called the Micozzi Beach on the north side of the east basin and is surrounded by trees. For this reason it became, for nearly a hundred years, a popular weekend resort for Bostonians who could access it by road or rail, picnic by the beach, stay in wooden cabins dotted among the trees, or just swim, sail or sunbathe during the summer. It was literally on the doorstep of Boston and the city dwellers could relax in the countryside in tranquil and idyllic surroundings. In its heyday festivities at the lake, particularly on 4 July, were crowd-pulling events. It is still popular and offers swimming, sailing, canoeing, fishing and many other sporting and recreational facilities.

The wooden cabins have now disappeared, however, and among the trees there are now expensive residential properties. On the north shore where there was once an Indian settlement, the site of which is known as Indian Hill and with which John Nutten once traded, there are now Colonial, Dutch and ranch style houses.

One can readily understand why since the 1960's the area has become sought after as a place to live. It is easy to access, being less than a mile east of the Northwest expressway (Route 3) which joins interstate roads leading directly to the north and more importantly straight into Boston in the south. It is only a couple of miles south of the shops in central Billerica and close to the many shopping malls and plazas in Burlington.

The fact that Pinehurst is a couple of miles from the shops in central Billerica will give the reader an idea of how spread out the town is. Whereas houses and shops in England are invariably built close to each other, apart from "out of town" retail parks, there are considerable gaps between most buildings in Billerica whether they be houses, shops, offices or factories. The overriding impression is one of space.

The only part of Billerica to which this does not apply is the area around the common in the centre of the town. The common itself is very attractive, with its bandstand, naval cannon, soldiers' monument and town flagpole. Down the west side of the common are a number of important or historic buildings, including, amongst others, the Bennett Public Library, the First Parish Unitarian Church, the Masonic Temple, and the Town Hall. On the south side of the common is the Clara Sexton house, built in 1723 and left to the Billerica Historical Society by its former owner, Clara Sexton in 1936. It now houses the town's museum.

My first port of call was the Town Hall where I was surprised to find that Billerica had a population almost the same size as Billericay. Because of the space between buildings this was not immediately apparent: minimum lot sizes in 1975 ranged from a minimum of 30,000 to 45,000 square feet. The town had one main shopping centre, the Billerica Mall, and two smaller centres, the Treble Cove Plaza in North Billerica and the Town Plaza in Pinehurst, all located on Route 3. The population of Billerica in 1975 was nearly 36,000, very much the same as Billericay and the highest point in the town was 316 feet above sea level compared with St. Mary Magdalen church in Billericay high street which is, I believe, approximately 322 feet above sea level!

The Boston & Maine Rail Road has a station at North Billerica which takes commuters into Boston some twenty miles away in much the same way as trains from Billericay take commuters into London some twenty five miles away. North Billerica also has a thriving commercial area with a large number of factories and head offices of substantial American companies. They have been attracted to Billerica because they have space in which to expand plus the benefit of easy access to major highways and the city of Boston.

Having come to the conclusion that the two towns were very similar in terms of population and composition I determined to find out more about the way in which Billericay acquired its name and what links, if any, existed between them. Although Christopher Martin and his family came from Billericay and had sailed on the Mayflower (probably the "May Flower") to America in 1620 they had not survived long enough to set foot on American soil and it had been left to later settlers to petition the court in Cambridge, Massachusetts in 1654 for a change in the name of the former Indian settlement, known as Shawshin, to Billericay. Their petition was granted in 1655 during the period that Oliver Cromwell was Lord Protector in England. Not long afterwards, however, the petitioners or their successors carelessly lost the "y" and the town has been Billerica ever since!

Fourteen settlers signed the petition and it is clear that at least four or five of them, including a Ralph Hill and a George Farley had emigrated from Billericay, which embraced Great and Little Burstead, and had persuaded the others to adopt the name of their home town when they colonised the area. My own suspicion is that William French who arrived in America in 1635, with his wife Elizabeth and four young children, as a servant of Roger and Eliza Harlakenden was also born in Great Burstead: the French family are still farmers in Great Burstead and Bert French from Great Burstead bears an uncanny likeness to Josiah French whose portrait appears in Hazens History of Billerica. Moreover, there is no trace of William French or his family in the area from which he is said to have emigrated!

They say that time and tide wait for no man and so, during Wednesday and Thursday, I visited the Town Hall, the town library and the museum and also paid fleeting visits to Lexington, Concord and Old Sturbridge village, intending to visit the outlying area more thoroughly when I returned to Massachusetts. Old Sturbridge village, being an excellent recreation of a typical New England village of the 1800s, merited much more time and attention than I could give it at the time.

Friday came around very quickly and I headed off to the Manning Manse Tavern, the meeting place chosen by the Rotary club for the presentation. The tavern had originally been a "garrison house" in colonial days when neighbouring farmers gathered together in times of stress for mutual protection. In 1696, when Indian outbreaks were still to be feared, Samuel Manning had built his sturdy and well-protected home by the Chelmsford road. By popular request he had not only provided shelter in times of danger but had also served meals to travellers. The Manning family had, so far as I could tell, been serving meals ever since!

On arrival I was greeted by Dick Corsetti, the President of the Billerica Rotary club, and by Gordon Brainerd not just as a visiting Rotarian but as "the guest of honor." I felt a slight sense of unease at being greeted in this way. "Why am I the guest of honor?" I thought to myself!

The Billerica town flag was duly presented at noon by Dick Corsetti to Michael Rea, the chairman of the Board of Selectmen and his fellow selectmen, Gordon Brainerd and George Gracie, in the presence of members of the Bicentennial Commission. It had been designed by a Mr. Nicola(s) Micozzi whose family name is associated with the beach at Nutting Lake and had been approved at a town meeting in 1972. The flag that had been commissioned by the Billerica Rotary Club was about seven feet wide and about five feet deep.

The design of the flag, which has been used for all subsequent flags, is impressive. It incorporates three vertical panels, two emerald green with a broader white panel between them. Imposed on the white central panel is a large shield in gold, outlined in black. On the shield is a large oak tree in the centre of which appears a representation of the shape of Billerica in green. The branches of the tree go beyond the representation of the town to the edges of the shield. On top of the green is superimposed a gold scroll, at the bottom of which is the name of the town in black on white and in the top left-hand corner of which is the date 1655. Above "Billerica" is a representation of a church steeple which extends above the shield giving the central white band a feeling of balance, given that the scroll is angled to the left.

The symbolism is explained thus. The oak tree represents Billerica's oldest "resident", having stood within the boundaries of the town for many centuries. George Washington is said to have rested in the shade of this particular tree, now called "the Washington Oak", when he stopped in Billerica on 5th November 1789 on his way back to New York after a tour of Connecticut, Massachusetts, New Hampshire and Maine. The date 1655 is, of course, the year in which the petition to change the name of the town was approved and the steeple is that of the fourth Meeting House built in 1789. The steeple survived a subsequent fire within the Meeting House and the entire building was completely restored in 1970: the steeple represents the past and the present of the town. I was to become very familiar indeed with the design of this flag, as I will explain later in this chapter.

After the lunch following the flag ceremony I duly presented my Billericay Rotary club banner and received one in return. I also received a scroll upon which were inscribed greetings from the Billerica club to my own, which I delivered on the following Monday. So far, so good! I was just about to sit down when Michael Rea rose and presented me with a Stock Certificate for $200 worth of Billerica Town Stock! As he handed it to me he whispered, but loud enough for everyone to hear, "Don't try to cash this!!" I assured him that I would not and had it framed to remind me of this, the first of many visits! There then followed presentations to myself of a Billerica Medallion (1776-1976) from the Bicentennial Commission and a volume of Hazen's "History of Billerica", published in 1883, from the Billerica Historical Society. It was all very unexpected and somewhat overwhelming.

After the presentations I had an opportunity to talk to Gordon Brainerd and passed on Bertie's kindest regards and best wishes. Gordon was obviously an extremely kind and charming person and held in high regard by everyone. He invited me back to his home for the rest of the afternoon, an offer I gladly accepted. It transpired that he was a great anglophile and proud owner of a three-litre Jaguar (pronounced "Jag-yew-arrh") which he lent me on a subsequent visit. He said he had connections going back to English emigrants in the 1630s and I promised to find out more about his ancestry when I returned to the UK. He insisted that, if I ever came back to Billerica, I should stay with him and this was the beginning of a long friendship. Both I, my two sons and a lady friend I took to Massachusetts, stayed with him in subsequent years and enjoyed the hospitality of Brainerd's "bed and breakfast", as he called it. It was on my visit with the lady friend in 1985 that she and I encountered the ghostly manifestation at his house, which I describe later in this chapter.

On my return I did indeed go to the Essex Records Office in Chelmsford and to Braintree town hall to check on Gordon's ancestry. It transpired that Daniel Brainerd was born in or near Braintree in Essex. He is said, in the Brainerd genealogy, to have been "stolen" from his native town "at about eight years of age and brought to America. He was "sold for his passage" to a William Wadsworth who, with his wife and four young children and young Daniel, emigrated to Hartford, Connecticut. The terms of sale were that he "be learned (taught) to read and write" and be given his freedom and "two suits of clothes" at twenty one years of age. His name and those of William Wadsworth and family appear in the passenger list of "The Lyon" which sailed to Boston in 1632.

It is clear that Daniel was Gordon's English ancestor. Further research revealed that, on gaining his freedom, Daniel moved to Haddam, Connecticut, became a highly respected member of his local community and married three times. By his first wife he had a son, William, who produced five grandsons and two granddaughters. They, in turn, generated over hundreds of descendants during the next three centuries, of whom Gordon was one! As far as his English ancestry was concerned I concluded that Daniel's mother was probably a lady by the name of Mary Northey, a widow who married a Thomas Branwood in Coggeshall in 1624. The surnames Branwood, Braynerd, Brainerd, Brainard, Brainwood and several other versions of what must have been the same family name appear in the parish records of the time. Because few of the parishioners could read or write their own names, semi-illiterate parish clerks wrote their names in the records as they were pronounced. Gordon, whose family were known to have come from Haddam, Connecticut, was delighted with my findings and I promised to visit him again in 1980.

Hazen's "History of Billerica", the weighty tome presented to me at the Rotary lunch, turned out to be a fascinating read: it was only when I dipped into it that I realised previous contact had been made between Billericay and Billerica in the 1870's. Although the citizens of Billerica had rather forgotten their connection to what might be considered their "mother" town in the eighteenth century, their interest had been aroused in the nineteenth century when, following the Centennial of the American War of Independence in 1776, the Reverend Edward G. Porter, from Lexington, visited Billericay in 1879. Like Henry Hazen I quote from his account of the visit.

"From London the journey is accomplished by rail on the Great Eastern line as far as Brentwood, (nineteen miles,) and then by the carriage road, a pleasant drive of about five miles. The roads are well made and well kept. Heaps of hammered stone may be seen at intervals, piled up in regular order, for use upon the road as occasion may require."

After a number of rapturous comments about the English countryside the Reverend Porter states that his carriage left the main road to Colchester "at a small hamlet called Shenfield, where there is a church, a shop, and two old taverns still bearing their ancient names of 'The Green Dragon and The Eagle and Child.'"

On arrival in Billericay he notes that "the High Street is "macadamized" and well-lit with gas, that in 1830 the population was about 2000 but that it had "fallen off since then, owing to the loss of the silk-weaving and coaching interests, which for a long period contributed much to the prosperity of the place."

He mentions that "the introduction of railroads was a blow to the ancient prosperity" of the town, being "left at a distance of several miles from the Great Eastern line. The brisk and profitable traffic which formerly passed directly through the town was thus diverted. The oldtime inns at which the coaches and teams stopped daily, may still be seen, though most of them are shorn of their glory."

Hazen's insertion in his book of the quite comprehensive record of the Reverend Porter's visit to Billericay reawakened interest in the town at the time and reminded the people of Billericay of their original links with the mother country. Although, doubtless, many other Americans visited the Essex area in the 1880s and 1890s the next recorded account we have of a visit to Billericay is that of Martha Hill Sage in 1898: I leave her to explain the reason for her visit in her own words.

"In the car which conveyed me from London to Billericay (probably a first class compartment on a Great Eastern train to Rochford and Southend) I met Colonel Brydges Branfil who told me that he had served in the English army in India thirty years and was now retired and living at Burghstead Lodge on the main street in Billericay." (This was the home of Basil Brookes and his wife who were killed in the Comet air disaster and is now part of Billericay public library).

"I told him I was a lineal descendant of Ralph Hill, one of the incorporators of my town, and that doubtless the American Billericay derived its name from the probable home of the first Ralph Hill here. And I was probably the first descendant of Ralph to visit his adorable English home.

"The Colonel was a most instructive travelling companion telling me many incidents of the route. As we crossed a little stream he said: 'This is the River Rom and the place is called Romford, so Dartford, Deptford, Wickford have derived their names and many other English towns, from being built around the ford of the rivers like Dart, Dept, Wick, etc.' He pointed out the spires of several Norman churches, built of English oak which, he said, were 800 years old. He showed me the wooded park belonging to Lord Petre who owns most of the land in and around Billericay. I have read that the first Lord Petre lived three hundred years ago and did not lose any of his landed property by confiscation by the Crown but kept on increasing it during the reigns of the Tudor sovereigns. His conscience, being as elastic as rubber, he was Protestant and Catholic by turns so as not to lose his landed property.

"A bit of water by the road was spoken of as being the only water in Billericay (this is probably the weir pond that existed in the Laindon Road at the rear of the Rising Sun). When the jubilee for the recovery of the Prince of Wales (the future King Edward VII) took place Colonel Branfil wished the event to be commemorated by placing curbing around the water on the road side: he was in the minority, and so, the village had a feast instead.(!!)

"How our English cousins would enjoy our beautiful Shawsheen and Concord Rivers for their eastern and western mounds, and what delight they would experience in boating and fishing and gathering lilies, had they our Nutting and Winning ponds."

She goes on to describe Great Burstead church in some detail and finishes her account by saying, "I sincerely hope, should any daughter of the English Billericay come to our town to see our things, that she may receive as kindly attention as I did from the Branfil family, the landlady of the Red Lion and others."

I could not let the generosity of everyone in Billerica go unacknowledged and when I returned to Billerica in April 1980 I took with me copies of maps of Essex from the Essex Records Office and a copy of the 1777 Chapman and Andre map of Billericay for presentation to the Billerica town council. For Gordon I took out a number of small china miniatures of the type of timber framed houses one finds in places like Coggeshall: I gave them to him to remind him of his Essex ancestry: he was so pleased to receive them and proudly displayed them on a shelf in his living room.

When I turned up at the town hall to hand the map of Billericay over I was politely told that I would have to come back the following evening at 7pm when Thomas Conway, the Town Clerk would be available to receive it. When I arrived the following evening I was confounded to discover that over eighty people, the town's top citizens, were in the council chamber!! Gordon had obviously been busy! I handed over the Billericay map and, in return, I was handed another copy of Hazen, inscribed by all the selectmen, and numerous reports and documents relating to the administration of the town. Since I already had a copy of Hazen I told the assembled gathering that I would present it to the Billericay Archaeological and Historical Society and the administrative documentation to Basildon Council. From that point onward things rather took off and I found myself acting as "unofficial diplomat" between Billericay and Billerica for many years thereafter.

It was during this visit in April 1980 that Gordon took me to Concord and Lexington to meet the Episcopalian minister for the Parish. I had expressed my interest in learning more about the reasons for the War of Independence. What the minister told me was revealing. He had seen the diary of the vicar of Bedford who, on the very day in April 1775 that the shot "heard round the world" was fired, wrote that he hoped the militiamen farmers who had gathered at the Buckman Tavern in Lexington would not get too drunk and do something they would regret.

The farmers knew that a detachment of Redcoats was on its way to Concord and Lexington to search for weapons, which they would confiscate. Because the soldiers were British and the settlers were British the officers in charge of these searches did not want to stir up trouble and usually sent someone ahead to make sure that no weapons were found. Unfortunately, the Redcoats were not able to do so on this occasion and had had to wade through one of the local rivers before arriving in Lexington. They were drawn up on the village green, feeling wet, hungry and fed up and awaiting orders from the officer in charge.

On hearing the Redcoats arrive one of the drunken farmers apparently left the tavern with his musket, squatted down behind a stone wall and took a "pot shot" at one of them. The bullet hit one of the soldiers in the wrist and, although the officer shouted that no one should return fire, the Redcoat standing next to the one who had been injured lifted his musket and fired back.

I am not sure, in the circumstances, which of the two shots "was heard round the world" – an incident that presaged the beginning of the American War of Independence, but it was probably that of the drunken militiaman farmer!

The background to all this was the resentment of the colonists at having to pay taxes to the British Government to cover, among other things, the cost of retaining troops on American soil once the threat of a French invasion had been removed. The French were in the north in Canada and in the south in Louisiana and had intended to build a line of forts between their two colonies that would hem in the British colonists and confine them to the eastern seaboard of America.

However, the defeat of Montcalm by Wolfe at Quebec and the success of the British in naval engagements with the French in the Atlantic and elsewhere had removed the threat of encirclement and the colonists did not relish paying further taxes to London if they could not have a say in how they were spent.

"No taxation without representation" became the cry. It was quite an understandable attitude given that the colonists were precluded from electing and sending members of Parliament to Westminster and the British government was short sighted in failing to acknowledge the genuine grievances of the colonists in this respect. It was an enlightening conversation and put subsequent history into quite a different perspective.

During my visit in April 1980 Gordon also introduced me to Professor Charles ("Charlie") Stearns whose distant ancestor, John Stearns, was one of the fourteen colonists to sign the petition to change the name of Shawshin to Billericay. Professor Stearns was the undisputed authority on the history of the town and he kindly invited me to dinner with his wife, Helen, and his daughters, Kate and Jeremie, to discuss Hazen's book and the links between our two towns and our two countries. He was aware, for example, that the citizens of Billerica had contributed in 1940 to a "Spitfire Fund" to help finance production of the famous fighter aircraft that had been at the forefront of the Battle of Britain. He wrote to me shortly after our first meeting setting out what he knew about the lives of a number of the fourteen petitioners and added, to my surprise, a postscript which read as follows: "And take care of Hill House. My Dad's correspondent was Mrs. Alice Cater." His father had corresponded with the lady in whose house I lived! That was quite a coincidence and a link with Billerica of which I had previously been unaware!

On my return to England I contacted the Billericay Archaeological and

Historical Society and made a formal presentation of "Hazen" to its Chairman, Donald Jarvis. I also presented all the administrative documentation from Billerica town council to Cliff Jones, the chairman of Basildon District Council. When I mentioned that I intended to return to Billerica with my children in August 1980 I was asked by both if I would take back gifts on behalf of them both. The Archaeological and Historical Society wished me to present to the Billerica Historical Society a fragment of a Roman mortarium that had been excavated in 1971 at a site now covered by extensions to Billericay school and the council wanted me to present an engraved Basildon District shield to Billerica Town Council. I was also asked to take a large greetings card signed by all the members of the Billericay Rotary club to their counterparts in Billerica. A mortarium, incidentally, is a bowl used in the preparation of food and was probably introduced into Britain by the Roman Army. It had a characteristic form with grit embedded in the inner surface to assist in grinding the food and usually had two spouts. Mortaria were usually white or cream being made from clay relatively free from iron: this particular mortarium had probably been made in Colchester, thirty miles away, in the latter half of the second century AD. It had been mounted on a wooden base and I prepared an attractive explanatory card so that it could, if desired, be displayed under glass as a historical artefact in a corner of the public library.

When, as a member of the Brentwood School scout troop I had applied for a passport for my very first trip abroad I had written "student" as my occupation in it. When, however, I applied for my second passport I had put down "travel agent" as my occupation. Because I looked younger than my years the word "student" had been useful in obtaining discounts for a relatively impecunious articled clerk and the words "travel agent" even more so. When I turned up at Heathrow with my two young sons for our flight to Boston and our three-week holiday on the east side of America, I asked the young lady clerk at the check-in desk whether there was any possibility of a free upgrade. I explained that my travel agencies at Shenfield and Chelmsford were IATA members, that we sold a large number of PanAm tickets (true) and that our tickets had been issued by my Shenfield office.

I have always operated on the principle that if one does not ask, one does not get! The clerk looked at the expectant faces of my thirteen-year-old and eleven-year-old sons and smiled. "I do not see why not. I am upgrading you free of charge to first class"! Without further ado we were ushered into the top deck of the Boeing 747 Jumbo jet where I and my sons were pampered throughout the entire flight by two very attractive air hostesses. Although I have never flown first class again this I thought is certainly the way to travel! I sat next to a Saudi-Arabian Sheikh who wore full robes and headdress. He was most impressed that I had, so far as he was aware, paid first class fares for my two sons when he had put his wife, or wives, and children in economy class! We must have played our parts well because he never realised that I was a travel agent who had, surprisingly and fortuitously, been rewarded for selling the airline's tickets!

Within a couple of hours of landing in Boston we boarded a flight to Washington and, on arrival, rented a car. We drove to Alexandria in Virginia which we made our base for a week. I have written about our strange experience in Virginia in an earlier chapter. After Alexandria, Washington and a trip to Luray in the Blue Ridge mountains we flew to Buffalo in order to visit the Niagara Falls and cross into Canada for a short time. It had been my intention to drive to Toronto during our full day in Canada, but my sons prevailed on me to stop "en route" and let them spend a few minutes at a "go cart" track. The few minutes turned into two hours and I had to abandon my idea of visiting the CN Tower. I had a gut feeling I could not explain that I should have pressed on to Toronto. Perhaps I was destined to meet Annette, my future wife, there. Fanciful perhaps, but it transpired that our paths had already crossed fleetingly in London some years previously although neither of us had attached any significance to the fact at the time. The meeting had registered in my memory, although not in hers, and it was only when we discussed the incident during our marriage that I could be certain it was her. From Buffalo we took a flight back to Boston where I rented another car for our week in Billerica and New England.

I had told Gordon when I stayed with him in April that I hoped to return to Billerica in early August with my two young sons. He had insisted that if I did so we must be his guests: there was no need to book accommodation in a local hotel. He would be delighted to have us stay in his home. He had written to me in July, however, to say that, as a result of an unexpectedly long trip to Australia and St. Lucia, Jacquie, his second wife, from whom he was estranged, would be returning to Billerica at roughly the same time as we were due to arrive.

The reason for her return was to finalise their divorce settlement and it would not be ideal for him, or comfortable for us, to be staying with him while possibly difficult negotiations took place. Gordon had previously been happily married to his first wife, Helen, a pillar of the local First Unitarian Church, for many years and, like many lonely widowers, had decided to remarry. If he had succumbed to loneliness on Helen's death and married for company then I can understand how he must have felt, having experienced living on my own, albeit with my two young sons, for many years. It would appear that his second marriage had not been as happy or successful as he and Jacquie had expected or hoped, and they had decided to go their separate ways.

If she should appear while we were staying with him Gordon promised to find alternative accommodation for us. In the event we spent three very happy days with him, my sons being particularly impressed by his double door refrigerator the like of which they had never seen in England at the time: it was massive!

Once again I had taken Gordon miniature china Tudor houses, also a number of wooden items purchased at craft fairs in the Billericay area. These craft fairs were populated almost entirely by amateur, part-time craftsmen and women who had converted a relaxing hobby into a profitable sideline. On retirement and wanting to do something with their spare time they had taken up woodwork, metalcraft, making pottery of various types and creating items out of wicker, cloth and straw. Some, in fact, had started their hobby pre-retirement while they had full time jobs, many in the City of London, as a way of relieving the pressures and stress of the commercial environments in which they worked. I knew quite a few of these people through my involvement in the leisure exhibitions I had organised for the local community. In addition to a number of impressive polished oak doorstops which are always useful I had taken him a "dibber" with which he was totally fascinated! It was the name of the implement as much as its function. I doubt whether he ever used it!

The imminent arrival of Jacquie led to our evacuation from the Brainerd household. But, true to his promise, Gordon had previously had a word with Professor Charles Stearns, the Chairman of the Billerica Historical Society, with whom I had been in correspondence since April. As a result we moved seamlessly into the home of Charles and Helen Stearns who were also pleased to look after us for the remaining four days of our stay. I had anticipated a possible "relocation" and took a number of Wedgwood china items to the United States which I was able to give to Helen and Charles Stearns and their daughters, Kate and Jeremie. Mrs. Helen Stearns had produced a lovely meal when I went to dinner with them in April and I also gave her a splendid casserole dish with which she was delighted. She wrote subsequently to say that "it sat in pristine glory on the pantry shelf, too clean to be abused. I cannot make up my mind which daughter will be the lucky one!" This was not quite what I intended and, hopefully, it did "see service" later! Charles Stearns indicated that his younger daughter, Jeremie, would be pleased to accompany us on our visits to Lexington, Concord, Sturbridge Village and the Plimoth Plantation during our stay and she proved to be a kind and thoughtful companion to my two sons when I, for example, visited the Billerica Rotary Club for lunch for a second time and attended the civic reception at which the presentations were made.

At the well-attended civic reception the engraved shield from Basildon Council was duly presented to Paul Talbot, the Town Manager of Billerica Town Council. At the request of Charles Stearns, the Chairman of the Billerica Historical Society, the mortarium, a gift to the society, was handed to the Chief Librarian of the Public Library to be placed on display in the library on permanent loan from the society. Both items were received with genuine thanks and appreciation and undoubtedly reinforced interest in and links between Billerica and Basildon District of which Billericay is part. I was later to see the mortarium on display, as intended, in the public library when I visited Billerica in 1985.

In return I received two framed aerial colour photographs of central Billerica, one for Basildon Council and the other for the Cater Museum. I had previously suggested the photos in correspondence with Paul Talbot and had also promised him that I would not return too frequently on "official visits" lest the representative organisations in the two towns run out of things to present to each other! In addition to the engraved shield, mortarium and greetings from the Billericay Rotary Club I had taken Essex Police insignia and a message of greetings from George Manning, the police inspector at Billericay, to the head of the Billerica P.D. The insignia were presented to the Chief of Police resulting, much to the delight of my two sons, in their being taken out for a couple of hours in a patrol car with two "gun toting" policemen. This proved to be one of the highlights of their holiday!

Shortly after I arrived back in Billericay the aerial photographs were presented to Ted Wright, the Curator of the Cater Museum and Cliff Jones, the Chairman of Basildon Council. As a result of the press publicity given to my April and August visits I received a stream of requests from people and organisations asking to be put in touch with their counterparts. I accordingly initiated contacts between the editor of the Billerica Minuteman, Cromwell J. Schubarth, Junior, a name one would be unlikely to forget (!) and the editors of the Billericay Gazette and the Basildon Recorder, between teachers in American and British schools with a view to collaborative art projects and pen-pal schemes, between selectmen, like Gordon Brainerd himself, and councillors in Basildon, like Councillor Horace Wilkins, between radio hams in the two towns and so on. During the next seven or eight years I hosted many citizens from Billerica when they visited Billericay, including Lieutenant Richard Strunk of the Billerica PD and his wife Barbara. A number, including Jeremie Stearns and one of Gordon's sons, stayed with me and my sons and I also acted as a conduit for messages and correspondence between residents of Billericay and Billerica. In fact, I had quite a busy time as an unofficial diplomat.

During my visit to Billerica in 1975 I was one of the few people who had taken a photo of the Billerica town flag. I did not think much about it at the time but when I returned in August 1980 I did wonder why there was no sign of a town flag anywhere. I made enquiries of one of the local Rotarians who told me that the original had been placed on the flagpole on the common on 4th July, Independence Day 1975, about two months after my visit, and had disappeared overnight. It had never been recovered.

I mentioned this in correspondence with Gordon in 1982 and he wrote back to me as follows: "About the town flag, you seem to know more about it than I did. Apparently, a replacement flag of smaller than original size was acquired some time after the 1975 disappearance date. The replacement flag (3 feet by 5 feet, it is thought) was in or at the public library much of the time and is believed to have been last flown on the common on Memorial Day, May 30, 1981 when, apparently, it was stolen. There are no current moves that I know of to replace it." This latter comment gave me an idea.

I had taken a photo of the flag and was aware that the flag makers to the Royal Family, Piggott Brothers, had a factory near Ongar, less than twenty miles from Billericay. I decided, in the circumstances, to ask the Queen's flag makers to produce two "Billerica flags" for me, one to replace the flag stolen from the flagpole on the common in July 1975 and another which would be mounted and framed for internal display. Hopefully the framed flag would not be stolen if it was attached to a wall in the public library or in the Town Hall!

I also commissioned water colour paintings of the churches at Great Burstead and Little Burstead from a well-known local artist, Joan Harvey, which I would donate to the Clara Sexton Museum, thereby reinforcing the links of the original settlers from Billericay with their birthplace.

Piggotts, as one might expect, were extremely efficient and produced for me an impressive nine foot by five foot six inch flag in superior quality nylon and wool bunting with the symbol of Billerica on both sides and a three foot by two foot presentation flag in superior quality satin with a screen printed design on one side only. By mid-1983 I had both flags and set about having the satin presentation flag suitably mounted and framed. I approached my friend Richard Sims, a Director of Killby & Gayford, joinery specialists, whose company fitted out banks and had, incidentally, provided the counters for my three travel agencies, and asked him for his assistance. He willingly agreed to assist and produced a very solid and attractive glass-fronted case for it. When I visited Billerica twenty-five years later the case was attached to the wall of the council chamber and looked as good as new, a tribute to the quality of his company's workmanship. By this time I had also received the paintings from Joan Harvey.

I wrote to Gordon at the end of 1983 telling him what I had done and asked him to keep the gifts a secret until I could finalise the date of my next visit to Billerica: it was not possible, at that point in time, to do so. I had intended to take the flags and the paintings out to Billerica in 1984 but commitments to my sons, to my work and to the various clubs, societies and organisations to which I belonged made it impossible to pinpoint a week during which a visit could take place. For example, Chris and Alex, being seventeen and fifteen years old respectively, had to sit important college/school exams in May and June and needed my support, encouragement and presence at home for the first six months of the year while they studied for them.

In the circumstances I wrote to Gordon telling him that, if he considered it appropriate, I would include in a seven-day holiday I planned to take in Boston with a lady friend at the end of May 1985 a visit to Billerica: the flags could then be presented to the town on the tenth anniversary of the original presentation.

Gordon wrote back and said that Memorial Day, 27 May 1985, would be an excellent date for a presentation, that we should forget about Boston and spend the week with him: he would be delighted to offer us the hospitality of his home for our holiday. I accepted his kind offer with thanks and in a subsequent letter in April 1985 he told me that the "wheels were in motion" for the presentation of my flags on Memorial Day. "Officials and various organisation representatives will be in attendance," he wrote, "as will many town citizens, veterans and probably the High School band and Police Honor Guard. Let us hope it doesn't rain as it did last year."

In his letter he went on to say, "I should prepare you for one thing. A couple of years ago a new organisation was formed and named the Billerica Avenue of Flags. With contributions from businesses and individuals it has acquired dozens of American, state and town flags which it displays on certain holidays on every utility pole in the Billerica Center area and in other places. So when you stand on the town hall steps and make your presentation you will be looking at scads of flags in every direction. This won't detract in any way from the effectiveness of your flag and its reception with sincere appreciation by everyone. I expect your flag will end up being the town's flag and will take its place on the main flagpole on the common after Memorial Day.". That was unexpected news, but I hoped that, notwithstanding this development, my efforts would be appreciated. And I am pleased to say that they were.

Gordon picked up my lady friend, Barbara, and me from Boston airport and drove us back to his home. For the next week he looked after us incredibly well. He took us to lunch with the Mayor of Rockport, famous for its clam chowders, and drove us out to historic Salem for the day. He could not have been a better host even though he was working and attending, at the same time, to his civic responsibilities as a selectman. The only sad news he broke to me on arrival in Billerica was that Helen Stearns had been tragically killed in a car accident in 1983. Charlie Stearns had not told me about her death and would be in Ireland researching his Irish ancestry with his daughters, Kate and Jeremie, when I was in Billerica. There would, unfortunately, be no opportunity to meet them and express personal condolences to them on their loss.

Memorial Day came round quickly. It was a dry and sunny day and several hundred citizens turned out for it. I was, to my surprise, appointed an honorary parade marshal! Gordon complained to me humorously that, in all his years as a selectman he had never been made one! When I handed over the flags at the beginning of the Memorial Day ceremony I was asked to say a few words. I explained that by a fateful coincidence I had decided on the spur of the moment to fly over to Billerica and visit the Billerica Rotary Club and had arrived on the very day the town flag was being presented by the club to the

Board of Selectmen. When I returned in 1980 I discovered that the flag had been stolen from the flag pole on the common on 4th July 1975, some weeks, I hastened to add, after I had left town! I decided to replace the flag by having one manufactured in England to the original design by the Queen's flag makers and here it was. I said that, to my surprise the town had already produced dozens of town flags and, on reflection, I should have guessed that they would have done so in the ten years since the original was stolen. I hoped nevertheless that the flags I had commissioned, one for the flagpole and the other for display in the council offices, would be accepted as a token of my sincere feelings of goodwill and as a reminder of the historic link between the towns of Billerica, Massachusetts, and Billericay, Essex. I also carried a message from the Youth Town Council in Billericay to mark International Youth Year and this was well received.

At the same ceremony, by coincidence, Nancy Strunk received the National Police Officer Medal of Honor for her late husband, Police Officer, Thomas Strunk, the brother of Richard Strunk whom, with his wife, I had taken out to lunch in Billericay. She received it from the Chief of Police, John Barretto, also a plaque from Michael Rae, now a State Representative. It was the same Michael Rae who had presented me with the Stock Certificate in 1975. Thomas, who had previously been a firefighter before joining the police, had died after interrupting a family errand to stop a suspected drunk driver. He had been killed while questioning the driver. A young man with a young family and a degree in criminal justice, he had been greatly admired by his colleagues and it is fitting that I mention him and the presentations to his widow in this chapter.

After the ceremony and my short speech, I joined in the parade. All the selectmen were in it, greeting people in the crowd that they knew, courting the massive Irish constituency in the town and mingling with the veterans. I was amused when Gordon, who was walking beside me spotted a group dressed predominantly in green standing at the roadside and shouted, "I'm Irish," when as far as I knew he wasn't, but that, I supposed, was politics! I have learned subsequently that when Sam, his son, had been researching the family genealogy many years previously he had discovered that, on the other side of the family tree, they did, in fact, have Irish ancestry. Gordon's great grandmother, Elizabeth Deacon, had come from Ireland and had been a Roman Catholic. As soon as Sam told his father of this tenuous link with Ireland and notwithstanding his lifelong membership of the First Parish Unitarian Church,

Gordon had gone straight down to the Irish American Club in Billerica and joined it. Now, THAT, as Sam has pointed out, was political!

The parade was headed by the Billerica Police Honor Guard and was split into four divisions. In the first division were the fire department, the dignitaries, the parade marshals, including myself as an honorary parade marshal, the Veterans and the "Gold Star Mothers". I assumed that they were the wives, widows and mothers of live or deceased members of the armed forces. They were clearly highly regarded and respected.

The second division was headed by the Elks Color Guard and included within its numbers members of the Irish American Social Club, the elementary school Band, a school of Irish dancing, who danced, and the Girl Scouts, Brownies and Bluebirds.

The third division was led by the Knights of Columbus Color Guard and included the middle school band, a baton corps, the Billerica "Sons of Italy" Lodge and the Boy Scouts and Cub Scouts. There was no sign of the Thomas Talbot Lodge of Masons which is broadly equivalent in its nature to Masonic Lodges in the United Kingdom, but I understand they appeared in later Memorial Day parades.

The fourth division comprised the impressive Billerica high school band, the Judy Ann Groves Twirletts who twirled energetically, a Billerica Soccer Association float and a number of other floats. The parade was the town's most prestigious and colourful event with several hundred young and old people and over thirty different types of participants in it. It was conducted with enthusiasm and a strong sense of social cohesion and I was delighted and honoured to be part of it.

When the parade was over the "Irish constituency" headed for a large marquee where drinks and, as I recall, food were served. Gordon introduced me at that point to a number of his Irish friends. I considered it prudent not to mention my own family's link with Southern Ireland, details of which you will find in a later chapter!

The paintings of Great Burstead and Little Burstead were received with thanks by the curator of the Clara Sexton Museum and the Billerica Historical Society and now hang in the section devoted to the town's historic links with Billericay, together with the maps I had presented on earlier visits.

On what I think was probably our last full day in Billerica, Barbara and I were waiting for Gordon to come home from his office in the centre of Billerica:

he was going to take us out that evening to a civic function.

Barbara asked me if I had brought anything out to America that might enable her to switch the power on her hairdryer from UK to US voltage: she needed a screwdriver or similar to do this.

I told her that I did not, but that Gordon had a workshop in his cellar which I had been to on a previous visit: I felt sure he would not object to us using one of his screwdrivers to adjust the power setting on it.

We both went down the wooden stairs to the cellar and stopped transfixed by what we saw. There in the grey stone wall on our left was a stone that looked like a faulty fluorescent tube: it was pulsing with white light: it was about two feet up the wall from floor level, about twelve to fourteen inches in width and about two inches in height. It just kept shining with this white luminescent glow.

Barbara was terrified. "I am getting out of here," she murmured, almost too afraid to speak, and disappeared up the stairs. It could have been hair-raising but I was more curious than frightened and stayed looking at the stone for a couple of minutes: it was very eerie standing in a cellar lit by a single light bulb with this stone emitting a pulsing white glow on the side of an otherwise dimly lit room.

When I came out of the cellar, with the screwdriver(!), I said "We must record this," and immediately wrote down a description of what we had seen: Gordon came home shortly afterwards. He was quite taken aback and wanted to see the stone himself.

"I have lived in this house for years and you bloody limeys come here and see that!" he declared. "I am going to ring 'GB.'" pronounced "Jeebie". GB was Gordon's son, Gordon Brainerd, Junior, and had studied mineralogy at university. "Maybe it is a pyrgo electrolysis," said GB. "What the hell is that?" asked Gordon. "When rocks are put under intense pressure they can generate electric current," replied GB. "I suggest you check it out."

With that Gordon and I went downstairs and prodded the now inert grey coloured stone with a broom handle: it moved slightly! No pressure there then! Gordon was absolutely baffled.

There had to be a reason, however, for this weird event and I came to a conclusion that might strike some as far-fetched: nevertheless it fitted in with my previous experiences of communications from people who had "passed on".

Having studied the background to the Salem witchcraft trials in 1692 I was very much aware that, had Barbara and I been alive in the 1690s and had we seen and mentioned a stone glowing in the basement of a house, we might have been accused of witchcraft or of consorting in some way with dark and unseen powers. We would possibly have been tortured and hanged!

Was the spirit of someone trying to get through to us from that period? I checked out the historical records of the Salem Witchcraft trials made famous by Arthur Miller's play "The Crucible" and, sure enough, a lady by the name of Martha Carrier, a former resident of Billerica, was accused of witchcraft in Salem. Several Billerica neighbours testified that they had been bewitched by her and she had been hanged in Salem. She was the sister-in-law of Roger Toothaker and he was the stepson of Ralph Hill from Billericay, one of the original setters who petitioned for the change of name of Shawshin to Billericay in 1654. Roger Toothaker, who had similarly been accused of witchcraft, died under torture in Boston Prison in June 1692.

Could this have been Martha Carrier? If so what was she trying to communicate? Why appear to people from Billericay, Essex, when she had not previously appeared to anyone who lived in America? Was it anything to do with the vaguely psychic "antennae" that Barbara and I appeared to possess? As you will be aware from the chapters on the haunted house and the haunted bed, I appear to have been able in the past to receive "vibes" from people who have died. At the moment the reason for the shining stone is a mystery and the event itself defies rational explanation: but it definitely happened: two of us witnessed it, and left Gordon with a record of it. My gut feeling that it was Martha Carrier has been reinforced by the fact that, in recent correspondence, Sam Brainerd, Gordon's son, has confirmed that Ralph Hill, to whom Martha was related by marriage, owned the land upon which Gordon's house was built from as early as 1652, before Billerica was founded.

The current house was built in 1740 by Ralph Hill's great grandson and did not exist when Martha was hanged. The cellar, moreover, was not added until 1910. There is nevertheless an intriguing connection between the land, Ralph Hill, Roger Toothaker and Roger's sister-in-law, Martha.

Once I had decided to set up a solicitor's property sales department in early 1986, had become preoccupied with it, and had taken on my future wife, Annette, as manager of it I had little time to pursue my links with Billerica in the 1980's. I did, however, manage a brief visit in May 1995 when I once again attended Memorial Day, this time as an honorary parade marshal and as bearer of the Standard of the Billericay Branch of the Royal British Legion in the Memorial Day parade.

A solemn service on the steps of the town hall preceded the parade: it started with the "Reading of General Orders" and was followed by the placing of wreaths, the recitation of a Memorial Day poem, "Old Glory", and the reading of a tribute to the dead. In this connection I have been able to obtain the names of the five servicemen from Billerica who died in the First World War. Their names, ranks and ages will be added to those of servicemen from Billericay read out at the Remembrance Day Service in November 2018 to mark the end, one hundred years earlier, of a conflict in which so many British and American servicemen lost their lives. I will not be alive to see the same thing occur, hopefully, in 2045.

Memorial Day remarks were made by Edward Hurd, Chairman of the Board of Selectmen. I was asked to say a few words. In the circumstances I mentioned the fact that British and American servicemen had fought side by side in two world wars and that, as an ex-serviceman myself and much involved in the local branch of our veteran's association, the Royal British Legion, it was a great honour for me to be able to participate in a ceremony in Billerica that was the same as our Remembrance Day Service and parade in Billericay. The service concluded with prayers, Taps and the American national anthem.

Gordon who, by this time, found walking for any length of time difficult, was delighted to have been made an honorary parade marshal and drove in the parade in an open-topped car behind the Royal British Legion Standard and the other Veterans' Standards, waving cheerily to the crowds who lined the main street.

Although I had had no contact with Billerica since 1995 I was approached in 2008 and asked to become chairman of the Billericay Mayflower Twinning Association. The Association had been formed in 1998 by Mrs. Hazel Morley. Much to her credit, it was she who had initiated a formal twinning link between the two towns. I was approached by Hazel Morley at the inception of the association and invited to join it but, at that time I was in the process of setting up my new legal practice in Shenfield and trying to get back on my feet financially after the Lloyds debacle, our foray into France and the failure of Resolve, details of which you will find in later chapters. There was, regrettably, no time to participate in it.

In May 2011 I led a group of members of the Association back to Billerica and rekindled my acquaintance with the town and with a number of its leading citizens. I once again took part in the Memorial Day Parade, as Royal British Legion Standard bearer.

While in Billerica I visited the First Parish Unitarian Church and was devastated to find a plaque on the wall of the Church dedicated to Jeremie Stearns who had taken her own life some years previously. There was also a plaque to Helen Brainerd, Gordon's first wife, who had played a leading role in raising funds for the extension which had been added to the church. I was not altogether surprised to find that a room in the town council offices had been named after Gordon who died in January 2001. He was such an extraordinary man, charming, kind and very capable.

During my visit I was also taken out to the Jessica Sachs Memorial Garden and it is a sobering fact and a sad link between the two towns that Jessica Sachs from Billerica and Carrie Clarke from Billericay were both working in the Twin Towers on 9th September 2001 and died in the terrorist attack. I and the members of the Association would very much like to place a similar memorial to them both in Billericay and, hopefully, one day there will be one: we are aware, however, of the wishes of Carrie's father and respect them. Perhaps, in time, he will be happy for us to do so.

20

Being a General Commissioner of Income Tax

From 1981 until 2009 I acted as Chairman of the General Commissioners of Income Tax for the Grays and Basildon Divisions, having been appointed a General Commissioner in 1976: for the last five of the thirty three years I was one of three members of the Lord Lieutenant's advisory committee for the appointment of general commissioners across the county of Essex. Both were interesting and enjoyable appointments which terminated when full-time tribunals were set up by the Government with highly paid barristers as chairmen.

Before the establishment of these full time tribunals general commissioners were men and women who gave their services free of charge to the state and acted as arbiters between the Inland Revenue and the taxpayer.

If a taxpayer thought the Revenue were demanding too much or being too strict in the application of the relevant tax legislation he, she or it (in the case of a company) could appeal to the general commissioners who would then hear the arguments put forward by the Revenue and the taxpayer respectively and determine how much the appellant owed or the latitude that should be granted.

One of my most memorable cases took place in the Grays Magistrates' Court. As commissioners we were sitting on "the bench" usually occupied by the magistrates and heard an appeal against an assessment of annual earnings of £4,000. This was in 1982 and the taxpayer argued that he only earned £2,900 a year!

I asked the taxpayer if he would mind our asking him some questions in order to clarify matters. He had no objection.

I started off by saying, "I note that you live in Emerson Park. I assume you live in a semi-detached house." "Oh no," replied the taxpayer." It is a detached house." My two fellow commissioners looked at each other and if looks could speak they would have said, "Emerson Park is one of the most expensive parts of Hornchurch" as I also knew full well.

"Do you have a family?" I went on and he confirmed that he had a wife and "dortah."

"I have had a look at your accounts and you only appear to have a van: is that not rather difficult when you want to go out as a family?" "Oh no," he replied, "I have got a Zephyr for that." The Zephyr was a top of the range Ford at the time. "I don't suppose you can afford to go on holiday as a family every year," I said. "Oh yes we can," he replied. "Where do you go?" "We go to 'Majjorkah'. " As a director of a travel agency I had a good idea how much that would cost him. Majorca was not exactly a low-cost holiday destination.

"One further question. Do you have a mortgage on your house?" "Oh yes," he said. "And how much is it for?" "Fawty farsand," he replied. "Is that with one of the major building societies?" "Yes, it is with the Leeds Permanent."

I thanked the appellant for being so helpful and asked him to withdraw while we considered his appeal.

The commissioner next to me could barely restrain himself. He was a farmer and knew exactly what type of business the appellant was in. "These people," he declared, "come round our farms and buy up poultry which have come to the end of their egg-producing lives. They then take them up to London and sell them in street markets as first-grade poultry. That man is on £16,000 a year if he is on a penny."

I happened to be the local agent for the Leeds Permanent Building Society in Billericay and knew exactly how much a mortgage of £40,000 would cost in terms of interest repayments. I also had a good idea of the minimum value of a detached property in Emerson Park, having been a residential conveyancing solicitor for many years.

We called the taxpayer back in and I addressed him as follows: "Mr So and So, we have heard your submissions and those of the Revenue and we have come to the conclusion that HM Inland Revenue were wrong to assess your earnings at £4000 per annum." At this the appellant looked very happy until I added, "We have concluded that, on the basis of what you have told us today, your income has to be no less than £8,000 per annum and we determine their assessment in that figure. Good day." It was a "foot in the mouth" case where the appellant would have been wise to agree the inspector's assessment of annual earnings of £4000 per annum, rather than dispute it!

What many taxpayers did not realise, moreover, was that the Inland Revenue had developed a series of "guide books" which indicated what any particular kind of business should be generating by way of profit: if the profit disclosed by the taxpayer was too low enquiries were made.

For example, if a business selling beds and mattresses was not making the usual level of profit on its sales the Inland Revenue checked the local newspapers (now the internet) for any advertisers selling new beds or mattresses on a regular basis from a private address. If one home owner seems to be selling either item on a regular basis on behalf of rather more adults or children than could possibly live at his or her address they have probably come from a shop where the proprietor is selling them on the side for cash!

One of the funniest cases to come before us was that of a businessman who had appealed to us against an assessment that he alleged was too high. "You have seen my books," he declared to the inspector, "and it is obvious you are charging me too much tax."

"That is right," said the inspector. "We have seen the books you submitted but we also happen to have received copies of your real books from your former secretary." It would appear that he was having a relationship with another lady as well as the former secretary and she had found out. Hell hath no fury like a woman scorned! "Collapse of stout party," as they say!

The earnings of second-hand car dealers always proved difficult to pin down and I can recall one taxpayer who was assessed for tax in the 1990s on earnings of approximately £42,000 on the sale of Jaguar cars that he purchased second hand and sold on. He, like others, was caught out by the number of sale advertisements he had placed in various newspapers and magazines for the different cars he had acquired.

When the inspector listed them all it was quite clear that he had a thriving business in "top end" second-hand Jaguars. "I am not going to be judged by this kangaroo court," he shouted at us and stormed out of the room. The inspector immediately asked if we would determine his assessment.

I told the inspector that since the appellant had left behind the evidence produced by the inspector we would do so if the appellant did not reappear before the end of our meeting. Sure enough, half an hour later, the car dealer requested permission to come back in. After he had tried to persuade us that there was, in fact, little profit in selling second-hand Jaguars and had realised that, if the inspector investigated his dealings any further, he might come across other undeclared dealings, he reluctantly agreed to accept the assessment, which was in all probability on the low side.

The inspectors, who now have a much greater ability to examine a taxpayer's business dealings and tax affairs, were invariably polite and well mannered and I can only recall one case where the Inland Revenue wanted to determine an assessment to earnings and where they had clearly not taken the true facts into account.

When the appellant came before us it turned out that he had lost his sight through a degenerative eye disease and that his wife had died within the previous twelve months: he had been unable to file an income tax return and, in any event, had lost his job. I asked the inspector whether, in the light of the facts, he wished to withdraw his assessment which had been based on previous years' earnings, making it clear that if he did not we would be determining the poor man's earnings in the figure of "nil". The inspector withdrew his assessment.

In many cases the taxpayers did not appear and this made it difficult for us to determine liability accurately: but in the twenty eight years neither appellants nor Inland Revenue appealed against any of our decisions by way of "case stated" to the High Court, even though on occasions we rejected the arguments put forward by the Inland Revenue and the inspector in question was clearly unhappy. In fact I recall a case where an inspector actually quoted me in a "case stated" when he had appealed a case brought in another division to the High Court.

I had told an appellant to our tribunal that "he had just shaded it" in his appeal against the withdrawal of his subcontractor's certificate but that if he ever submitted his tax returns late in future we would have no hesitation in rejecting any appeal made by him. He had failed to pay tax on his employees' earnings on a regular basis, as required, and had put forward as an excuse the inadequacy of his former accountant.

He pointed out that without a subcontractor's certificate he would not receive the full price of subcontract work: he would only receive 70% and since he had over forty employees it would mean his having to lay off staff: he would not be liable to pay the Inland Revenue the full 30% retained by the main contractor and the resultant loss of income until he recovered any overpayment would mean the laid-off staff having to try to find employment elsewhere.

The appellant's new accountant was present with him and gave the necessary assurances that tax would be paid promptly in future. We had to balance our judgement on a number of factors. The appellant was clearly in the wrong. He had apparently remedied his failure to pay tax promptly by taking on a new accountant: employees would undoubtedly be laid off and the future of an apparently successful business would be at stake.

We determined that he could have his subcontractors certificate but that if he ever defaulted again, he would lose it.

The appellant went away and behaved in exactly the same way as he had before. He knew, however, that there was no point in appearing before us again so when the inspector withdrew his certificate again he appealed the withdrawal of his certificate before general commissioners in the adjoining division. He deployed the same arguments and they, like us, let him have his certificate. At this point the inspector requested a "case stated" to be sent to the High Court. A "case stated" is a summary of the facts of the case and the law applicable to those facts, the details of the appeal and the reasons for the commissioners' decision. The High Court would determine whether the decision was correct.

The inspector quoted my final warning on the first appeal and the High Court agreed that the subcontractors certificate should be withdrawn. Why the appellant took no notice of our warning I cannot say but his business doubtless suffered immensely as a result of his ignoring it.

In the early 1990s we were urged to expand the pool of general commissioners to reflect the "make-up" of society: in other words we should ask members of ethnic minorities to volunteer their services as general commissioners. I took this to heart and approached an Indian accountant who had a busy practice in the area.

"Would you consider becoming a general commissioner of income tax?" I asked him. "I would," he said. "How much will I be paid?" "You do this job for free but it is usually only one morning a month and it is a vital part of the tax system, ensuring that taxpayers are able to appeal assessments that are harsh or incorrect." "I could not do it for less than £120 per hour. That is my hourly rate," he replied.

I then tried the owner of two well-established Chinese restaurants in the area. "Would you consider becoming a general commissioner of income tax?"

I explained what the job involved and he looked concerned. "Does this mean that I would have to sit in judgement on appeals made by members of the Chinese community in the area?" "Yes." I replied. "They are taxpayers like everyone else and are entitled to appeal to us as are all other taxpayers."

"Oh, I could not do that," he replied, presumably worried he might upset other members of the Chinese community.

After another couple of unsuccessful efforts to persuade members of ethnic minorities to become general commissioners I gave up. Not long after this, however, I cornered Lord McKay, the then Lord Chancellor, at an accountancy conference in London where he was guest speaker and told him about my experiences.

He looked sympathetic. "It is the Anglo-Saxon ethic, dear boy," he said. "Only Anglo-Saxons appear willing to give up their time to do this type of job free of charge. At least you tried." With that he moved on to speak to someone else. The reader is left to draw his own/her own conclusions from this.

The difficulty in widening the field of general commissioners may have had some influence on the introduction of tribunals, headed by paid chairmen and the concentration of appeals on a reduced number of venues for them. All I can say is that local general commissioners knew their areas very well and did an excellent job free of charge to the community: they were accessible to the people living in their localities. Nowadays appellants have to travel large distances to appear at appeals and the whole system is much more distant and bureaucratic. Such is progress and such, frankly, is the lack of appreciation shown by Government for the unpaid and time-consuming work carried out on behalf of their communities by general commissioners and by magistrates.

21

The Consequences of Cheek

It is strange how one thing leads to another! As a schoolboy between the ages of eleven and thirteen I was considered very cheeky by the prefects at my school: they could only punish me by putting me in "drill" on a regular basis. This meant that about once a week I had to turn up after school, outside the masters common room, in singlet, shorts and plimsolls to run round the school fields twice. This was the only penalty they could impose on me for my lack of respect!

My Housemaster must have seen me through the windows of the Common Room and thought to himself: "I will have to put Hughes, Pagram, Alleyn and Norris (all in my House and all doing the same penance) in the House cross country team because they are getting plenty of practice." And so it transpired that three or four years later I became Captain of my House cross country team and developed, thereafter, a real love of running! I kept running through my university days and have, in fact, been running ever since!

But I digress! Having opened travel agencies in Billericay and Shenfield in 1968 I was invited to fill the transportation category in the local Rotary Club. In those days there was a single representative from each trade, profession or vocation in each Rotary Club whose international motto was "Service above Self."

I was much attracted to this concept of service above self and within two years I was helping Jack Wilson, a fellow Rotarian and retired headmaster of a local junior school, organise a leisure exhibition for Billericay. The aim of the exhibition was to show the residents of Billericay what opportunities existed for recreation and leisure within the local community. We located over fifty clubs, societies and charities in Billericay and gave them each a stand at the exhibition in a local secondary school.

The exhibition took place in 1971 and proved a successful blueprint for two later exhibitions in 1976 and 1981. Jack Wilson left the area shortly after the 1971 exhibition and I was left in charge of organising the two subsequent events.

The exhibition which took about a year to organise was held during the school's Easter holiday break in 1971. The main hall of the school accommodated about half the stands while the remainder were located in classrooms on the ground floor of the building. Entry to the exhibition which lasted for three days was free but members of the public could purchase, at a nominal cost, a printed programme which listed all the exhibitors by category, indicating the location of their stands and giving the names, addresses and telephone numbers of the contacts for each of the exhibitors.

The exhibition attracted considerable local interest and publicity and all the exhibitors reported increases in membership. It proved to be a successful blueprint for future exhibitions which we decided to hold at regular five yearly intervals.

The 1976 exhibition was more successful than its predecessor because more local organisations saw the benefit of appearing in it: the number of exhibitors crept up to the mid-seventies. What was lacking, however, was a live activities aspect to what had previously been static exhibitions and in 1981 we incorporated new features. In addition to the static exhibition we added live activities with everything from sub-aqua and motorcycle displays to a tennis tournament and a scrabble competition. There was also a separate craft exhibition at which local crafts people advertised their wares. The entrance fees the crafts people paid to appear in a hall nearby, paid for the cost of manufacturing proper display stands in the leisure exhibition itself. The idea of a craft fair was seized upon by others and ultimately resulted in the creation of a massive permanent craft fair at Barleylands on the outskirts of Billericay.

Over one hundred local organisations appeared in the 1981 leisure exhibition which took about eighteen months to organise and nearly 23,000 people visited the two three-day exhibitions, approximately half the population of Billericay at the time.

Not long after the exhibitions I was approached and asked to become

President of the Billericay and Wickford District Scout Association, a position I have held with pride since 1981.

My involvement in the community, including the (Royal) British Legion which I joined in 1975, gave me access to many local personalities and organisations and, like my father before me, I tried to develop a community rather than a political focus to all my activities: as a solicitor I was dealing in any event with all types of human problems and my work similarly led me away from espousing any particular party or cause.

As an innate pragmatist and an inactive member of the local Conservative Party I was, moreover, much influenced by the warning of Prime Minister Harold MacMillan that he detected a North/South Divide growing in this country and that everything should be done to prevent this division getting more pronounced.

When, therefore, Arthur Scargill led the miners into a bloody confrontation with the Conservative Government causing untold misery not only to the general public but to the families of the miners themselves I decided to show that we, in Billericay at least, did not subscribe to a North/South divide: nor did we lack the common humanity that appeared to be missing from the way in which the dispute was being conducted, particularly by the leadership of the National Union of Mineworkers. I advertised the fact that we were collecting clothes and toys for the wives and children of striking miners.

I quickly gained support for this initiative but was equally quickly thrown out of the local Conservative Party! If the local Conservatives had realised that most miners were extremely reluctant to go on strike and very hard up as a result of it they might have reacted differently. But they displayed an inbuilt prejudice which, although understandable, did not reflect well on them at the time.

With an estate car bursting at the seams with clothes and toys I drove to Easington Colliery – just above Newcastle upon Tyne – and met members of the local Lions Club who put me in touch with the NUM secretary for the Colliery. He was one of the most genuine people I have ever met: from my army days I had always liked "Geordies" and he was no exception.

He freely admitted that the strike was a disaster, that Scargill was destroying the NUM and that his own ability to help his members had been completely negated by the lack of money and resources available to him. The "Social" – the community centre for the workers at the colliery – had had to close, youngsters were breaking the windows of it and the strong bonds of loyalty that had previously existed between miners were being undermined by lack of pay and accusations of "scab" labour from the leadership of the NUM. I knew then that I had done the right thing. Sadly the colliery had to close not long after the strike but my admiration for people from the North-East, including my co-director at my travel agency in Shenfield, Gordon Forster, remained undimmed.

After the dust had settled on the miners' strike I was readmitted to the Billericay Conservative Party, only to be thrown out again in 1997: but that is another story which you will find in a later chapter.

Among the people who joined me in this initiative were Francois Talou, who generously lent me his brand new estate car, and Rod Hutchison who had, in his day, been an eminent race walker. He was still pretty fit at the time and subsequently participated in running events with me, including the Worthing marathon.

After one of our runs we commented on the lack of a running club in Billericay. We had both seen so many people run round the town on their own but there was no local running club for them to join. "Why don't we try and start one," I said. "Why don't we include a race walking section in it, as well?" he replied: and that became our plan.

The next step was to set up the club and find members for it. We therefore approached the Amateur Athletics Association (A.A.A.) representative for the area, a Howard Williams, and sought his advice. His immediate reaction was that forming a club for the town would be a very good idea and he gave us some helpful advice on how to make it comply with A.A.A. regulations and requirements.

But what would we call it? Rod and I would have to propose a name that embraced running and race walking. We came up with "The Billericay Striders", a name that found favour with the thirty or so runners who turned up to our initial meeting.

From that initial meeting in 1986 a steering committee was formed and the club literally took off from that point: it is still going strong over thirty years later. It has its own premises and a large membership. I could not be more proud of the way in which the club, of which I became the first chairman and subsequently founder president, has developed since that first meeting.

Unfortunately Rod Hutchison had to leave the area by virtue of relocation of his employment shortly after the club was formed and a race walking section was never established.

Being cheeky as a schoolboy led me to this outcome and, on reflection, my advice to any reader would be this: be yourself and seize the opportunities for good that come your way: do not be influenced by the prejudices of other people and be true to your own feelings. In this way you will discover yourself "warts and all", as Oliver Cromwell once said. You will probably be an asset to your family, friends, and society at large and will undoubtedly enjoy the years given to you. You will also, hopefully, be able to reconcile yourself to your Maker during your lifetime!

22

Lifeline: Essex Radio

In 1985 I was approached by the Reverend Peter Elvey, the Vicar of Great Burstead Parish Church, just outside Billericay and was asked whether I would be prepared to join him on a weekly "phone in" programme being broadcast by Essex Radio on Sunday evenings between 10pm and midnight. I would be appearing "pro bono", that is to say without being paid. The programme called "Lifeline" was designed for young people who faced dilemmas in their lives and who needed genuine pastoral advice in relation to social, legal and personal problems.. I would be appearing with him and a social worker on a fortnightly basis. Another solicitor from the Southend area would alternate with me.

I was pleased to accept his request and for three years turned up to a virtually empty radio station in Southend late on Sunday evening to try and give sensible advice on a wide range of issues. The three of us sat round a central console with earphones attached and listened to all the calls that came in. Throughout the three years we never ran out of calls, which were broadcast seven seconds after they came into the studio – so that we could put a block on anything offensive or libellous and ensure that it was not broadcast.

Peter Elvey was the most extraordinary vicar I have ever met: he was a complete extrovert. He would occasionally get up from his chair while I or the social worker were answering a call and waltz, with earphones attached, around the studio. It was very difficult for either of us to answer questions seriously when he was being humorous but we did our best!

He also had an "earthy" sense of humour and when a "spoof" call came in he would always be ready with a funny response: In fact one of our problems was differentiating the spoof calls from the serious ones: we were well aware that the pubs in the Southend area closed during the first half of our programme and when we could hear giggles or muffled laughter in the background we knew that the caller was doing his best to amuse his friends by asking us a question, usually of a sexual nature which he (always a male) thought would embarrass us.

One young man, for example, told us that he had bought his recent girlfriend a handbag. When he gave it to her he asked her whether she would go to bed with him. Whereupon she hit him with the handbag. What advice could the panel offer? Quick as a flash Peter Elvey told the young man that in a real relationship one cannot buy sex like that and that if he wanted to continue the relationship he should not buy her a bigger handbag!

We had to be careful to sort the wheat from the chaff and genuinely help the young people who really needed help. We all joined in most of the responses but there were a number of times when specific legal advice was requested, particularly in relation to young people renting flats and to a lesser extent on the division of property during the breakdown of a relationship. They were told how and where to get the advice they needed after brief comments on the legal principles involved: they could not refer to the internet in those days as young people do today.

The format of the programme was changed radically, however, after a very sad incident. One evening a fourteen year old girl rang in and told us that she was desperately upset and intended to commit suicide. In this type of case – where there was a genuine crisis of some sort – we did our best to keep the caller on the line while the police, whom we contacted immediately, tried to locate the call box or phone line from which the call was being made. Someone, usually the social worker, would leave the studio and speak directly to the caller from another room while the programme continued.

In this particular case the call was traced to a phone box just outside the entrance to Southend Pier but by the time the police arrived the young girl had disappeared. She had, in fact, climbed over the entrance gates to the pier and thrown herself off it. Tragically her body was found in the sea the next day.

The radio station felt it should no longer be involved in this type of programme: the format should be changed and, instead of giving advice directly to young people phoning in, generic advice in the form of talks by experts on different types of problem should be broadcast. The station clearly felt that the reputational damage that might be caused to it by our speaking directly to young people would be too great. I was not convinced that it need to have responded in that way but, in any event, Peter Elvey was appointed vicar of a parish in Chelsea not long afterwards and there was no one who could have taken his place.

    I enjoyed appearing in the programme and being able to help many young people. Few solicitors in Southend had ever heard of me at the time and I was also aware that I would not be taking bread out of the mouths of my fellow solicitors in the area! All in all it was a very interesting and satisfying experience for me and, I hope, one that helped some of our young callers.

23

Life with Annette

It is fair to say that I have known many extraordinary women in my life but none so extraordinary as my second wife, Annette.

I claim no credit for giving a sense of direction or purpose to my first and second wives but Vivien, who had studied photography at art college before I met her and who did not have any defined goals during our marriage, went on, after we had separated and divorced, to obtain a teaching qualification and a first class honours degree in the history of art. She has subsequently lectured worldwide on the subject.

Similarly Annette, who had one "A" level (in religious knowledge) when we met acquired a doctorate in psychology and consultant status (in obsessive compulsive disorders) as well as becoming a director of education, training and workforce development at an NHS mental health trust hospital. She also achieved university status for her trust and, but for her tragic death from cancer at the age of fifty six, would undoubtedly have represented the United Kingdom on the global health programme of Yale University in America.

Maybe they looked at me and thought, "If he can get an M.A. (for which I admittedly paid nine guineas – one of the perks of getting a B.A. from Cambridge) and pass the Law Society's finals why cannot we do equally as well?" Quite how I passed all seven heads of the Law Society's qualifying exams at one go mystified my principal at the time and occasionally mystifies me but I am fortunate in having had, for many of my earlier years, a photographic "card index" memory. In fact, as previously stated, I was once described by a business colleague as being an encyclopaedia of useless information!

The way in which Annette and I came together shows how fate can take a hand in shaping our lives.

When I qualified as a solicitor in 1965 I appreciated that no solicitor in his right mind would employ someone who spent so much of his spare time organising student travel. More to the point, the starting salary for an assistant solicitor in the City of London in 1965 was £1,150 per annum and I was already earning well over £3000 a year from my student travel activities! The only sensible option was to set up on my own as a sole practitioner and concentrate solely on the areas of the law that I had experienced during my articles (the three-year period of training before one could take the Law Society's qualifying exams); these were residential conveyancing, wills and probate.

My father who worked in the legal department of Basildon Council very kindly recommended me to a number of the staff in his and other departments and for two years I worked on a small scale from the marital home in Noak Hill Road, Billericay on various legal matters for them. My clients from Basildon Council had to walk past a row of "Hughes Overland" Ford Transits and Land Rovers parked in the drive until I moved to an office in Billericay. They must have wondered about my legal abilities and my commitment to the law at the time but they were evidently satisfied with the service I provided because more and more of them kept coming!

The growth of the student travel business had already enabled me to rent a room at 24 High Street Billericay for administrative purposes and following the successful opening of Shenfield Travel Bureau in 1968 I was able to open two more travel agencies, County Travel in the main precinct at Chelmsford and Hughes Travel Bureau at 106 High Street, Billericay.

Hughes Travel Bureau had offices over it that I then used as a solicitor's office and thereafter – until I moved offices – as an administration centre for the student travel business and the three travel agencies.

Once in a high street location, however, the legal practice burgeoned and I was obliged to move the student travel business and the head office of Hughes Overland to Chelmsford.

The increased exposure of my legal and travel activities in a high street location did cause many people to wonder whether I was a solicitor or a travel agent! In order to avoid confusion and since the travel agency was less profitable than the legal practice and since I had an opportunity to purchase "Foxcroft," a children's home, at 100 High Street Billericay, I closed the travel agency and assigned the lease of it to an electrical goods retailer.

Foxcroft, a large Georgian building in the middle of the high street had twelve large rooms, a number of smaller rooms and a cellar – altogether ideal for a legal practice in terms of office and storage space.

It had become clear to me from the early 1970s that unless I could give the student travel business my undivided attention the days of my involvement in student travel to Greece, Italy and Turkey would have to end. It was very demanding in terms of my having to travel all over England at weekends and whenever I could get away from the office during the week to meet college representatives and put up travel posters on college notice boards.

With a manager in charge of Hughes Overland working out of offices above County Travel in Chelmsford I decided to concentrate on my legal practice in Billericay and on the administration of my retail travel agencies in Shenfield and Chelmsford both of which had managers who dealt with the day to day sale of package holidays, cruises and airline tickets and running the businesses there.

Within a short period and with the spacious office accommodation provided by Foxcroft the legal practice expanded to the point where it offered residential conveyancing, wills and probate services, advice on matrimonial law, criminal law and commercial law matters and undertook civil and criminal litigation generally. By the mid-1980s the practice had nearly twenty staff and provided all the services one would normally expect from a firm of high street solicitors.

At this point – in 1985 – I went up to Scotland to see and stay with an ex-Army friend, "Sandy" Green, in Bo'Ness, not far from Linlithgow. While there I noticed that many solicitors in Scotland had "Solicitors and Estate Agents" in gold lettering on their windows or embossed on brass plates by the front doors of their practices. The thought crossed my mind, "Why cannot solicitors do the same in England?"

With my nearly twenty years of experience in running travel agencies I had acquired a lot of knowledge about retail selling, advertising and promotion: adverts for our services and the holidays we offered appeared in the same local papers as the services of estate agents and the properties they offered for sale. I suspected that many solicitors would regard the idea of selling properties as "unprofessional" but it was an idea worth exploring.

Shortly after my return I discovered that a legal practice in Lincoln,

Messrs. Langleys, had had the same idea and had actually opened a property sales department, as an adjunct to their conveyancing practice – in the teeth of opposition from the Law Society. Moreover they were offering other solicitors advice on how to do the same and how to meet the stringent "professional" requirements of the Law Society.

The opportunity to find out more was too good to miss. Why should we not be able to offer a complete house sale or house purchase package, incorporating our solicitors' conveyancing charges in the usual estate agency commission on house sales? We would only be doing what solicitors in Scotland had done for a very long time!

Having paid Langleys a visit it became clear that one needed a special type of person to run a property sales department – someone who would maintain the reputation of the practice and the profession while doing what most estate agents do (!) and who would be able to adapt to a legal environment. Enquiries revealed that a really capable, charming and professional estate agent by the name of Annette Talbot worked at Edward Charles, estate agents in Billericay High Street: she had been there for only eighteen months, having previously worked in Toronto as a realtor. In Canada realtors combine the role of selling properties and preparing the actual contracts of sale and she appeared to be an obvious choice.

I contacted her and invited her to visit Langleys with me to gauge whether she would be at all interested in this new concept. I explained that I was considering opening a property sales department and that, if I did so, I would need a manager for it. Since it was a new venture the manager would have a completely free hand in pretty well every aspect of it – from setting it up, to operating it and to sharing the income from it. Its proposed layout, decoration, style of literature and sale boards would be in the hands of the manager and the venture would be funded by myself.

Annette, was, fortunately, very impressed by Langleys' approach to house sales and purchases and I was sufficiently impressed by her obvious abilities to ask her to drive my car back from Lincoln. She had previously indicated that her driving instructor had been a police driving instructor and I thought I could concentrate on asking her for her thoughts on the concept while she drove.

Her ideas were imaginative and her driving was faultless! I subsequently had to endure being "corrected" by her on my driving on many later occasions

– as all our children will confirm: my driving standards were admittedly not as high as hers!

Within a short time she had accepted the position of property sales manager and we set to work on setting up the property sales department on the ground floor of my Georgian office building: it proved a great success under her management and we got on very well together.

In fact, after about twelve months I realised that my feelings for Annette extended beyond those of a business associate: she had, moreover, during those twelve months finalised her divorce from her first husband in Canada. There was, however, a seventeen-year gap between us and I did wonder whether she would be at all interested in overtures from myself. On the other hand, there did not appear to be such a gap in our ages from the point of view of our personal appearances.

She was slim, a former health and fitness instructor in Canada, attractive and intelligent: I was still slim, with brown hair (!) and had run the London marathon in under three and a half hours in 1987: we were both equally energetic and shared the same sense of humour.

Despite the age gap, therefore, there was little doubt that we were attracted by and attractive to each other and that we could meet and fulfil each other's emotional needs.

As a result I took my courage in both hands and proposed to her. Somewhat to my surprise she accepted my proposal and we discussed a possible marriage date. I put it to her that we should not marry until we and our five children could all get to know each other better: her children, James and Zoe were at boarding schools and Lucy appeared to have been badly affected by her parents' divorce: she was very much a "Daddy's girl". Annette, on the other hand, felt that we should marry as quickly as possible.

Although I did not appreciate it during our twenty-one years of marriage, Annette did, in fact, have a compelling reason for wanting to do so. At the time I proposed to her Annette was receiving sufficient maintenance for her three children to enable her to send James and Zoe to boarding schools and consequently to be free to work full time.

She already knew, however, from a previous relationship she had had on her return from Canada that, as soon as her ex-husband became aware of our engagement, he would undoubtedly stop paying maintenance for them; he had threatened to do so before.

When discussing a marriage date Annette had gone so far as mentioning the previous relationship and the name of the person concerned but had not explained why that relationship had ended.

I was not surprised that she had been out with other men: she was only thirty three years old when I first met her and very attractive. I assumed their relationship had ended because, as she emphasised to me at the time we first discussed marriage, her prime concern was the future happiness and wellbeing of her children, given the traumatic effect on them of the sudden and unexpected breakdown of her previous marriage. She wanted to ensure that any permanent relationship would be a happy one for them as well as for herself. Since I felt the same for my two sons I reassured her on this point: moreover, the age gap did not appear to matter too much to her.

By another of those strange coincidences I have experienced throughout my life I was instructed some years after Annette's death to act on a landlord and tenant matter where a landlord was being rather negative in enabling two of my clients to surrender part of the premises they had leased from him. The landlord was represented by a legal executive whose name I immediately recognised as the person with whom Annette had had the relationship.

After resolving, quite amicably and easily the landlord/tenant problem I asked the conveyancer "Did you, by any chance, know someone by the name of Annette Talbot?" His reply surprised me. "I left my wife and children for her," he replied. "So what happened," I asked him, "because I subsequently married her in 1988."

"Well," he said, "I turned up at her house, as arranged, with just a suitcase, intending to move in with her but I did not get much further than the front door."

"Why was that?" "When I arrived, Annette was on the phone at the time to her ex-husband in Canada and at the end of their conversation, he asked to speak to James." "James, who was only five, told his father excitedly that "Uncle Mike" had come to live with them. At this point Annette was summoned back to the phone and was told that if "Uncle Mike" moved in all maintenance for the children would cease forthwith. Annette appreciated that "Uncle Mike" who had left a wife and children of his own would never be able to support her three children as well and told him, with great sadness, that the children came first and that in the circumstances he could not move in and that she could not continue with the relationship.

"What happened then?" I asked him. "I lived out of the suitcase, sleeping on friends' sofas for a year until my wife took me back," he replied. "I never saw Annette again."

I concluded that their relationship could not have been a strong one: on the other hand Annette's reaction to her ex-husband's threat did not really surprise me. She had tried throughout our marriage to compensate for the trauma caused by the breakdown of her previous marriage by what I considered was "over generosity" towards her children and by shielding them as much as she could from painful realities.

In fairness to Annette she had told me from the outset that her children had to be her first priority, given the manner in which her former husband had rejected her and their three children in favour of another woman with two young daughters, and I accepted this. In fact, given what I learned about Annette during our twenty one years of marriage, I have concluded that her former husband had been unable to cope with such a feisty woman: she was just too challenging!

It would have been more honest of her to have explained why "Uncle Mike" had never moved in and why the relationship had ended but I suspect she found out subsequent to that telephone conversation that consent orders for the maintenance of children could be registered and enforced in Canada: I probably mentioned the fact myself and she had hoped I would apply for registration of her consent order in Canada.

Annette was and had been very much into astrology when we decided to marry. She was a "Gemini" and to the extent that certain characteristics are attributed to Geminis I have to admit that she exhibited all of them throughout our marriage. She proved capable of "moving in two directions at the same time" and showing contrasting attitudes, for example wanting constantly to move to London while remaining resolutely attached to her home in Billericay or being quite uninhibited in spending too much money on credit card purchases while running a department of an NHS hospital incredibly capably from a financial standpoint!

Rather than explain the problem she faced – an immediate withdrawal of maintenance for the children once our engagement came to knowledge of her former husband – she produced astrological charts she had prepared: they were based on our birth dates and showed that we were highly compatible. She also announced that the ideal time for people with our star signs to marry was "under a Cancer moon"!

Since I proposed to her in November this meant marriage in just over four months. In retrospect, that was probably as long as her finances would hold out if her ex-husband pulled the plug on the children's maintenance!

Lest the reader think I am simple-minded I have to point out that Annette was a sales person of the highest calibre – as will become evident later. I was also very attracted to her and did not want to lose her or alternatively prejudice our future relationship.

Notwithstanding the panic attack I had a week or so before the wedding it went ahead as planned. The only unexpected feature of it was that I married a blonde instead of a brunette! Without mentioning her intention to do so Annette had changed her hair colour the day before we married and it was only when she arrived at the register office that I found out about the change!

In the same way Annette subsequently abandoned the plain gold wedding ring, which we had both chosen, for a platinum ring with gold bands.

Being somewhat traditional I thought that a honeymoon was an occasion when newly-weds went away on their own to somewhere rather romantic.

Annette agreed with the "going away" part of the honeymoon but insisted that we take the five children as well. We must therefore be one of very few couples who took their five children on honeymoon with them. She wanted the children to "bond" – a laudable aspiration!

Some years later we discovered that the four eldest children did indeed "bond" without telling us. After an evening meal together we would return to our two adjoining holiday homes. Each had two bedrooms: little James slept in one of our bedrooms while the other sons and our two daughters each had twin bedrooms in the other holiday home.

We would be woken up pretty early by James and would go next door to wake up the other four, all of whom seemed dead to the world and who grumbled at our making them come over to us for breakfast.

It was only when they had all married and left home that they admitted to waiting until they knew Annette and I were asleep and then disappearing off to a local night club! No wonder they were all so shattered at 8.30 am every morning!

As anticipated by Annette the maintenance for her children came to an abrupt halt when her ex-husband found out about her engagement and despite registering the consent order in the Canadian courts he found ways to avoid paying maintenance thereafter.

As long as the property sales department continued to grow this would not have been a problem and we could have maintained the lifestyle Annette wanted for her children.

24

The Disaster Phase

Within five months of our marriage, however, we received devastating news: Annette's mother had been diagnosed with inoperable cancer. Annette was distraught: her father had died at the age of fifty three when she was only ten years old and she had relied on her mother for emotional support from that age onwards. She had not really wanted to be so far away from her mother when she went with her husband and three children to Canada and kept in constant touch with her when she returned to the United Kingdom.

Such was her feeling for her mother, on hearing the news, that she insisted her mother come to live with us until she died, despite the fact that her three older sisters all lived much closer to her mother and were much more able and equally willing to look after her.

I put it to Annette that she should not object to her sisters taking care of their mother: none of them had the commitments we shared. I told her that we should concentrate on our marriage, our five children and our professional commitments. She was well aware that I had invested a great deal in the property sales department and that it needed her presence there as the only property sales negotiator. In the circumstances it would be very difficult for us to look after her mother as well: on the other hand we could drive up to Staffordshire to see her on a regular basis.

Annette would not listen to my point of view: she insisted that, of the four sisters, she was the closest to their mother, having lived with her for some years after the others had all married. She was therefore going to care for her whatever I thought and whatever the consequences. Fiercely divided in our attitudes we drove up to Staffordshire to collect her mother.

Her determination to override the wishes of her sisters led to a break with them for some years, and her determination to put caring for her mother before what I considered should be her priorities, namely our family, our marriage and our joint enterprise nearly led to an early divorce. Not only was her income, out of which she paid her children's school fees, dependent on the continuing success of the property sales department of which she was manager and principal fee earner, she had immediately prior to our marriage employed my eldest son, Chris, as a trainee with a view to his becoming another permanent member of her sales team. As a result of my opposition to bringing her mother to Billericay, and whether by force of circumstances or design, she decided to terminate his employment. Chris and I both took her decision badly: within a week Chris had moved out of our home, followed by his brother, Alex, who left in sympathy.

As a result, moreover, of her absence from the office the property sales department ground to a halt; our relationship which was already strained became even more strained and her poor mother spent her last few months in an atmosphere I would not have wished upon her.

I, frankly, was appalled by her disregard of the views and feelings of myself and her sisters and her insistence that I should not attend her mother's funeral in Staffordshire in view of the fact that I had originally opposed her coming down to Essex to live with us. I, therefore, made my displeasure more than evident by serving a divorce petition on her once her mother had died in an effort to make her realise what she had done. I did not really want to divorce her but I had to put a stop to her lack of consideration for our marriage and oblige her to respect the views of others. She appeared to be taking out on me the pent-up resentment she felt towards her former husband.

I could sympathise with her feelings about her mother but not the lack of respect for her sisters, myself and my children and her determination to ride roughshod over the feelings of others.

Ironically, however, it was that same determination and commitment that led to her insisting many years later that I be resuscitated – after a serious brain haemorrhage even though she was told by doctors that she would probably be nursing a vegetable for the rest of my life.

At this point, Annette who had resented my stance throughout, not surprisingly, lost virtually all interest in property selling. In the circumstances I felt I had no option but to advertise for an alternative manager which led to even more resentment on her part and a very noticeable cooling of our relationship – virtually to the point of breakdown.

I knew there really was no one, however, who could take her place and as a consequence I decided to dispose of the property sales department, which, having to fund Annette's salary and the salaries of the other member of the department without sufficient income from sales of properties, was losing money heavily. I had to stem the loss and give up the idea of a solicitor's property sales department. It could have been a great success if Annette had been more flexible but, without her commitment to it, it could not.

The difficult situation was compounded by my practice partner handing in his notice: he felt that in the months leading up to our marriage, Annette and I had been concentrating too much on the financial requirements of the property sales department to the detriment of the practice and that, as a result of our marriage, his views would inevitably carry even less weight. There was an understandable perception on his part that he would be side-lined in the decision- making process. This perception, at the time, of our marriage was, however, not the only reason he handed in his notice. He had previously told me that, in his view, as a married man with two children, living in a semi-detached house with admittedly a very nice Mercedes car he had achieved "total mediocrity". Moreover, as a former college law lecturer he had come to dislike dealing face to face with the general public: he had developed an aversion to clients! This is a dangerous aversion for any solicitor whose ability to communicate with clients, however difficult they might be, is absolutely critical to the successful outcome of a legal transaction and the reputation of his practice.

Annette's increasing influence in the early days of setting up the property sales department and her subsequent lack of commitment to the practice, when added to his dislike of clients prompted his decision to seek employment as a costs draftsman where he would only have to deal with costing files and never have to meet the clients to whom the files related.

One might reasonably say that, having lost my sons and my legal partner and having initiated divorce proceedings against my wife my life had reached a low point in terms of relationships. Not only that: I also had the problem of restoring the fortunes of the legal practice and disposing of a property sales department, if that was indeed possible.

The only way of resolving the marital issues – one way or the other – was to continue with the divorce proceedings. Annette, of whom I was still extremely fond, might just see that her attitude towards our marriage was wrong. It was outside the entrance to the Southend Divorce Court that she had her "light bulb" moment: she asked whether, in view of what we still felt about each other, we really had to go through a divorce. I told her that if she could see her way to cooperating in making the marriage a success I would meet her more than half way in doing whatever was necessary to do so: up until then she had acted very much as an individual and not as a marriage partner.

The attraction between us was still there and it would be a pity, I said, if we parted. Over a cup of coffee outside the court she accepted that what I said was true and we agreed to give our marriage another chance. I went in and told the judge we would not be proceeding with the divorce.

Over the next few weeks I found a purchaser for the property sales department, but without a practice partner and no job for Annette the situation still looked bleak. On the other hand I had become an underwriting member of Lloyds of London in 1986 and expected to receive my first dividend, based on the value of my Georgian office which I had put up as security for my underwriting activities.

The time had come to review our lives and our marriage, which had been rescued at the last gasp and decide where we should go from that point onward. Annette and I, having restored amicable relations, had a serious heart to heart talk on what we wanted from life in future.

"What do you want us to do?" I asked her. "I would like us both to do something more fulfilling than spending our lives in Billericay. I do not want you to become a boring old Solicitor." I could accept "old" but I thought that in view of my active involvement in so many aspects of the life of Billericay, "boring" was rather unkind! How, moreover, she thought I would be able to support our family without spending a great deal of time and effort in keeping the practice profitable I was unable to fathom.

"Why don't we go abroad and open a finishing school somewhere in France?" she asked. "Don't you think this type of educational need is already well catered for in Switzerland?" I replied, being aware that my first wife had been to a finishing school there. "We could be different and less expensive," was her response to that.

"Then I suggest you do some serious research and come up with some costings showing how viable such a project might be."

We were soon knee-deep in brochures from virtually every finishing school in Europe! Her enthusiasm was boundless and, after considering all her facts and figures, I decided to meet her half way as I had promised. I would meet her half way by putting my practice up for sale and by applying for a legal job which gave me much more freedom. We would buy a property in France and concentrate on teaching French in a property that had sufficient accommodation for twenty or more students and we would emphasise the value of learning business French given that Britain was in the Single Market. We would take young ladies from the United Kingdom and, in effect, give them the language skills they needed to work in France with English companies or in England with French companies: we felt there would be a growing demand amongst employers for young women with an ability to understand business French on both sides of the Channel. In retrospect it was all rather naive but Annette was very persuasive!

The anticipated income from Lloyds and the rental income from my Georgian office building plus the legal income would exceed my income as a sole practitioner having to pay the salaries of so many staff. I could also sell County Travel in Chelmsford, substantially improving the capital base for the proposed venture. I have never been afraid of taking a chance in life or exploring a new business venture and if this was going to make my new wife really happy I would take that chance.

I did make it clear, however, to Annette, that I would have to live a substantial portion of my time in England and commute from England to wherever we were located in France for two reasons: the first to keep sufficient legal income coming in to maintain our home in England as a base and, the second to advertise in the United Kingdom for clientele. I did not realise it at the time but a third unexpected reason was the requirement to be able to purchase and transport Marmite, baked beans, cornflakes, tomato ketchup and all the staples of British student life to the property we purchased in France!

I advertised the sale of the County Travel and quickly had a number of major travel companies bidding for it: I sold it to Lunn Poly who later merged with another major tour operator

25

Our Foray into France

Having sold County Travel my next task was to find a purchaser for my legal practice. It was not difficult to do so and within a period of months I had sold the practice and leased Foxcroft, my Georgian offices to a firm of solicitors in Southend.

In selling my practice to them and not using another firm of solicitors to represent me I made a serious mistake: just as there are dangers in doctors treating themselves, solicitors should never assume that they know how best to protect their own interests. The terms of the sale were straightforward enough: the purchasing practice would enter into a lease of Foxcroft at a market rent: it would pay the purchase price of the practice itself by ten annual instalments: for a maximum period of two years I would remain as a consultant in order to effect a smooth transmission of my clients to the purchasing practice.

The purchasing practice was given every opportunity to carry out due diligence and appeared to be completely satisfied with its acquisition: all I can say is that appearances can be deceptive as I discovered subsequently.

I was not to know how shabbily I would be treated some two years later, but having successfully disposed of County Travel and my practice and in anticipation of an income from my membership of Lloyds of London I felt we were in a good positon to look for a property in France.

Annette had decided that the best place to look was the Dordogne: we would find a suitable property and open a college there. During the summer we therefore drove down to Perigueux, the principal city of the region in order to find out whether there was anywhere suitable for our purposes. There were a number of chateaux for sale in the Dordogne but the property that caught our eye was in a village called St. Agnan.

It was a maison du maitre (a house of the master) and belonged to the Commune de Bondy, a local authority in Paris. It had been used by the local authority as a children's holiday home and had accommodation for forty two persons.

The property was called "Le Pavillon de Bonheur" (the House of Happiness) and had been well maintained by the commune: the only drawback was that it came with a housekeeper, a Madame Brehzinski, who had probably deterred most earlier prospective purchasers by her aggressive attitude. She had an irrevocable tenancy of an apartment within one of the buildings constituting the Pavillon de Bonheur and had controlled all the linen, bedding and household items used in accommodating the children, which, ostensibly, the commune was including in the sale price. We never saw these items after we purchased the Pavillon because she refused point blank to let us enter the storeroom in which we suspected they were located on the grounds that the storeroom contained only her personal possessions. She was, in every way, a most unpleasant and uncooperative lady who regarded us as "intruders". Fortunately she moved out after about six months, taking whatever was in the storeroom with her.

The Pavillon itself was quite beautiful – a large nine-bedroomed house with a fountain in the front lawn and a large range of buildings around three sides of a courtyard: these were used for the accommodation of children during the holidays and, of course, for Madam Brehzinski. We fell in love with the house as soon as we saw it. It was set in seven hectares of gardens and woodland – about eleven acres – all surrounded by a high stone wall. On the wall were two iron crosses where partisans had been shot by Germans during the way. They were a grim reminder of the Second World War.

The village of St. Agnan is very close to the Chateau D'Hautefort, one of the principal tourist attractions in the Dordogne and when, during the Second World War, the Germans had occupied the chateau as their regional headquarters, the Baron of Hautefort had been obliged to move into the Pavillon, a property owned by the family.

The baron was, according to the locals, an unpleasant man who had treated his wife, the baroness badly: they had no children and rumours abounded as to his sexual orientation. All I can say is that one room in the Pavillon, interconnected with the baron's old bedroom (as opposed to the baroness's old bedroom – they slept apparently in different rooms) did have a noticeably strange and rather chilling atmosphere.

Most people will go into a house and be able to say whether or not it has a warm and welcoming atmosphere, as they do at 37 Stock Road, Billericay, and I may have a more developed sensibility than others to this aspect of houses. But the baron's old bedroom was the best in the house, overlooking the front lawns, the fountain and the entrance gates and we used it as our bedroom, going into the room next door, a private bathroom, only as often as was strictly necessary!

Having decided to purchase the property our next task was to obtain a mortgage to help pay for it, and also ensure that we had the right legal framework for the purchase. It was here that Annette's extraordinary negotiating skills came to the fore: although, at that stage, she could not speak any more than "O" level French she persuaded Credit Agricole, a major French bank, to lend us the bulk of the purchase price.

Once we had received an offer of a mortgage in principle and confirmation that the commune was agreeable to selling the Pavillon to us we flew to Paris and set up an SCI – a French property company to own the Pavillon and an SARL, a trading company to operate the college.

The negotiations relating to the purchase and the setting up of the companies took some months and it was not until the end of the summer of 1990 that we were ready to move into the Pavillon. Annette's children had left their boarding schools at the end of the summer term and their great adventure, and ours, was about to begin.

I purchased a Renault Trafic van and started moving essential items from Billericay to St. Agnan. By leaving Billericay at 6.30 am, and using the Dover/Calais ferries, I could be in St. Agnan by 10pm the same day – a long and lonely drive via Paris and Vierzon but on good roads as far as Limoges. Annette took her "Property Department" Mercedes with her and used it all the time we were in France.

Annette was full of energy for her project and located suitable teachers in the area, English and French, and I managed to sign up a number of young ladies for our finishing school by advertising in the British Press. Our young ladies were accommodated in the bedrooms around the courtyard and were taught in the main building or in a room we had converted in one of the courtyard buildings. We had converted another courtyard room into a student common room and, from the students' perspective, their accommodation and living conditions were very pleasant.

Annette, who worked incredibly hard to set up a viable framework of teaching for the finishing school, also had to organise the catering for the students, the laundering of their clothes and bed linen, the cleaning of the buildings and the maintenance of the gardens and the property generally. The "labour pool" in the area was not great and we had mixed fortunes with the French staff we employed. One of the cleaners, for example, stole clothes from the laundry room where we had a battery of washing and drying machines because her brother-in-law had been seriously injured in a car crash and, as a consequence, had lost his job and his income. It was only when the students complained about the mysterious loss of their clothes that we were alerted to this and fired the young woman in question!

Annette had, from the outset, the aura of a headmistress and it was not difficult to see her in the role of Directrice of the College: she also mastered French in record time – a case of having to do so!

In an effort to boost numbers I flew out to Hong Kong and visited some of the private girls' schools there: the heads or directors of these schools were, however, not too impressed by the location of the college or the fact that it had only recently been established and I flew home empty-handed.

In fact what Annette and I rapidly discovered was that it was not easy to break into the finishing school market and that we had not done our market research property: we had a good product in a lovely building in the wrong place!

On the other hand the children had quickly settled into life in France and into speaking French, the quality of life was excellent and Annette had become highly respected in the area: so much so that she was invited to become a member of the Syndicat D'Initiative for the Hautefort area (the local tourist council) and a member of the British Chamber of Commerce in Bordeaux.

It had become apparent after a few months that her concept of a finishing school in the Dordogne would not work, and here we were with a capacious well-equipped college but not enough pupils. In the circumstances I suggested to Annette that we adopt a different approach. Britain had entered the Single Market and we should offer courses in business French to British men as well as women, and English courses to French children. She was not happy at abandoning her favourite project but she could see it was not working as she had hoped and we once again set out advertising the new courses in the British

Press.

Teaching business French to UK business people was only partially successful because equivalent courses were on offer in Bordeaux, a more cosmopolitan location: the British, moreover, appear to have a natural aversion to speaking any language but their own! We did, nevertheless, find some applicants for them. We also discovered to our surprise that our English courses for young French children were very popular – particularly during the long summer "vacances" when families, mostly from the Paris area, came down to spend the summer in the Dordogne and wondered what to do with their children for several weeks.

An "English style" college in the area with a very talented and charming "Directrice" and safe grounds appealed to them. The young French children also loved our two Scottish sheepdogs and our Burmese cats that had made the journey to France with us. Had it not been for a series of disasters we might have made a success of the college and remained permanently at the Pavillon. My unusual life story would then have ended with Annette and I running a college in France.

But just as we were beginning to gain recognition for what we were doing at the Pavillon we received two shocks: the purchasing practice which, by this time, had stopped paying me a consultancy fee "decamped" from Foxcroft, my Georgian office building without giving any notice and Lloyd's of London collapsed almost immediately thereafter with losses of eight billion pounds. I faced potentially immense claims as an underwriting member for asbestos-related health problems, the "Exxon Valdez" oil spill in Alaska and the "Piper Alpha" disaster in the North Sea.

Although I did not realise it at the time I joined Lloyd's of London, Lloyd's underwriters had encouraged a very large number of people with valuable properties to become members of their syndicates in a comparatively short space of time. It became clear, in retrospect, that we were "cannon fodder", members whose assets would defray the gargantuan losses that mysteriously appeared from such woodwork as existed in the Lloyd's building!

At the interview for membership of Lloyd's in the splendid wood panelled boardroom at the then new and shiny Lloyd's building at One Lime Street in the City of London we were advised that we "could be liable down to our last pair of cufflinks" but were then cheerfully informed that Lloyd's had not made a loss for the last 320 years! What splendid actors the interviewers were! Or, alternatively, how ignorant they were of the effect of the massive claims that were just about to erupt, like a pent-up volcano, beneath their feet on the floors below!

The purchasing practice, the firm from Southend, added insult to injury by moving into offices in Billericay owned by the underwriter who had introduced me to Lloyd's of London in the first place. As a result I owed money to Lloyd's of London instead of being in receipt of income from it.

I remonstrated with both the purchasing practice and the underwriter of whose syndicate I was a member. The underwriter, an extremely wealthy man for whom I had acted in numerous successful transactions, had not bothered to tell me that my tenants were moving into his premises and invented a "cock and bull" excuse for allowing them to do so: he was clearly not concerned about the duty of care he owed to a member of his syndicate or about undermining my security: he was more concerned about finding tenants for his offices and the additional rent my former tenants would pay him.

The purchasing practice must have concluded that it could take my practice elsewhere in Billericay and thereby avoid being obliged to pay more than a sixth of the value of it: its excuse for doing so was that the practice was not as profitable as it first thought and that if I wanted to recover anything from it I would have to sue the firm, primarily a bunch of litigation specialists, for it.

The "knock-on" effect of these two disasters was very serious, as the reader will doubtless appreciate, and was only mitigated by the fact that, after my consultancy period had ended, I had been able to obtain self-employment with the Law Society as an Intervening Agent. The self-employment involved my being sent to the offices of solicitors in default by virtue of dishonesty or incompetence and doing my best to ensure that the clients of their practices were protected and compensated for any financial losses they had incurred.

Since I was, in effect, my own boss, billing the Law Society on an "ad hoc" agency basis for each intervention, this particular form of self-employment enabled me to divide my time between living and working in Billericay for periods of roughly two weeks and driving down to St. Agnan (and back) for up to one week. When at the Pavillon, apart from keeping a very busy Annette company, checking the college finances, decorating rooms, mowing the lawns and driving into Perigeux or Brive for the shopping I did not have a great deal to do! On the other hand, living apart from Annette was not easy and I did appreciate the time I could spend with her.

When the twin disasters occurred I had to decide whether we should spend valuable years of our lives trying to recover money from the practice in Southend and suing the underwriters: we risked losing our remaining assets – our home and my travel agency in Shenfield. The additional stress would be enormous. Alternatively, should we cut adrift and move on?

The Pavillon was not yet self-supporting, we had substantial mortgages on Foxcroft and on our home and the loss of rental income from my office and of the Lloyds income that had supported the college spelt the end of our French adventure. The only advantage of all these disasters would be that we could go back to living together all the time in England.

Annette was devastated by these two events after all the effort she had put into the college and, again, our marriage which had been strained by our living apart came under intense pressure. She felt that if I had sold our home in Billericay and had used the proceeds to pay off the mortgage on the Pavillon and if I had disposed of the travel agency in Shenfield, and Foxcroft ,when the Lloyd's losses I had incurred were known we could have remained in France.

I took the opposite view, that we should weigh a doubt against a certainty and stick to the certainty, namely our assets in England. There was no guarantee that the Pavillon would provide an income for us in the future and I did not want to keep commuting to the Dordogne.

Although the closure of the college and our sad retreat from St. Agnan pushed us both emotionally and financially to the limit and although, as a result of the stress caused by it we separated for a short time on our return to England, the bands of gold we wore on our left hands held us together. It was a nerve- racking and tumultuous time – another very close call – but we survived as a married couple and learned a lot from our experiences in France.

One of the major things Annette learned was how students interact with each other in a "closed environment" and how attractive the young ladies under her care were to the young French men in the area! They were attracted to our finishing school students (and to our daughters) as bees are to honey! Annette had to use all her motherly powers of persuasion to prevent or try to prevent our young women from succumbing to the blandishments of these amorous young men! In fact she developed quite an interest in psychology which subsequently led to her stellar career in the NHS.

For my own part I discovered that French employment tribunals invariably come down on the side of the employee and that French policemen are craven when confronted by a bunch of irate farmers on tractors.

When we opened the college and took on staff we asked them to accept British Bank Holidays in lieu of French National Holidays: they all willingly agreed to this. When we closed the college they took our SARL, our trading company, to an employment tribunal claiming double pay for the French National Holidays they had voluntarily agreed to waive. As I sat in the tribunal chamber waiting for their case to be heard a friendly looking man sitting next to me asked me in French why I was attending the tribunal: I told him and he looked at me sympathetically and said, "Has no one told you that employees always win?"

"The employees are entitled to recover double wages from the SARL," the tribunal judge boomed, and the man sitting next to me gave me a pat on the shoulder and said, "I told you so." I did not bother to tell the judge that the SARL had nothing left in its bank account and that I was on my way back to England immediately after the hearing: there did not seem a great deal of point in doing so.

As for the police, Annette had asked me to drive into Brive one day for some shopping. The city of Brive was about twenty miles away and when I had driven about half way I found the road completely blocked by tractors: I walked the fifty metres or so to the front of the blockage and found a French gendarme standing there smoking a cigarette.

"Is there in France," I asked him, "a right to pass along a road?" (Un droit de passage). "Mais oui," he replied. "Then why are you not enabling motorists to pass?" He looked at me with a resigned expression, gave the usual Gallic shrug and carried on smoking his cigarette! He was not going to argue with the farmers or attempt to enforce the law.

Unlike the British, who appear almost obsessive at complying with the law, however absurd or bureaucratic, the French have no hesitation in sticking up two fingers to authority if they are not getting their way! The nearest we get to this type of vaguely anarchic behaviour is taxi drivers blocking the streets of London who may well have learned this stratagem from French counterparts while on holiday abroad.

The other thing we both learned was that, although most French people proclaim "Liberty, Fraternity and Equality" and some deride what they consider class consciousness in Britain they can be very status conscious themselves and can even be quite neurotic about it! One evening there was a knock on the front door of the Pavillon. The Chef de Police, very smartly dressed, was standing there: "I regret to inform you that your son, James, was caught riding on the back of a motorbike which is against the law: we had to make him get off it." Annette and I looked at each other and thought, "We and James must be in trouble." "In the circumstances," said the Chef de Police, "I have brought him home in a police car. I apologise for troubling you." With that he doffed his cap, ushered James into the hall and left. We concluded that he would not have been so polite if we had not been living in the Pavillon!

On the other hand the French can be incredibly kind and also very entertaining. When Annette was unwell one day and I had to catch a plane from Bordeaux early in the morning a friend, Mr. Ratinaud, got up at 5 am to drive me to the airport some fifty miles away. He would accept nothing for his kindness and I will never forget this generous act on his part.

Annette also had an enjoyable and illuminating time at the Syndicat D'Initiative (the local tourist council). The meeting would start at about 7.30 pm and the items on the agenda would be discussed: it was not uncommon, however, during the often heated discussions for someone who disagreed vehemently with the decision of the committee to slam his papers on the table and storm out of the meeting room: the rest of the committee would carry on as if nothing had happened!

After a few minutes the person who had stormed out would re-enter the committee meeting, sit down and, like the others, carry on discussing matters, again as if nothing had happened! At the end of the meeting the mayor would go up to a large and impressive cabinet at the back of the room and bring out a number of bottles of wine and glasses. Annette said she usually left when they started hugging each other as if they were all the best friends in the world! There was a touch of "Don Camillo" about the whole proceedings.

Annette had mounted "Art Exhibitions" in the Pavillon, had allowed couples to use the building and gardens for wedding celebrations and photographs and it was such a pity we had to leave such a beautiful location and head back to Billericay and a very uncertain future.

Myself at 40 years of age

Shenfield Travel: the scene of the theft

Hughes & Co staff photograph

Annette as Manager of the Property Department

Annette at home

Hautefort: view of the Pavillon du Bonheur

The Pavillon as "Hautefort College"

Annette and myself as family mediators

Myself "on the stump" as the Loyal Conservative Party parliamentary candidate in the 1997 General Election

Vivien at the time of our marriage

Vivien the actress, as "Anastasia"

Myself (front, third left) as Cedric (Ceddie), Little Lord Fauntleroy, in "Angels in Love"

Grandfather Somers: Royal Artillery, 1917

Robin Tilbrook, Chairman of the English Democrats and a fellow solicitor, with myself at Court

Annette at the Doctorate ceremony

26

Resolve Mediation and Counselling

When Annette and I returned after two and a half years in France somewhat battered and bruised by our unfortunate experiences and facing a potentially catastrophic (and, at that stage, unquantified) bill from Lloyds of London we had to decide what to do with our lives.

At the time I still had the Law Society appointment as an Intervening Agent which I knew would not go on for ever but which would cover our overheads at home for the time being. We both had to re-establish long-term career paths, however, and decide what to do with Foxcroft.

Despite the risk inherent in "putting all our eggs in one basket" we nevertheless wanted to do something together if we could and the one area on which we were in complete agreement was the trauma of separation and divorce: we had both had personal experience of marriage breakdown.

During my thirty years of practice as a solicitor I had, moreover, been involved in some very harrowing divorce cases where the solicitors acting for the other spouse had appeared more interested in encouraging dispute than in resolving it, thereby earning substantially more out of divorce than was ever necessary or appropriate. As a member of the Institute of Arbitrators whose primary role is dispute resolution without the need for litigation I had heard of proposals for the mediation of divorce and we both became aware that this concept was being incorporated into the Family Law Act 1996.

While at the Pavillon de Bonheur Annette had developed a strong interest in psychology. Annette felt she should catch up on her misspent youth and decided to develop this interest by studying cognitive behavioural therapy

(CBT) and applying to the Open University to read for a degree in psychology.

Our convergence on the subject of matrimonial breakdown led us both to sign up to a course on family mediation being offered by John Haynes, a famous American expert in this field: the course had been arranged by Alastair Logan who had previously devoted many years of his career as a solicitor to securing the acquittal of the "Birmingham Six", wrongly convicted of planting bombs at the "Mulberry Bush" and the "Tavern in the Town" in Birmingham.

The course was very successful: Annette proved to be a natural family mediator and I developed into one after I had suppressed an innate desire to "lead" the process, as I had done in litigated divorce!

We both qualified as family mediators and as a result of the fact that there was no family mediation organisation, as such, several members on the course decided to form a mediation organisation: I suggested, as a name, the British Association of Lawyer Mediators (BALM for short!). Lord Mackay, the then Lord Chancellor, liked the name and BALM would doubtless be in existence now but for the 1997 General Election.

Annette and I could see a couple of major flaws in the concept of family mediation: the first was that many divorcing couples are in such a state emotionally that they find it almost impossible to be rational about the immense decisions they have to make: women tend to use the children as bargaining tools, some husbands tend to regard wives as possessions to be discarded or try to conceal their income and assets in order to pay as little maintenance as possible to their outgoing spouse: many, though not all, husbands also try to evade financial responsibility for the children they have brought into the world.

In short, husbands and wives would invariably benefit from counselling of a "down to earth" and practical nature before they ever embark on divorce.

The second flaw was that the mediator should be independent of the couple seeking mediation, each of whom should refer to their own solicitor for legal advice: a mediator is not there to offer legal advice to couples, merely to facilitate discussion and mediation between them.

In a mediation session we were taught to "triangulate" by keeping a table between husband and wife: the spouses should be sufficiently far apart so that neither could assault the other across the table and the family mediator should be sufficiently far from the couple as was necessary – to avoid him or her being assaulted during the mediation process!

How was this problem to be overcome? Annette and I decided to set up an organisation called "Resolve Mediation and Counselling Services Limited" which offered counselling and mediation in that order, on a national basis: it also offered a national referral system whereby couples could be referred to independent family mediators, but retain their own solicitors for necessary legal advice.

We worked very hard on the concept of family mediation being linked to counselling and travelled all over England promoting "Resolve": the solicitors who came on our courses paid a fee to attend and we covered our overheads in this way. Annette proved an excellent communicator and we could see interest building in our approach to family mediation.

Once again, however, fate took a hand and before the mediation provisions in the Family Law Act could be implemented Tony Blair had ousted John Major as Prime Minister and "Derry" Irvine, Blair's Lord Chancellor, had put the mediation provisions in the Act on "hold": they were not to be activated thereafter for many years.

This was a great disappointment and one might think that we would be "punch drunk" by the series of misfortunes that had befallen us: this proved not to be the case.

Annette decided to pursue a career in the NHS and obtained employment with the South Essex Partnership Trust (SEPT), the largest Mental Health Trust in Essex. Before long she had acquired a formal qualification in CBT and was enjoying her new role: the story of her amazing career from this point onward is told in a later chapter.

I reluctantly decided to return to general practice as a solicitor and to utilise the offices I had acquired in Shenfield for the intervention work and Resolve as a Solicitor's practice. I had renewed my practising certificate every year while acting as a Law Society Intervening Agent and had been much involved in untangling the practice affairs of dishonest and incompetent solicitors since 1989: it was therefore no great effort to set up in practice on my own account. In fact I was, ironically, earning more from my three-person practice in Shenfield than I had earned from my practice in Billericay where I employed nearly twenty members of staff: the overheads were minimal and I cut out every aspect of general practice that was time-consuming, namely litigation, divorce and criminal legal aid work.

As anticipated the Law Society decided, after some years, to instruct larger practices to carry out intervention work and collected the many thousands of client files I had been steadily working through in an effort to locate deeds and documents that should be retained or distributed and to ensure that cases in the files had been property handled and closed: my experiences as an Intervening Agent appear in a later Chapter entitled "The Third Phase".

27

Political Experiences

My first indirect contact with politics came in 1959. My father, as Assistant Town Clerk of Billericay Urban District Council, had once again been deputed to organise the count for the General Election that year with his secretary, Joyce Norris, formerly Joyce Carpenter. Joyce whose family had lived in Great Burstead for many years had married Sammy Norris, a survivor of the infamous Burma Railway. She was later awarded the MBE for her outstanding services to Billericay and Basildon Councils.

My father and Joyce were both good organisers and in 1955 had succeeded in getting the election results for Billericay constituency out first nationally: this was no mean feat because at the time the constituency comprised four towns – Billericay, Wickford, Laindon and Pitsea – and was the fourth largest in land area in the country.

In 1955 Alma Hatt, the ambitious Town Clerk of Billericay and a qualified barrister had hit on the idea of Billericay getting its election results out first: he felt it would put Billericay "on the map" before it was absorbed into the New Town of Basildon and it certainly did.

In order to ensure that the ballot boxes reached the most central point in the constituency without delay three vehicles were waiting at each polling station to whisk the boxes at 9 pm to the school at which the count was to take place: one vehicle carried the ballot boxes, the other two were "back up". In those days cars were not as reliable as they are now! Both my father and Joyce calculated that the maximum time likely to be taken for the journey was nineteen minutes and the projected time for the count itself was somewhere between thirty and forty minutes.

A large wooden tray-like structure – rather like a massive "roll a penny" table subdivided into three adjoining sections – was placed in the middle of the counting area and the counters of the votes were seated at a number of trestle tables in the school hall around it. Scrutineers from the respective parties were able to walk between the tables and check that the votes were being properly allocated. The candidates and their electoral agents were also able to check the counting process. The votes, when counted, were bundled into hundreds for each candidate and then into thousands and placed on the large wooden tray: it was possible, in this way, to see if any particular candidate was moving ahead of the others and to see immediately who had won the Billericay constituency.

In order to expedite the count rehearsals were held with dummy voting slips in the weeks before the actual election and these rehearsals resulted in a very efficient and streamlined counting system on the night of the count itself.

It was no wonder, therefore, that in 1955 the result for Billericay was broadcast first on national radio. Richard Body, the Conservative candidate (later Sir Richard Body) was elected as successor to Bernard Braine (later Lord Braine of Wheatley).

In 1959 my father got me a job as a "vote counter" and I thoroughly enjoyed the experience and felt so proud of my home constituency coming out first, once again, with the election results. "Billericay" was really on the map now: coming first in 1955 had been no "flash in the pan". This time Edward Gardner, the Conservative candidate (later Sir Edward Gardner) was elected to represent the constituency and the whole process from closure of the polling stations at 9 pm to the declaration of the result took 59 minutes: Billericay was getting rather good at counting votes!

Between 1961 and 1963 I lived for about eighteen months from Monday to Friday in a flat in Lewisham with the owner of the flat "Ike" (Isaac) Ascher and two other young men, Harald Munthe-Kaas whose father was, I believe, a university professor in Norway and Chris Beeby, whose father was a High Court judge in New Zealand. Harald went on to become a journalist and an expert on Communist China and Chris went on to be New Zealand Ambassador to France and one of his country's most distinguished lawyers and diplomats. "Ike" who was a lecturer in economics and politics at Goldsmiths College was employed to assist Professor Robert Mckenzie, a famous sociologist and political commentator, at general elections during the BBC "all night" coverage of the results. It was Robert McKenzie who refined the "swingometer" that has been used on all subsequent general elections I have to say that the flat was a very interesting place to be during the week with Ike providing a lot of background information on how election television broadcasts were organised in those days.

By 1964 I was back in Billericay full time and my father appointed me a deputy returning officer for the count at the general election in that year: he had asked me to concentrate on keeping the Press happy because, by this time, we actually had the BBC Television cameras in the Archer Hall, the scene of the count.

Once again Billericay produced its results first but, although Edward Gardner's winning margin was in excess of 1500 votes, the Labour candidate demanded a recount. I was standing next to Raymond Baxter, the BBC's motoring correspondent on the stage of the Archer Hall at the time. He was anxious to have the result announced first but, to his annoyance (and that of most people in the hall) the Labour candidate demanded a second recount. By this time it was clear that a political game was being played – because the majority was obvious from the bundles of thousands and hundreds of votes on the massive wooden tray. "We have been nobbled," Raymond Baxter shouted to me. He was incandescent because the Billericay result was delayed until Salford, a Labour constituency, announced its result: the Labour party wanted a Labour result to be first to reflect the expected national swing to Labour. After that and in view of the deaths of Alma Hatt and my father and the revision of the electoral boundaries no subsequent efforts were made to compete for "first place" and the Billericay result lost any significance.

In relation to the revision of the electoral boundaries and the growth of Basildon as a New Town it is worth commenting on the enterprise of Alma Hatt. He was an extraordinary man who, appreciating that the New Towns Commission was charged merely with building the New Towns and nothing more, put it to the councillors and staff of Billericay UDC that both would benefit enormously by relieving the Commission of any responsibility for setting up a new Basildon Council and by taking over all aspects of administration of the New Town.

The salaries of local government officers were assessed on the populations they served and the councillors would get in "on the ground floor" of political representation for the New Town.

Alma therefore rented Keay House in the new Town square at Basildon and moved the administrative staff of the council "lock, stock and barrel" to Basildon!

After the prestige gained by getting its election results out first and its string of eminent Members of Parliament, Billericay had subsequently to endure the considerable loss of face caused by Ian Dury and his song, "I'm a Billericay Dickey"!

This was compounded by the "exposure" of Harvey Proctor as someone whose sexual proclivities were unacceptable to the electorate he served, albeit that, as Member of Parliament for Billericay, he had been responsible and diligent in representing his constituency between 1983 and 1987.

In 1987 the local Conservative Party looked for someone who would reduce any stigma attached to the town and the constituency and selected Teresa Gorman. She had obtained a double first in biology and zoology at University College, London (a first class degree), had been an elected member of Westminster City Council between 1982 and 1986 and had run a business selling teaching aids: she was also involved in property development. She probably looked an ideal candidate, but it was in fact the ninth seat she had tried for!

What she failed to mention, when selected and adopted, was her true age. She claimed to have been born on 30 September 1941, rather than 30 September 1931 – her true date of birth – believing, correctly, that this would increase greatly her chances of being adopted!

Having been elected with the very substantial majority of 17,986 votes as MP for the Billericay constituency she clearly believed that her position was secure for the rest of her political career and rapidly embarked, as a Eurosceptic, on a policy of opposing the Government's attempts to improve our relationships with Europe. In 1992 she increased her majority to 22,494. In 1994, however, she had the Conservative Whip withdrawn for refusing to back the European Community Finances Bill and she became a leading figure in the rebellion over the Maastricht Treaty that nearly brought down the Government, earning herself the soubriquet of "bastard" from John Major: she was one of nine Conservative MPs who voted against his policies on a number of occasions ("the Whipless nine") and caused him great embarrassment as Prime Minister.

It was not just her attitude to John Major, however, that led me, as one of the many who felt she was not representing the views of her constituents, to stand against her in the 1997 general election.

It was her lack of respect for Billericay and the effect that her actions were having on the reputation of the town: the last thing Billericay wanted after Ian Dury's song and Harvey Proctor's behaviour was another highly controversial Member of Parliament as its representative voice and image.

Having created a maverick image for herself it was not surprising that she came to the attention of programme makers at the BBC and that she was invited to appear on "Have I got news for you". Watching MPs trying to be jocular or at least self-possessed in the face of humorous and cutting remarks from Ian Hislop and Paul Merton makes for good television and can often help the public profile of the MPs themselves: Boris Johnson is a case in point. It became pretty obvious, however, from the outset that she had accepted rather too much "hospitality" from the BBC in the infamous "green room" before the show. Being light-hearted is one thing, being embarrassing is another. As a result her behaviour did her no credit and did nothing to enhance the reputation of the constituency she represented.

I telephoned her after the show and asked her not to let herself and Billericay down by drinking more than was wise before any future radio or television programme. She laughed off my request and said I was taking her behaviour and appearance too seriously.

Since it was clear that she had missed the point of my call and indicated that she had no intention of acting any differently in future I told her that, if I ever saw her, as MP for Billericay, somewhat the worse for wear on TV I would try to preserve the reputation of the town by standing against her, as an Independent Conservative at the next general election: once again she laughed off my comment.

It was not long after that conversation, however, that she appeared on the "Mrs. Merton Show" and, once again, it was painfully obvious that she had accepted rather too much "hospitality" before the programme: she allowed herself to be ridiculed and did nothing to enhance the reputation of her constituency. So I rang her up and told her that, in the circumstances I would carry out my promise and would stand against her at the next general election.

"You wouldn't do that, would you?" she said and when I confirmed that I meant what I said there was a stunned silence at the other end of the line. "I am coming round to see you, now," she replied.

Not wishing to be inhospitable I did, in fact, open a bottle of "bubbly" when she arrived about half an hour later and we consumed it between us! But we were not on television and it would have been my word against hers if she had said anything detrimental about our meeting.

I explained why I was going to stand against her, although at the time I had no idea how I was going to do it. I had spent more than twenty-five years trying to enhance the reputation of Billericay whereas she appeared to have little loyalty towards her constituents or even her own party. In the eyes of the nation she represented Billericay and what the nation thought of her it thought the same of us. During about an hour's conversation she did her best to deflect me from standing against her. It was only when her charm offensive had failed that she said, "If you do stand against me I can say all sorts of nasty things about you," to which I responded, "Then you had better go ahead and say them." With that she departed!

I did not add that I would have had more nasty things to say about her than she would have had to say about me!

As a former protégé of Dame Shirley Porter she was not really in a position to engage in any form of mud-slinging and, in fairness, neither of us did so.

Although I was not aware of it at the time, questions did remain unanswered relating to her property interests until 2000 when she was suspended from the House of Commons for a month for failing to disclose on the Register of Members' Interests between 1984 and 1994 three rented properties in South London and for her failure to register two rented-out Portuguese properties from 1987 to 1999. The House of Commons Standards and Privileges Committee also found that she should not have introduced a Ten Minute Rule Bill in 1990 proposing the repeal of the Rent Acts (which protected tenants) without registering and declaring a financial interest.

All I had read in the papers or heard about in 1997 was that her solicitors had been threatening her with bankruptcy for the alleged non-payment of a substantial legal bill incurred during a widely reported planning dispute she and her husband had conducted with Thurrock Council. They had made a substantial number of alterations to their constituency home, a listed Tudor farmhouse, without the necessary listed building consents. After being fined £3000 for breach of the listed building regulations they had reluctantly had a new porch demolished. Why they thought they could flout the legislation which protected historic buildings we will never know!

Having thrown down the gauntlet I had to mount an effective challenge.

But how on earth was I actually going to be able to oppose her? How was I even going to get my name on to a ballot paper? I found out that Teresa Gorman had done something very similar: she had stood as an independent "Anti Ted Heath" Conservative in Streatham in 1974 when he was the Prime Minister. She had polled 210 votes. Could I do any better?

I decided to approach my fellow Striders and ask if any of them would be prepared to add their names to the list of nominees I required in order to stand as a candidate. To my relief and surprise I had no difficulty in filling the nomination form with the requisite number of supporters. The completed form, plus my £500 deposit, was delivered to the electoral returning officer and I was accepted and registered as the "Loyal to John Major, Independent Conservative Candidate" for the Billericay constituency.

At this point the local Conservative Party reacted with fury. Despite the fact that I had held a membership card the Press were informed that I had never been a member of the Conservative Party, that if I was a Conservative I was disloyal in opposing the MP chosen by the local Conservative Party and that, if I was not, I was a trouble-maker, probably working for the Labour Party, etc, etc. It was all very predictable!

I began to wonder whether I had bitten off more than I could chew but shortly after the newspapers started publicising my candidature and publishing these broadsides from the local Conservative Party I received a telephone call. "Derek Greenfield here," said the caller. "You are Teresa Gorman's electoral agent," I replied. "What do you want?"

"I'm not her agent any more," he said. "Do you want an agent? If so I would be happy to act as your agent." I could hardly believe my ears. "Of course I would like you to be my agent." What a stroke of luck! Her own electoral agent could not accept her brand of right-wing Conservatism and had decided to resign from her team. What I came to appreciate quickly thereafter from the guarded telephone calls I received from a number of Conservative county councillors was that my intervention was not unwelcome and that, whatever the attitude of the local Conservative Party towards her, they wished Derek and I well.

Once he arrived at my home the first thing Derek and I had to do was design and print electioneering literature and posters. We applied ourselves to this with enthusiasm. A local resident whom I had known well through Scouting also offered to build a temporary arch over the entrance to my drive with a

"Party Headquarters" sign on the top of it. A number of local businessmen who had no time for Teresa Gorman also came forward with offers of financial and logistical support. The assistance I received was very heartening.

At the same time, however, I started to receive threatening phone calls, undoubtedly from supporters of Teresa Gorman, in which the callers stated that they knew where I lived and that I, and my family, would be, "In serious trouble" if I continued to stand against her. I put the phone down very firmly on these people – all male – with appropriate responses from myself!

Having printed our election posters and several thousand leaflets and having also purchased a large number of wooden stakes upon which to attach our posters, the next step was to find suitable places to locate the posters and to distribute the leaflets: it was here again that my fellow Striders rallied round. Being runners and living in different parts of the constituency they were only too happy to distribute them around their localities: in this way most parts of the constituency were leafleted whereas Teresa Gorman could only rely on coverage and limited support from people who, for the most part, lived in Billericay.

Putting up and maintaining our posters on the stakes we had purchased proved a time-consuming exercise: many local residents were only too happy for us to put stakes and posters in their front gardens. We had to do this every morning throughout the election campaign because Teresa Gorman's supporters ripped the stakes out of the ground at night. It is no exaggeration to say that I learned quite a lot about political "dirty tricks" during the campaign!

In terms of electioneering her views were much more right wing and anti-European than my own: in fact she bore with pride the accolade of the "most right-wing member of Parliament" bestowed on her by the Guardian columnist Polly Toynbee. I stuck very much to the John Major line over Europe, namely that whatever one felt about the obvious deficiencies of the European Union it was better to argue a case for reform from the inside rather than shout at it from the sidelines.

In fact Teresa Gorman was remarkably quiet and reticent about expressing her views to her constituents: she probably chose not to advertise her opposition to John Major in public as she had in the House of Commons: she did not appear at any joint party political hustings and it was, ironically, left to me as an inexperienced non-political Independent to represent the Government's views!

Because she had such a large majority she probably felt her position was invulnerable and that she really did not have to do anything to hold on to her seat: she had, after all, the unwavering support of her local Conservative Party (less Derek Greenfield, her former electoral agent) and must have assumed that her rebellious behaviour would be condoned by the bulk of Conservative voters in the constituency. But it was not acceptable to many and there was no real reason why it would be so.

My rationale throughout the election campaign had been that if I could get enough people who felt that she was not good for the reputation of the constituency to vote for me it was more than likely that, at a future election, she would be deselected. Someone less controversial would be adopted as Conservative candidate and the tarnished image of Billericay would be restored. A protest vote that did not unseat her but caused her backers to think again about choosing her to represent the constituency in future would be enough.

And so it proved. Her majority of 22,494 in 1992 was slashed to 1,356 in 1997 and the number of voters who supported her fell from 37,406 in 1992 to 22,033 in 1997. If I had polled another 700 votes she would have lost her seat! I polled 3,377 votes and retained my deposit. As a result of the election she was deselected as a future Conservative candidate by the local Tory party.

At the count it is usual for each losing candidate to congratulate the winning candidate – which I did. The winning candidate then pledges to represent the interests of everyone in the constituency and says a few complimentary words about the other candidates. Not surprisingly, what she said about me was very uncomplimentary indeed and quite provocative. As a result, her braying supporters howled me down and, as I stepped off the platform, closed in on me. At this point a somewhat concerned police superintendent stepped forward and asked whether I needed any assistance. "I can look after myself," I replied and walked straight through the middle of them. "If this is politics," I thought, "I can do without it!"

John Baron was adopted as Conservative candidate for the next election and proved a very good community MP – even though I did not agree with his stance on the E.U. He enhanced the reputation of the constituency, rather than the reverse and this is all that was required.

What happened to Teresa Gorman? She tried to stand as Conservative Mayor of London but her attempt was blocked: she subsequently became involved in local politics in Grays, in Essex, but that is all.

She died in August 2015 intestate, leaving an estate of worth £2.8m: she had refused to make a will because she did not want to countenance her own death.

During her lifetime, however, she had made donations to the HMS Beagle Project charity and had expressed a wish that the figurehead on the prow of the replica of HMS Beagle be a bare-breasted likeness of her and that the bust of the figurehead be enlarged in line with her feisty nature! The replica of HMS Beagle on which Charles Darwin had travelled to South America will one day replicate the voyages he made and her "immortalised" effigy will travel with it!

In a strange way her interest in biology and zoology and her declaration that she regarded herself as "St. Teresa of the Menopause" and the "Angel of HRT" have come together in this unusual request!

My subsequent short political career as a pro-European Conservative candidate in the 1998 European parliamentary elections was interesting but hardly deserving of more than a fleeting mention. Although I joined a party that was expressly formed and designed to promote the Conservative "Britain in Europe" case and met some really interesting pro-Europeans, the campaign was poorly handled and the "party" sank without trace. It made no impact because the Conservative Party insisted that it was pro-European and challenged the existence of the newly formed party on the basis that it merely replicated Conservative Party policy at the time. It is interesting and ironic that less than twenty years later the Conservative Party is leading the country into Brexit and out of the European Union!

28

Lessons Learned: Marriage

It has been said that marriage is the process whereby your wife finds out the type of man she would have preferred to marry: there is an element of truth in that!

I have come to a number of more serious conclusions about marriage both from personal experience and from acting as a divorce lawyer and qualifying as a family mediator.

The first and most obvious is that people marry for the right reasons or for the wrong reasons: the people who marry for the right reasons are more likely to have longer and happier lives than those who do not. The right reasons, are unfortunately not too obvious to young people and by the time the reasons become clear they may well have lost the person to whom they would have been best suited.

The wrong reasons, like feeling one is "on the shelf" and must get married to someone in order to have children and financial security, or needing a wife for status or as a replacement mother figure invariably lead to a sense of dissatisfaction with the marriage.

The second conclusion is that marriage is a matter of tolerances: some fortunate couples enter into marriage and have no difficulty in living with their spouse, essentially because they both want the other to be happy. Because they have the best interests of the other at heart the relationship deepens and strengthens as does the feeling of love or respect they had for each other when they wed. This type of relationship is normally capable of withstanding difficulties and traumas, laying down firm foundations on which to base a successful family life. The children of such marriages learn about happy or contented relationships from their parents and, from my experience, the children of these couples usually replicate that happiness and contentment in their own relationships.

Other less fortunate couples enter into marriage in the expectation of happiness but find that their "other half" is not what they expected. It is usually as a result of the other half putting himself or herself first rather than his/her spouse. Disillusion on the part of one or both spouses sets in. Very often, however, unhappy spouses remain in marriages because they have a greater tolerance level than others: they grit their teeth, conclude that they have "made their bed and must lie on it."

In this respect many marriages become a compromise – a relationship which is partially unfulfilled but which is tolerable and maintained very often for the sake of the children of the marriage and for reasons of comfort or security: it is often a "trade-off" between providing the income for a married state and being provided for, between simply maintaining a home or having children and enjoying the comfort and financial security that marriage offers or implies.

Most young people do not like to feel that they are being left "on the shelf" and most older people do not relish the idea of solitude in later life. It is not unusual, therefore, for couples to enter into marriage without actually "loving" each other: in the case of the male, the acquisition of a wife, or in the case of the female, the opportunity to have children in what she considers a secure environment are the rationales for marriage.

The couples in which one spouse discovers that he or she cannot tolerate the behaviour of the other usually finish up before a divorce judge or a family mediator: the behaviour of the spouse and the tolerance or otherwise of it varies a great deal: not surprisingly some people have low tolerance levels while others have higher levels and some couples who stay together have one spouse with a higher tolerance level than a spouse who seeks divorce.

I have also come to the sad conclusion that the amount some young couples spend on their marriage ceremony and the attention they give to it is often an indicator of how long the marriage will last – because the ceremony becomes an end in itself and its relevance to the longer term relationship is overlooked, sometimes completely ignored.

I have to acknowledge that, being the child of a happy marriage, I did rather assume that my first wife would tolerate my spending so much of my time on building up my travel business and legal practice in the interests of our long-term security: having had a less happy childhood and feeling overlooked she could not.

My rationale had been that marriages often go through "sticky patches" – particularly in the first few years when adjusting to the demands of young children and the need to provide a decent home for the family. There is also a steep learning curve in adjusting one's behaviour to what is acceptable in a married relationship. I took too much for granted: I was not what she expected and we had a consensual divorce.

It was a hard lesson to learn and one that I realised had to be applied to my second marriage.

29

Legal Career, Phase 3: Sorting out the "Baddies"

The third phase of my legal career opened my eyes to the problems encountered by clients and banks in dealing with certain members of the legal profession.

Having sold my practice in 1988 and having come to the end of my consultancy period I decided to retain my practising certificate and offer my services to the Law Society as an Intervening Agent. An Intervening Agent is rather like the person who clears up after the Lord Mayor's Show! Dishonest, bankrupt and deceased solicitors have a habit of leaving a lot of mess behind them and that mess has to be sorted out by someone or some practice with the necessary skills and experience to do so.

By 1989 I had been involved for over twenty years in most aspects of the work of a high street solicitor and had a reasonable understanding of what was required: I felt confident I could carry out this particular role because I had already experienced intervention work during my consultancy period.

When, in the 1980s and 1990s the Law Society got wind of dishonest or highly questionable behaviour on the part of a particular solicitor or firm of solicitors, usually as a result of letters of complaint, it used to send investigators from its offices in Stag Place in the West End of London or from Leamington Spa to check what was going on. This investigative function was subsequently taken over by the Solicitors Regulation Authority (the SRA).

If either fraud or dishonesty was detected, for example by comparing the monies that were in each individual client's ledger account with the monies that were actually in the client account of the practice at the bank, the Law Society would decide without further ado to appoint an Intervening Agent. Although nothing would necessarily have been said by the investigators during their visit to the solicitor or the practice in question immediate steps would have been taken to close the practice down by freezing the solicitor's bank accounts.

There were, of course, other reasons why an Intervening Agent should be appointed, particularly in the case of sole practitioners. The sole practitioner could have died or had a nervous breakdown or been seriously injured or killed in an accident. Alternatively, he or she may have been unable to secure the necessary professional indemnity insurance to enable him or her to continue in practice or been made bankrupt.

Even if a sole practitioner could afford the annual professional indemnity insurance premium he or she might not have been able to afford the cost of "run off" cover if he or she wanted to retire and was unable to sell his or her practice. No solicitor in private practice can obtain a practising certificate without professional indemnity insurance cover and no sole practitioner can retire without "run off" cover. "Run off" cover was (and is) intended to protect clients by enabling them to sue a solicitor who has retired should any negligence on his or her part come to light at a later date.

Faced with the prospect of paying a premium of somewhere between £20,000 and £30,000 in order to cover this ongoing risk some solicitors keep on working until they drop! You cannot sue a dead solicitor!

Professional people who live on their wits, with the prospect of being sued if they make a mistake, often succumb to mental or physical problems or resort to alcohol as a prop and solicitors are no exception. Financial and marital stresses brought about by constant Government cut-backs in the justice system and the need to work harder and longer for less salary have caused many provincial solicitors to wonder whether or not he or she should be abandoning a vocation in the law in favour of something less onerous and a very small proportion fall prey to the temptation to take client monies. It is for this reason that there are robust systems to remedy any problems that might arise.

The larger practices that fail tend to do so as a result of incompetent management and it is probably not unfair to say that solicitors, by and large, are not as good businessmen as they are lawyers. A number of major firms have in the past overreached themselves and come to grief: others have been caught out by changes in Government policy – particularly in the fields of legal aid and personal accident litigation.

Having been appointed the first thing an Intervening Agent does is pay a perhaps not unexpected visit to the practice in default with a representative of the Law Society (now the Solicitors Regulation Authority), secure the premises and remove the defaulting solicitor or solicitors where fraud or dishonesty is suspected.

In the case of my first intervention the sole practitioner had already vacated his offices, leaving me a clear field: it had, in fact, been quite a busy practice and the solicitor had been helping himself to client monies for two or three years: he had worked out that if he delayed the redemption of building society mortgages by anything up to two months and merely paid the interest on the late repayment of the mortgages he could take and use redemption monies received on later sales to pay off monies outstanding on earlier redemptions: in other words he was "robbing Peter to pay Paul."

He was able to get away with this stratagem while the volume of sales and redemptions was rising but there would inevitably come a point when the monies in the client account at the bank would not be enough to pay off all the outstanding mortgages he had to redeem. At first the building societies would not have complained when they received redemption monies late because the amount they received correctly included the payment of late mortgage instalments and interest. The solicitor covered his tracks by explaining to the respective building societies that completion had been delayed by the failure of the purchaser of the property to come up with the purchase monies on the contractual completion date: his clients, having cancelled their standing order on the original completion date were allegedly paying the outstanding instalments out of the balance of the proceeds of sale. He told the purchasers' solicitors that the sellers' building society was being very slow in confirming the redemption of his clients' mortgage: at the time, some building societies were indeed slow at doing this and no awkward questions would therefore have been asked.

In the meantime this particular solicitor was living the high life, and, for some unknown reason, spending quite a lot of his clients' mortgage redemption monies on promoting his image with the British Percheron Horse Society. He wanted to become an influential member of the society, albeit that he did not apparently have a Percheron horse. These magnificent creatures were best known for pulling brewers' carts through the streets of London before motor vehicles replaced them.

According to a former magistrate friend of mine who happened to own two Percheron horses and to be a member of the society at the time, our "dodgy" solicitor would turn up at annual meetings of the society with a Land Rover and a large horse box, but no horse! Inside the horse box were bottles of wine and champagne and expensive food, delicacies which he would proffer to everyone attending the meetings! It is reassuring to know that he never achieved any office in the society and that his unsubtle attempts to curry favour with the members of the society came to nothing!

Where client monies had been misappropriated it was my task, as Intervening Agent, to work out how much, approximately, was missing and refer clients to the Solicitors Compensation Fund for reimbursement of their losses. Where, alternatively, the client was involved in litigation I would contact the relevant court and the solicitors for the other party and secure an adjournment of proceedings pending the appointment by the client of another solicitor to represent him or her. I would advise the client to seek representation elsewhere since it was not my role, as Intervening Agent, to take over the work of the defaulting solicitor but merely to facilitate the transfer of any clients' matter to another practice. The Intervening Agent was "on the side of the angels" charged with maintaining the reputation of the profession as a whole: it was not up to him or her to do anything more than that or become otherwise involved in any way.

My second intervention was not so straightforward. I appeared at the main offices of the solicitors in default with the representative from the Law Society: it was quite a large practice with three offices. Two partners ran the main office while two experienced legal executives were in charge of the smaller branch offices. Having summoned all staff to the main office of the practice the Law Society representative announced that the practice was being closed down without further notice and asked everyone to hand over their keys to all three offices.

The senior partner demurred but the Law Society representative insisted and asked all fee-earning staff to leave the premises immediately: they did so grudgingly. It was suggested by the Law Society representative, however, that I retain certain members of the secretarial and accounts staff to assist me with the task of locating client files and client balances and I accordingly retained seven or eight of them on a temporary basis: the three offices must have employed at least twenty five staff in total at the time.

I arrived early the next morning to let the retained staff into the main office and we all set to work. The first thing was to establish which sales and purchases of property were imminent and whether the practice was in funds to complete them: this entailed a visit to the solicitors' bank to find out exactly what monies were in the client account and from whom the monies had been received. Because it was only possible to identify about the last two weeks' payments in and out of the bank account I had to operate on a "last monies in, first monies out" system. It rapidly became apparent that the credits on client ledger accounts bore no relationship to the monies in the client bank account: there was a deficit of at least £1 million.

Where client monies could be identified they were used to complete transactions and reimburse clients but where the monies that should have been in client ledger accounts had disappeared, the clients had to be notified and helped to make a claim on the Compensation Fund.

The Compensation Fund is a fund to which every practising solicitor contributes: it is administered by the Law Society and ensures that no client of a practice in default incurs loss as a result of the misuse of his or her funds by virtue of the dishonesty of a solicitor.

The milkman arrived shortly after the office opened: he had come to ask for his weekly bill to be paid. I explained that the practice had been closed down by the Law Society and that the solicitors and legal executives to whom he had been delivering milk would not be needing or paying for any more milk. I did, however, point out that the Law Society wanted to retain certain members of staff for a short time to help deal with the closure and asked him if he would be so kind as to deliver a limited number of bottles each day, for which the Law Society would, of course, pay. He agreed to do so.

"I hope you do not mind my mentioning this, sir," he said. "But as I came down the high street at 4.30 am this morning I noticed that all the lights were on in the main office and that three gentlemen in suits appeared to be working in it." One of the partners had clearly retained one or more sets of keys and the three of them were removing incriminating evidence. From that intervention onward the locks of the offices of solicitors in default were changed immediately on my arrival!

This particular firm of solicitors may well have started off down the slippery slope by trying to keep their three offices fully staffed when the downturn occurred in the property market in the late 1980s and early 1990s. Because their profits from legal fees or income from other sources did not match their office overheads they had probably been tempted to use client monies in the hope that house sales and purchases, their principal source of income, would revive and they would be able to pay back what they had misappropriated.

Whatever may have been the original reason, by the time I arrived they were engaged in full-scale fraud and I discovered enough dishonesty to send the two partners to prison for some years. Apart from just pocketing clients' money where they thought no one would notice they engaged in two frauds which could have been difficult to spot.

The first required two offices, a dishonest surveyor and a "man of straw", someone who, for a payment, would hold himself out as a purchaser of a property, sign some mortgage documents and then disappear. These transactions were called "back to back" sales and purchases.

The fraud, although bare-faced, was quite simple: take a probate property where the solicitors were executors. Ask an accomplice surveyor to "down value" the property for probate purposes. In valuing a property for probate surveyors invariably come up, in any event, with a value lower than the actual market value for equivalent properties: there is nothing unusual about this.

As executors the solicitors controlled the sale and, provided the low valuation was within the expectation of the beneficiaries, no questions would be asked by them about the sale price.

One office of the practice would act on the sale of the property at the value determined by the surveyor: the sale file would look completely normal and "above board" but for one single feature.

The other office would act for the bogus purchaser, the "man of straw" who, for a modest payment would allow his name to be used on an application for a 100% mortgage to buy the property. For the purchaser the same surveyor would produce a high valuation of the property that enabled the bogus purchaser to obtain a mortgage well in excess of the sale price. In this way a fairly substantial margin was created, which the surveyor and the solicitors would share after payment of the stamp duty and Land Registry fee and the payment to the "man of straw" usually foreign, who had signed the necessary mortgage and contract documentation. .

The sale would have been completed, the beneficiaries would have received the proportion of the estate of the deceased person to which they were entitled under the will of the deceased, albeit that it was less than they originally hoped and the building society mortgage would have been registered against the property.

It would only be after two or three months that the building society would realise that no interest payments were being received from the "man of straw", the borrower. He would have disappeared, without trace and, after fruitless attempts to find him, the building society would have repossessed the property and would have sold it. The dishonest solicitors would not have been involved in this aspect of matters post completion, having registered the charge in favour of the Building Society and having sent the title documents to it.

The challenge when going through the sixteen thousand files for this particular practice was to spot the fraud and to find the same property appearing in the records of both offices.

There might have been nothing untoward in one office having acted on the sale and another office having acted on the purchase of the same property: this sometimes happens where there is no apparent conflict of interest. And if a "house purchaser" had spotted a bargain then good luck to him or her!

But, having located the files for the two transactions there was always one giveaway sign. The reader may have guessed what this might be, bearing in mind that the bogus purchaser was a "man of straw" with not a penny to his name.

The giveaway sign was the lack of a payment of a ten percent deposit on exchange of contracts: if there was no record of a deposit passing between one office and the other suspicions would be aroused. There would otherwise have been nothing on the sale file to show that a fraud was being committed and nothing on the purchase file to show that the purchaser was bogus.

The stamp duty and the Land Registry fee on the purchase would appear to have come from the purchaser, although like the "back hander" to the "man of straw" it came out of the surplus generated by the differing valuations. The subsequent failure of the borrower to repay the mortgage would not have appeared on the clients' purchase file and in a difficult market which had led to the intervention, the odd mortgage default from someone who failed to make repayments on a 100% mortgage would not have been particularly noticeable.

Once located the files in each case relating to the "back to back" fraud were passed to the commercial fraud department of the Metropolitan Police for further investigation.

Since the 1990s this type of fraud has become impossible as a result of the introduction of money laundering regulations, stricter ID and income checks and the Law Society's conveyancing quality scheme: unless residential conveyancers have been accredited under the scheme they are not admitted to the conveyancing panels of building societies and this, in itself, has been extremely effective in preventing dishonesty of this type.

Building societies, moreover, carry out much more comprehensive checks on potential borrowers, and the purchase of a property by someone who wanted a 100% mortgage but had no discernible assets would not now be possible.

The second stratagem was probably even more lucrative and, again, very simple. When dealing with the probate of an estate worth say, £800,000, the solicitors would file with the Revenue an inheritance tax return in which it was stated, incorrectly, that the estate was worth £650,000. The solicitors would assure the beneficiaries of the estate that a supplementary return would be filed when all the remaining assets had been gathered in: the beneficiaries would, of course, receive their share of the estate worth £800,000 when those assets were paid into their practice client account.

Not long afterwards, they would confirm that this had taken place and would make a final distribution of the estate to the beneficiaries, assuring them that a supplementary return had indeed been filed and inheritance tax paid on the outstanding £150,000: except that the 40% tax due to the Revenue on that amount had not! It was only when a beneficiary of one particular estate wrote directly to the Revenue insisting that a mistake had been made in calculating the inheritance tax due from the estate that the "underpayment" which the solicitors had shared between themselves came to light!

It is more than likely, moreover, that, as previously indicated, in some cases this practice had pocketed the entire proceeds of estates where they had been appointed executors and there were no obvious beneficiaries: they had done this rather than instruct a specialist agency to carry out the necessary research and trace missing heirs.

One of my tasks, as Intervening Agent, was to try and track down client balances and although the solicitors in this particular practice had removed a number of client ledger account cards with up-to-date information on them they had overlooked during their "night visit" earlier ledger cards upon which balances appeared. To this day, for example, I will never know what happened to a balance of approximately £120,000 in favour of the estate of R C Harrison deceased which appeared on one of the cards they had forgotten to remove.

Despite a thorough search the probate file itself had disappeared without trace and must have been removed.

In this particular intervention I collected approximately sixteen thousand client files from the three offices and had to check each file in order to extract "ongoing" leases, wills and other documents that should have been stored separately, and ensure that no further work had to be done on them. There were so many files from this and the other interventions I was dealing with that I had to rent a large farm building on the outskirts of Billericay to house them! Checking all the client files proved a time-consuming exercise!

Of the sixteen interventions I carried out only one or two others stand out.

In one I attended the offices of a sole practitioner in Regent Street, London who had been made bankrupt. When I arrived at his offices the bailiffs who had gained access to them before I arrived had tipped out the client files, office records, deeds and documents all over the floor of the offices when removing the office furniture. The mess was indescribable and all I could do was pack everything into black plastic sacks and transport it back to the farm building in Essex for sorting.

On another occasion I was Intervening Agent in the practice of a sole practitioner who had gone to his local police station on the Saturday morning of an August Bank holiday weekend to hand himself in. He had taken £30,000 from his client account, had subsequently been consumed with guilt and had decided to "do the honourable thing." You can imagine his surprise when the desk sergeant told him that he appreciated his attending the police station but that since no-one from CID would be on duty until the following Tuesday would he mind coming back then!

In view of the fact that there were so many thousands of client files from the various interventions to be checked I enlisted, with the consent of the Law Society, the services of my wife, Annette, to go through them with me when she returned from our disastrous foray into the Dordogne. She proved remarkably adept at spotting "back to back" transactions where the same address alone would appear on files from two different offices – once on a sale file headed with the name of the sellers, usually executors although they were not necessarily named as such, and again on a purchase file in the name of the "man of straw" in another office. The address was the only clue to the existence of a "back to back" transaction.

It was as a result of our spotting as many of these as we could that we came into contact with the commercial fraud department of the Metropolitan Police at Richbell Place, just off Southampton Row in London. As with the ticket thefts from Shenfield Travel, fraud of a commercial nature was referred to this department by police forces within the Greater London area.

Annette and I were therefore frequent visitors to the department, taking "matching" files from two offices with as much information as we could gather from client ledgers and bank statements relating to each transaction. Given that this was, at the time, a novel type of fraud as far as the police were concerned our presence at their offices and our explanations were much appreciated.

One afternoon we were sitting at the desk of a detective sergeant explaining a case of "back to back" fraud we had located when a bell rang: it was just after 4 pm and, being one of nature's innocents, Annette said, "Oh, does that mean it is time for afternoon tea?" "No, dear," replied the sergeant. "It means the bar is open!" With that he opened the top drawer of his desk and drew out a half-empty bottle of whisky and three glasses! The hard drinking "macho" culture of the 1970s and 1980s obviously still permeated the department at the time! It has doubtless disappeared in the twenty-plus years since my role of Intervening Agent came to an end!

The role of the police was to identify dishonest behaviour that might lead to a successful prosecution for theft or fraud but, as Intervening Agent who reported dishonest activities to them, I was constantly reminded of the difference between dishonesty in the eyes of the law and the mental dishonesty of so many people, not just solicitors, in so many walks of life.

Anyone who, for example, deliberately overcharges someone else for a service or product is just as guilty and should be brought to book. Sometimes, however, this type of mental dishonesty is difficult to pin down, as in the case of the divorce lawyer who, instead of aiming to resolve a matrimonial dispute quickly and with the least trauma to a separating couple, deliberately inflames tensions between them in order to boost his or her fees. It was, in fact, my disgust with this type of solicitor that led me to qualify as a family mediator and to promote family mediation through Resolve which Annette and I had created (see earlier chapter) and to give up litigated divorce.

A solicitor who, during the 1990s, took money from a client but who rendered a fee note for his or her services, declared his income to the Revenue and paid tax on it could only be censured if he or she overcharged and if the client subsequently complained.

At the time a client could indeed complain that he or she had been overcharged and report the solicitor to the Law Society: the Law Society would review the client's file and determine whether the charges made were reasonable, usually within the context of charges made for time spent at the average hourly rate by a solicitor of his or her level of experience.

The average hourly rate included those of City solicitors as well as those of provincial solicitors and was invariably higher than the amount solicitors outside London would have been inclined to charge. The maximum sanction therefore that this sort of solicitor might expect would be a "slap on the wrist" and a fine in most cases. The overcharging would have had to be blatant for anything worse.

Fortunately complaint mechanisms and client care procedures have improved a great deal since the 1990s and I will refer to them in the next chapter.

As a footnote, a magistrate at Billericay Magistrates Court, a Mr. Roderick Watt, a former law lecturer, who had been impressed by my performances in the court, subsequently instructed me to act on his behalf on the sale of part of his garden to developers, the sale of the house itself and the purchase of a farm in Suffolk. He purchased and kept a number of Percheron horses at his farm and it was he who told me about the behaviour of the solicitor in whose practice I had intervened.

We became good friends and he asked me if I would be prepared to take over from him as legal adviser to a charity, the International League for the Protection of Horses (ILPH). It would mean a long drive up to the headquarters of the charity in Snetterton in Norfolk every few weeks to attend board meetings but I had no objection to this and for about a year I attended board meetings chaired by Andrew Parker Bowles, the former husband of Camilla Parker Bowles, now married to Prince Charles. Andrew Parker Bowles was a most kind and courteous man, an excellent chairman, and I liked him a lot. At the boardroom table I sat next to Baroness Soames, the youngest daughter of Winston Churchill, and opposite and around me were several members of the House of Lords and the aristocracy generally. The patron of the ILPH is Princess Anne and I attended an AGM when, as guest speaker, she addressed the meeting extremely fluently and knowledgeably for nearly half an hour on equine matters. The charity, however, wanted advice on some agricultural matters, not within my sphere of knowledge, and I referred them to a large firm of solicitors in Norwich and gracefully withdrew. It had, however, been a most interesting experience and one that I would not have missed.

30

The Legal Career, Phase 4 :
On the Council of the Law Society

When the Labour Party came to power in 1997, "Derry" – Lord Irvine of Lairg, who had been appointed Lord Chancellor by Tony Blair – put the introduction of family mediation on "hold" Annette and I realised at that point that our well-advanced plans for Resolve, our combined mediation and counselling service for divorcing couples, would have to be shelved, possibly until a later date but probably for ever. We were too far ahead of what the Labour Government was prepared to endorse and activate at the time.

The Family Law Act, passed by the previous Conservative Government in 1996, had embraced the concept of family mediation on divorce: it was to be an optional alternative to the dismal prospect of having to engage in litigation to secure an outcome which, in terms of finance and access to children, many couples would undoubtedly have been prepared to accept without the abrasive and divisive nature of correspondence between solicitors and appearances in court.

Family mediation had been introduced in recognition of the fact that it would take a lot of the unnecessary heat and stress out of divorce. Why the Labour Government was not inclined to support this sensible piece of legislation I cannot say. The Family Law Act had made family mediation on divorce an option: ironically some twenty years later it has become a requirement that separating couples at least consider mediation before engaging in divorce litigation. Annette and I had added the counselling element, which is now also belatedly being acknowledged as a good idea and which some "pods" of lawyers and others involved in matrimonial breakdown are including in a combined approach to the problems that arise on divorce. Sadly, our own efforts were "water under the bridge" at the time and so it was back to the law full time for me and to the NHS full time for Annette.

The fourth phase of my legal career began, therefore, in 1997 and continued for over twenty years.

Because I considered myself bound by the terms of the sale of my practice in Billericay, despite the fact that the purchasers of the practice had no such scruples about breaking the terms themselves, I decided to start from scratch in Shenfield, a suburb of Brentwood, a few miles up the road from Billericay.

It was familiar territory that I knew well from my ownership of Shenfield Travel Bureau. I had already leased an office there for Resolve and, prior to that, for my Law Society intervention work: it seemed a sensible and obvious location in which to set up once again as a high street solicitor.

A mass circulation of leaflets announcing the arrival of a new practice in Shenfield proved very successful and immediately attracted a number of prospective clients: not only that but many of my former Hughes & Co. clients from Billericay who had not been well looked after by my successors instructed me to act for them as soon as they heard that I was back in full-time practice.

I was also fortunate enough to be able to take on an excellent trainee solicitor and to recruit secretarial staff who were absolutely first class. My trainee (and subsequently assistant) solicitor was Sarah Walker, a dynamic and extremely personable young lady whom (and I hope she will forgive me for mentioning this) I had only once previously encountered as a two-year-old, vigorously pushing her wooden trolley with a doll in it along the hall of her parents' home in Billericay in the 1970's!

Between us we attracted quite a following and it was only a matter of months before I was receiving an income from a practice with four staff that was greater than the income I had received at Billericay from a practice with nearly twenty! This was because Sarah and I concentrated primarily on conveyancing, wills and probate, as at the start of my career some thirty years previously, with a smattering of divorce cases.

As soon as the practice was up and running I joined the committee of the Mid Essex District Law Society and was rapidly elected treasurer, a position disliked by most lawyers. It involved writing to all the firms of solicitors, including a number of sole practitioners like myself, in the mid Essex area, requesting and usually chasing for membership subscriptions and payments for events organised by the society: it was an unenviable task but one which brought me into regular contact with many local solicitors.

As a result of my involvement in the society, I was elected President of the Mid Essex District Law Society in 2002 and it was in that year that Trevor Murray, the Law Society Council member for Essex decided to step down half way through his term from representing all the solicitors and practices in his Essex constituency. Although at the age of sixty six I would only have been eligible to represent the constituency as a Council member until the age of seventy according to the rules of the Law Society at the time, my district Law Society nevertheless suggested that I should take his place and nominated me to stand as a candidate for election.

Holding the post of Council member would mean that I represented all the solicitors in the constituency including the three district Law Societies within it. The position would entail, as part of the role, visits on a regular basis to the committees of the three district Law Societies and attending events organised by them. It would involve keeping their committee members informed of developments at Chancery Lane, the head office of the Law Society, and feeding back the views of these district Law Societies and their members to the Council of the Law Society in London.

Two other solicitors stood as independent candidates but my previous experience in generating publicity for my various ventures, plus the fact that many solicitors in both the other districts were aware of my seven-year stint as a Law Society Intervening Agent, undoubtedly counted in my favour and I was voted in as Council member by a substantial majority of the votes cast. This appointment at the age of sixty-six led to a really interesting ten-year involvement in the administrative and political activities of the Law Society.

In order to give worthwhile feedback to the three district Law Societies and constituents generally and to represent their interests in these activities one clearly had to become involved in various aspects of the policy and rule-making functions of the Law Society itself and this proved, for me, the most time- consuming aspect of being a Council member.

The policy and rule-making functions of the Council were, at first sight, quite distinct from the executive functions of the Law Society although one obviously fed into the other. It was a bit like the Government and the Civil Service. The Executive, like the Civil Service, performed the functions that the governing body, the Council, authorised it to perform.

As in the famous television series "Yes Minister", however, the Council usually told the Executive to do what the Chief Executive had intended it to do in the first place! Many were the times that Council was pushed – stampeded might be a better word – into taking decisions that were thrust upon it by the Chief Executive without any real opportunity to debate them properly.

The Executive, led for much of my time as Council member by an exceedingly capable Chief Executive, Des Hudson, was responsible for running a complex organisation with well over 100,000 solicitor members: its tasks were to produce policy documentation for discussion and determination by the Council, its boards and committees, regulate the profession, collect millions of pounds in respect of practising certificate fees, and compensation fund contributions, make sure that everyone had professional indemnity insurance, organise conferences, administer regional offices, and provide secretarial facilities for all the boards and committees of the Council, etc. In this description I am only scratching the surface of what it had to do.

Perched on top of this massive organisation were the President of the Law Society, its elected officers and the Council members with their four boards and numerous specialist committees. The Management Board ostensibly oversaw the management of the Society, the Regulatory Board, its rules and regulations, the Membership Board the interests of its members and the Legal Affairs and Policy Board, its promotion of worthwhile legislation and the lobbying of organisations and parliamentarians. Much of the latter's "firepower" was provided by the specialist committees where really well-informed solicitors in specific areas of practice contributed their expertise to proposals that would assist Parliament in framing legislation on their particular area of the law. It all looked very impressive!

I concluded over a period, however, that for the most part the Executive, which carried out a lot of the research, provided the bullets and the President and the Council fired the gun and this conclusion led me into scrutinising how the relationship between the Executive and the Council worked and how it might be improved: but more of that anon.

I should explain that when I joined the Council in 2002 it was about one hundred strong: about sixty per cent were geographical members representing solicitors in counties and in the major cities while the remainder represented specific areas of the law, such as family law or special interests such Black and ethnic minorities.

The mix of male and female Council members was relatively well balanced, for 2002, and during my ten years on the Council there were some outstanding male and female Presidents and Vice-Presidents. There were one or two, like David Mackintosh and Paul Marsh, who spoke pure unadulterated common sense and to whom I will refer later. One particularly eminent female President was Dame Fiona Woolf, DBE, the first female Lord Mayor of London and for a short time the Government's second choice to chair the massive and wide-ranging independent inquiry into child sexual abuse – (IICSA) – across the spectrum of society including the rich and famous It was her associations with the latter, and in particular Lord and Lady Brittan that led to her replacement: she was deemed to be too close to them to be impartial. In my view, however, she, like the first choice for the post, Baroness Butler-Sloss, would have been an excellent chair, quite capable, like any judge, of putting personal views and associations on one side while she led the inquiry.

Inevitably because of work and family commitments most Council members were in their mid/late forties or above, but, again, there were some extremely impressive younger members who were clearly destined to have a marked impact on the Law Society and its future direction of travel.

If I had to summarise how I viewed the Council members when I first arrived at Chancery Lane my initial impression was one of a degree of complacency among those in the "magic circle", encompassing top lawyers in the City of London, the Law Courts and the West End, frustration among provincial lawyers, to which I will refer later, and a burning desire on the part of special interest lawyers for change and reform.

Overall the Council members were the more vocational members of these three groups: they felt that they were committed professionals and deserved some degree of respect for the years they had spent in qualifying and practising – whether those periods were long or short – and for what they had managed to achieve. They also felt they had something worthwhile to offer and, as a representative body, the Council did reflect what was good and decent in the profession.

There were, of course, some who were, and I make this observation charitably, more interested in leading the Council than reforming it: the majority, however, were foot soldiers who took up different causes and did their best to promote them.

I would merely comment that the leaders who remained as Council members after their moment of glory as President and remained committed to the reform of the law and the Law Society itself deserved the greatest respect.

What most Council members did not appreciate at the time was that waiting in the wings was a Sir David Clementi, soon to throw a cat among the pigeons (or perhaps the dovecotes) of Chancery Lane and promote an irreversible change in the fortunes of the Council and of the profession.

In addition to keeping three district Law Societies informed on what was happening at Chancery Lane (which, regrettably, Trevor Murray had not done) and representing the interests of individual solicitors within the constituency I had to decide in which way I would become involved in the board and committee structures of the Law Society. My previous involvement with the society had been in connection with the investigation of misconduct and I therefore gravitated towards professional conduct, professional standards and scrutiny of the way in which the boards dealt with the work within their individual remits.

My first appointment, therefore, was as a member of the Professional Standards Appeal Panel where the panel determined, in essence, whether a solicitor who had been unable or had failed for whatever reason to renew their professional indemnity insurance and had thereby fallen into the "assigned risks pool" should be allowed a period of grace within which to practise and earn enough to pay the outstanding premiums to the Solicitors Indemnity Fund and sort out their affairs.

This was not dissimilar to my role of General Commissioner of Income Tax and I was impressed by the even-handed way in which the chairman of the panel dealt with all the solicitors who came before us some with harrowing stories of unfortunate personal circumstances who deserved support and others who really had little excuse for the situation in which they found themselves.

This panel was wound up when the Solicitors Indemnity Fund, the Law Society's own professional indemnity insurance scheme was wound up and solicitors had to purchase cover in the open market. From that moment there was to be no period of grace for those who could not come up with the necessary indemnity insurance premiums.

Shortly thereafter I became a member of the Council Members Conduct

Committee which monitored the way in which Council members should behave towards one another: there were the occasional contretemps where breaches of rules and conduct were alleged. They were, fortunately, few and far between and apart from the odd moan by one Council member against another I do not recall anything so serious as to result in anything more than a word in the ear of the person against whom the complaint was made. There were one or two Council members, like my predecessor, whose views were highly controversial but these people were usually persuaded to moderate their annoying, publicity-seeking behaviour. As a result we did not meet very often!

The committee in which I became highly involved, however, was the Scrutiny Committee. This was a rather unpopular committee because it examined the work programmes of the four boards of Council and pointed out to them and to the Council what they had overlooked or failed to achieve during the year. Scrutiny, as a concept, had been imported from local government and was felt, by many board chairs to be inappropriate and the reader can imagine how they viewed a committee that drew their omissions to the Council's attention. We were regarded as "nitpickers"!

But, to put our role in context, the four boards to which about forty members of Council belonged, each produced a work plan at the beginning of year. Some board chairmen were more ambitious than others, some more efficient than others. Our role was to draw to the attention of the boards and Council the omissions in work programmes by comparing what boards had announced they were going to do at the beginning of the year with what they had actually achieved.

There were never many omissions but such as came to light were reported to the boards and to the Council for their information and for inclusion, if necessary, in the following year's work programme of that particular board.

After I had completed the two years left on Trevor Murray's four-year term of office I was re-elected as Council member in 2004, only two years before, according to the rules of the Law Society at the time, I would have to retire.

However as a result of my regular attendances at district Law Society meetings, the updates I had given them and the representations I had made on their behalf at Chancery Lane, the committees of all three district societies decided that the "retirement at seventy" rule would have to be changed! I was heartened, therefore, when, at the annual general meeting of the Law Society in London in July 2006 representatives of my three district societies came to the meeting and proposed a rule change, which was carried unanimously, removing the upper age limit of seventy for membership of the Council.

I was even more heartened when I was elected chairman of the Scrutiny Committee by the other members of the committee for a three-year term in the same year.

It had always struck me that pointing out oversights and omissions after the event was a bit like closing the stable doors after the horses had bolted: doing so, however useful, could never be any more than a "tidying-up" exercise: I could well understand why board chairs resented being told what they had failed to do some time after the event!

It would be more sensible, in my view, to have a regular ongoing performance review of the work programmes of each board without actually "stepping on the toes" of the board chairs while they were implementing their respective programmes. For this to be a reality I would need the cooperation of the Executive, the approval of the Council on whose behalf we acted, and the support of my committee who thought very much along the same lines as myself.

Des Hudson, the Chief Executive whom I consulted on the matter, was very much in favour of the prompt dissemination of board minutes to board and Council members and the traffic light system of review that I and my committee proposed: there would be a "green" sign in the board minutes alongside a programme if the work had been satisfactorily completed, an "amber" sign for work satisfactorily in progress and a "red" sign for work which was not progressing satisfactorily or had not even been started. Not surprisingly the board chairs were not at all keen because they would have to acknowledge during their years of tenure as chairs the lack of progress made on projects that they had optimistically included in their work programmes at the beginning of the year!

By imposing time limits on the approval by chairmen of their board's minutes (which they could otherwise string out) and on the production by their secretaries of more intelligible minutes after such approval (which, again, could be delayed) everyone would be informed more promptly and last-minute "ambushes" due to the late production of important policy-related board minutes would be reduced.

Naturally most of the remaining one hundred members of Council welcomed the ideas my committee had proposed and at a conference of

Council members in Cardiff in 2009 I was able to persuade Council to give my committee additional performance review powers (most of which the board chairmen managed to scale back when I retired from the Council in 2012!!).

Although, according to the rules, the term of office of a committee chairman was three years, my committee pointed out to me that, under exceptional circumstances, the term could be extended to six years: it had decided that the exceptional circumstances existed, namely the implementation of performance reviews, and I was accordingly unanimously re-elected in 2009 for another three years! This was probably because no-one else on the committee wanted to accept the extra work load involved, but I did not object and it is fair to say that during those three years board minutes were given a better shape, made more intelligible, and produced and disseminated more promptly.

On the broader stage, however, during my last six years as a Council member some fairly momentous changes were taking place in the profession as a result of the Clementi report on legal services. The Government had decided that lawyers should not be left to regulate their own affairs and Sir David Clementi had been tasked with a review of regulatory structures in the legal profession generally.

His wide-ranging review recommended that the Law Society should delegate its regulatory powers to a new subsidiary body, the Solicitors Regulation Authority, and stick to representing solicitors: the regulation and policing of the profession should be left to a body of which he considered the majority of board members should not be solicitors!

To the extent that the Law Society already had robust regulatory, disciplinary and compensatory procedures it was difficult to comprehend, at the time, how transferring them into a separate authority was going to do any more than add an unnecessary layer of bureaucracy and considerable cost to what already existed. Many solicitors regarded the recommendation as nothing more than a veiled attempt to undermine the independence and the status of the profession: they could see that diverting a large proportion of the annual practising certificate fee to fund the administration of a separate authority would affect the ability of the society to represent its members and to advise on proposed law reform, two of its principal functions.

What really upset the Law Society and the profession, however, was Sir David's observation that solicitors were just part of the "Legal Services Industry". They were not viewed by him as a profession with the expertise and integrity associated with the word "profession" but as part of an industry. Classifying solicitors in this way has coloured the approach of every subsequent Government to the legal profession and has substantially diminished the respect in which the public previously held them.

Industries sell commodities and making the administration of justice a commodity and downgrading the profession in the eyes of the public cannot be helpful: it will ultimately undermine the rule of law. Moreover, successive Governments since the Clementi report have steadily cut down access to justice by abolishing most forms of legal aid and raising court and employment tribunal fees, thereby making justice something for those who can afford it.

The price to the consumer and the cost to the Ministry of Justice, rather than quality of service and level of expertise, have become the principal drivers in the minds of Government Ministers in the provision to the public of legal services and the independence and quality of the judiciary itself will inevitably be affected. Judges in most tiers of the court system are, as at the date of writing this book, already overworked to a not inconsiderable extent by having to listen to litigants in person who have to conduct their own cases, relying sometimes on inexperienced "Mackenzie friends" (amateur helpers) rather than being able to call on the services of trained barristers and solicitors. The effectiveness of the judicial system is steadily being eroded and this impairment will become even more marked when competent and hardworking members of the judiciary retire as early as they can and bright young prospective barristers and solicitors conclude that it is not really worth their while to qualify as such.

The upshot of the Clementi report was the passing of The Legal Services Act in 2007, the setting up of the Office for Legal Complaints (the OLC) and the appointment of the Legal Ombudsman: as a result of the legislation the Law Society was obliged to split itself in two and delegate the regulation of solicitors to the Solicitors Regulation Authority whose board members are, for the most part, not solicitors but people who, however august in their various fields, have limited understanding and little experience of the way in which the wider profession operates. In addition to the cost of funding the new Solicitors Regulation Authority solicitors were also expected to contribute the bulk of the cost of the Office for Legal Complaints, the Office of the Legal Services Ombudsman and the pre-existing Solicitors Disciplinary Tribunal: it was bureaucratic "overkill".

One can well understand the frustration of provincial solicitors, most of whom one would describe as high street solicitors, with their professional body: it had not been fighting their corner in relation to civil and criminal legal aid where their fees had not been raised for nearly 15 years and it had not adopted the robust approach to these new impositions that they expected. Access to justice was being curtailed, many firms were going out of business and those that remained bore the brunt of public dissatisfaction at the fees they had to charge in order to cover their increasing overheads. As a representative body the Law Society did not appear to be doing a very good job. But again, I digress!

During the "Blair years" the Labour Government decided to force through the introduction of Home Information Packs (known as HIPs) which Ministers considered would speed up the house sales process: it was evident that they had not a clue about what was involved in selling a property that was in a chain of transactions, as is usually the case. In the circumstances the Law Society decided to set up a task force to offer advice to Government on the conveyancing process in an attempt to mitigate the adverse effects of this misguided project.

Nine Council members were required for the task force and I applied to join it as an experienced conveyancer. I was accepted as a member and joined five former Presidents of the Law Society, including Paul Marsh, the senior partner of a large and well-known practice in the Home Counties and three other Council members with substantial long-term experience in the bulk sale and purchase of residential properties.

In collaboration with experienced members of the Executive of the Law Society we formulated the Society's observations on HIPs: we set out in as objective a manner as possible the disadvantages and possible advantages of what the Government proposed. We rapidly discovered, however, that John Prescott, the Minister in charge of the project, did not really appreciate any of the disadvantages of HIPs and that a somewhat doctrinaire Yvette Cooper, his successor, thought that we were just trying to protect our position in the field of residential conveyancing and, in doing so, to "feather our own nests". She was completely impervious to the reasons we gave her for modifying or dropping the proposal.

Paul Marsh, our principal spokesperson, pointed out that obliging a seller to carry out searches for a future prospective purchaser before putting his or her house on the market was not going to expedite a sale if a chain of prospective sales had to be assembled before the various transaction could all proceed: moreover, most searches and enquiries could be made by a purchaser within the time it took for a survey report and a mortgage offer to be received by that purchaser.

The production by the seller of an HIP also stood uneasily alongside the long established legal principle of "caveat emptor" (let the purchaser beware). In essence a residential property is sold as seen and it is up to the purchaser to inspect and survey it and to make all necessary enquiries of the seller before exchange of contracts. In this respect the Law Society has over the years developed a comprehensive set of pre-contract enquiries which, if answered correctly, will elicit everything a purchaser needs to know about a property and which, if answered incorrectly, opens up a seller to a claim of misrepresentation and substantial damages. Apart, therefore, from the production by the seller of an energy performance certificate which might have some marginal influence on a prospective purchaser's decision to proceed with a purchase, the HIPs initiative by the Labour Government was a complete white elephant and mercifully abandoned, to the relief of almost everyone in the conveyancing field, by the subsequent Cameron administration.

During my membership of the task force and acting entirely on my own initiative I formed a limited liability company by the name of "Law Move Limited" which I offered to the task force and the Law Society as a prospective alternative to Rightmove, the only website offering houses for sale at the time. It did not cost me much to do so and I could see that the Law Society would require additional sources of income to continue to act as an effective representative body should the Solicitors Regulation Authority, as a burgeoning bureaucracy, demand an increasing proportion of the practising certificate fee.

I explained to members of the task force that all that my concept needed was for it to be taken up by a large company like, for example, the Daily Mail and General Trust, with the Law Society promoting it within the profession and receiving a proportion of the income generated by it. My idea was considered far too commercial, however, and far too oriented towards house sales to be appropriate for a professional body!

I felt duly chastised but I have never been afraid of coming up with ideas and concepts which push the boundaries of what is possible. Since I formed, and sadly wound up Law Move Limited, alternative house sale platforms, such as Zoopla, have emerged to compete with Rightmove.

The only other service I was able to render to my fellow Council members was to point out, in my closing address to Council as chairman of the Scrutiny and Performance Review Committee, that seventy five should be the retirement age for them. Having removed the upper age limit some of my contemporaries might be tempted to remain as Council members until they were literally carried out of the Council chamber! Young blood was essential to meet the challenges faced by the Law Society.

Having retired as a Council member I was not to be let off the hook entirely and served subsequently as President of the Southend on Sea District Law Society: at the end of my allotted year I was surprised to be elected President for a second year, the first time since 1947 that someone had been elected President for consecutive years. I thoroughly enjoyed both years and they marked for me, a very pleasant and satisfying wind-down from the previously heavy involvement in Law Society matters.

Throughout my years on the Council I had continued to act as a solicitor in private practice both as principal of my own practice until 2007 and, following my subarachnoid aneurysm (brain haemorrhage) and the sale of my practice, as a consultant solicitor to the practice of the purchaser, Sanjay Panesar.

Despite the difference in our ages and background he and I established an immediate rapport and I have worked very happily in a multicultural practice for well over ten years. Sanjay considers himself a "fourth son", a sign of affection and regard that I have wholeheartedly reciprocated.

Shortly after I left the Council of the Law Society I was approached by the person at whose property I parked my car. He asked me whether I could possibly help him, as a member of a workers' committee formed by a group of Visteon employees who felt they had been treated shabbily by the Ford Motor Company (Fords) and left to their own devices by their union (Unite), which should have been fighting on their behalf.

Fords had apparently put their spare parts division into a separate company called Visteon and had indicated at the time that the employees of Fords who opted to remain in the new company would suffer no diminution in their pension entitlement and lose none of the privileges they had formerly enjoyed as full-time employees of Fords: they would, for example, continue to have the right to purchase Fords' vehicles at a discounted rate.

When, however, Visteon found itself in financial difficulties and was forced by creditors into liquidation Fords stated that its former employees would not, after all, be entitled to the pensions they would have enjoyed had they remained as employees of Fords. I asked the former Visteon employee for proof of his assertions and after reading through the paperwork he provided concluded that the workers' committee had a case: the "volte face" by Fords was basically unfair. I appreciated, however, that the Visteon employees would need a high-powered "no nonsense" advocate to argue their case if they were to stand any chance of success.

I therefore approached David Mackintosh, a former President of the Law Society, a former President of the City of London Law Society, an honorary QC and a former senior partner of a leading firm of City solicitors, and asked him whether he would be interested in helping them. He was semi-retired but he asked me to send him the papers for consideration. Once he had read them he was, like me, appalled at the way in which the Visteon employees had been treated. Although he had, in the past, acted for major companies and not their employees he took on the Visteon employees' case and, with single-minded determination, commenced proceedings against Fords, threatening to sue not only Fords but the union, which should have been fighting for its members. As a result he secured an impressive settlement with Fords that substantially improved the pension rights of the former employees of Visteon: he was extremely capable, forthright and patently committed to their cause and earned the complete respect and, indeed, affection of the members of the Visteon workers' committee who, prior to his arrival on the scene, felt that they stood little chance against a monolithic company like Fords with its ability to call on the services of batteries of barristers and solicitors.

I have always been well aware of my own limitations and, as a solicitor, have never hesitated to refer clients elsewhere if I have felt they would get a better service from someone else and this was a case in point. Some clients, however, have been with me since 1965 and to many I have become "Uncle Brian" or a sort of substitute grandfather! That has been very satisfying and also humbling. Fifty years in practice as a solicitor has taught me a lot about human nature and I have been extremely fortunate in gaining the confidence and respect of so many clients.

Communication is the key to good relationships with clients and I have never had much time for solicitors who fail to communicate or regard themselves as somehow superior to the clients for whom they act: they tend not to keep their clients very long!

As a footnote, my brain haemorrhage was undoubtedly brought about by my trying to do too much in my work and community life and I was extremely lucky to survive. I would nevertheless urge every reader to regard whatever talents they have as gifts, to be used in the most satisfying and balanced way as possible. They will not then consider, before they pass on – as we all do – that they have wasted any of the time allocated to them.

My late wife, Annette, and I have both tried to make good use of our time and our talents and although I have regrets they do not relate to my various work and community activities.

31

A Close Encounter with Death

One of my "philosophies" has been that if you are going to lead a busy life you need to stay fit: the body is, after all, just a machine that demands careful use plus regular maintenance and servicing if it is to function effectively. The Ancient Greeks advocated "nothing too much" and can be rephrased as "everything in moderation". It is not a bad rule to follow even if one cannot stick to it all the time!

Keeping fit is even more relevant when you are married, as I have been, to someone who is seventeen years younger than yourself and a former health and fitness instructor!

Another "philosophy" has been that since you only live once, you might as well enjoy and make the most of life: this particular philosophy was challenged when I had myself "regressed" in my forties into what appeared to be someone else's life in a previous century. But that is another story and one about which I hope to write a second book after I have checked at the National Archive whether what I experienced during my regression might just be true and not a figment of my imagination.

As an amalgam of sole practitioner with a busy legal practice, a member of the Council of the Law Society, the Governing Body for all Solicitors in England and Wales, chairman of one of its committees, a married man with family commitments and someone actively involved in the community including the single-handed management, on behalf of the Royal British Legion, of a hall that was let out to a number of local organisations, it was essential that I balanced mental with physical exertion.

By 2004 the pressures of my various roles were building up, together with the stress of ensuring that the practice stayed in the black. In the circumstances I decided to add to my regular running activities by swimming thirty lengths every Thursday evening after work at a local pool.

This "balancing act" seemed to be going well until Saturday 14th February 2007, when, at the age of seventy one and while sweeping up leaves on the patio, I felt as if I had suddenly been kicked in the back of the head. It was a massive disorienting blow which brought me to my knees. I could do nothing but stagger into the lounge, kneel on the carpet and put my head on the sofa. It was about 2.30 pm and Annette was up in London seeing private patients at her Harley Street practice.

The light was hurting my eyes and, after about thirty minutes, I decided to go to bed and await her return. Not long after her return I was violently sick and Annette phoned our family surgery: she was advised to purchase some anti-sickness medication.

It was only after two days of my constantly being sick and losing well over half a stone in weight that the doctor to whom Annette had spoken was prevailed upon to pay me a visit and it was only at Annette's insistence that the doctor reluctantly agreed to my being admitted to hospital.

The doctors there diagnosed severe dehydration and food poisoning and after two days on a saline drip and medication to settle my stomach I was discharged. The diagnosis was completely incorrect despite the fact that the nurses at the hospital had accurately noted my symptoms on my patient notes on my arrival: these notes were later to prove very important.

What I had suffered, and discovered the name of later, was a "sentinel bleed" – a warning sign that something was seriously wrong with my brain and that worse would follow. On release from hospital, however, I felt better and went back to work and to my usual activities, including swimming. I had no reason to think the diagnosis of food poisoning was incorrect because, like many males, I tend to ignore "sell by" or "use by" dates on food products! Annette was constantly telling me off for doing this and I felt I had got my just deserts.

On Thursday 1st March 2007, I therefore turned up at the swimming pool at Brentwood School where I had become a member of the fitness club and started my usual thirty lengths.

I had got to the end of length eleven (the deep end of the pool) when I disappeared from view: the pool attendant who was sitting on a high chair wondered why I was not churning my way back down the pool, got down from it and went to have a look. I was on the bottom of the pool!

The attendant shouted for help, apparently, and I was fished out unconscious but still alive: he gave me artificial respiration and called for an ambulance that I understand arrived about twenty minutes later. The ambulance driver radioed to A&E at Broomfield Hospital, which informed him that the hospital could not take any more emergencies: he should take me to the Queen's Hospital in Romford. This proved fortuitous.

On arrival at the Queen's at about 8 pm I was given a brain scan that revealed I had suffered a subarachnoid aneurysm – an artery in my brain had ruptured sending blood to all parts of my brain. The hospital immediately put me on "life support" while the doctors decided what to do and while Annette was consulted on my medical history: judging by my physical condition they were apparently surprised that was I was so old.

At 10 pm my heart stopped and I was resuscitated: it stopped again at midnight and I was resuscitated once again. At this point the doctors told Annette that they could detect no sign of brain activity. The maximum number of times the NHS will resuscitate is three times: if my heart stopped for a third time did Annette want them to resuscitate me again? They said that if they did and, if I survived, she would probably be nursing a vegetable until I died. The choice was hers. Without hesitation Annette said that they should resuscitate – she would take the risk and the consequences of her decision. Some two hours later my heart stopped for a third time and, on this occasion, I was resuscitated with some difficulty. At this point the doctors asked if I had any religious affiliation: "Church of England," said Annette. "In that case we will get hold of the Chaplain," they replied.

The Chaplain arrived at 3.20 am and gave me the Last Rites: as soon as he had done so the life support system was removed and I was taken into a side room: "Your husband will pass away peacefully within the next two hours," one of the doctors told Annette and they left the room to attend to other patients.

My entire family, wife, children, sister and brother-in-law sat in that side room with the Chaplain who decently decided to stay until I passed away.

At 6 am the Chaplain had to leave to prepare for a Service that day and at 6.30 am I groaned opened my eyes: Annette and my sons immediately summoned the doctors.

"Oh, is he still alive? We thought he would be dead by now. We had better put him back on life support." You can always rely on the sympathy of doctors in NHS Hospitals!

The hospital decided, in the circumstances, to clear the chlorine from my lungs and the "spilt" blood from my brain and repair the ruptured artery. Nine days later they passed a coil through my thigh and heart and placed sheaths inside the ruptured artery, a bit like repairing a puncture from the inside. The Queen's Hospital had a specialist in this type of operation whereas Broomfield Hospital did not.

The operation was a success and nine days after my aneurysm my memory returned: Annette who had held my hand for the first forty eight hours after her arrival at hospital breathed a sigh of relief tinged with a slight element of sadness. She said later: "Brian, during the nine days you were not really with us, you were so nice. You told the nurses what a splendid job they were doing and how much you loved us all, and, now, you are back to normal!"

My eldest son who had read me articles from classic car magazines while I was unconscious in the hope that I would hear him, and who had always had reservations about Annette since she fired him from the property department, said later: "Dad, if I ever doubted that Annette loved you those doubts were dispelled by the way she acted during your time in hospital – her firm decision to resuscitate you and her obvious love for you throughout." That was a heart-warming moment for me: something good had come out of all that trauma.

In fact Annette took three months off from work to look after me and ensure that the practice continued to operate efficiently. From my point of view the only ironic and vaguely irksome aspect of her arranging for the practice to be supervised and her reorganising it during my absence was that it actually earned more when I was not there than when I was! She was clearly not such a "soft touch" as myself!

As a result of the aneurysm I decided the time had come to sell the practice – for the second time – and not to put Annette through any further traumas, should I not live for very long.

My survival was described as "one in a thousand" and apart from a slight deterioration in mental ability and a temporary lack of sensation in the upper part of my left leg there have been no adverse long term effects. In other words I have been extremely lucky!

I wrote, of course, apologising to the Chaplain for wasting his time: he was very understanding about it and wrote back a humorous letter!

After my return to work, moreover, I was discussing my miraculous escape with a fellow lawyer who specialised in medical negligence: we were both on the Committee of the Mid Essex Law Society. He asked if I would allow him to obtain a copy of the notes the nurses made at the hospital since he felt there was something wrong with the initial diagnosis. I had no objection and a few weeks later he asked me to pay him a visit.

The doctors had ignored the nurses' notes, and in particular, my observation that I could not stand the light after what he confirmed was a clear "sentinel bleed." He showed me the "medical bible" which highlights what symptoms indicate the likely existence of certain medical conditions: the book works on a "traffic light" system and it would have been quite obvious what had happened by checking the symptoms that appeared on the notes and which were all at "red" in the book.

He offered me a conditional fee agreement and I recovered compensation from the hospital after three years of protracted litigation. My fellow solicitor undoubtedly recovered in costs more than I received by way of compensation and it brought home to me the fact that, if the hospital had employed competent doctors (both of whom disappeared abroad during the litigation) in the first place and if the hospital had admitted its mistake at the outset instead of spending a fortune on denying liability, an awful lot of NHS money could have been saved and put to other more productive uses. There has to be a better way of dealing with cases of negligence on the part of doctors.

32

Reflections on Survival

When one has survived in this extraordinary way the temptation is to think that one has been spared for a purpose. I tell my friends that St. Peter said, "We don't want him here," and the Devil said, "We don't want him here either – at least not for the time being."!!

But staying alive after experiencing a subarachnoid aneurysm in a swimming pool, with no obvious brain or body impairment is pretty unusual and maybe I am meant to say or write something. But if I do say or write something it has to be sensible and my reasons for doing so have to be explained.

The explanation lies in my education and in my life experiences and to quite a large extent in a little red book. That little red book (and I am not talking about Mao Tse Tung's little Red Book!) was entitled "Memoranda" and was handed to every boy at my school. It contained a selection of poems and extracts from books and plays which we were meant to learn by heart during our school careers. The idea was that we should become impregnated with the thoughts and the wisdom of people who had lived in previous centuries. I have learned most of it and can still recite parts as if I had learned them yesterday and the book is one of my most treasured possessions.

To me one extract from the "Spectator" in about 1710 (yes, about 1710) stands out and at the risk of boring the reader I set it out below: it was written by Joseph Addison, (1672-1719) the editor at the time.

"For my own part, though I am always serious I do not know what it is to be melancholy; and can therefore take a view of nature in her deep and solemn scenes with the same pleasure as in her most gay and delightful ones.

By this means I can improve myself with those objects which others consider with terror. When I look upon the tombs of the great every emotion of envy dies in me.

When I read the epitaphs of the beautiful every inordinate desire goes out. When I meet with the grief of parents upon a tombstone my heart melts with compassion: when I see the tomb of the parents themselves I consider the vanity of grieving for those whom we must quickly follow.

When I see Kings lying by those who deposed them; when I consider rival wits placed side by side or the Holy men that divided the world with their contests and disputes I reflect with sorrow and astonishment on the little competitions, factions and debates of mankind.

When I read the several dates of the tombs of some that died yesterday and some six hundred years ago I consider that great day when we shall all of us be contemporaries and make our appearance together"

With that extract and with extracts from works of John Milton, Sir Henry Wotton, Charles Dickens and others firmly lodged in my brain as reference points you will not be surprised at the way in which I have approached life.

Within that orthodox framework I have had some fairly radical thoughts: various strange things have occurred to me during my life that have caused me to have these thoughts and I will set them out for the reader's consideration below.

The first event that affected my thoughts occurred while I was still at school. As editor of the Classical Society magazine I was approached by a fellow pupil and asked whether I would publish in the magazine an article he had written on "Comparative Religion". I read the article and found it most interesting. I referred it to my co-editor who, being a more doctrinal Christian than myself, was appalled by it and said that he would resign if I published it. I thanked him for his assistance with the magazine in the past and accepted his resignation.

The article, written by a pupil called McFarqhuar, stated, in essence, that primitive religions had been translated or transformed over the centuries into the religious beliefs one finds in the world at the present time and that these beliefs were and have been adapted by the societies in which they were or are practised: Knowledge and custom have affected them: he pointed out, for example, that the outward manifestation and interpretation of Christian belief has differed markedly between, say, the twelfth and twentieth centuries. I could see nothing wrong with the article as a genuine expression of sincerely held views and I believe McFarqhuar subsequently read for and obtained a degree in divinity at university.

The next "intellectual missile" hit me at university.

The study of international law constituted one of the building blocks of a law degree. International law is the system of law that regulates the manner in which countries relate to each other: one hears of treaties between countries from the sixteenth century onwards and this network of treaties gradually acquired an established format that has been refined and adapted over the centuries.

One thinks of "non treaties" like the piece of paper Neville Chamberlain brandished when he got off a plane in England after a visit to Hitler in 1939 and real treaties like the treaties of Rome and Lisbon: these are an interlocking system of legally enforceable agreements created for the convenience and benefit of the countries that have entered into them.

What is the relevance of this? A Dutch lawyer by the name of Grotius, provides the clue. What he said was that nothing is perfect: everything in life is an approximation to the absolute: mankind being anything but perfect tries to attain the absolute in whatever it does. No one or no thing, he considered, could ever attain the absolute – whether it be beauty, purity, the law between nations, even religious belief, apart from our Creator.

I tend to look at what he propounded in this way: if we were ants we would imagine that God was a "super ant": as humans we perceive everything in human terms, whatever the real truth, whatever the absolute. Man's arrogance, moreover is reflected in his perception that we are in the image of the Creator of everything in the universe and beyond.

Being persuaded by McFarqhuar and Grotius that every religion is an approximation to the absolute and that religious expression is very much a human construct it appeared fairly obvious to me that one has to look elsewhere for the answer to why we exist and why religious beliefs have such an important place in our lives.

My previously held Christian convictions were also affected indirectly by my classical history studies and by an interest, in particular, in the corn supply to Rome. At this point you may think that I have gone off my head but it was fairly obvious to me that the worst time of year for a Roman Emperor to hold a census was in the middle of winter when many roads and tracks throughout the empire would be impassable and when the population would have difficulty in returning to their home towns or villages – as Mary and Joseph would have had to do during the reign of Augustus. Augustus was known to have been an astute emperor who would have decreed that the census be held at the most convenient time of year.

The most convenient time of year for anyone growing crops, and, in particular, corn upon which Rome relied, would have been between the sowing and the reaping of crops. I hope you get my drift! On that basis April/May would probably have been the best time for the census and the birth of Christ would have taken place during one or other of these two months.

It is well known by theologians at least that Christmas, as we know it, is a fabrication of the Christian Church: the early Christian Church wanted to get rid of the Feast of Dionysius, the mid-winter festival that was deeply rooted in Romano-Greek culture and replace it with a Christian festival a few days later: hence the creation of Christmas as a token date for the birth of Christ.

The next "intellectual missile" to hit me was a book by Robert Graves, the author of "I, Claudius" which I read at university. He advanced an interesting and entirely plausible theory. He stated that when people are crucified they do not die from pain: they drown.

Flogging, plus the position in which people are placed on the cross, causes a build-up of liquid in the lungs to the point where the lungs no longer function. This proposition – when taken in conjunction with the fact that large nails were probably quite expensive items to produce in the non-industrial early Christian world and would, in any event, have been little or no use in attaching someone to a cross for any length of time – led him to consider the following possibility.

Christ was probably attached to the cross by ropes tied tightly around his wrists and ankles: if nails alone had been driven through his hands the tendons and muscles in his hands would have torn by virtue of the weight of his head, chest and torso: they would probably not have been sufficient to hold his body in position.

After he had been on the cross for a comparatively short time a Roman centurion is said to have pierced his side with a spear. According to Robert Graves the centurion pierced a lung thereby enabling the liquid "build-up" in his lung to escape and thus allowing the lung to function. Christ's followers managed to get him down quickly while he was still alive and put him in a tomb which they could access but which was hidden from view.

Robert Graves theory may be fanciful but having experienced a "one in a thousand" survival I dismiss nothing out of hand. What if Christ did survive? He would have been faced with a dilemma: "Do I let it be known that I have survived, in which case the Romans will come looking and will make sure I die or do I disappear? Do I go East or West and how do I ensure that what I have preached about God and spirituality is not ignored in such a pagan world? Do I take my wife and family with me? Would they be forced to disclose what actually happened to me if I left them behind?" If one follows Robert Graves' train of thought Christ would have gone to the East with his family – across the nearest border of the Roman Empire: he had a trade as a carpenter and could have made a living.

In a previous age Robert Graves would have been branded a heretic but scientific knowledge has expanded enormously in the last fifty years and has had a profound impact on the way in which society views what were once considered central tenets of Christian belief: I have to admit that in the light of science and the increase in knowledge of genetics and DNA structures I do not feel at all comfortable with the concept of the virgin birth.

In fact, it was at school that our R E teacher, the Reverend R. R. Lewis ("Tusky" to the boys because he had two rather pronounced molars) taught us not to believe in miracles. "Take the miracle of the five loaves and fishes, for example," he said to us. "I was in Palestine (now Israel and Jordan) during the war and I saw how people lived in the Middle East. When they go out into the desert they always take some food with them. When the five thousand followers went out into the desert with Christ all but a few took something with them. When, therefore, Christ called for contributions of food for those who had been incautious enough to go into the desert without any, sufficient was quickly found to feed them. That was no miracle," said the Reverend Lewis, "and the same goes for other miracles"!

One can hardly be surprised, in the circumstances, that I have approached Christianity and Christian teaching, to which I subscribe in, hopefully, a more honest way as a pointer to spirituality, with caution!

When Joseph Addison referred to "the Holy men that divided the world with their contests and disputes" he did not mean just Christian holy men: he meant the holy men from all faiths – Christian, Muslim and so on and the subtext to what he said is, I believe, his view that these particular holy men have overlooked the one element that should be reflected in all faiths, namely spirituality. Spirituality is common to all beliefs and it is spirituality that all faiths try to "anchor" in holy writings, sacred buildings and the sayings of prophets. In its most recognisable form it is the manifestation of goodness and charity wherever it appears: in its more revered and human form it is, perhaps, what we in the West call saintliness.

It is fairly obvious to me – and I hope my thoughts are shared by others –that there is no one faith that has a monopoly on spirituality or access to whatever lies beyond the grave: that would be to condemn everyone who has not subscribed to a particular faith to some sort of oblivion which is not shared by the subscribers to that particular faith.

In this respect Christ and Mohammed both talk of a heavenly state: "In my Father's house are many mansions," says Christ. But can we, as rational human beings imagine a place beyond physical life where literally billions of people live, where spiritual accommodation is provided for everyone who has believed in a certain prophet? I cannot envisage this though many can.

I have tried to rationalise the existence of spirituality and the after-life and I have started by trying to see everyone on earth as a candle: we come into the physical world each with the candle of spirituality: the candle flickers initially in the darkness of the world and the way we live our lives determines whether it glows brightly or goes out. Sometimes it glows very brightly indeed in the holy men who really want to impart the existence of spirituality, of something beyond just getting through life: these holy men try to leave a permanent imprint in what they say, what they write and what they build.

All the time these holy men are up against the corroding effects of our primal animal instincts and the ways in which, for a variety of reasons, we prefer to ignore the candle that, in many of us, is often extinguished. It is undoubtedly extinguished in those who subvert for their own purposes the teachings of all the holy men and women who have ever graced the Earth.

So what is life all about, we ask ourselves and how do we use whatever spirituality is in us? I leave that to the theologians! I have referred to the arrogance of mankind in thinking that we are in the image of God: this personification is given credence in Christian teaching but we should not overlook the relationship of Earth in its size to the rest of our universe and all the other universes that exist, nor the length of time "sentient" mankind has been on the Earth and the comparatively recent grown in religious beliefs – in probably not much more than the last 30,000 years.

As far as the place of the Earth in the universe is concerned it is totally insignificant, although perhaps unique in many respects. Our development from ape-like creature to sentient human beings is also extremely recent in time terms and why we should think that the Creator of this and all the other universes should wish to manifest itself in the shape of something that has been around for less than half a million years on just one of the many planets that must exist I have never been able to understand.

33

The Extraordinary Annette

As I stood in the state of the art lecture theatre Annette had designed and which had subsequently been dedicated to her memory I reflected on the sad loss to the world of such a prodigiously talented person at such a comparatively early age.

When she died, at the age of fifty-six, she had been a Director of Education, Training and Work Force Development at one NHS mental health trust and a consultant psychologist at another: she had split her time between the two.

She was, in fact, one of the most extraordinary women I have ever known – good-looking, charming and extremely clever. She had an air of confidence about her which was very reassuring and which made people put their trust in her and respect what she said.

Her headmistress, Miss Farrer, at Clayton Hall grammar school, Newcastle-under-Lyme, recognised that, behind the façade of rebellious teenager, there lurked a formidable talent and had tried to direct it towards a career in teaching: it was Miss Farrer who used her influence to get Annette, with her one "A" level in religious studies into Redlands teacher training college in Bristol.

Annette went to Redlands when she was eighteen and, during her first year there was sent on teaching practice for a term to a junior school in Islington: one of the children she encountered there was the daughter of the well-known author, Shelagh Delaney, and it was the difficulty of coping with her and the somewhat unruly children she encountered there that led her to question whether teaching was for her. It had been a baptism of fire as far as she was concerned!

On the other hand, she discovered while at the college that she was good at motivating her fellow students and organised and led a Students' Union demonstration against Margaret Thatcher's decision to dispense with milk for schoolchildren. In many ways she was probably still as rebellious as the children she encountered during her teaching practice!

During the summer vacation in 1972, at the end of her first year at Redlands, she found herself a job in London working behind the bar of a well-known public house just off Oxford Street and it was there, apparently, that she met her first husband, Graham: in the words of one of her sisters he looked like a "Greek God," tall, blond and extremely handsome. Annette was bowled over by him.

It did not take her long to appreciate that marriage to a talented, good-looking young university graduate who played tennis for his county and whose parents were quite wealthy trumped any thoughts of becoming what Miss Farrer had hoped she might become. She left Redlands without completing her teacher training course and they were married shortly thereafter.

A few years later saw her in Toronto with three children and a seemingly happy marriage. She had applied her restless energy to her children, to her home, to becoming a qualified YMCA health and fitness instructor and a "star" negotiator for a major property selling company, W.H. Bosley & Co. Ltd, realtors. It must, therefore, have come as an immense shock when her husband came home from work one evening and calmly announced that he was in love with someone else and wanted a divorce. She had been persuaded by him to move to Canada in order to progress his career in I.T. management and to leave her widowed mother, to whom she was devoted, and the rest of her close family. It must have been a crushing blow for her.

As her second husband I have often had pause for thought over his decision to "look elsewhere" and have concluded that he was unable to cope with her high intelligence and her remarkable creativity. I was often accused by her of acting more like a father than a husband but one had to be very sure of oneself to be able to withstand her persuasive insistence that what she wanted to do was right, whether it was or not: she could be very determined! It was this determination that stood her in good stead when at the age of forty she decided to embark seriously on her chosen career.

Having returned from our ill-fated venture in France we faced considerable financial uncertainty as a result of my membership of Lloyds of London and the disastrous losses incurred by syndicates in which I had been involved. This had subsequently been compounded when our efforts to create Resolve, a mediation network for divorcing couples, were scuppered by the decision of the newly elected Labour Government in 1997 to put the provisions of the 1996 Family Law Act relating to family mediation on hold.

Although there was no discernible outcome from either of our joint ventures Annette's experiences as the directrice of a language college in the Dordogne and as a qualified family mediator had, nevertheless, given her the sense of direction she was looking for.

As a result of her experiences with our language students she had decided to study psychology and, when qualifying as a family mediator, she had defined the field of psychology in which she was most interested. While, therefore, we were trying to set up Resolve as a national body and were touring England and Wales promoting the concept of family mediation she had been taking courses on cognitive behavioural therapy (CBT) and had become a member of the British Association of Counselling: she had also approached the Open University with a view to taking a degree in psychology. She started a three-year course in 1993 and obtained a 2.1 degree in 1996.

During those three years I had been acting as a Law Society Intervening Agent and could choose the hours I worked: I could therefore help around the house and with the children while Annette was studying for her degree and "cutting her teeth" on counselling work. At almost the same time, however, as Annette was awarded her degree the intervention work came to a halt and I had to go back into full-time legal practice.

This meant that Annette had to get herself a full-time job: she applied to the South Essex Partnership Trust (SEPT) and was employed as a mental health therapist, specialising in C.B.T.

I had completely supported Annette's desire to underpin her new career with a proper qualification of some sort when she had first applied to the Open University: she told me at the time that she desperately wanted to make up for her misspent youth – smoking in the school toilets and having a good time when she should have been studying for her "A" levels – and that obtaining a degree would compensate for her lack of academic achievement to date.

Although we had three children to look after, whether they were at home or at university, during those three years we had found time for her to study and achieve a good degree. If, however, I thought that was enough for her I was very much mistaken. On receiving notification of her degree she said, "That was not too difficult, I think I will try for a masters (an MSc) in psychology".

This was going to be quite a challenge for her because she now had a full-time job and I was having to try and build up a legal practice from a standing start in Shenfield: it was demanding a lot of my time. Nevertheless, by sharing the household and family tasks and by my cooperating with her as much as I could she pressed on with her studies and achieved a master of science degree in psychology with a distinction in her dissertation on Counselling Psychology from City University.

Annette was clearly cut out to be a Counselling Psychologist: I could see that she had worked incredibly hard to gain an M.Sc. A distinction in her dissertation emphasised her latent talent. Her mastery of her subject revealed an ability to analyse problems and produce clear and coherent responses to them.

This analytical ability was to reveal itself soon after she had gained her M.Sc. I walked into her study one evening where she had been preparing work for the next day. "I have had a great idea," she said. "I will go to see Patrick Geoghegan, the Chief Executive, and put it to him that he has made his way up the career ladder from a lowly position in the NHS to become Chief Executive. He had been self-motivated, like me, to succeed. But there is no reason why everyone working in the NHS should not be given the opportunity to advance their career prospects by taking courses that would help them to do so. I will suggest that I devise these courses for everyone from the hospital porters upwards and that we sell these courses to other NHS trusts. In this way we will be able to cover the cost to our trust of the staff required to monitor the progress of the applicants for the courses within our own trust. The same staff can also monitor applications from senior staff, specialist doctors, psychologists, psychiatrists and others for additional training in their particular areas of work."

This sounded like a good idea to me: it also sounded an excellent idea to Patrick Geoghegan, the ebullient, charismatic and extremely "switched on" Chief Executive of SEPT: from having one personal assistant Annette rapidly built up a department of about thirty staff, half of whom dealt with the career advancement of the staff and half of whom sold the courses to other NHS trusts.

Although Annette thoroughly enjoyed this aspect of her work she started to miss dealing with patients and approached Patrick Geoghegan with a request.

Would he mind her spending one day a week at another hospital where she would be able to treat patients? It was very difficult for her to combine two functions at the same hospital. He readily agreed, and Annette approached Dr. Naomi Fineburg at the Queen Elizabeth II hospital in Welwyn with a request that she act as a member of her team of psychologists dealing specifically with obsessive compulsive disorders (OCD), one day a week. Dr. Fineburg was delighted to accept her on this basis.

After working at the QE II hospital for about a year Annette told me that she had had another "great idea". "What is it this time?" I asked her. "Well, at the moment about forty five per cent of the OCD patients do not turn up for their appointments so I sometimes spend half a day sitting around at the hospital doing nothing. But what if I got eight patients together and gave them all a three-month course on treating obsessive disorders, then even if only half of them turned up after the first session, I would not be wasting my time and I would be saving the NHS a lot of money. It would also free me up to do other things as well."

This, again, seemed a very sensible suggestion and Dr. Fineburg thought so as well. Annette therefore arranged for eight OCD patients to attend the first group session and explained what she intended to do: it would be entirely up to the patients if they wished to participate in the group: otherwise they could be treated individually. Not surprisingly they liked the idea of being part of a group: they all turned up for the second session and every session thereafter: she had virtually a one hundred per cent attendance for the entire twelve-week period and at the end of the three months she turned to me and said, "I seem to have produced eight budding amateur psychologists! They have all become so involved in the subject of obsessive compulsive behaviour that they are advising each other on their individual symptoms!"

Meeting as a group helped them realise that they were not alone: there were many other people like themselves: it gave each group member the confidence to discuss their symptoms with others: it was not like going to an appointment on their own and being worried that they would be put under a microscope by a psychologist. There was reassurance in being part of a group.

Having established that group OCD treatment worked and was, in fact, very successful, Annette turned to me once again one evening and said, "I think I will try to obtain a doctorate and base it on the results of my group OCD experiment." "Hang on a minute! How on earth are you going to have time to study for a doctorate?" I asked her. "Your life is full enough as it is, what with your work at SEPT and everything you do at the QE II." "I feel sure I can do it," she replied, "provided we pull together and you help out with the family as you have done before."

I could see that she was quite determined and that achieving a doctorate meant a lot to her: her mother had, apparently said to her when she was much younger, "Annette, your ambition terrifies me." I knew exactly what her mother meant although I would have substituted "determination" for "ambition." Annette was not to be deflected once she had made up her mind to do something!

As we walked out of the Guildhall in London after the City University 'Degree Giving Ceremony' Annette turned to me and said, "Do you know, I am the only person not on the teaching staff of the university to have received a doctorate?" It was a very proud day for her and for our entire family. She was unstoppable! It was not long after she achieved her doctorate in counselling psychology that she was appointed a consultant at the QE II and to her great pleasure and delight was able to park in the consultants' car park!

Although the concept of group treatment for sufferers from OCD was her own she was not at all selfish about sharing her ideas with others and was quite happy for other specialists in OCD to take advantage of her findings as set out in her doctoral thesis. The concept was subsequently adopted by Professor Paul Salkovskis and others as a viable way of cutting costs and treating a number of OCD patients at the same time.

Annette did, however, have the warm and reassuring personality to make the members of her groups feel comfortable and there is no doubt that any psychologist undertaking group therapy would require teaching skills as well as confidence and substantial experience if he or she was to do so successfully.

Once Annette had achieved her doctorate and consultant status her thoughts turned to another project she had in mind. As usual it was prefaced by her comment to me, "I have had another great idea."! By now I was becoming used to her great ideas. "What is it this time," I asked her.

"I do not think that NHS trusts are particularly well managed: they could do with some expert advice. I am going to fly to Yale University and ask some professors from the health management school to come over to England and give courses on health management to the chief executives of NHS trusts and to the heads of strategic health authorities. I will also find some headline speakers from the UK to help sell the courses".

This, again, struck me and her chief executive, Patrick Geoghegan, as a very good idea and off Annette flew to Yale. As already indicated, she could persuade anyone to do just about anything and it was not long before Yale had agreed to participate: forty two executives signed up for the first course and by the time she died the courses, which are held every November, had attracted keynote speakers from the head of Monitor, the Government's health "watchdog", downwards. Annette had also been asked by Yale to act as UK representative on their global health programme: unfortunately, this was after she had been diagnosed with multiple myeloma.

Even after she had been diagnosed she continued to work incredibly hard to raise the profile of her NHS trust: she felt strongly that mental health trusts should be allowed to achieve university status and, with Patrick Geoghegan, went to discuss with the Under-Secretary of State for Health the possibility of her trust doing so.

The Government had previously been against mental health trusts achieving university status but after an hour of persuasive talk from Patrick Geoghegan and Annette there was a surprising change of attitude: the Under-Secretary agreed that they should, after all, be allowed to do so. Annette told me that, as they left the room in which they had met, the Under-Secretary took her on one side and said quietly to her: "My dear, have you thought of coming into politics?" Alas, she could not have done so even had she wanted: she died shortly after university status was conferred on the South Essex Partnership Trust.

Why did she succumb to cancer? Sadly she could not be dissuaded from working so hard before cancer was diagnosed: contrary to my advice she insisted on working through two attacks of shingles and doubtless reduced her body's defences to cancer as a result. On the other hand, by working so hard, she doubtless achieved more in her sixteen years in the NHS than most people would have achieved in twice that time.

She was, in my view, destined to achieve high honours had she been able to slow down and been more inclined to take care of herself. But she would not take my advice and became really annoyed with me when, for example, I tried to insist that she come to bed reasonably early for the sake of her health.

Many people have commented on the fact that it was her restless energy and my own that made us so compatible – once we had survived the traumatic adjustment stage at the beginning of our marriage. That is probably right. We each respected what the other was trying to achieve and this mutual respect generated a very strong bond between us.

As readers will doubtless have gathered I was immensely proud of Annette's achievements and admired all her good points – including her single-minded determination. I was aware, however, that, under all that apparent confidence and assurance was a sense of insecurity. I was able, in the circumstances, to give her the stability which, after the death of her father when she was only ten years old and after the manner in which she had been cast aside by her first husband, she really needed: I acted as an anchor for her.

Perhaps, therefore, she was not so far out when, occasionally, she would complain that I treated her more like a daughter than a wife! I was, after all, seventeen years older than her!

She was a fantastic example to any woman who wonders whether, after having children, she can make a career for herself. She would definitely have endorsed former President Obama's favourite exhortation "Yes, you can!"

34

Background and Education

When one considers what a cheeky and workshy young boy I was at the age of twelve and how much I disliked Latin and Greek until I started to study ancient history one cannot but marvel at the transformation brought about by the schoolmasters at Brentwood School. My final school report gives an indication of how affected I was by the encouragement they gave and the support I and the other boys received from them.

From Final School Report: Summer 1954: *Form Master:* "He has done well, shown himself a leader and, by his example, been a great help to the Form: I hope he may have won a State Scholarship. My warmest wishes for his future."

Housemaster: As Senior Librarian, Praepostor (Prefect), Colour Sergeant in the CCF and Secretary of the Classical Society he has set, by his readiness to take responsibility and to work selflessly, an outstanding example of service to a Community. The whole house wishes him every success in the future." [In 1995, Brian was awarded an MBE for service to the community.]

Headmaster: "He has shown a real sense of responsibility and loyalty: he goes forward to University with our sincere hopes for his success."

But to start from the beginning. I was born in 1936 in a council house in Warrington Road, Dagenham about a mile from my cousin, Dudley: my father, then twenty four years of age, worked as a legal assistant in the town clerk's department of Dagenham Council. As previously mentioned, my grandfather, William Owen Hughes, had been so mean that my father had had to go to school (Westcliff High School for boys) in his Scout jersey: he never had a shirt, a tie or a blazer while he was at school and had been obliged to leave school after matriculating and gaining his school certificate: although he was bright there was to be no further education for him: he had to go to work at sixteen.

On the other hand, my father was determined to ensure that, to the best of his ability, his children would receive a decent education: the unfulfilled hopes and aspirations of my mother and father were reflected in their desire to ensure that my sister and I took full advantage of whatever education was on offer and did well at school. We were both very much aware of this and it did put a certain amount of pressure on both of us throughout our time at school.

Dudley's mother, Ada and my father were brother and sister and Ada incurred the displeasure of her father, my grandfather, by running away from the family home in Westcliff on Sea and marrying a humble platelayer on the railways by the name of John (Jock) Moore: hence Ada and Jock were living in a council house in Dagenham at the same time as my parents.

Ada had been her father's favourite daughter and he, initially, was very upset by what she had done. "Never darken my door again," was his attitude until his grandson, Dudley, started to make a name for himself at school. As we now know, however, Dudley was an extremely talented child and defied all the odds: he was a brilliant pianist and, as a result of his musical abilities, gained an organ scholarship to Magdalen College, Oxford. His achievement was so remarkable that his school gave all the children a day's holiday when his scholarship was announced. Once he was at Oxford his future was assured and his career thereafter as a musician, comedian (Dud and Pete) and film star ("Ten", "Arthur" etc.) is well documented.

My father was very fond of his sister Ada and I can remember our visiting "Ada and Jock's" home when I was between twelve and fourteen years of age and Dudley being told to play something for "uncle Alfred and auntie Gertie." Dudley who was about fourteen or fifteen at the time would grimace and play some Chopin or similar quite beautifully on the family piano.

Barbara, his sister, was older than Dudley and I can recall her, tall, attractive and dignified, coming in later in the afternoon after work. She married Bernard Stephens, an RAF officer who retired as a squadron leader after being a regular in the RAF.

Having been in Dagenham from the date of his marriage, it was not long before my father changed jobs and obtained employment with Hornchurch Urban District Council: we therefore moved when I was nearly two years old to a new house in Alma Avenue, Hornchurch in 1937. However, war was looming and my father sensibly decided to find employment in Kettering in a pleasant part of Northamptonshire: the RAF fighter base at Hornchurch was only a few hundred yards away from our home in Alma Avenue and was likely to be attacked by the Luftwaffe which, in fact, it was.

In the circumstances my parents rented their house in Hornchurch in 1939 to a Mr and Mrs Steadman (who never paid the rent!) and moved to a rented house in Kettering, the rent for which was, I believe, thirty shillings (£1.50) a week. I have so many childhood memories of living in Kettering that it would bore any reader to death if I recounted them: they would constitute a book in themselves!

Suffice to say I enjoyed my time at Hawthorn Road primary school and passed the "8-plus" scholarship to Kettering grammar school. Until 1945 children were admitted to grammar schools at the age of eight: I can vividly remember sitting on the stairs at our home in The Broadway and being asked by my mother whether she or I should open the letter containing the result of the examination: I opened it and read it with some relief.

Kettering grammar school was an "all boys" school, immediately adjacent to its counterpart, an "all girls" grammar school. We were all children from ordinary backgrounds: no one was better off than anyone else: the war was a great leveller in this respect. I made many friends there and felt very much at home in the Midlands.

When I was ten, however, my father was on the move again, this time to Billericay where he was appointed Assistant Town Clerk to Billericay Urban District Council at the age of thirty four: he had no legal qualifications and this was to tell against him later. But in 1946 the lack of any legal qualification was no problem: he was an efficient administrator with eighteen years' experience of local government: that was enough.

The Steadmans had "done a moonlight flit" at the end of the war and we moved back into our home in Hornchurch after the bomb damage had been repaired: a German V2 rocket had landed behind the house and destroyed a number of houses in the next street, causing blast damage to our own. The Government made grants towards the cost of repair of war-damaged properties and we lived for several months in a "war requisitioned" bungalow – "St. Olaves" in Homestead Road, Ramsden Bellhouse, about four miles from Billericay. The bungalow has long since disappeared and was notable only for the adder's nest we found under the floorboards of my sister's bedroom!

The problem for my parents was where to send me to school. They did not want me to go to the local secondary school in Billericay where the progress I had made at the grammar school would not be maintained: on the other hand my father could not afford to pay for me to attend Brentwood School, an independent grant maintained public school nearby: the fees were a whopping £20 (nineteen guineas) a term!

In desperation he obtained a letter of recommendation from the headmaster of Kettering grammar school where I had consistently come in the top four or five in my class and borrowed enough money to pay the fees for two terms at Brentwood School. The school accepted me into the preparatory school on the basis of the letter of recommendation but my father told me that unless I passed the "eleven plus" in the following February I would have to leave and go to a secondary school.

As a child I felt that having to take and pass the "eight plus" and the "eleven plus" was a bit unfair but the Butler Education Act introducing the eleven plus had been passed in 1945 when I was nine years old and I had fallen between two stools academically. Suffice to say I passed the "eleven plus" and my worries and those of my parents were over as far as the cost of school fees were concerned.

As indicated earlier I moved upwards through the school in fits and starts academically, gained an Essex county major scholarship and a place at London University at the age of seventeen and finished up with a state scholarship in classics and a place at Downing College, Cambridge at the age of eighteen. I put down my success and that of the other pupils in my class (five state scholarships and an exhibition in classics at Trinity College, Cambridge out of the eight of us) to the excellence of the teaching. It was really superb.

The school left a very deep imprint on me: it made me appreciate how lucky were young people like myself whose parents were not wealthy but who were able to receive such a good education as a result of the "eleven plus", and how indebted we were to society for this chance in life. It also brought home to me how useful grant maintained schools were for exploiting the talents of young people who, but for the "eleven plus" and the free education it offered, would not have had the chance to achieve places at good universities and thereby be of benefit to aociety.

At Brentwood School there were boys whose parents paid fees to get them in and then there were "us" (called "the Grammar bugs")! It was only because

I had been to a grammar school where we had all been equal that I noticed the divide between the "haves" and the "have nots" at a public school like Brentwood: it was quite marked between the boys in the lower forms and we "have nots" were rather looked down on until academic achievement rather than the wealth of our parents separated and distinguished us.

This divide was rather amusingly emphasised when I met Dudley backstage at "Beyond the Fringe", the smash hit comedy revue in the West End. He and Alan Bennett shared one dressing room, Peter Cook and Jonathan Miller another. As Dudley introduced me to Peter Cook and Jonathan Miller he said, "We are the grammar school boys, they are the public school boys. They keep themselves to themselves."!! It was a humorous dig at them – because all four were from Oxbridge – but he and I were both aware of the unconscious sense of superiority of those whose parents paid their public school fees over ourselves whose parents paid nothing, notwithstanding the fact that our abilities were just as great as theirs!

35

My Fall from Grace

If I did not believe in fate in my early years I have become increasingly convinced that I am very much a creature of fate and that, in so many ways, I am living out a life that was predestined.

I am reminded, in this respect, of the elderly Chinese palm reader in Kowloon who accurately and uncannily told me about my past and future life, including how many children I had and how close or otherwise they would be to me.

Why, otherwise, would Mr. Martin have decreed that I should study Greek and why, for example, should I have been the "one in a thousand" to survive a brain haemorrhage and escape drowning in a swimming pool? Why, some thirty-five years after I had lost the love of my life, should she suddenly reappear? Why indeed, should I be writing this book as a result of my many experiences?

The guiding hand of fate or chance, as the ancient Greeks described it, does not relieve me of responsibility for whatever I have done in my life and goodness only knows that I have a lot of regrets and have done many things I should not, but my achievements and failings have clearly fitted into a pattern that has not been entirely of my own making. My psychic experiences and antennae have added to a sense of being "semi-detached", half in control of my life and half not!

If I am to try and put this life puzzle into some sort of context I should perhaps start at the beginning of it. I was born at Epiphany, in the reign of King George the fifth, of God-fearing parents who were such keen supporters of their local Church that I was christened on Easter Sunday. From the ages of eleven to thirteen I regularly attended the "King's Own Bible class" in Billericay. The "King's Own", led by Peter Braun a keen evangelist, was an interdenominational Christian organisation where Peter and his associate, Norman, told us stories from the Bible, taught us how to pray and got us to sing "happy hymns"! Most importantly, these two men taught us to be kind to others and not to ignore or look down on people less fortunate than ourselves: for example, they welcomed to the Bible class an older boy, Joe, who shook uncontrollably all the time, keeping his left arm as close to his body as he could while walking with a permanent shuffling limp: whether he had had a stroke or similar I cannot say. It was clear that although he was years older than us he loved coming to the Bible classes: he was a regular attender and was accepted by us all.

When, as a family, we moved into Pink Cottage, my parents also took me quite regularly to the local parish church, St. Mary Magdalen, in Billericay where, I have to confess, the Reverend Smith gave what seemed to me as a child, some incredibly boring sermons! At the same time I attended chapel at Brentwood School and was confirmed at the age of fourteen.

During my National Service in Edinburgh I regularly attended the Church of Scotland, in preference to the Episcopalian Church, with my friend Kenneth Gubbins, attended the first of two Billy Graham rallies and somehow managed not to use any swear words during my National Service. Church attendance continued at university, not only at Great St. Mary's (or "Great St. Mervyn's as it was called, after Mervyn Stockwood, the Vicar, later to become Bishop of Southwark) but also at the college chapel. As an anecdote, I can vividly recall one particular occasion when the college chaplain, Frank Telfer, asked me to look after the Bishop of Ely. "Sit next to him and make sure that he is all right,",said Frank. "He is not used to giving sermons. He may be a bit nervous.". After the "odd" introduction to which I have referred in an earlier chapter the bishop and I sat together in a corner of the chapel and, just before he was due to give his sermon, he bent over and drew a small silver flask from his trouser pocket and took a swig of brandy (from the smell of it) out of sight of the congregation!

One might reasonably say that I was in a bit of a spiritual straitjacket during my early years: my interpretation of the twentieth century version of Christianity was, as previously indicated, tempered subsequently by what had been expounded by Grotius and Robert Graves and by what I knew about ancient Rome but my adherence to it as an anchor for spirituality was still strong after I left university and has continued ever since.

Picture, therefore, an earnest, albeit humorous and socially aware, twenty three year old, someone who had had no real girlfriends although he had been the good friend of a number of lovely young women at university, somewhat straitlaced and with absolutely no experience of sex: to him the nearest he ever got to romance was to sing to the occasional young lady he took out! He enjoyed singing! It was of course, the era of "No sex please, we are British" – before the "liberal explosion" of the 1960s and relationships were at that time very proper!

So when did the course of his life change so dramatically and when did this fall from grace occur?

One might say that it began when I decided to join the local operatic society. I will reflect on the unfortunate outcome of that decision shortly but not before I have mentioned my trip to Greece in 1960 and its aftermath.

When I left Cambridge in the summer of 1959 I had intended to take a break from academia and spend a couple of weeks in Greece before starting work at Rowe Swann & Co. My godfather, however, would not hear of it. "You have been at university for the last three years enjoying yourself and having a thoroughly good time," he said. "If you want a job in my firm you will have to start work the week after the degree-giving ceremony at the end of June." I detected a note of "green eye" in this but that is what I did: I gave up thoughts of a holiday in 1959 and started work early in July.

I was determined nevertheless to go back to Greece in the summer of 1960 "by hook or by crook", as they say, and it was on the return leg of my three-day train journey from Athens in that year that I met a lovely young lady whose first name I will give as Andrea. Having only a fortnight's holiday I spent three days leading one party out to Athens via Brindisi and three days bringing another party back via Belgrade: this gave me eight days in or around Athens. I felt it worthwhile despite the discomfort of long distance travel by train and boat. I had not therefore travelled out with Andrea's "four week" party but was returning with it and, apart from seeing her and her friends off from Victoria Station, had not met her before.

She was reading classics at Cambridge and we hit it off immediately: in fact we stood talking in the corridor of the train for much of the homeward journey. She invited me to her twenty-first birthday party in the West Country a few weeks later and I stayed with her family for two days. Although I was immensely attracted to her I was somewhat overawed by her patrician father, a much respected academic, his highly intelligent and intellectual wife and their other "blue stocking" daughter, Andrea's sister, a lecturer at London University. I was also a trifle disconcerted by Andrea's brother who, at the age of twenty three, introduced himself by swinging, like a gorilla, down the bannisters from the first floor into the hall! I had always regarded myself as somewhat eccentric but, apart from Andrea who appeared to be completely normal, they gave the impression, at least, of being more eccentric than myself!

Andrea was very much involved in her academic studies at Cambridge, and I was working during the week for stockbrokers and spending most of my weekends on my student travel programme: the opportunities to meet her in Cambridge and in the West Country were limited. Nevertheless we promised to keep very much in touch and to see each other whenever we could. I was really smitten by her: in fact I had fallen in love with her.

However, something had occurred only four months before we met that prevented me from declaring my true feelings to her: that event determined the course of the rest of my life.

At this point I have to return to the summer of 1959.

Once I had sent my three student parties to Greece in the summer of 1959 and had seen the last of them safely return to England at the end of September I found myself at a loose end in the evenings and decided to join the Billericay Amateur Operatic Society: they were advertising for members so I applied to join. I had always enjoyed singing and was accepted as a member of the chorus in their March 1960 production of "the Waltz Dream". Not wishing to appear too much of a novice I started to take singing lessons in order to improve my voice projection and singing technique.

There were about eighty people in the Billericay Amateur Operatic Society in 1959, approximately fifteen in the orchestra, fifteen in the production team and fifty who performed on stage. There were slightly more female than male "performers" but not noticeably so and the ages of members, across the entire society, ranged from early twenties to late fifties: they were, without exception, good-natured and enthusiastic, although there were one or two "prima donnas" – an occupational hazard of many local operatic and dramatic societies – and I thoroughly enjoyed the weekly rehearsals.

Once auditions for the principal parts had taken place and leading roles had been allocated rehearsals started in the hall of a local secondary school where, accompanied by a solitary pianist and under the watchful eye of the musical director we learned our singing parts, initially with the musical scores in our hands and later without.

As the weeks went by I began to appreciate the complexity of an operatic production. The musical director had to work "hand in glove" with the producer in order to integrate the singing, dancing and acting with the orchestra who were practising elsewhere. A lot of movement and choreography was involved and it was not surprising that it took from mid-October to the end of February to perfect the moves of the actors and the routines of the dancers and the chorus.

As the name implies the "Waltz Dream" had choreographed dance sequences and, once we had learned our words and had achieved a sufficiently high standard of singing in the school hall, we moved on to the dance sequences and to getting used to performing them on stage. The production itself took place over four days at a hall in Billericay which had a large stage and an audience capacity of about four hundred and fifty people. We rehearsed there during the month leading up to the week of the production itself in early March. As usual the show was a sell-out.

During the last month we were measured up for our costumes and the wardrobe mistress had a busy time ensuring that the costumes that had been hired for all the members of the cast fitted us properly. The wardrobe mistress brought one of her daughters along during the final rehearsals to help her and we got chatting. She was blond, attractive and worked as a secretary in the City and was happy to talk to me when she was not helping her mother with the costumes.

I liked her a lot and when, during the final performance I mentioned that, the following Saturday, I was going to an Epstein exhibition in London I asked her whether she would like to come. I admitted to her that I did not know much about Epstein's work. I had been to the National Gallery and the Tate Gallery and a number of art exhibitions elsewhere and had seen a lot of paintings and sculptures during my trips abroad but had not previously come across his work: I felt it must be similar to the work of Picasso. She said she would and on that fateful Saturday we set off for London

The Epstein exhibition proved my undoing as, in some respects, it was for my pretty companion also. I had no idea that, with his own work, it would feature so much of the primitive and erotic art that he had collected and I regret to say that we were both carried away by it.

In fact we were both so carried away that when I offered her the alternative of being dropped off at the bungalow at which she lived with her parents or coming back with me to my home, Pink Cottage, she chose to come back with me. My parents had gone to the weekly family gathering at my grandparents' home and were not going to return until late. During the drive back from London I had expressed the hope that she had not been offended by the explicit nature of some of the statues in the exhibition: she had not. Somewhat emboldened by this reply I had then asked whether she had had sex with anyone before: she admitted that she had. When her parents had gone to bed she had regularly slipped out of her ground floor bedroom window and met a young man to whom she had lost her virginity. Her parents had been completely unaware of these late-night assignations. Was he a boyfriend? He was not, but she was still seeing him.

As someone totally inexperienced as far as sex was concerned, I did rather assume that she would have warned me if there was any risk in our making love that evening: it was to be the first, and as it turned out, the last time I did so before I married five years later. I have to admit that, as I drove her home, I felt uneasy at what had occurred. To have had unprotected sex, even with someone who appeared to know far more about the subject than myself, was completely out of character and very irresponsible. We had both foolishly given way to urges generated by an exhibition of primitive art.

At the time I could have no idea of the massive consequences of that particular Saturday. Ironically, few of the extraordinary things that have happened to me in the subsequent fifty years would have happened but for that exhibition. There is not a great deal of point in acknowledging this rare lack of discretion in one's younger days unless one is prepared to accept the reaction to and the consequences of it. In this respect the reproach of any reader would be superfluous when, as in my case, I reproached myself for the next forty five years for this lack of self control in my youthful and less mature days.

We shall call the young lady Jane and, as a result of the time we had spent together that Saturday, she subsequently made a point of getting into the same compartment of one of the early morning trains to Liverpool Street whenever she could. A couple of my rugby club friends, Richard Shipton and Stanley Ball, with whom I usually travelled to London, did rather look down their noses at my inviting Jane into our compartment and at my chatting happily to a lowly "secretary" but, being the perverse individual that I am, their attitude towards her made me all the more determined to talk to her and be friendly to her when she got into our compartment.

Jane got into our compartment quite regularly after that until one morning in June she thrust a note into my hand as she got out of the train and asked me not to read it until she had left us. As soon as she started walking up the steps out of the station towards her office I read it. "You know what has happened between us," it read. "I do not want to see you again." I raced up the steps after her and caught her up. "What has happened?" I asked her, although I suppose I had already guessed. "I have missed two periods: I am pregnant," she replied.

"You cannot cope with that on your own," I told her. "You must let me come and talk to your parents." "I don't want you to talk to my parents about this. It is my problem and I will deal with it," she replied. If that was what she wanted I told her I would not see her but she must contact me as soon as she told her parents and I would come and see them. After that brief conversation she turned and walked away leaving me totally shocked, mortified and ashamed at what I thought I had done. Given that one cannot really conceal pregnancy for very long I concluded that when her parents noticed it they would get in touch. I would have to face up to the situation at that point and we would both have to decide what to do. I could not help feeling that it was unfair that on the one and only occasion in my life that I had been sufficiently aroused to make love to anyone I should have made Jane pregnant. I resolved there and then never to be so stupid again.

Her revelation presented me with an immediate dilemma in terms of a decision I would have to make in my personal life. In less than seven months' time I could be looking at a totally different future to the one I had hoped to enjoy. After my appearance in the "Waltz Dream" I had been approached by a member of the Billericay Folk Players (the local amateur dramatic society) and asked whether I would be interested in taking one of the lead parts in a play they were putting on in November 1960. The play was "Angels in Love" and was all about Cedric, Little Lord Fauntleroy, who knew nothing about the facts of life and whose mother, Lady Fauntleroy, had asked a close female friend to explain them to him in as explicit a way as decently possible.

Lady Fauntleroy was concerned that, after nine months of marriage her son did not appear to have a clue about sex. Fate was clearly playing games with me! This "little Lord Fauntleroy" obviously needed no further education on that particular subject! The production for which rehearsals had already started was in five months' time. Should I stay away, indeed was it likely that I could stay away, from Jane's family as she wanted? Should I risk public ridicule if the news of the pregnancy leaked out before or during my appearance in the play in November?

I decided to take the gambler's option to press ahead with the play and risk it: if I had to leave Billericay in shame and disgrace and married to Jane I would have brought the outcome on myself. People might, I thought, even confuse the fiction of the play with the fact of my bringing a baby into the world! From the moment that Jane handed me the note I lived in trepidation of a phone call from her or her parents. The facts that she said she wanted no contact with me and that, from end July, I had fallen in love with Andrea as a result of my trip to Greece, added to my confusion, to my state of anxiety, to my shame and, more significantly, to the feeling that I had thrown away my future happiness. Of course, I could not be absolutely sure I was the father but I assumed I was.

Remarkably there was no phone call during those nerve-wracking five months but after I had appeared in the play which, incidentally, won the Jobson Trophy for the best amateur production in the area, and was sitting watching television one evening a note dropped through the letterbox at Pink Cottage addressed to me.

I told my parents it was about the operatic society but it contained a terse request to meet Jane's parents. This is it," I thought. "The balloon goes up at this point."

I met her parents immediately and they told me what had happened.

Incredibly Jane had concealed the pregnancy and had given birth to a daughter, much to the astonishment of her parents, shortly after hauling the family's boat up a shingle beach the previous weekend. She had admitted to them what had happened after our trip to the exhibition and they wanted me to acknowledge that I was the father of the child. I repeated what Jane had told me about her late-night assignations and that their daughter was not a virgin when we had made love: I could not be absolutely sure that I was the father.

They were clearly disconcerted by my reply but Jane's mother expressed her firmly held view that from the baby's appearance, there was little doubt who the father was. It was me! I asked whether, for my own reassurance, I could see Jane and the baby but was told I could not. As a result of that refusal

I wondered for over forty five years whether I was indeed the father but, at the time, I saw no further point in questioning the matter of paternity.

They asked whether my parents were aware of the pregnancy. I told them they were not. Was anyone else aware? The answer, again, was no. I confessed to being ashamed and mortified by what I had done and said that I would marry Jane if she and they considered it the honourable thing to do: they felt, however, that this would not be in the best interests of either of us. The baby would have to be adopted immediately.

In fact they went on to say that since only four of us knew about the birth my parents should not be told and that we should all continue to live our lives as if nothing had happened. Her mother expected me, however, to pay for the baby clothes she had purchased and to sign the birth certificate, both of which I did. I have to say that I was genuinely astonished and humbled by the attitude of Jane's parents who were about as understanding and lenient as any parents could be in such circumstances.

It was only well over forty five years later that my daughter, who had apparently been named "Heather" by Jane and who had been adopted by a well-educated couple in Middlesex tracked me down and was able to tell Annette and I why she had been put up for adoption so quickly. Some time previously she had traced and met Jane. According to Jane her parents had apparently made plans for a holiday that they did not want to disrupt. That had been the principal reason for Heather's rapid adoption.

Heather told me that Jane who, regrettably, I never met again after our terse conversation on the steps at Liverpool Street Station, had gone on to marry and have children. She, like me, had had the opportunity to meet her daughter and establish a loving relationship before she died and she, like me, had been touched by Heather's determination to contact her birth parents.

My relief at this total reprieve was palpable at the time. I had already sworn never to have any form of sexual relationship until I married and I had been given the chance to redeem myself. Henceforth I would revert to being a useful and responsible member of society and try to lead a blameless life. My resolve in this respect was all very well but what was I to do about Andrea? How could I possibly tell her about what had happened four months before I met her? I carried on seeing her, albeit spasmodically, until mid-1961 but decided it would be unfair to expect her to accept me, a fallen and disgraced man, as a husband and equally unfair not to tell her why I was not seeing her as much as

I really wanted.

For someone who was so confident when dealing with the practicalities of life and the "ways of the world" it was doubtless a lack of confidence in the emotional sphere that led me to turn my back on what was undoubtedly the best relationship I could ever have enjoyed. Had I been open and honest with Andrea and had the relationship been as good as I hoped it was then I would doubtless have had nothing to fear: I would not have been rejected. But feelings of guilt and shame overrode rational thought and I could not face up to rejection. That was a big miscalculation as I was to discover many years later. The word "love" had never been mentioned by either of us: we had so much enjoyed each other's company but we were both too restrained to say those three essential words that, had I known it at the time, would have transformed the situation. As a result my life moved on without Andrea but, as the reader will discover, that was, by no means, the end of my relationship with her.

But by mid-1961 I had a lot of other things on my mind: my travel parties to Greece were becoming increasingly popular with students in universities across the country, my work life at Rowe Swann & Co. was not progressing as I had hoped. I had just failed the final exams of the Chartered Institute of Secretaries and, as a result of my appearances in the operatic society and in the amateur dramatic society, had been approached by both societies to take roles in other productions. Having been captain of house rugby at school I had also just finished playing during the winter for Billericay Rugby Club and choices and decisions had to be made.

Jane's mother had said that we should continue to lead our lives as normal but I decided that it would be prudent to give the operatic society a miss for the time being. If I appeared in a couple of plays no one would think anything of my absence from it for a year or so. I therefore agreed to take the part of Armand, the adulterous brother, in Jean Anouilh's play, "Colombe" and the part of Eiliff, the unpleasant son of Mother Courage in Bertolt Brecht's play of the same name in 1961 and 1962.

As far as work was concerned it was becoming increasingly clear by mid-1961 that it would take me years to become a partner, if at all. As indicated above I had also just failed to qualify as a chartered secretary from whose ranks were drawn the company secretaries of many major companies, including those in the Stock Exchange "Footsie" index.

When I was moved from the general office of Rowe Swann & Co. where I had been introduced to the mechanics of buying and selling stocks and shares, preparing contract notes and learning settlement procedures in late 1959, it had occurred to me that, if I was going to qualify as anything, it would be sensible to qualify as a company secretary. It would be an appropriate qualification because, as part of my job in the statistical analysis department, I was constantly reading company reports and analysing trading figures and results: it could also lead to another well-paid job in the City if progress through the ranks of Rowe Swann & Co. proved difficult or impossible.

I had signed up to a Rapid Results College course which was, in fact, very good and had passed the final economics papers of the institute with flying colours. To my chagrin, however, I had just failed the final law paper because I had assumed, incorrectly, that I would be able to rely on the knowledge of the law I had acquired when studying for a degree in the subject.

My father's advice to get a professional qualification behind me still held good and I would continue to follow it. In the circumstances a change of direction was required!

The only other viable qualification was that of solicitor provided I could obtain articles of clerkship. Studying for the seven heads of the Law Society's final examinations would also take my mind off Andrea and my self-imposed estrangement from her. But could I afford unpaid or low-paid articles? In either case I could only survive if I used the money I had made by buying and selling shares and could bring in some income from organising more student parties. Solicitor's practices in the City of London were paying meagre amounts to articled clerks and what they paid would not cover travel by train to London every day and all my other living expenses: I would have to find very cheap digs in London during the week and use my father's aged 1936 Austin Ascot de Luxe which he sold to me for £60 at the weekends for my university visits and any social activities.

I therefore approached the Cambridge University Appointments Board who helped me find a firm of solicitors in the City of London prepared to offer me articles and pay me, however small the amount, rather than me having to pay them. Once, with their assistance, I had obtained an offer I handed in my notice with some trepidation to Rowe Swann & Co. My two years with them had not, after all, been a waste of time because I had learned a great deal about the Stock Exchange and the City of London and the profits on my share dealings made it possible for me to live for the next three years on a very low trainee solicitor's salary.

Although I have referred in previous chapters to the nature of my work in the City of London as an employee of a firm of stockbrokers and as an articled clerk at Bircham & Co. I have not dwelt on the personal aspects of my life between December 1960 and December 1962.

For much of my spare time I concentrated on my student travel programme which was expanding fast. In this respect there was a distinct pattern to these two years and the ten years that followed. First of all fares and costs had to be ascertained – of train and boat tickets, of coach tours in Greece and of the accommodation I reserved for members of my parties for their first two nights in Athens. When this information was to hand the dates of the train and train/boat parties and of the coach tours were finalised and incorporated into the programme and the necessary reservations made for the accommodation of the male students at the Hotel Marion, managed by my good friend Babis, and for the female students at the XEN, a modern and well-equipped YWCA hostel in the heart of Athens.

Having to make advance bookings of the train seats and couchettes, to notify the shipping lines of the likely number of passengers on the Brindisi Piraeus crossings and to estimate the requirements for hotel/hostel accommodation meant that a limit had to be placed on the size of each student party in the programme. Once the travel programme had been printed, posters had been designed and produced and the handbook had been brought up to date it was then just a matter of filling the parties! In order to do this I would set off most weekends during the first half of the year to put up posters on student noticeboards in colleges and universities across the length and breadth of the country. Over the years and, in order to assist the promotion of my parties, I developed a network of "College Reps" in universities from as far afield as St. Andrews and Exeter. These reps were all students who had been particularly enthusiastic about their previous trips to Greece with my parties and who had invariably contributed additional useful information to the handbook on Greece.

When masses of letters started to arrive at Pink Cottage from prospective travellers, usually from April onwards, I had, of course, to answer them all, send out promotional information and booking forms, collect deposits and subsequently send final payment requests with instructions on where and at what time to meet for the train journey from London and the coach tours from

Athens. Every student also received a printed card, giving the necessary details of where and at what time they should appear for their homeward journey at whichever point they had indicated they would join or re-join their party. Nothing was left to chance and no one was ever going to be stranded abroad provided they followed my instructions!

Over the years I also developed a round "BH recommended" window sticker which I asked leaders of parties to persuade the proprietors of restaurants and tavernas throughout Greece to display if the leaders had received good value and the restaurants or tavernas were friendly to our students: most of these recommended eating places were mentioned subsequently in the handbook, which I revised every year. The proprietors were only too happy to display the window sticker since it clearly brought them a lot of custom. Such was their popularity the parties quickly filled up and, to my great relief, all travel arrangements and coach tours over the fourteen years I organised them went according to plan without a serious incident or delay.

As an aside, however, there was, in 1963, a massive earthquake in Skopje which devastated the railway lines through the city and my mother and I spent all night making identity armbands for the fifty-odd students in three groups who were due to travel on the Tauern Orient Express via Skopje not much more than two days after the earthquake occurred. It was vital that the students stayed with the leader who held their particular group ticket against which alone their "contremarque" (a small brown coupon) was valid when they were transported by army truck or bus from one side of the city to the other.

The armbands displaying their party numbers worked well and no one was lost or misplaced during the somewhat chaotic journey across the stricken city in the makeshift transport provided by the Yugoslav authorities.

On the social front I threw myself back into acting and singing and after appearing in the two plays and, after the judicious two years' absence from it, I rejoined the operatic society in October 1962. Thereafter I spent time learning my lines and rehearsing my part in "Die Fledermaus" in which I appeared as "Alfredo", the unfortunate suitor who lost out to someone who was much more attractive to Rosalinda, the leading lady, than he!

Whenever I had a spare hour or so in the evening, whether it be on my return from work or late in the evening, I would go for runs of between four and six miles around the areas in which I happened to be at the time: they were the only occasions on which I could gather my thoughts and review how my life and my various activities were progressing. They were and continue to be an immensely useful means of contemplation and winding down from the stresses of the day.

Throughout this two-year period I kept thinking about Andrea and shortly after "Die Fledermaus" in March1963 I plucked up the courage to drive up to Cambridge and explain why I had not been in touch with her for such a long time. I decided I would tell her how deep my feelings were for her but that shame had kept me away.

I would at least find out her reaction to what I had done and whether, hopefully, our relationship could be revived.

When I arrived at her digs on the outskirts of Cambridge and went up to her room on the first floor she was sitting cross-legged on the bed with the other young man who had been at her twenty-first birthday party: let us call him Stephen. Before I could open my mouth to say any more than "Hello", Andrea said, "Brian, I want you to be the first to know that Stephen and I have become engaged." Although shaken to the core by this unexpected announcement I managed to congratulate them both. But her words were like being hit over the head with a blunt instrument and shortly after listening, with a sense of disbelief, to their wedding plans I left crestfallen by what I had heard.

I had to acknowledge that as a result of my own neglect of her I had lost the only woman I had ever fallen in love with and that I had received my just deserts. My inbuilt reluctance to be dishonest to her when added to my inability to be honest with her had brought this situation about. I had not been in touch with Andrea for nearly two years while I confronted this moral dilemma. She was an extremely attractive young woman and there was no reason why she should have waited for me to reappear, if, indeed, she thought I was going to do so. Nor, in the 1960's, was it the "done thing" to try and persuade a betrothed young lady to break her engagement. My already forlorn hopes of marrying Andrea, had she been prepared to accept me, were, sadly at an end. "Alfredo" and I clearly had a lot in common!

To me the moral of this disastrous turn of events was all too obvious: you must lead a blameless life if you can, but above all you must be honest with yourself and others and take the opportunities that present themselves: do not hesitate if you encounter something good in your life. Be courageous and go for it!

Losing Andrea was cathartic: it made me realise that one cannot play about with emotions and put them on "hold" to suit one's own convenience while forgetting or ignoring the fact that the emotions of other people are involved and are being affected at the same time. In this respect I was probably a typical young man of the period.

The result of this serious bit of introspection led to my seizing an unexpected opportunity which presented itself and which resulted in marriage to another attractive young lady: it came about in this way.

A few months after my fateful meeting with Andrea I was watching a religious programme on ITV when I saw a beautiful young lady, a member of the public, being interviewed: she was serene, composed, with classic features that could have come from a 15th century Italian painting. I felt she was someone I would very much like to meet. I therefore rang up the producer of the programme, Jan LaChard, and asked for the young lady's name and address. Nothing ventured, nothing gained, I thought!

Jan LaChard was amused by this somewhat "cheeky" phone call and said she would let the young lady in question know she had an admirer. About three weeks later I was surprised to receive an invitation to the engagement party of a Miss Caroline Seaman at an address in Richmond. She had penned a note saying that, as I was one of her admirers, she would like to meet me!

The Seamans were close friends of Norman Parkinson, the famous society photographer, and Mrs. Seaman was an acquaintance of a Mrs Hilary Lack, the mother of my future wife Vivien: they had known each other some years previously when Caroline and her daughter, Vivien, had been at the same school and had bumped into each other in Peter Jones in Sloane Square, one of the John Lewis department stores, shortly before the engagement party. Mrs Lack had indicated that her daughter was at a loose end after attending a finishing school in Switzerland, and Mrs. Seaman generously invited Vivien to attend her daughter's engagement party at Norman Parkinson's home: there were sure to be a number of eligible young men present!

When I met Caroline I was indeed impressed by her but she did not measure up to Andrea and she was, in any event, very much engaged: in fact I thought that she and her fiancée, another trainee solicitor, made a lovely couple. She clearly had a great sense of humour in inviting me along. I sincerely hope that they have had a long and happy life together.

Of course I knew nobody else at this rather exclusive party but it was not long before I spotted another attractive young lady who appeared to be very much on her own: that young lady was Vivien Lack. Vivien had known Caroline in the distant past but knew none of her current friends. We finished up talking to each other for most of the evening. We left the engagement party at the same time, at about midnight, and sat in my car, by now a Wolseley 1500 with a sporty MG engine under the bonnet, talking for another couple of hours.

I am not sure who confessed first but it transpired that we had both had children who had subsequently been adopted. None of her relatives, family friends and acquaintances had known about her pregnancy because she had been sent to stay with a vicar and his wife in Norfolk as soon as the first signs of pregnancy appeared. Our mutual experience had to be the most extraordinary coincidence and I drove home highly relieved that I had, at last, been able to tell someone whom I would probably never see again, about my fall from grace. All I can remember of the journey home was that I passed the Royal Exchange, opposite the Bank of England at 3.15 am and was back in Billericay well before 4 am! In those days there were no speed cameras and, at that time of night, the roads were deserted. I had come out with my burdensome secret to someone and felt so much better for doing so!

I did not pursue Vivien after that meeting but a couple of weeks later she appeared one Sunday afternoon in her mother's Austin A35, saying that she had "just been visiting friends in the area"! I did not question that statement at the time but it transpired that she had, in fact, no friends in Essex at all! But as the reader will have gathered I have always been a bit naive where women are concerned!

She said that she had very much enjoyed our meeting and that she would like to see me again. I was flattered by the pursuit. I was also aware that, at twenty seven years of age, I should be thinking in terms of marriage if I intended to get married before I grew too set in my ways! Vivien was only twenty years old but we did appear to have a lot in common: we were both interested in art and in the theatre, in literature, poetry and photography: she had studied photography at Guildford Art College before she had been obliged to drop out of her course and was working for a professional portrait photographer at the time we met.

She came, moreover, from an impressive professional background: her father, a Fellow of the Royal College of Surgeons and also a Fellow of the Royal College of Physicians, was head of child psychiatry at the London Hospital and church warden of his local parish church. Her grandfather, Professor Lambert

Lack, had been head of ear, nose and throat surgery at the same hospital. I discovered, in later years, that Vivien's father had numbered Marilyn Monroe among his private patients: she had consulted him when she was filming in England during her marriage to Arthur Miller. Lest any journalists prick up their ears at this observation I have been assured that, being very professional indeed, he destroyed all the papers relating to his private patients when he retired!

One of Vivien's uncles was Deputy Lord Lieutenant of his county, another was professor of ornithology at Oxford and her aunt was a senior examiner at RADA. Having lost Andrea and having chanced, in the most extraordinary way, upon someone keen to pursue me, with much the same interests in the arts, theatre and literature as myself I slid, without any great reluctance, into engagement and subsequently marriage to an attractive young woman who was clearly looking for a stable life outside that of her immediate family.

I realised soon after I met her parents for the first time that, although her father possessed a formidable talent, he had not been a particularly understanding father and this conclusion was borne out when, about three years later, Vivien's younger brother ran away from home at the age of sixteen, never to return to it. Dr. Lack's children had, unfortunately, been brought up in what I can only describe as a sterile atmosphere without the close interaction between parents and children that I had encountered with my parents and that occurs in most well-adjusted families.

It was not really his fault. Vivien's father had been brought up by a series of governesses when he was a child and he rarely saw his own parents. When it says, in the Bible, that "the sins of the first shall be visited unto the seventh generation" that is, in my view, shorthand for acknowledging that habits inculcated in one generation take seven generations to work themselves out of a family. He was just the product of an upbringing where personal professional attainment and involvement in one's children's lives were poles apart. At the time, however, entrance into her family was heady stuff for a trainee solicitor with uncertain prospects who earned only £8 a week!!

When we became engaged I recall Dr. Lack expressing the view that he would rather I was in a profession rather than "in trade" and that I should concentrate on passing my Law Society final examinations in preference to developing my travel interests. In order to emphasise the point that I should become a professional and join the elite of society he subsequently took me to his club, the Athenaeum in Pall Mall, where members of the great and good in society seek sanctuary from the world outside and where, on the one occasion I visited, a purple-smocked bishop, sitting in a high-backed chair placed immediately opposite the entrance, glared balefully at everyone as they came through the front doors of the club. I half expected him to object to anyone as young as myself entering its hallowed precincts ! "Favete linguis"!

The fact that, like my prospective father-in-law, I had been to Cambridge helped gain his consent to our marriage but his detachment throughout our subsequent marriage was exemplified by one incident that took place shortly before it.

When we married in April 1965 I wanted us, as newly-weds, to move straight into the three-bedroomed semi-detached house I had found for us on the outskirts of Billericay: it was not ideal but it was as much as I could afford at the time. When one took into account the fact that we had been able to purchase little more than a bed, a table and a few chairs it was actually more than I could afford and I decided to ask my future father-in-law whether he could possibly lend me a thousand pounds for a year while we got onto our feet financially. I was aware that my travel activities would bring in enough to repay him and that the house was not going to have much furniture in it without his temporary assistance.

His response was: "I will ask my solicitor to draw up the necessary loan agreement for you to sign. I will not, of course, charge you interest." Well, that was decent of him! I queried whether a formal loan agreement was really necessary. "Imagine," he said, "you or I are dead: think of your executors or my executors dealing with the repayment of the loan." He was an extremely wealthy man and I could hardly see him chasing his daughter for one thousand pounds in the event of my death within the twelve months after our marriage. Although I signed the agreement and repaid the loan within the year I never expected or received any favours from him again. I felt my bank would be more confident in my ability and intention to repay a short-term loan than he!

Of my first marriage I will say little. We produced two remarkably well-balanced sons who came to live with me and who I looked after on my own for nearly seven years prior to my marriage to Annette. They assured me, in their teens, that they did not intend to make the same mistakes in their marital relationships as I. I should have felt duly chastised at the time but I do not think I did!

It is fair to say, however, that I undoubtedly concentrated too much on establishing a secure financial future for us. Vivien's assertion that, since her parents were rich, we (she) would inherit a lot on the death of the survivor of them and that there was consequently no need for me to work so hard now cut little ice with me. I wanted to create my own future without having to rely, at some point, on whatever wealth might be passed on to us (her) in the wills of her parents. Moreover, I was "not what she expected". Her expectations, in this respect, may have been a trifle unrealistic and unduly romantic.

Nevertheless, we had some good early years and I did introduce her to the Billericay Folk Players where she excelled as an actress, playing many leading parts, for example that of Eliza Doolittle in George Bernard Shaw's Pygmalion", subsequently made into the film "My Fair Lady", Anastasia in the play of that name and Sarah in George Bernard Shaw's "Major Barbara". To the extent that we both enjoyed going to the theatre and loved acting in plays we were, of course, very compatible. Our approach to performing, however, was not quite the same. I tended to learn my lines, often to the despair of the producer and the rest of the cast somewhat late in the day and enjoyed adopting the roles of a variety of characters from creepy to comic albeit only on stage and in rehearsals, whereas Vivien studied her lines intently from the outset and lived the part she was playing. When she was cast as Anastasia, the woman who had tried to persuade everyone that she was the daughter of Tsar Nicholas II and that she had not been murdered at Ekaterinburg in July 1918, she literally became Anastasia and I was treated at home as a sort of Russian serf rather than a husband! It was a trifle disconcerting to be living with someone so regal.

By her second marriage which similarly ended in a consensual divorce (I do not think he was what she expected either!) she has produced another two talented and charming sons, one of whom has taken leading roles in plays on the London stage and at the Royal Shakespeare Company in Stratford-upon-Avon and who appears regularly in cameo roles in films and on television. There is clearly a strong orientation towards drama generally running through her family's genes.

Having rejoined the local operatic society for Die Fledermaus in 1963 I remained a member until 1970. During those seven years I took the parts of Camille, the Count de Rosillon, in "the Merry Widow", Strephon (half man / half fairy) in "Iolanthe", the Honourable Lawrence Lyell, the disappointed suitor, in "Gypsy Love" and Nanki Poo, the Mikado's son disguised as a wandering minstrel, in "The Mikado". They were all significant or leading tenor roles and my singing lessons had clearly paid off.

Between 1963 and 1978 I also appeared in a number of plays. Among other roles I took the parts of the treacherous and opportunistic Richard Rich who gave evidence against Sir Thomas More in Robert Bolt's play, "A Man for all Seasons", the murderous husband, Simon Mostyn, in Agatha Christie's play "Death on the Nile", the hot-headed Sir Francis Verney in "The Young Elizabeth", the idiot Major Colin, in Noel Coward's "Nude with Violin" and the gullible opera composer, Roger Lennox, in Ronald Millar's end of season romp "They don't grow on trees".

I found learning lines for my parts in plays written by George Bernard Shaw and Noel Coward, for example as the urbane Charles Lomax in "Major Barbara", as sailor boy Billy in "This Happy Breed" and as 'would be' lover Morris Dixon in "Present Laughter", very easy: the words seemed to flow and be exactly what the character concerned would have been expected to say quite naturally in the particular circumstances.

By comparison the lines in the Agatha Christie play were carefully engineered to the point at which they became tortuous and difficult to remember: there was a precise order in which each word in each line had to appear so as to complete the jigsaw that was the plot. The best moment in my "varied" acting career was probably in "They don't grow on trees" when the audience, already bent double with hysterical laughter, could only stamp their feet on the floor at one point in the play. The "buzz" one gets as an actor is immense: to have the audience completely in one's hands is a very satisfying feeling. I am sure professional comedians and comic actors would all agree!

I finished off my acting career by appearing as the theatre critic, Birdboot, in "The Real Inspector Hound" (a "spoof Agatha Christie" play by Tom Stoppard) and by producing another of his humorous "one-acters". Acting and singing had been a thoroughly enjoyable pastime and I was sorry when I no longer had the time to continue with either. I had learned a lot about stagecraft during those seventeen years and the knowledge gained has enhanced my appreciation of the many plays I have seen subsequently.

By way of final comment on my marriage to Vivien, I had not seen her for quite a long time when I met her for a Christmas celebration at one of our sons' homes in 2016. I was taken aback when she turned to me and asked, without apparent guile or unpleasantness, "Brian, can you remember why we got divorced?"! This question called for a diplomatic response, as close to the truth as possible but without prejudicing the festive atmosphere. In the circumstances I acknowledged to her that I was eighty per cent at fault and she only twenty per cent responsible for the breakdown of our marriage and nothing more was said.

But, I had, during our marriage, repeatedly told her that I was trying to build up an independent and secure future for the two of us and our children and that every marriage goes through "sticky patches". It was a matter of tolerances and her tolerance of my behaviour was not as strong as mine was of hers. If my heart had been more in the marriage it could well have lasted longer, but not necessarily so, and that is why I attributed the breakdown of what could have been a viable relationship largely to myself.

My heart had been with Andrea and in the next chapter I will reveal how and when we met and what happened thereafter.

36

The Intervening Years

In previous chapters I have commented on the beneficial effect of a secure and loving family environment and how the attitudes and upbringing of great grandparents and grandparents are reflected in the lives of parents and their children. One cannot, of course, ignore the genetic structure of each individual person and the fact that genes and external factors influence behaviour.

From my point of view, however, and in the light of my various experiences, children who are brought up in a sterile atmosphere at home can often find it difficult to relate to those brought up by loving parents and vice versa.

As a lawyer I am always inclined to question the validity of assertions of this nature without evidence or justification and I should, perhaps, attempt to justify them, without hopefully boring the reader by revealing some of my background.

My parents were loving and did everything possible to provide a secure and happy home for my sister and myself within the limited resources available to them. In fact, when they did not have enough to cover the cost of my trip to Greece with the Brentwood School Scout Troop in 1954 my mother, as mentioned in an earlier chapter, applied for a job at the local Post Office and did a post round over the Christmas period in order to raise the necessary money for it.

My mother was strong-willed, quite fiery, highly intelligent and, as indicated previously, an extraordinarily capable manager of the family finances which she controlled literally "to the penny". A local butcher whom I got to know well through my membership of the local Rotary Club told me that, if she came into his shop and asked for 2/3d. worth of liver and he said,

"That comes to 2/6d", she would reply, "No, I want 2/3d. worth." He always tended to put a bit more on the scales than the customers had asked for but she would have none of it. She knew exactly how much she could afford!

If I had to name a fault it was that she was extremely possessive of me. Evidence of this can be found in the fact, for example, that before I moved out of Pink Cottage in the autumn of 1961 she threw away all the personal letters I had received from young female friends and acquaintances during my university days. I had kept them in a cardboard box in a wall cupboard high up on my bedroom wall and, when challenged about their disappearance, she asserted that she needed the space "for other things": she was obviously very jealous of any relationships I might have had, however fleeting or inconsequential, with other females.

I regarded this act on her part as an unwarranted and unforgiveable intrusion into my personal space and my relationships with others and I vowed I would never do the same thing to any child of mine. It was the possessiveness of a mother for her son that I later encountered in Annette's relationship with my stepson, James, after she and I married in 1988. In her case, however, I could much better understand her desire to protect and support him in whatever way she could after the manner in which she and her children had been cast aside by his natural father.

As controller of the family finances, moreover, my mother had throughout my life effectively determined what I could or could not wear until, that is, I arrived at university and was in receipt of an annual scholarship grant from the state. In her opinion my clothes had to be practical and hard-wearing, namely grey or corduroy trousers, black multipurpose shoes and one tweed jacket and not anything frivolous like jeans or sneakers, until I could afford to buy them for myself!

Although assertive within the home my mother, being very house-proud and somewhat insecure, did not welcome visitors, other than close relatives into it. Nor was she particularly sociable and consequently made little or no effort to engage with my father's circle of friends although, in fairness, she did attend at least two formal dinners when he was Chairman of his local Branch of NALGO and Master of his Masonic Lodge.

When I asked, for example, whether I could invite my friend, Kenneth Gubbins with whom I had been in the army in Edinburgh and who was now up at Cambridge to stay with us for a few days one would think that, by asking, I was betraying her in some way! The house was not sufficiently well decorated, apparently, for visitors she did not know well, etc. The house was always immaculate and she was making a great big fuss about nothing! At this point my father took me on one side and said, "What your mother does not appreciate is that when people come to the house they come for our company. They do not come to inspect the paintwork! Don't take any notice of your mother. If you want to invite Kenneth, you invite him." Which I did. Despite the furious denunciation of myself as some sort of traitor before he arrived she was sweetness and light during his stay and when he left her comment was, "What a delightful and charming young man." I could have throttled her!

In my mother's case her insecurity and lack of confidence in her own ability to hold her own socially can probably be traced back to her grandparents.

On her mother's side the Langley family who lived in St. Helens in Lancashire and who were Roman Catholic had been wealthy. John Langley had a glass factory in St. Helens and had invented and produced the system of glass tubing used in siphoning beer from barrels to the taps from which it was dispensed in public houses across the country. Before John Langley died his son, Henry, my mother's grandfather, had married a young lady from Colchester in Essex. Her name was Elizabeth Anne Roberts and she was a member of the Church of England: they had six children of whom my mother's mother, my grandmother, was one and they were all brought up as Roman Catholics in St. Helens. Although John Langley was sober and hard-working and undoubtedly a very shrewd businessman, his son Henry was not. Within a couple of years of his father's death and notwithstanding the fact that he had a wife and children, Henry Langley had gambled away the entire family fortune, mortgaged the factory to pay off his gambling debts and had then sold the factory and the business without disclosing the mortgage to the purchaser.

In order to avoid arrest and prosecution he fled to the Stratford area of London with his wife and children, changed his own name from Langley to Clare, became a member of the Church of England and found employment in a glassworks there. Unfortunately he died of pneumoconiosis in his early thirties, leaving his widow destitute: she had to survive in Stratford with her children as best she could. My grandmother, therefore, had a grim childhood and it is not surprising that her upbringing and her attitudes had a profound effect upon her daughter, my mother.

My maternal grandfather, John Somers, moreover, was the son of Henry Bolton Somers, a former head teacher of a school near Moate in County West Meath, now in Eire. Henry had been threatened with death by the local Feinians: I believe he was a prominent member of the Orange Lodge in the area. On hearing of the threat the local gentry had clubbed together, had given him thirty guineas and told him to migrate to England with his wife and young children. John Somers had been born in 1881 some time after his father arrived in London with his other children and had settled in the Stratford area. Although he had been obliged to leave County West Meath, Henry's brothers and sisters remained in Southern Ireland and their descendants are there to this day.

Fate clearly brought my maternal grandparents together in the Stratford area. They met, married and rented a house there. In view of their similar family circumstances and experiences they were determined to provide a stable and secure home for their children. It must have come as a heart-stopping moment for both of them when, in 1916, and at the age of thirty five my grandfather received his "call-up" papers, forcing my grandmother, like so many other young mothers, to raise and look after their three young children on her own. My mother, the oldest of the three, was four years old at the time.

My grandfather was conscripted into the Royal Artillery and was sent to the Western Front in France where, after serving as a member of a team responsible for bringing horse-drawn guns up to the battlefront, he was assigned to laying telephone lines across "no man's land" to forward observation posts (F.O.Ps.) from which an officer would be able to direct artillery fire onto enemy positions. It was a highly dangerous task and he told me that he was very much aware of what would happen to his wife and three children if he was killed. His widow would be left in very much the same position as her mother. He realised that German snipers would be on the "lookout" for any British soldier who had ventured out beyond his own trenches and took as few risks as possible. He had been extremely lucky to survive given the hazardous nature of what he had to do.

After the Great War my maternal grandparents had two more children, making five in total. My mother, my two uncles and my two aunts were a happy close-knit family during their childhood and kept in close touch with each other once they had grown up. Every Saturday evening, apart from the

Second World War years, they congregated with or without their "other halves" and children at the three bedroomed council house in Becontree to which my grandparents had been located in the early 1930s. Between the ages of ten and eighteen, therefore, I headed there after school late every Saturday afternoon: we had lessons on Saturdays at Brentwood School from 9.15 am to 12.30 pm followed by sport, either cricket, rugby football or soccer in the afternoon: it was lessons and sport, or the cadet force, six days a week with homework on Sundays!

My parents and sister would normally arrive by car at about the same time as myself and I really looked forward to seeing my kind-hearted grandparents and to the lively company of my uncles, aunts, cousins and their boyfriends (later husbands) who would make a point of turning up weekly to talk, to laugh, to express their views on everything from football to politics, to debate history, my Uncle Gerald's favourite subject, to enjoy a splendid "fry up", courtesy of my grandmother and Uncle Gerald and to drink gallons of tea!!

Because there were not enough chairs or sofas for everyone in the lounge and the dining room which had folding doors between them, my cousins, all female, had to sit on their boyfriends' laps – not that they seemed to mind!

Occasionally my grandfather would get out his accordion, if pressed to do so, and play tunes we could all sing along to – as had his comrades in the trenches. There was consequently a terrific sense of family at all times and Saturday nights at Sheppey Road were probably very much the same as a typical Irish family gathering of the 1940s and 1950s, minus the Guinness! My bachelor Uncle Gerald who lived with and supported my grandparents financially bought a television set in 1953 in order to watch the Coronation but the set was rarely turned on: any television programme would have had to be fairly momentous to compete with and drown out the noise and laughter generated by my talkative family!

The contrast between my two sets of grandparents could not have been more extreme. To me, as a child, my paternal grandfather was a distant, disapproving and somewhat austere figure: I can only recall meeting him and my paternal grandmother, Ada, once or twice before they died. According to my father, my grandfather only really had time for two of his nine children, his daughter, Ada, who ran off with John (Jock) Moore, Dudley's father, and his son, Billy (William Owen Hughes, the third!) who died of a collapsed lung while working in a missionary bookshop in Zanzibar. The other children were not particularly well regarded or looked after by him. As previously indicated, my father never had a shirt or tie while he was at Westcliff High School for Boys and had to wear his Scout uniform all the time. The children also had to share one swimming costume between them, (although they were all of different ages, sexes and sizes) when they wanted to go for a swim from the small beach at Leigh on Sea where the family lived until the early 1920s. Fortunately it was a one piece garment which could be worn by boys and girls alike! My grandfather appeared to expect affection from his children but gave little back in return.

As for his character he was entrepreneurial, ambitious, clever, pretentious and insofar as he wrote and "self-published" books on such subjects as "Self Healing by Divine Providence" and similar (in the back of which he advertised correspondence courses) he appeared to prey very much on the hopes and fears of a small section of the general public. I could see that his books might have superficial appeal to elderly widows and people with illnesses or conditions for which, at the time, there was no known cure or treatment but they really imparted little of significance or merit to the reader: to me he appeared, in the words of Joseph Addison, rather like "the mountebank who sold pills which (as he told the country people) were very good against an earthquake!"

His background, however was much more interesting. His ancestors lived in Llangedywn in North Wales and in the 1840s his grandmother, one of the daughters of the mill owner there, had gone to work as a lady's maid at Llangedywn Hall, the home of Sir Watkin Williams-Wynn: the mill was virtually opposite the Hall and I suspect that she and her parents wanted her to find out more about the gracious style of living of the aristocracy in such a splendid household. Be that as it may, she must have been an attractive young lady because it was not long before Sir Watkin "had his way" with her. When she told him she was pregnant he paid for her to leave Llangedywn and live elsewhere on the understanding that he would offer her financial support until she died, provided she never returned. It was, apparently, quite a common arrangement among members of the aristocracy who made their female servants pregnant! She went to Liverpool where her baby son was born: she called him William, in acknowledgement of his father's family name and Owen, after Owen Glendower who was descended from or related to Cadrod Hardd a twelfth century Welsh chieftain. Her son, William Owen Hughes, moved south when he was old enough to do so and became a boiler-maker for steam ships in the dockyards near the city of London. It was probably a reasonably well-paid job at the time.

My grandfather was a draper's assistant when he married in 1900 but, being ambitious, managed to qualify, unlike myself, as a company secretary!! Thereafter he became the company secretary of the Anglo Baku Oilfield Corporation which exploited the production of oil from wells in the area of Russia close to the Caspian Sea. There were a number of eminent aristocrats with influence on the Board of the Company and my grandfather became quite wealthy. In a fit of breathtaking "hubris" he even bought himself a Victorian "mock castle" near Ryhl in North Wales – which he subsequently sold to an American during the Great War at a substantial profit – and approached the College of Arms for a family crest! It was, at this point, however, that an investigation into his "lineage" revealed that his grandfather had been conceived "on the wrong side of the sheets"! The crest, which had actually been produced, was consigned to an attic cupboard and the whole grandiose project was quietly shelved!

Unfortunately, the Bolsheviks and the Soviets after them did not approve of the foreign control of one of their country's most important resources and took over the oilfields, leading to the collapse of the company. In 1920 or thereabouts the Russian Government gave my grandfather and the other shareholders in the company bonds to the value of their respective shareholdings but the bonds were never redeemed and, as a small child, on the one and only time I visited my grandfather at his home in Hornchurch, I can just recall seeing a pile of splendidly ornate certificates in the bottom drawer of his writing desk. Being inquisitive I had started to open all the drawers – much to his annoyance! I have noticed my own grandchildren doing exactly the same and I admit it can be nerve-wracking!!

On the loss of his position as company secretary he moved his family from Leigh-on-Sea and used the money he had managed to put together to purchase two large houses in Canewdon Road in Westcliff-on-Sea: one was intended to accommodate his family, the other to provide an income from holidaymakers. However, the 1920s were not a particularly good time economically for the owners of boarding houses and he was ultimately forced to sell both the properties and move elsewhere: By the mid-1930s he was living in Hornchurch with my paternal grandmother who died of cardiac asthma in 1940.

My paternal grandmother also appears to have had an extraordinary ancestry – all conceived on the right side of the sheets – which I only found out about in my late seventies. Dudley Moore's niece, my second cousin, had done a lot of research and presented me with an authenticated family genealogy for "grandmother Hughes" which went back to 1123AD. I did some further research and took it back to Yves II Seigneur de Bellesme and Alencon and de Creil who was born 940 AD. His granddaughter was Mabille Talvas D'Alencon and her grandson Sir Rainauld de Baliol came over with William the Conqueror and was granted the fiefdom of what is now Shropshire! The Creil family were described by the Historian, Walter Ashe, in 1876 in the following terms: "although a fierce, proud, warlike and cruel race they were gifted with the chivalric virtues of valour and generosity". It would have been quite an ancestry to have to live up to as far as chivalric virtues are concerned had I known about it earlier!

My father, unlike his own father, had always been very sociable, the life and soul of any gathering: he proved to be a loving, kind and thoughtful parent. Aware of the disinterested manner in which his father had treated him he went out of his way to ensure that I and my sister received all the encouragement and support he could give us. I can recall that from the age of six he bought books for me on a variety of subjects including history, geography and science and, in view of the fascination of a child during the war for all things military, he also brought me books published by the Ministry of Information on various branches of our armed services.

One book, in particular, deserves a mention and that is Sir Thomas Malory's "Morte D'Arthur" as retold by Waldo Cutler. My aunt Lily read it to me from cover to cover as a bedtime story while she lived with us during the war. I think she enjoyed reading the stories of King Arthur and the Knights of the Round Table as much as I enjoyed listening to her doing so. I am sure that I was much influenced by the stories and that the influence of them is reflected in my later life.

My father's problem was his health. In his early twenties I suspect that a surgeon had inadvertently damaged one of his intestines when removing his appendix and this was ultimately to result in his death at the age of fifty three, only four days before his fifty fourth birthday in August 1966. As a consequence of the botched operation a colic fistula, a hole, developed in his intestines as a result of which the benefit of much of the food he ingested was lost. This weakened his body and led to bronchitis, pleurisy, pneumonia and double pneumonia between 1939 and 1948: his family had a tendency to asthma and his chest was the first to suffer from the lack of nutrition.

By the summer of 1948 he had dropped to six stones in weight and was skeletal: at this point the newly formed NHS came to his rescue. He was told that he had less than three months to live unless he allowed an eminent surgeon at the London Hospital, a Mr. Herman Taylor, who turned out to be a colleague of Dr. Lack, to carry out an operation that had never been attempted before, namely the complete removal of my father's intestines, the cutting out of the "bad bits", sewing together the "good bits" and inserting them back into his stomach. Faced with certain death in about three months, in any event, and immediate death if the operation failed my father accepted a lifeline which could not be guaranteed. He survived the operation with almost half his intestines removed: it gave him a fighting chance to survive for many years.

While I was in Cyprus in 1956 doing my National Service he succumbed to tuberculosis and spent several months, I believe, in East Grinstead hospital, formerly the hospital at which Sir Archibald McIndoe had carried out plastic surgery on disfigured RAF pilots and other servicemen suffering burn injuries to their faces and other parts of their bodies. He was nursed back to health but his lungs had lost their elasticity and he became extremely vulnerable to cough and cold viruses: he finished up, after TB, with, in effect, half a stomach and half a chest until he died in 1966.

Some two years before my father died Babis who, until the incident of the haunted bed, visited Billericay regularly every November commented in private to me, after visiting Pink Cottage, that, in his view, my mother appeared to demonstrate the same characteristics as his uncle. She was not moving well, her face muscles had become stiff and her face was becoming less and less expressive. He suspected that she might have Parkinson's Disease.

That was observant of him and I was instantly reminded of an incident in 1962 when my mother, an inveterate painter and decorator, had been wallpapering the main bedroom. When descending the stepladder she had inadvertently put one leg through the rungs of the ladder and had fallen back, without being able to save herself in any way, hitting the base of her skull hard on the floor. She had been very shaken up by this incident and took some time to recover from it. Could the impact have affected her base ganglia which control the production of dopamine, the lubricant for muscle and brain activity? It was the lack of dopamine that caused Parkinson's Disease. When she visited her Doctor, Dr. Pamela Butcher, however, she was told that she was suffering from rheumatism.

In April 1965 Vivien and I married and, following the wedding, Dr. Lack had taken me on one side and expressed the view, without wishing any diagnosis to be attributed to him, that my mother was suffering from Parkinson's Disease. Since Babis had said exactly the same thing I told my father and a subsequent visit to the local hospital confirmed that it was not rheumatism: it was indeed Parkinson's Disease and my mother would, in the fullness of time, need full time nursing care.

The diagnosis affected my father deeply: he had relied so much on my mother's support throughout his various illnesses. Being in poor health himself the prospect of the inevitable decline of his wife into someone who would need constant care and attention was daunting. They were only fifty three years old and their futures looked bleak.

Nevertheless being a mentally resilient and courageous person who had overcome so much ill health he was determined to look after his wife to the best of his ability. I was surprised therefore when I received a panic-stricken telephone call from my mother on 16 August 1966 at about six o' clock in the evening. "Brian, please come down to the house straightaway. Your father is in bed and there is something seriously wrong with him." When I arrived I went straight into my parent's bedroom. It was clear that he had just died. His body was still warm but there were no signs of life.

At the coroner's inquest I explained that my father, a committed Christian, was a cheerful and optimistic man who would never have contemplated taking his own life. He had come home early from work, feeling very unwell and after a minor contretemps with my mother who, as previously indicated, could be somewhat fiery, had retired to bed. It transpired that he had taken four sleeping pills, not enough to kill a healthy person. Half a stomach, when taken in conjunction with a weak chest, had however magnified the effect of the pills on him and had caused his death. A verdict of death by misadventure was recorded.

At his funeral I recall my mother looking round at a packed church and asking, "Who are all these people?" To which I replied, "They are his friends." Which, of course, they were. He had been a wise, kind, non-judgemental and very humorous confidant of so many of those who knew him.

His death at the age of fifty-three left my sister, Angela and me responsible for our mother who, only four months older than her late husband, was slowly but perceptibly succumbing to the debilitating effect of Parkinson's Disease. Vivien and I had been married for just sixteen months when he died and she was expecting our first son, Christopher. Angela had a baby daughter of her own and it would not have been practicable for our mother to come and live with either of us.

She was, in any case, a determined lady who loved her home and who preferred, while she was still mobile, to live on her own. For the next six years, therefore, she soldiered on at Pink Cottage with Angela and I visiting her and taking her out as often as we were able. We both phoned her every day to make sure that she was all right and, in particular, she was eating properly. Other members of the family frequently came to see her and we also arranged regular visits from the district nurse and social services.

My sister and I were both aware, however, of the gradual decline in her mobility and when, early one morning, I telephoned and got no answer I immediately drove down to Pink Cottage. The front and back doors were bolted, this being her normal procedure before going to bed, and heat was literally pulsing out through the kitchen windows. She had slipped over on the highly polished kitchen floor while making a cup of tea. She had put an aluminium kettle on one of the rings on the top of her electric cooker. The kettle had boiled dry and the ring was glowing red. She had been unable to get up and turn the cooker off. I called out to her and told her that I would have to break a window – to which she objected vehemently! But I broke it nevertheless, climbed in through the window and switched the cooker off.

That was the first ominous sign of real physical incapacity and it was followed not long afterwards by an even more disturbing incident. I made my usual early morning call. Once again there was no response. Fearing the worst I raced down to Pink Cottage and let myself in. She had, fortunately, listened to my strictures about bolting the front and back doors! This time, however, I found her, literally blue with cold, lying in her nightie on the bedroom floor. She had slipped sideways off the bed while trying to get into it the previous evening and, being economical, had already switched off the central heating for the night. She had been unable to get up and had been on the floor all night. It was patently obvious that she could no longer live on her own, however much she wanted to do so.

By this time Vivien and I had two children, Christopher and Alexander, and Angela three daughters. Realistically the only option was a residential care home in the locality with nursing facilities. But would the proceeds of the

sale of her house, plus attendance allowances and any other sources of income be sufficient to cover the cost? She was scarcely sixty and her life expectancy, even with Parkinson's Disease could well be seventy, possibly more as new drugs were developed to combat the debilitating side effects of it. In point of fact she lived until she was seventy four.

In the circumstances I proposed a solution that, if acceptable, could be beneficial for all of us. Given that she might well live beyond the point at which the proceeds of sale of Pink Cottage were exhausted and she had no more money for a private care home, I suggested that, if she was prepared to allow me to put the proceeds of sale of her home towards the purchase of Foxcroft in Billericay High Street, I would pay her care home fees for the rest of her life.

My sister Angela was happy with my proposal since it removed the worry of her having to help finance our mother's care home fees at a later date: so was my mother to whom it offered the assurance of permanent accommodation in a care home. Having larger and more prestigious offices in the High Street would enable me to expand my legal practice and thereby ensure that I could cover the care home fees. Paying them for so many years turned out to be a major consideration for me financially but it was a responsibility that I assumed at the outset and which I fulfilled. Pink Cottage was sold for £32,000, a ludicrously small amount when compared with its current value but that is what it was worth at the time on the open market.

On the personal domestic front I had moved into Chapel Court Billericay on the sale of the former matrimonial home: the maisonette was spacious and very close to my office in the High Street: it had ample accommodation for myself, my sons who, for about two years, stayed there on alternate weekends and a guest. But it was a leasehold property and I very much preferred a freehold.

In November 1976, therefore, I sold the maisonette and purchased my very run-down "haunted house". Not only was I looking for a freehold but I was also looking for a project: restoring a neglected property was something that I, as a single man, could take on. Not many married couples in suburban Billericay would care to rise to the challenge of converting three primitive flats in a leaky, cold and sorry-looking building into a family home. Despite its neglected condition it had real potential and I was used to living in uncomfortable surroundings!

My two sons had liked my maisonette in Chapel Court and I was relieved when they also took to a somewhat Spartan existence in my new home where conditions, at the outset, were indeed very basic. Within three years of the purchase, having for that period spent most weekends with me, they came to live with me on a permanent basis. My former wife, Vivien, had remarried not long after we divorced and had produced two more sons. With two young children and a new husband she must have felt that if I was already looking after them most weekends I might just as well have them all the time. Whatever she may have felt, it was a solution that had my wholehearted support because I really wanted to be with them and I knew that they were happy to be with me.

The reader may be wondering why I did not remarry until 1988, many years after my divorce in the mid-1970s. I did not, in fact cut myself off from female company. In the words of Francis Thompson in "The Hound of Heaven" I "pleaded outlaw-wise by many a hearted casement, curtained red, trellised with intertwining charities" but none of the ladies I met before my sons came to live with me, however charming or attractive, struck me as potential long term marriage prospects and, once my sons were living with me, none I met subsequently appealed to them, whatever I may have felt! They had had enough insecurity in their lives and because I wanted them to feel completely secure with me there could be no remarriage until they were older and could accept the prospect of my meeting someone I wanted to marry.

Looking after sons is not, as I subsequently discovered, anywhere as difficult as looking after daughters and I had no problems over the next seven years in doing so. As far as feeding them was concerned I insisted on giving them a cooked breakfast every school or college morning which set them up for the day. Evening and weekend meals may not have had as much variety as they enjoyed when living with their mother. We tended to live on fish fingers, sausages, baked beans, chips, vegetables and Cumberland pie followed by Angel Delight or tinned fruit but they have both grown to be over six foot tall and built like barn doors – in fact Alex has subsequently played touch rugby for England on thirty four occasions – so were brought up healthily and have remained healthy ever since!

Their arrival on a permanent basis called for quite an adjustment in my life, including giving up acting and singing but I was more than content to become, in effect, a single parent responsible for such mundane tasks as washing their clothes and ironing fifteen shirts every Sunday evening in front of the television! Five for each of them and five for me!! Chris and Alex were allowed to drink alcohol, beer or wine – with meals on special occasions from about the age of fourteen – which meant they did not develop any great craving for it when they were in their later teens.

In this respect they were encouraged to be responsible for themselves. For example, Chris was allowed to cycle with a friend from Billericay to Castle Hedingham in the north of Essex when he was fourteen and to stay overnight in a youth hostel provided he took a puncture repair kit and promised to telephone me to confirm that he had arrived safely at the hostel. His mother would probably have been horrified and no one could let a child do that sort of thing nowadays. He had the expected puncture, repaired it and rang from the hostel as promised. It was character-forming. I had complete faith in his common sense and it was an adventure he has never forgotten.

My first task with Alex when he left junior school close to my former wife's home and came to live with me was to get him into Brentwood School, if that was possible. At first the school declined to take him because he had missed one term of learning Latin. But since I had a scholarship in classics and undertook to bring him up to the same level as the other boys of his age by the beginning of the next term the school accepted him. Alex did not welcome having to learn some Latin, particularly over the Christmas period but I had previously taught my future brother in law enough Latin to get him into Cambridge University when it was an entry requirement for virtually every subject one could study there, including estate management! So teaching Alex the basic verbs, nouns and declensions that the other children of his age had already learned was no problem and when he joined the school he was as proficient in Latin as the other boys in his new class.

With Alex I took involvement in his personal activities further when I told him, at the age of sixteen, that he and I would be flying out to Greece for a fortnight with rucksacks and sleeping bags. When we arrived there we would be exploring the country in the same way as my students in the 1960s, sleeping on roofs, travelling by local buses and eating typical Greek food in the tavernas we came across. It turned out to be a memorable holiday and I trust the reader will allow me to digress into it and describe a couple of its unforgettable moments.

On arrival in Athens we headed for the Hotel Marion and my Greek "brother" Babis. He thought I was mad to want to sleep on the roof of his hotel in a sleeping bag but, once committed to a certain course, there could be no turning back! And Babis had no idea how wonderful it could be, sleeping out in the open air on the top of a building or on the deck of a ship with a vast canopy of glittering stars above. Of course one had to ensure that no one wandered off with one's rucksack during the night and that it was possible to have a wash and a shower somewhere in the building the next morning but that was all.

Having paid the obligatory visit to the Acropolis and having eaten at one or two of the restaurants mentioned in my student "Handbook on Greece" we headed off to Delphi by local bus. The driver threw the bus round the bends on the mountainous roads as if his life depended on getting to Delphi before the Apocalypse which seemed all too close as we sat in the back seats and looked out many times at the void beneath us! The back wheels of the coach must have been inches from the edge of sheer drops on one side or the other of the road on several occasions. It was a bit like being on a fairground roller coaster without the safety harness!

When we arrived in Delphi we found a private house – pretty, white, with pots of flowers outside, in one of the side streets of the village where we could stay the night for a few drachma and went off to a local taverna. Although Delphi is famous as the navel of the ancient world most tourists turn up in air- conditioned coaches, gaze at the classical ruins for an hour or two and then disappear. Delphi was, at the time of our visit, still very much a village community. Being in a private house for the night was, in fact, a "step up" for me because the last time I had stayed there as a student I had actually slept among the ruins!

The next morning I told Alex we were going to ascend the Phaedriades, the massive cliffs overlooking Delphi because there was an amazing view of the Vale of Crisa from the top with the gleaming waters of the Gulf of Corinth in the distance. The Phaedriades were called the "shining rocks" by the ancient Greeks because they caught the sunlight all day. There was a goatherd's track which took one precariously from the bottom of them to the top. His mother and I had used it when I brought her to Delphi some years previously. My confidence in my ability to locate the starting point of the track proved misplaced!

I told Alex that if we started to climb up the cliff in front of us we would be sure to hit the track at some point: my mistake was to start climbing up a fairly steep slope at a point which, we discovered later, was about one hundred yards to the left of the track which headed off to the right and not to the left!

At about five hundred feet we concluded that we had somehow missed the track and had to decide what to do. We could try to descend slowly and carefully to the base of the cliffs or carry on upward. At this point Alex sensibly indicated that the gradient on his left did not appear to be as steep or as difficult as the one we faced and I told him to take it. I would continue to climb upwards on a gradient that was not quite vertical and would meet him at the top of the Phaedriades from which, in classical days, the ancient Greeks hurled to their deaths those who did not believe in the Gods.

After another five hundred feet or so, however, the cliff became vertical and I found myself having to use hands and feet to make progress, and I still had a long way to go. There was now no choice. I had to keep climbing and, at this point, I really began to worry. What if Alex was having the same problem? What if he fell off the cliff? What would I say to his mother if he did? What would he do if I fell to my death? There was absolutely no point in peering downwards: there was just a massive drop beneath me and the likelihood of vertigo if I looked down. I just had to keep going and hope for the best! But within a hundred feet or so of the summit the cliff developed an overhang and I could hear scorpions scuttling through the rocks ahead. We had started at 8.30 am but by now it was past eleven o' clock and the sun was beating down on the cliff face and on me.

That is all I need, being bitten by a scorpion as I hung, dehydrated, to the cliff face. I was not, I thought, in a good place! At this crucial juncture some "helping hand" must have come to my aid because I managed to cling on and negotiate the overhang without being bitten. No sooner had I crawled over the top of the cliff than I collapsed in a heap on the ground, absolutely shattered. But where was Alex? There was no sign of him. After a brief rest I made my way across the top of the mountain and came across him nonchalantly sitting on a rock. "What kept you, Dad?" was his greeting! I did not know whether to laugh or to cry at the sheer relief of finding him unscathed and none the worse for his experiences. I thanked the Gods for our survival! We found the goat track for our descent and each drank a great deal of water when we arrived back in the village!

From Delphi we took a number of local buses to Kalambaka in the Meteora in the north of Greece via Thermopylae and visited one of the monasteries perched on massive pinnacles of rock. In mediaeval times the only access to them was by a man-sized basket which was winched up from the ground to the monastery a couple of hundred feet above. If the monks did not like the look of the person in the basket they just took their hands off the winch and let the basket drop! End of unwelcome visitor!

In our case we got a taxi to the one monastery that could be reached from a road. When we got there Alex was going to be allowed in straightaway but the monk dressed in black robes with his tall black orthodox priest's hat barred my entrance." "Why can't I come in?" I asked him in Greek. "Because you are wearing shorts. Young boys in shorts can come in but men in shorts cannot!" Not being someone prepared to be deflected by this rebuff I went straight back to the taxi driver who was waiting to take us back to Kalambaka. "I will give you an extra hundred drachmas if you will lend me your trousers." He was short, quite fat and startled by this request. Nevertheless he lent me his trousers and I was admitted to the monastery with his trousers at "half mast" and me clutching the surplus rolls of them in my left hand!

Alex and I then headed off to the island of Thassos in the north of Greece via Thessaloniki and the port town of Kavalla. We spent a week there relaxing in a wooden cabin in a German holiday village which Babis had found for us, not that Alex or I spoke any German! We kept ourselves to ourselves and, early every evening, walked the mile or so to the town of Thassos and ate at one of the local tavernas. We made our way back to our cabin guided by the light of the moon and the stars: it was an extraordinary holiday in which we bonded more than on any of the previous holidays I had spent with Chris and Alex – and they had been good. It was a great experience for both of us.

But I have digressed and must now return to Andrea!

As Chairman and subsequently President of the Billericay Branch of the Royal British Legion I used to spend the Friday evenings and Saturday mornings before Remembrance Sunday each year running round the pubs in Billericay with trays of poppies and collecting tins on Friday nights and standing in the High Street on Saturday mornings topping up what I had collected the previous evening. Pubs on a Friday night were particularly good for donations to the Poppy Appeal when people had had a few drinks and Saturday mornings were also good for spotting friends and clients I knew and having a chat while collecting a donation from them and handing them a poppy!

In 2012, the last year in which the head office of the Royal British Legion allowed individual collectors to know how much they had been able to collect I managed to collect £659.71 (somewhat less than the £731.11 in 2007), between 8.30 pm on Friday and 12.30 pm on Saturday. Quite why the RBL did not want its collectors to know how much they had collected I cannot say but, for me as a competitive runner who always wanted to improve on his last P.B. (personal best) it was a disincentive!

Imagine my surprise when on a Saturday morning in November 1996 one of my clients, Caroline Wilson, came up to me in the High Street and said "I have recently met an old flame of yours: her name is Andrea and she has very fond memories of you. I met her at the university where I am studying for a degree.

"How did you meet?" I asked Caroline. "Well one of the tutors turned up late for a lecture and, while we were waiting, I started to chat to her: we happened to be sitting next to each other". "She asked me whether I had had to travel far from my home to attend the summer school and, when I told her I lived in Billericay she asked me whether I knew a solicitor by the name of Brian Hughes. I told her that he was our family solicitor and had been so for over twenty years. She then asked to be remembered to you."

What an amazing coincidence. "Are you going to see Andrea again?" I asked Caroline. "If so, please do give her my kindest regards." Which is exactly what Caroline did and not long afterwards I received a long letter from Andrea telling me what she had done and where she had been since 1961. Annette commented that it must have taken some guts to write as she had and I agreed. I wrote back a similar letter giving Andrea a summary of my life over the past thirty give years and when Andrea telephoned my office a couple of weeks later and asked whether we could meet I agreed to do so because I wanted to explain to her in person why I had not continued our earlier relationship. I told her I would be in touch to arrange a convenient date for a meeting.

I did not consider it sensible to tell Annette because I had no wish to worry her about a relationship that had existed thirty five years previously and when, some weeks later, Annette flew to Ireland to stay for a week with a friend she had made on her Open University degree course I met Andrea for lunch.

It was patently obvious, however, when we met that we were still very much in love with each other. She was the missing piece in the jigsaw that made up my life. "You silly man," she said. "Why on earth, did you not tell me about

Heather at the time? I would have married you anyway and would have been more than happy to adopt Heather if that had been possible. I thought you must have gone off me when you stayed away for nearly two years and that you had moved on to someone else."

"Why did you marry Stephen?" I asked her. "Because I did not know whether as a Classics graduate I would find anyone once I left university and because, at twenty three, I thought I would finish up on the shelf. Stephen, who had been at Cambridge with me had been very attentive and, although he was a couple of years younger than myself, I thought we could make a go of marriage. We have made a go of it but my love for you has never diminished and never will, whatever happens from now onwards."

Our meeting and this forthright declaration knocked me back on my heels because I had no desire to discard my relationship with Annette and I could not, in all conscience, undermine her own longstanding marriage to Stephen. I had to make a seriously hard and painful decision for both of us. If you really love someone, as it is clear that I did, you do not want them to be harmed by your own feelings and desires, however understandable. The person you love comes first and that applied to Andrea as much as it did to Annette.

After a good deal of thought and, in the circumstances, I wrote a letter to Andrea the precise content of which I set out below.

" 'The moving finger writes and, having writ, moves on: nor all thy piety nor wit shall lure it back to cancel half a line nor all thy tears wash out a word of it'. I am sure you are familiar with this stanza from the Rubaiyat of Omar Khayam.

I regret so much having to write to you like this because I do understand how you feel and do not want to hurt you. But when I said "adieu" I meant "adieu".

It was lovely to "go for a walk down memory lane" and to catch up on what has happened to you over the past thirty six years and to discuss what might have happened. But what might have happened did not happen and the past cannot be recreated.

The present realities are that we are both married with families and commitments. I am very happily married to Annette and my aim is to make the most of my relationship with her and to give her my sole and undivided love, attention and support.

In fact, our meeting brought home to me in a very forceful way the importance of working hard to improve the family relationships I currently enjoy and to concentrate on making the most of my marriage and whatever the future may hold. Life is not a dress rehearsal – it is a one and only opportunity to create and enjoy a happily married state and family values. I have no wish to impair my relationships or to have any other tangential involvement in my life, however tenuous, decorous or distant.

All I can say – as I have said before – is that you should count your blessings, concentrate on your children and on Stephen, give them your love and support and enjoy what you have. Be happy and don't look back and have regrets for what might have happened in the past. The moving finger has written and moved on.

Perhaps I cropped up on the path of your life, once again, as part of your destiny to remind you that we carry our destinies in our own hands, that we make mistakes and take wrong turnings but that, with all this said, we have to live for the moment and make the most of what we have. Paradoxically you have done this for me.

In the circumstances and, despite your entreaty, I do not intend to pen any more letters but I do, with utmost sincerity wish you all the very best in your future life and in your family relationships. "Adieu", once again and take care."

For the next thirteen years I had no contact with Andrea and concentrated on my marriage to Annette and on my family. It was so difficult to write that letter, given how I felt but I knew it was the right thing to do for both of us.

37

Conclusion

Having made the "right" decision and having, so I thought, resolved, by my letter to Andrea, the dilemma of being committed to my steadily improving relationship with Annette, while being aware of my continuing love for Andrea, I was left with the uncomfortable feeling that, once again, I was "letting go" of a person with whom I shared an extraordinary affinity.

There was no doubt about that. The years since we had last seen each other had just melted away when we met in 1997. Nor was there anything immature or fanciful about what we clearly felt for each other. We were no longer young lovers in the first flush of a romance. There was something totally uncomplicated and natural about the way we talked and laughed about the same things, held hands and shared interests. It had transpired during our meeting that we had, for example, both sung and acted in amateur theatrical productions at the same time.

We were both Classicists with a love of English literature and poetry and appeared in many respects to be the male and female counterparts of each other, like two sides of the same coin. It goes without saying that, notwithstanding the obvious compatibility, I would never have seen Andrea again, had not Annette died. There was never any question of being unfaithful to Annette or splitting up another family.

Andrea and I both had families and commitments and, once again, our courses through life would have to diverge but with one important difference. We both knew that the feelings we had for each other in the 1960s were genuine and that the years we had spent apart had not affected them in any way. We were, however going to have to lead separate lives once again and make the very most of what we had. There could be no return to the past. Andrea would be the love I lost through a few moments of irresponsibility and that would have been that.

Although, moreover, Annette was highly oriented towards her career and undoubtedly put her career and her children before myself, she and I had, during the many years of our marriage developed strong bonds of loyalty, companionship and mutual interdependence. We respected each other and what we were each trying to achieve. She relied to a considerable extent on my support – both financial and emotional – and I on her good-natured and lively company and rare humanity.

Where I felt there might be incompatibility I did my best to avoid it. She had, for example, a deep-seated antipathy towards Freemasonry. She never explained why but it appeared to relate to her childhood in Stoke-on-Trent and the proximity of her home to a local Masonic hall. I did not, therefore, pursue that particular interest until after she died. On the other hand. she supported all my other activities including, albeit grudgingly, my standing in the 1997 General Election in opposition to Teresa Gorman and shared to the full my anxieties and disappointment over the Lloyds debacle.

Her love for me was not as spontaneous or unconditional as that of Andrea. There had doubtless been an element of self-interest in her agreeing to marry someone seventeen years older than herself and I cannot deny that there must have been the same in myself but there had always been a definite attraction and love had developed out of our mutual desire to make our relationship work and not to fail, for any reason, for a second time in our lives.

Annette also had a spiritual dimension which she rarely displayed: it manifested itself when we visited religious sites in Italy and France: she would sit, lost in thought, in the peace and quiet of an empty church or chapel, undisturbed by myself for many minutes: I always wondered what was in her mind but left her to her private thoughts: she would have told me about them had she wanted to do so.

In much the same way she differentiated between her private and public "personas". Although she would freely discuss her work when at home, she would never allow me to intrude in any way upon her position and status as director of an NHS Foundation Trust hospital although I was well aware that the husbands and wives of other directors attended a number of social functions organised by it. By the same token, she had no long-term friends from earlier years whereas I had many. There was a subconscious barrier within her that did not exist within Andrea.

The ten years from 1997 to 2007 were, by and large, happy and productive years with the children growing up and with Annette and I pursuing our respective careers and interests. It was only my brain haemorrhage in 2007 and the diagnosis of Annette with multiple myeloma later in the same year that cast their dark shadows over her life and mine.

But before I mention those last two harrowing years I really should mention three significant events that occurred between 1997 and 2007, two of which were relevant to the period post 2009.

In my late fifties I had been suffering for some time with an embarrassing and debilitating health problem encountered by many men of the same age, namely an enlarged prostate. After a particularly painful episode I was whisked off to Orsett hospital in the spring of 1996 where I had an operation that effectively rendered me impotent. The operation need not, apparently, have been quite so drastic but I have learned to live with the inhibiting effects of it and it could conceivably have saved me from cancer of the prostate. I only mention it in the context of what happened many years later.

In the year I met Andrea I also had a second genuine health crisis which, had it occurred twenty years earlier, would have left me blind. I was running round Billericay on one of my twice-weekly five-mile evening runs when, a couple of miles from home, a whorl of blood appeared in my right eye. It curled in a lazy circle round my eyeball as if it was being stirred slowly by an invisible spoon. I stopped running immediately and decided to walk slowly home. First thing next morning I visited a local optician and asked him, on a scale of one to ten, how serious it was. "Ten," he replied and packed me off straightaway to Harold Wood hospital which, in turn, referred me immediately to Moorfields Eye hospital in London.

Examination by a consultant the same day revealed that the retinas of both of my eyes were becoming detached: the retina in my right eye was also torn, resulting in the bleeding. There was nothing for it but to have laser surgery there and then. It was at this point, as I waited for the eyesight-saving laser treatment, that I recalled John Milton's poem on his blindness and the despairing nature of the first few lines of it.

" When I consider how my light is spent
... in this dark world and wide,
And that one Talent which is death to hide,
Lodged with me useless...".

I speculated that John Milton, Oliver Cromwell's equivalent of a modern "spin doctor" and eminent writer and poet, might well have suffered from detached retinas as a result of the copious amount of time he spent working in candlelight at all hours of the night. My treatment was successful, but it brought home to me very forcibly how precious a gift eyesight is and how one should not abuse it. I took great care thereafter to ensure that I worked in adequate light and that my staff at Hughes & Co. did not suffer from any form of eyestrain. I thanked God for the fact that I did not have to "serve" by "only standing and waiting".

The third event was my meeting with Andrea's daughter. Although I kept my word and had no personal contact with Andrea between 1997 and early 2010 she had apparently mentioned me to her daughter in nostalgic terms on a number of occasion over the years and had then told her, in confidence, about our meeting. It came as a great surprise, therefore, when her daughter, on her own initiative, contacted me out of the blue some two years later and asked whether I would be prepared to appear in a surprise video she was preparing for her mother's sixtieth birthday. After some thought I told her that it would indeed give me great pleasure to appear as "an old flame" and we met for lunch. Andrea's daughter was so like her mother that I recognised her before she spotted me. She had no photo of me but eye contact was all that was necessary. We had such an enjoyable afternoon together that she could have been a daughter.

Although she wrote to me afterwards and wanted to correspond I felt it politic not to write back. The temptation to open up an indirect line of communication with Andrea would have been too great and I avoided it. But I was very heartened and gratified, nevertheless, by her open and friendly nature and the way in which she treated me.

The diagnosis of Annette with multiple myeloma came as a great shock: she had been complaining for some weeks of severe pains in her side and since she suspected the problem was muscular I arranged for her to see a specialist consultant in that field. He confirmed, however, that her problem was not muscular and telephoned a consultant colleague who was able to see her the same afternoon at another private hospital. The second consultant immediately referred Annette to the medical assessment unit at Basildon hospital.

A diagnosis was carried out overnight and the next day the source of the pain was disclosed to her – some twenty eight gall stones! But the diagnosis also revealed that she had multiple myeloma, cancer of the bone marrow. Her life expectancy, without a transplant, was a maximum of two years. After she was diagnosed in December 2007 Annette faced her illness with great bravery and when, after an unsuccessful stem cell transplant, she realised that her days were numbered she set about making the most of them. She still wanted to work and achieve great things for her NHS trust but she also wanted to spend time abroad in her favourite countries, Italy and France.

In this latter respect I drove her in 2008 and 2009 to her favourite hotel on Lake Maggiore, Italy, and to the Bordeaux region of France: we also went on other holidays to Suffolk and to Rome: we came back from a holiday on Lake Maggiore less than three months before she died but just after she had obtained university status for her mental health NHS trust, the first such trust in the UK to obtain it. In fact, she worked until four weeks before she died, such was her level of commitment to the trust. One of her last achievements was the design and equipping of the "state of the art" lecture theatre at Rochford hospital that I have mentioned in an earlier chapter and that was subsequently named after her.

Her death in November 2009 shortly before my seventy-fourth birthday blew a huge hole in the lives of myself and our children and for the next three years I wore her expanded wedding ring above my own in order to have something of hers close to me. Annette had told me, before she died, not to grieve for her and to get on with the rest of my life, even to find companionship elsewhere if I felt so inclined. But I could not help grieving and attended bereavement counselling for nearly a year. It took me longer than that to adjust to her loss.

I inserted a "circular letter" with news of Annette's sad passing in all the Christmas cards I sent to family and friends in December 2009 and included Andrea and Stephen in the circularisation. I received a letter of sympathy from Andrea suggesting that, if I considered it appropriate, we could meet some time in the New Year. In fact, we met for lunch in March 2010. It was lovely to see her again and to be able to reaffirm our feelings for each other but I made it clear that I did not want to disturb her marriage in any way. On the other hand I saw nothing wrong in a seventy-four year old and a seventy-one year old having lunch together occasionally in order to keep in touch and abreast of what was happening in our respective families. I would also value her wise counsel. We therefore agreed to meet once every three months.

We met like this for over three years, from the middle of 2010 until the end of 2013, just before my seventy-seventh birthday. During that period we met for lunch, invariably at a country pub with restaurant facilities followed by a visit to a nearby National Trust or English Heritage property or by a long walk in the countryside. It was only after three years of meeting like this that I concluded it might be possible to see Andrea a little more often and be reassured that, in doing so, I was not prejudicing her marriage in any perceptible way.

I had noticed, however, that during those three years Andrea had become more and more alive and happy and no longer prepared to surrender to old age. In fact we both had something to live for. In early 2014 I therefore suggested that, in view of our advancing years, it might be a good idea to meet and enjoy each other's company on a more frequent basis. The joy of our being together, even for a few hours was immense and we never ran out of things to talk about. We were leading separate lives but these occasional meetings were wonderful highlights for both of us. Andrea heartily agreed. We decided to meet once a month for lunch and also attend occasional evening lectures of interest to us both at the British Museum.

We did this for about eight months until, by an extraordinary twist of fate, I succumbed to what was later diagnosed as Lyme disease, an inflammation of the brain caused by tic bites. While walking with a Holiday Fellowship Group in August 2014 in the wooded hills above Church Stretton in Shropshire and following the downward path of a stream I noticed that blood was trickling down my left hand and that a large black fly was on my wrist at the point the blood was seeping out. I flicked it off and mentioned the incident to our group leader. He said it sounded like a horsefly and that I might get a rash, which, indeed, I subsequently did. Twenty minutes later the same thing happened: more blood and another black fly!

There was no physical reaction to either until, roughly ten days after the holiday, I drove one evening to Harwich to meet the steering committee of the ill-fated Harwich Mayflower Project. As Chairman of the Billericay Mayflower Twinning Association I felt it would be a good idea to find out how much actual progress the committee was making in the construction of a full-size replica of the Mayflower to sail the Atlantic in 2020, four hundred years after the original vessel made its historic voyage.

On the homeward drive I did not feel at all well, and since it was well after 10.30 p.m. before I arrived back in Billericay, I decided not to eat but to go straight to bed. During the night my feet and the lower parts of my legs started itching for no apparent reason and, since sleep appeared impossible, I got up at about 1 a.m. thinking that I would go downstairs and make a cup of tea. I got no further than the landing when I collapsed, hitting my head so hard on the floor that I must have knocked myself out.

When I came round I discovered, to my horror, that I could not move my arms or legs, They would not respond to my brain: in the circumstances I would have to remain lying on the landing until I could move them or someone found me. All I could do was wait and see what would happen. I am not sure how long I lay on the floor. It seemed like hours but was probably less. The ability to move my limbs ultimately returned and I was able to stagger back into the bedroom and collapse on to the bed.

The experience of that particular night made me realise how quadriplegics must feel when they discover that, however hard they try to make their limbs move, nothing happens. They find, like Christopher Reeves who played the part of Superman in a number of films, that they have no control over their bodies and are trapped within them. It is a terrifying sensation.

At what I thought was 8.30 am I got up, feeling distinctly groggy, and went downstairs to the kitchen only to be surprised a few minutes later by a knock at the front door. It was my son, James, who immediately asked me how I was. When I replied that I was surprised he had come round so early in the morning to ask me that, he interjected, "Dad, it is ten minutes to one. I have come round because the office phoned me. They were concerned that you had not shown up for work." James was brief and to the point. "I can see there is something wrong with you. I am calling for an ambulance." Despite my protestations he summoned an ambulance and I was taken down to the same medical assessment unit as Annette at Basildon hospital.

Whether the doctors were rushed off their feet or did not appreciate the significance of the symptoms I displayed – and by this stage the red rash on my lower left arm was quite obvious – I was released after four hours. James was very surprised and decided to stay with me after he had collected me and had driven me home. Not being prepared to accept the hospital's assessment that there was nothing wrong with me he asked other members of my family to come round and confirm his view that I was anything but well. They agreed with him and James rang the NHS "out of hours doctor" service for an urgent home visit.

The doctor arrived and checked me over. He also gave me the senile dementia test. I told him, as I had told the hospital, about losing control of my limbs after hitting my head on the floor the previous night and he withdrew to discuss matters with my family. While he was out of the room I got up from the sofa and tripped over his black medical bag, collapsed onto the floor and started having a major seizure. This time it was really serious. I went into convulsions, ground my teeth and "lost it" mentally. James had been absolutely right and I was readmitted immediately to the hospital.

There then followed three further seizures at the hospital in the space of eight hours. My brain was addled and I could not control my body. I involuntarily ground my teeth during the seizures, necessitating subsequent dental repair, and could not stop myself trying to look over my left shoulder, also trying for some reason to straighten the sheets covering me. It was all very weird and unreal and, of course, incredibly worrying. What was happening to me? As a student on holiday in Greece I had once witnessed a young woman on a train from Athens to Piraeus having an epileptic fit and foaming at the mouth while three men in the carriage tried to pin her to the floor but this was different. My brain was being attacked by some sort of virus.

I was sedated initially and then put on a ten-day "round the clock" regime of antibiotics which, mercifully, started to work after about three days. There were no more seizures but, mentally, I was still in bad shape and very confused. In fact, I was so confused, during those first three days, that I texted gibberish to my office about my condition and mistakenly sent a garbled text about the treatment I was receiving to Andrea instead of to James. On receipt Andrea realised that I was in hospital and became extremely concerned about my mental and physical state. She desperately wanted to see me and to find out what was wrong with me. Her daughter who happened to be visiting her the day the text arrived told her mother, without a second's hesitation, that rather than have her worry about me she would drive her the sixty miles to Basildon hospital straightaway.

As a result Andrea and her daughter arrived completely "out of the blue" while my son, Chris, was visiting me. Chris already knew about Andrea but had never met her or her daughter. It could have been an embarrassing meeting for everyone but, to my relief, they were all more than happy to greet and talk to each other. My son and Andrea's daughter agreed that it would be a good idea to go and have a cup of coffee and leave Andrea and I on our own. Over coffee they decided to swap telephone numbers in case Andrea or I should be affected by health emergencies or problems in future. Chris was, in fact, as impressed as myself by the daughter's kind and forthright nature and by Andrea's obvious concern for me. My unfortunate illness led, therefore, to an encounter which I had not planned or expected but which proved, paradoxically, to be entirely beneficial. I have to put the meeting, as I have put many other things, down to fate!!

The upshot of my spell in hospital was that, in view of the fragility of our lives and uncertainty over what the future might hold in store for us, Andrea and I decided that we should meet more frequently while we could: being seventy eight and seventy five respectively it was a matter of, "Gather ye rosebuds while ye may"! We would follow our hearts while doing our very best not to disturb our existing family relationships. We knew that we loved and cared deeply about each other and that time was not on our side. And so we did meet more frequently and expanded the range and variety of the places we visited, including theatres, exhibitions at the British Museum, other museums in the capital and historic houses elsewhere. I also arranged for Andrea to visit Billericay and meet Heather, who came over for the day. They took to each other immediately and both regretted that they had met so late in life! How very ironic!!

Because, from the end of 2014, Andrea had begun to pay far more attention to her appearance and was so much happier than ever before and because, despite her seventy five years, she had literally "blossomed" Stephen concluded that she must have a lover and, in early 2016, he could not resist asking her whether there was anyone else in her life. In response to his question she confirmed that, indeed there was and that the someone was myself. She reminded him that he had met me at her twenty first birthday party over fifty five years previously and at Cambridge in 1963. She had fallen in love with me in 1960 and had been in love with me ever since.

She explained the extraordinary way in which she had found out where I lived, how we had briefly been in touch in the 1990s and how I had only contacted them subsequently by Christmas card on Annette's death. We had met regularly since 2010 and had realised that our love had not faded over the years. It was as strong as ever. She had not wanted her love for me to affect Stephen or their family and had made efforts to prevent it doing so. But she could not help her feelings for me and, if he could not accept the situation, she would leave him and join me. That was certainly not what he wanted. Given that what she said came as quite a shock he was nevertheless impressed by her candour and her constancy. He recognised and accepted the strength of her feelings and her obvious love for me. He said he was quite relieved in a strange way that it was me and not someone she had met during their marriage.

From my experience as a former divorce lawyer and family mediator a wife who "looks elsewhere" for emotional fulfilment and a degree of happiness during her married life is invariably dissatisfied with what her husband had been able to offer, whether it be in terms of understanding, affection or support. She often falls out of love with her spouse, if she was ever in love with him in the first place as a result of that dissatisfaction.

By contrast a wife who by an unexpected twist of fate encounters or rediscovers late in life the person with whom she was in love before her marriage is in a very different position. She faces the excruciating dilemma of having fallen in love with one man and being committed by marriage to another. Reconciling the two conflicting situations has to be extremely difficult, if not impossible.

As a result of her forthright admission Stephen had recognised the strength of Andrea's feelings for me. He also recognised, however, that he had done nothing sufficiently serious to prompt his wife to wish to leave him or "look elsewhere" during their fifty odd years together. He appreciated that he had unfortunately married someone who had previously lost her heart to another in the same way as I had lost mine to Andrea before I married Vivien.

It is probably fair to say that there must be many couples in the same positon at various stages of their lives together who, whether previously in love with their partners or not, have accepted a less than satisfying relationship because they have high tolerance thresholds and no wish to prejudice the stability of the families they have created. The paradox, in our case, therefore, was how, if possible, to resolve the situation in which we found ourselves. Stephen faced losing his wife if he could not come to terms with Andrea's love for me and mine for her. The time had come for some serious soul-searching all round.

Stephen admitted that, in retrospect, he had married Andrea in his now distant younger days, not because he was madly in love with her but because she was very attractive, highly intelligent and would make an excellent wife and mother. He had genuinely hoped at the time that love of the kind that existed between Andrea and me would develop. He conceded, moreover, that, having won her hand, if not her heart, he had subsequently taken his marriage somewhat for granted and had concentrated rather too much on his own career and outside interests, as I had myself in my first marriage. Andrea, for her part, had married a younger man because she was afraid of being "left on the shelf" once she left university.

Whatever their original motivations he and Andrea had developed a relationship that worked and, whatever may have been its emotional deficiencies, he had no wish to disturb and thereby destroy their marriage. In fact we were all agreed on that. Given our respective life expectancies it was a matter of coming to a "modus vivendi" that would keep Andrea happy and Stephen and me relatively so, if at all possible.

Andrea was able to assure Stephen that, in view of my age of eighty and my impotence as a result of my prostate operation some twenty years previously, and her own age of seventy seven our love for each other had necessarily to be platonic and limited in duration. She also confirmed that, apart from her brief and occasional absences caused by our meetings about which she would tell him in advance, there would scarcely be a detectable ripple on the outward surface of their domestic and family life.

Bearing in mind that I was obviously good for Andrea, had re-energised her and made her very happy, Stephen indicated that he would be prepared to extend the hand of friendship to me on condition that we accepted "ground rules". He still had many outside interests that he wished to pursue and he would consequently continue to be away from home quite a lot. He now appreciated that leaving Andrea on her own as he had done on many occasions in the past while he did what he wanted to do was not particularly fair. He could understand her desire for company when she was left on her own and the pleasure she must have derived from doing things with me, like visiting museums, exhibitions, theatres and historic houses, going for walks and discussing literature, poetry and the classics in which he was not particularly interested.

If he was able to leave Andrea with someone with whom she could share her interests, whom he could trust to look after her and who would not attempt to undermine in any way his own relationship with her then he would be reasonably content, if not entirely so. We were, he said, to treat each other as "best friends". We could be with each other when he was away but Andrea had to be in the marital bed when he was at home. He was not prepared to be left at home on his own. What we did when we were together was down to us but he expected me to act in a gentlemanly manner at all times.

From his perspective it was a pragmatic solution to the situation in which we found ourselves in advanced old age. From my perspective I was happy to accept whatever companionship Andrea was able to offer without risk of upsetting or antagonising Stephen. I never had any desire to undermine their long-standing marriage. By being circumspect, even helpful where possible, and in no way demanding I was able to establish a rapport with him which I believe has been of benefit to both of us. It certainly made him more appreciative of Andrea and everything she had done for him over the years. Forbearance, mutual respect and consideration for each other's position resulted in a civilised way of ensuring the least emotional upset all round.

Indeed Stephen went so far as to say that, but for my love for his wife and hers for me, we could have been good friends!

What others will make of this unusual arrangement I have no idea but as far as Andrea, Stephen and I were concerned it had to be a careful balance of emotional needs where we all tried to do the best for each other, while acknowledging the difficult situation in which we found ourselves. Andrea, as at the date of this book, has continued to be a conscientious wife, a superb grandmother with a contented heart and the focal point of her large family. We are all realistic about what has occurred and is likely to occur and appreciate that, given our ages, our relationship can only continue until infirmity or death intervenes. I leave it to the reader to decide whether, unexpectedly reunited, Andrea and I have been foolish to follow "the devices and desires of our own hearts" as the Book of Common Prayer might describe them or whether this is a heart-warming tale of true love being acknowledged by the three of us and it working for the benefit of us all.

All I can say is that our chance reunion in 1997 and our meetings since 2010 have definitely been beneficial for Andrea who would otherwise have steadily retreated into old age, reading books most of the time, and who would have lacked any incentive to look forward to emotional fulfilment and the good things that life could still have in store for her. None of us expect our children or anyone else to regard our relationship as one which others should adopt or approve but the members of my family who have met her can see the love between Andrea and myself and cannot gainsay it. They think she is a delightful person, particularly good with grandchildren and a pleasure to meet. They regard us, perhaps slightly irreverently, as the "Charles and Camilla" of the family and one of my daughters has been prompted to present me with a plaque which I display in the hall. It reads, "Remember: As far as anyone knows we're a nice normal family!"

Nice perhaps! Normal, probably not! "Whatever" – as a well-known Royal might have said – "normal may be"! Everyone has a conception of what is "normal" and the word and the concept probably have as many interpretations as there are thinking people on the planet. Considering myself somewhat eccentric I have never wished to be categorised as such and I leave it to the reader to decide whether, after reading what I have to say about life and death I am or not!

As far as a personal philosophy is concerned I have always wanted and tried to add something to whatever sphere of activity or relationship I have embarked upon because I firmly believe that one gets out of life what one is prepared to put into it and that one should not be afraid of doing things that others might choose to avoid for fear of criticism or ridicule. Everyone makes mistakes and everyone encounters problems: it is how one copes with them and learns from them that matters. My life has been characterised by near-death events, paranormal experiences, tragic losses of family and friends, financial disasters, unwise involvements and relationships. But it has also been productive, happy and full of optimism for the future.

The future now has to be limited to a somewhat short life-span, and, having reached my eighties, my thoughts have naturally turned to what there might be beyond death. Although I cannot claim to have led the life of the idealised person in Sir Henry Wotton's poem on the "Character of a Happy Life" I have always had the poem at the back of my mind and, like so much of the poetry I have absorbed over the years, it has acted as a constant reference point. I will not bore the reader with the entire poem but set out the first few lines.

"How happy is he born and taught
That serveth not another's will;

Whose armour is his honest thought,
And simple truth his utmost skill!!
Whose passions not his masters are;
Whose soul is still prepared for death,
Untied unto the world by care
Of public fame or private breath;"

My father often repeated to me the exhortation "To thine own self be true… thou canst not then be false to any man." and the poem and the exhortation have universal resonances. "Be honest with yourself and try to be in control of your own life and destiny."

When the poet says, "Whose soul is still prepared for death" he clearly presupposes that we all have souls and that death is not the end of our individual existences. Nothing, apart from one's soul survives because our bodies are discarded and either burned or buried and all earthly possessions and human relationships are stripped away from us. One's soul, if it exists and has survived the journey from birth to death, is freed from whatever human condition it has suffered or enjoyed. Having encountered ghosts I am quite sure, in my own mind, that there is some sort of existence beyond the grave and that many souls remain in the "here and now" possibly as a result of concerns, like Ada Rolfe who sent me a "mint" silver Victorian threepenny piece, or trauma, like Miss Clements who died in her beloved brass bed.

The concept of what is beyond death is, for most people, predicated on what they have been taught or led to believe and what they have accepted as a result of the religious creed or faith they have followed during their lifetimes. There are, of course, those whose views are entirely negative as far as some sort of existence beyond the grave is concerned. All one can say with any certainty is that, if the soul survives, it will find itself very much on its own in a different paradigm of existence.

As indicated in a previous chapter I have views on spirituality that are controversial but I start from the point that people's religious beliefs are invariably predicated on the environment in which they have been raised. From infancy they have been taught to believe that the way to an afterlife, if they believe what they have been taught and if there is one, is through one or other faith. Faiths, however, are being constantly redefined. A twelfth century Christian or Muslim would doubtless encounter a big difference in the interpretation and application of his or her religion between 1100 AD and 2000 AD. The reason is that, as Grotius pointed out, all religions across the millennia are and have always been approximations to the absolute.

The one common factor, however, that all genuine religions have displayed and continue to display, whatever their teachings on life after death, is their emphasis on spirituality. It is an element believed to reside in the soul of human beings which reflects itself in love, kindness and self-sacrifice. Christians speak of the Trinity of which one is the Holy Ghost, the spiritual element that other faiths acknowledge in different ways. In Christian terms it is in essence the doorway through which the soul passes to another existence. All genuine faiths and religions act as spiritual anchors for humanity by which the spiritual element can be maintained and nourished. It would, in my view, be illogical to conclude that spirituality was exclusive to any one particular religion or faith, as has been claimed by one or other religion over the centuries.

There are those, of course, in whom an element of spirituality no longer appears to be present and whose views are entirely negative as far as the prospect of any future existence beyond the grave is concerned. Indeed there are many people who would say that the concept of people having souls is, in itself, a human construct, that mankind has developed an awareness that there are beneficial and advantageous ways of interacting with each other and there are harmful and disadvantageous ways, characterised as "good" and "evil". In every age there have consequently been men who have not been afraid to advise or warn people to be good and to avoid evil, even at the risk of their own lives. They have held out the notion that unless people accept good, renounce evil and acknowledge their faults they will not discover what is beyond death and the end of their earthly existence.

I am not so dismissive as to say that the soul does not exist and believe that, in addition to the purely animal instincts bequeathed to us by our primitive ancestors, mankind possesses an element within itself which it has defined as spirituality. It has accepted that spirituality, as propounded by wise and selfless men and women, is the key to the essence of ourselves as "homo sapiens", and having become aware of this element it has attributed it to something we call the soul. It has then gone on to deduce that its presence within us is due to a Creator.

It was and always has been logical for mankind to assume that someone or something was responsible for the creation of the Earth and, at the same time as it began to think this way, it attributed qualities and personalities to whoever or whatever did so. Such is mankind's need for reassurance, even possibly arrogance, that we, as human beings, should have envisaged a God or Gods as having an earthly form or forms, but whoever or whatever created a vast universe in which Planet Earth is a mere speck on the periphery of it is not going to be in human form.

I cannot help feeling that our ancestors reluctantly acknowledged this when they accepted, thanks to Copernicus, that the Earth was not at the centre of the universe: the Christian Church, which found this particular fact difficult to grasp in the Middle Ages, has always considered a Creator in human form as useful "shorthand" for whatever our Creator may be. Looking rationally and dispassionately, however, at the insignificance of mankind in the life of our planet and looking then at the insignificance of our planet in the firmament of the universe we, as a species, have to be somewhat presumptuous to think that the Creator of it all chose to take the form of a late development of a primitive form of ape that first appeared on one of probably a number of planets less than half a million years ago. I proffer sincere apologies to the "Son of the Creator" if I am mistaken in this respect!

In the Christian, Jewish and Muslim faiths, the Creator is defined as one God whereas in many other religions creation has been attributed to more than one God. According to these faiths God or Gods live or have lived in an alternative dimension known, in the case of the Romans and the Greeks, as Elysium and what we, in the West, call Heaven. The concept of Heaven has always puzzled me because, in my very mortal view, it cannot be a vast celestial housing estate where the souls of billions of people from every period of history and every religion that has promoted and nourished spirituality intermingle, and having been reunited with those nearest and dearest to them in an "after-life", wait around, metaphorically speaking, for Eternity.

Certain basic questions come to mind. How would souls recognise each other? Would souls have a young or old appearance? What vestiges or earthly existence would souls retain? If a person died of senility, dementia or Alzheimer's disease what "mental capacity" would his or her soul possess? Ask any priest or holy man and you will receive a variety of answers! Most people do not like to face up to death or seek answers to these questions but, apart from the payment of taxes, death is the only certainty one can expect from life, whatever may follow. It is a pity, therefore, that some souls cannot come back from wherever they may be and tell humanity about it, although one or two mortals have expressed a view or had a good guess! But if they were to come back and tell us is it likely that anyone would believe them? It will clearly not be long before I find out myself!

I cannot claim to be any sort of theologian or philosopher and I mean no disrespect to those who are. I also expect what I say to be roundly denounced by them. As, however, those who are must appreciate and, as the reader will have gathered, I am just an inquisitive old lawyer who has been exposed throughout his life to a variety of experiences, events and influences that I have sought to explain and rationalise. As far as Eternity is concerned the only moment anyone and every living creature knows is "now" – the moment I am writing this and the moment you are reading it. And that moment, in my humble submission, is probably Eternity when taken out of the time frame of the world and universe in which we live. As Henry Vaughan poetically expressed it:

"I saw Eternity the other night,
Like a great ring of pure and endless light,
All calm, as it was bright;
And round beneath it,
Time in hours, days, years,
Driv'n by the spheres
Like a vast shadow mov'd; in which the world
And all her train were hurl'd".

The "roundness" observation appears to chime with a number of religious beliefs and Eternity could well be "now" with the time element subtracted.

It is incredibly difficult to speculate on what, if anything, there is for us all after death but I have a sense that, apart from spirits or souls who, for whatever reason, choose to remain in the temporal world – like Ada Rolfe until I had sorted out the problem of the stairs – most souls merge back into a sea of spirituality and that our souls and our spirituality are recycled. Recycled spirituality enters children of each generation when they are born and stays with them as they grow into adults: it remains with them until they die or reject it at some point. On this basis "redemption", in Christian terms, would presumably be the re-entry of spirituality into someone after such rejection. There is little doubt in my mind that mankind's obsession with materialism which has developed over the past twenty thousand years has deadened awareness of the spiritual element that resides or has resided within us.

Why do I sense this? The Romans took the view that the souls or spirits of the dead would linger in our present temporal world as long as people remembered and honoured them: on another side of the world ancestor worship appears to be an attempt by later generations to keep the souls or spirits of their ancestors with them. I have referred to my own horror of the First World War, as if the spirituality or soul of a soldier killed in it had entered me. I have also had the experience of my regression into the previous life of someone which may or may not be based on fact.

I can also remember quite vividly the shocked atmosphere in the air when I unjustifiably, and now deeply regret doing so, criticised my maternal grandmother for not allowing my cousin, Jacqui, to take the "11 plus" exam. I sensed that her soul or spirit was present, perhaps keeping an eye on me and that I had really upset her. It was not just conscience on my part or any form of interaction with the person to whom I was speaking at the time. What, moreover, would be the point, for example, of a twelfth century Christian or Muslim wishing to remain in Eternity if his or her spirit could return to human existence once again?

In summary and before I "head for the exit" myself I would merely exhort everyone to keep an open mind on the things that he or she does not understand but accept that guidelines for the soul, in terms of spirituality and good living, exist. We all have an opportunity to make the most of life until it is taken away. Mistakes are inevitable: we have to try and learn from them and, above all, be honest with ourselves. We can only be a credit to humanity if we do this.

I can do no better to close this concluding chapter than by referring the reader to Shakespeare's Sonnet on Mortality which has resonances for all of us, and particularly myself.

When I have seen by time's fell hand defaced
the rich proud cost of outworn buried age
When sometime lofty towers I see down razed
and brass eternal slave to mortal rage.

When I have seen the hungry ocean gain
advantage on the Kingdom of the shore

*and the firm soil win of the watery main
increasing store with loss and loss with store.*

*When I have seen such interchange of state
or state itself confounded to decay
ruin hath taught me thus to ruminate
that time will come and take my love away*

*This thought is as a death which cannot choose
but weep to have that which it fears to lose.*

*Since brass, nor stone, nor earth nor boundless sea,
but sad mortality o'ersways their power.
How with this rage shall beauty hold a plea,
whose action is no stronger than a flower?*

*O, how shall summer's honey breath hold out
against the wrackful siege of battering days
when rocks impregnable are not so stout,
nor gates of steel so strong, but Time decays?*

*O fearful meditation! Where, alack,
shall Time's best jewel from Time's chest lie hid?
Or what strong hand can hold his swift foot back?
Or who his spoil of beauty can forbid?*

*O, none, unless this miracle have might,
that in black ink my love may still shine bright.*

www.ingramcontent.com/pod-product-compliance
Lightning Source LLC
Chambersburg PA
CBHW060048230426
43661CB00004B/702